THE FOOTL[...]

SOUTHERN INDIA

C000147514

THE footloose GUIDE

Southern India

MELISSA SHALES

Series Editor: Andrew Sanger

SIMON & SCHUSTER

LONDON·SYDNEY·NEW YORK·TOKYO·SINGAPORE·TORONTO

First published in Great Britain by
Simon & Schuster Ltd in 1992
A Paramount Communications Company

**Simon & Schuster Ltd
West Garden Place
Kendal Street
London W2 2AQ**

Simon & Schuster of Australia Pty Ltd
Sydney

A CIP catalogue record for this book is
available from the British Library
ISBN 0–671–71003–6

Typeset in Sabon & Futura by
Falcon Typographic Art Ltd, Edinburgh
Printed and bound in Great Britain by
HarperCollinsManufacturing, Glasgow

CONTENTS

For Stephen
with thanks for being a wonderful travelling
companion, and for keeping me sane and keeping
me working on the numerous occasions when I
was prepared to give up

ACKNOWLEDGEMENTS

A great many people have helped me both with my travel arrangements and with information while I have been compiling this book. In particular, I should like to thank Ashley and Jane Butterfield of Butterfield Indian Rail Tours for my first introduction to India; Dr Dandapani of Indian Railways for his constant interest, and for providing a rail pass and a stream of detailed information; Oberoi Hotels for providing me with regular and much needed oases of clean living, air conditioning and hot water; Dr Salwan, at the Indian Tourist Office in London, for armfuls of books and other literature, and a great deal of helpful advice; my editor, Andrew Sanger, and Richard Wigmore at Simon & Schuster, for their endless patience.

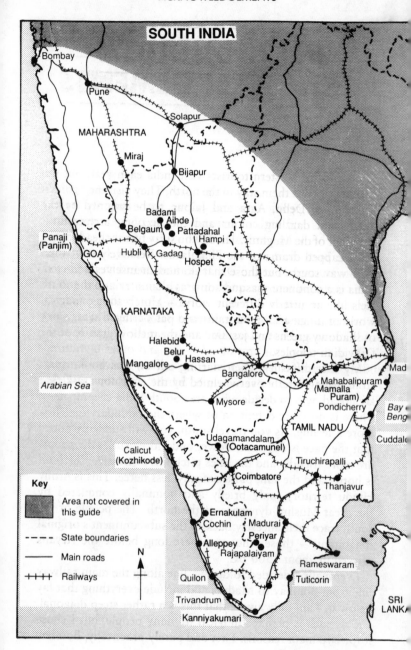

INTRODUCTION

Thousands of Western tourists visit India each year, but the vast majority of them stay in the north. They visit the "golden triangle" of Delhi, Agra and Jaipur, to be stunned by the desert and dazzling colour and the dizzying architectural grandeur of the Mughuls. Those who stray further head for the snow-capped drama of the Himalayas. Relatively few wend their way south, but those that do find themselves addicted. India is a continent masquerading as a country and the south feels like an utterly different world – a marvellous, magical world of jungle-clad mountains and palm-fringed seas, a riot of shadowy greens and jasmine and the mellow granite of the Dravidian temples.

My first difficulty when starting out on this book, apart from feeling utterly overwhelmed by the enormous task that lay ahead, was to decide what area South India encompasses. There is no strict definition of where the boundary lies, it is more a feeling. As you travel south, you will suddenly notice that the pace is different, slower and more gentle; the people are more friendly and the sales pitch less aggressive; the food is hotter and the sun, paradoxically, less fierce. This is firmly Hindu territory, only briefly and nominally conquered by the great Muslim dynasties of the north. The people of the south trace their ancestry back to the sub-continent's original inhabitants – those who were here long before the Aryans arrived in about 1500 BC.

Eventually I decided to draw a line along the main railway line from Bombay to Madras and include everything that lay below it. I am fully aware that this is a rather steep diagonal, and as such is perhaps illogical to many people, but I chose it for two main reasons. First and purely practically, Bombay is the major starting point for almost any tour of South India. A book that did not include it would be infuriating for the traveller. Second, while southern Maharashtra was conquered by the Muslim empires, it never fully absorbed the Muslim culture. It feels like part of the south. Hyderabad to the east, although geographically just south of Bombay, is a predominantly Muslim city, firmly rooted in the north.

The first time I visited India, I spent about a month reeling from city to city in a state of shock. Everything was so utterly different from anything I had known before. Not only was I faced by the noise, the chaos and the confusion that is India's normal way of life, but the only history I recognised (to my shame) began with Clive of India and the British Raj. Each time I arrived in a new city, people were speaking a different language and had totally different cultural roots. I was also faced by the temples and mosques of several different religions; I had the haziest idea of Islam and was totally ignorant of the others. I obediently made my way round sight after sight, appreciating the architecture but understanding nothing.

To survive in and understand India, even at the simplest level, is exceptionally difficult, and without a basis from which to start you will at best miss many of its glories, at worst be utterly miserable. I have therefore chosen quite deliberately to stray not only from the standard format of the Footloose Guides, but occasionally even from the geographical boundaries that I had set for myself. This book contains a far more detailed section than others in the series on the practicalities of travel in the hopes that you might avoid some of the pitfalls by which I learned – the hard way. I have also included a background information section on Indian history, society and main religions. Lack of space permits nothing but the briefest and most superficial overview, but I hope that it will help you to understand at least something of the sights you will be visiting. Finally, I have not included any listings for bars and nightlife. This is chiefly because bars, clubs and discos hardly exist. Where they do, most are in the luxury hotels built and run for foreigners and they are totally outside the Indian experience.

Even South India is a huge area geographically (about the

same size as Western Europe), with a formidable cultural heritage. It would take an army of researchers several lifetimes, and enough books to fill a library, to cover it fully. The constraints of time and space have forced me to be selective and there are inevitably some gaps, although I hope that none of these is major. Nor have I been able to inspect every hotel and restaurant in the region, although I have included a reasonable cross-section across the price ranges in each place. Every effort has also been made to ensure that all the information contained in the book is accurate and up to date, but the constantly fluctuating situation inevitably means that some things will have changed since we went to press. I apologise in advance for any shortcomings. Please write in with any comments, suggestions, changes and additions you would like to see included in the next edition. Meantime, I wish you an interesting, trouble-free trip and hope that you will come home loving South India as much as I do.

Melissa Shales, 1992

SOUTH INDIA TODAY

Indian society is a heaving, throbbing mass of paradox and contradiction. Basically, society seems to have divided its psyche in two. The public/state side is completely modern and secular, based on Western principles inherited from the British, while the private side remains locked into traditional and religious values. Most Indians seem happy to live this schizophrenic existence, and few even recognise that there is a problem with it. Only bewildered Westerners, trying to impose their own logic, become seriously confused.

THE POPULATION

The current population is estimated at around 850 million, and is still increasing at the rate of at around 12–15 million a year. Although the cities are huge, and growing at a furious rate, over 80% of the population still lives in rural surroundings, scratching out a living from traditional smallholdings.

The vast majority of people (around 80%) are Hindu, while over 80 million (13%) are Muslim. There are also around 19 million Christians, 10 million Sikhs, 5 million Buddhists, and 3 million Jains, plus small populations of Jews and Parsees. India has 65 officially recognised languages and over 550 distinct dialects.

Some 45 million people (around 7% of the population) belong to a variety of minority tribes. Mostly in remote areas, many of them still live traditional lifestyles.

GOVERNMENT

In theory India is a model of liberal democracy. On paper

the constitution could be a blueprint for the perfect system. Educated Indians have a passion for political debate that erupts on every street corner and station platform, but whatever their politics they all believe equally passionately in democracy. As a result, the government has managed to **remain stable** against astonishing odds, including war, riot and assassination. Of course, it is a slightly odd form of democracy. There are literally dozens of political parties but only one, Congress, has enough support to form an effective government, and there seems to be a need to cling to the security of hereditary rule. Members of the Nehru family have been Prime Ministers for 38 out the last 45 years.

The only real threat to Congress is from the Bharatiya Janata Party (BJP), a backward-looking Hindu fundamentalist group that is calling for India to become a religious state under Hindu law. The BJP brought down the last government and although it is still in opposition, it has enormous – and growing – popular appeal.

In practice, government works surprisingly well given the enormous odds against it. There is complete freedom of speech and the media. There is some political intimidation, but not enough to jeopardise the system. There is corruption, but remarkably little of it in comparison to other developing countries. The legal system has flaws, but is basically fair and impartial, and while the bureaucracy is cumbersome in the extreme, it works – eventually.

There are just too many people, too much poverty, too many factions and too little money. In the struggle to feed people, there is little left over for social welfare, for providing clean water or a roof for everyone. Traditional divisions between religions, castes and tribes are papered over in a fragile peace which crumbles every so often into bloodshed, and it is difficult to legislate against traditional practices which are carried on behind the closed doors of the family home.

THE ECONOMY

India's popular image is of a country surviving on a knife-edge of poverty, with few resources and even less development.

The Constitution

India is a presidential, federal republic within the Common-
wealth. Central government has two houses of parliament. The
lower house, the *Lok Sabha*, has up to 500 members, and
represents the people, while the upper house, the *Rajya Sabha*,
with up to 250 members, represents the federal states.

The constitution is secular, based on universal suffrage,
bans untouchability, enshrines an American-style declaration
of human rights and equal rights for women, and even reserves
some jobs for the lower castes.

The leader of the majority party, as Prime Minister, is the
chief executive of government, backed up by a cabinet. The
president normally acts only with the approval of Prime
Minister and parliament, but does have the power to take
direct control of central government should the parliamentary
process fall to pieces.

Central government retains sole control of defence, foreign
affairs, railways, ports and currency. The states, each of which
has its own parliament, have control of education, agriculture,
industry and the police.

But while India has poor people by the million, it is not a
poor country. Behind the pictures of despair beloved of TV
cameramen, India is now one of the world's top ten leading
industrial producers. And as India inherited almost no industry from the British, it has created this huge manufacturing
base in only 45 years.

Perhaps the country's most impressive achievement, however, is that it is still self-sufficient in food, if only just. People
might go hungry, but it is a long time since there has been true
famine, in spite of a population that has quadrupled in the last
40 years.

Since the 1950s, Indian companies have been encouraged
to save precious foreign currency and produce both raw
materials and machinery themselves. As a result, the country's
manufacturing base too is almost totally self-sufficient. The
few foreign companies that have been allowed in have to
have Indian partners. There are some imported goods in the
shops, but there are local versions of everything, from TVs to
tanks. Most famous was the round-topped Ambassador, the
"People's Car", created by Sanjay Gandhi in the 1970s, but

there is even a local version of Coca Cola: Thums Up. About the only thing they can't make for themselves is oil.

Alongside this picture of success, however, millions still live bleak, hopeless lives. The country has some of the world's richest men, living in the sort of oppulence few but an Oppenheimer could aspire to, but the majority scratch out a living, supporting their whole family on less than Rs200 a month. The free market economy has been left to flourish with as few restrictions as possible. The result is rampant pollution, and a minimal regard for workers' health, safety and living conditions and rates of pay. Labour is so cheap and so plentiful that the unions have won few improvements. Desperate workers who borrow from their employers at vast interest rates find themselves unable ever to repay their debts or to leave their jobs until they have done so, and effectively spend the rest of their lives as slaves. Children are put to work in factories from the age of seven, and are even mutilated by parents who have discovered that a disabled child can earn more in a day begging from soft-hearted tourists than their fathers can earn in a week. The rich are very rich indeed, the middle classes do nicely, and the poor get exploited.

CASTE

The middle classes at least are eager to assure any visitor to India that the caste system is dead. Officially it is, and to a very few really has stopped having any relevance. In the marriage ads in the papers, surprisingly large numbers say "caste no object" – but then how many lonely hearts ads in a Western magazine would even dare mention class? In practice, the caste system is still alive and well and has an iron grip on Hindu society.

It is an infinitely complex and rigid system. There are four main groups: the *brahmans* (priests); *kshatriyas* (warriors and rulers); *vaishyas* (cultivators); and *shudras* (untouchables). Within this basic framework are literally thousands of sub-castes, based on occupation, financial and social status.

Caste is an integral part of the Hindu religion, hedged around by laws and taboos. It is hereditary. By religious law, you cannot marry a person of a different caste – or, amongst the most orthodox, even eat with them. You cannot leave your caste – your only hope of improvement is if, over the generations, the social status of the entire sub-caste changes. Even if your sub-caste rises in status, it is impossible to shift from your main caste.

The only real challenge came in the 1920s when Gandhi began to champion the cause of the untouchables, whom he christened the *Harijan* or Children of God. Under his protection, they were given a political voice for the first time, together with some access to education and a chance for economic improvement. In the post-independence constitution, they were given equal rights in law, together with a degree of positive discrimination in terms of jobs. Some 22% of all government jobs are currently reserved for the Scheduled Castes, as they are now known.

There has been some progress. Today, economic and professional status no longer depend entirely on caste. A few people from the Scheduled Castes are highly educated, in positions of authority and have good incomes. Nevertheless, the few who have climbed their way out of the gutter are the exception rather than the rule. The lower castes still hold all the most menial jobs, have far less access to education, and make up the poorest sections of society. Even within the government job reservation system, it is far easier for a *Harijan* to get a job at the lowest end of the scale than to secure a management position, and you would never find someone from an upper caste working as a cleaner. Every small advance has been made in the teeth of fierce opposition. Efforts by the National Front government of 1989–90 to reserve another 5% of jobs for the Scheduled Castes led to violence across the country that eventually helped topple the government, while the fundamentalist BJP, with its desire to turn back the clock and reinstate Hindu religious law, has gained much of its support from upper castes fearful of losing their privileged place in society.

WOMEN IN INDIA

Since the Civil Disobedience campaign of 1930, women have played an active and prominent role in the political life of the country. When Indira Gandhi became Prime Minister in 1966, India became one of the first countries in the world to have a woman premier. In law, they have equal rights in all things, including inheritance, while the Hindu Marriage Act of 1956 banned polygamy, and provided women with access to divorce, along with alimony or other support payments. Birth control is actively encouraged by a government desperate to bring India's population explosion under control. Women of all classes work, and the wealthier amongst them have access to every level of education.

In spite of all this, the Hindu ideal of womanhood remains that of unquestioning obedience to father and husband, and only a handful of women would dare challenge the concept. For an Indian woman to lose her virginity before marriage is truly a social catastrophe. A large proportion of marriages are still arranged, with the bride often still in her early teens. She has the right to object, but is rarely given the right to choose for herself. She is handed to her husband along with a dowry and

The Origins of the Caste System

The caste system was brought to India by the Aryans in about 1500 BC. There were three divisions: *kshatriyas*, the warriors and rulers; *brahmans*, the priests; and *vaishyas* or cultivators. The Sanskrit word for caste was *varna*, which meant colour. The original inhabitants of the sub-continent were of a different colour (dark-skinned). The Aryans called them *shudras*, or outcasts. The three Aryan castes were thought to be twice-born — or in a higher state of spiritual development than the *shudras*.

Government was in the hands of the *kshatriyas*, but only the priestly *brahmans* could give divine status to the kings. As a result, they gradually gained absolute authority and became the highest caste, a position they still hold today. To preserve their status, they made caste part of the religion, surrounding it by laws and taboos. Cleanliness had always been a part of the religion, but by the seventh century AD, the Brahmans began to talk of ritual purity. The *shudras*, who were thought to be spiritually unclean, were barred from the temples. Finally, the Brahmans claimed that they would be polluted even by the touch of an outcaste and the concept of untouchability came into being. There was little further change for the next 1,200 years.

as this has to be returned to her family if the marriage breaks up, but not if she dies, all too many women die early and mysteriously. Suttee (the traditional custom that forced a woman to throw herself on to her husband's funeral pyre) has been banned for over 200 years, but still happens occasionally.

Even upper and middle-class women are rarely included in social activities in public places. You will almost never see an Indian woman dancing and will never see one drinking alcohol or smoking. The loose woman in Hindi films is usually the one wearing Western dress. Her repentance of her wicked ways at the end of the film is heralded by her appearance, looking suitably modest, in a sari.

Women travellers will have a chance to meet and talk to plenty of local women. They regard female Westerners with some awe and a great deal of amusement and are as eager to chat as the men. However, only the most highly educated and Westernised would dream of talking to a strange man.

RELIGION

HINDUISM

Although it only got its name in the nineteenth century, Hinduism has evolved over the last 6,000 years, and began to take shape properly with the arrival of the Aryans in about 1500 BC. The word Hindu simply means "Indian" in Persian.

It has no one holy "rule book", but there is a collection of classic literature written over the last 3,000 years, including the *Rig-Veda*, the *Upanishads*, the *Ramayana*, and the *Mahabharata* – the world's longest poem.

Beliefs

Hinduism is more a state of being than a religion. You are born and die a Hindu. You cannot become one, or stop being one. Beyond that, it has plenty of concepts, but few rules.

It divides human society into four castes (see page 12). You are endlessly born and reborn and your actions in this life decide your *karma* (fate) in the next. If you behave well, you will be reborn into a higher caste, so these are known as the "twice-born". During each life, you have four aims: to live properly, make money, satisfy desire, and to arrive at the end of the cycle of rebirth and merge with *Bhagvan*, the soul of the universe.

Main Gods (Devas)

At first, there seem to be an endless number of gods, but most of them are just different aspects of Vishnu and Shiva, and their families. The main ones are:

Brahma

The Creator, once the most important of the gods, but now only a shadowy background figure. Also known as **Bhagvan**, the one-god or soul of the universe.

Vishnu

The Preserver, a wise, benevolent figure who comes down to earth when the world is in great need. So far he has appeared in nine different incarnations, or *avataras*. In art Vishnu is usually shown carrying a discus, conch shell, mace and lotus blossom. Different incarnations are represented by a fish, a boar, a tortoise, a man-lion and a dwarf. Vishnu rides a half-man, half-eagle called **Garuda**.

Krishna

The 7th incarnation of Vishnu. He is said to have been brought up amongst the peasants, loved women and was full of fun, so is very popular amongst the poor and lower castes. He is often painted blue and his temples usually have a number of statues of beautiful women and can include erotic carvings.

Rama

The 8th incarnation of Vishnu. Hero of the epic poem the *Ramayana*, he is seen as the ideal princely man and chivalric hero. He was married to Sita who, ever obedient, loyal and subservient, is considered the ideal of Hindu womanhood.

Other important incarnations of Vishnu include **The Buddha**, who is thought to have been the 9th, and the 10th, **Kalkin**, who is worshipped, but hasn't yet appeared.

Lakshmi

Vishnu's main wife, also the goddess of good fortune and prosperity.

Shiva

The Destroyer, also worshipped under a number of names, each one reflecting a different aspect of his character. He can be loving and gracious, but is also the destroyer. He is the god of dance (**Nataraja**), the god of animals, and the god of procreation.

His most common symbol is the *lingam* or phallic symbol. Shiva has a third eye in the middle of his forehead, a sign of wisdom and his power of destruction, as it is capable of blasting his enemies with fire. Other symbols include the bedraggled hair of an ascetic and a crescent moon. Shiva rides a bull, **Nandi**.

Parvati

The wife of Shiva, the sister of Vishnu, and the centre of the mother goddess cult. She is also known as **Durga**, depicted riding a tiger and carrying weapons in all ten hands, and as **Kali**, the goddess of destruction, the most terrifying of all the gods.

Ganesha

The popular elephant god and son of Shiva and Parvati is god of wisdom and prosperity.

Hanuman

The monkey god is also popular but less powerful. He is best known as Rama's companion on his journey to rescue Sita from the demon king of Sri Lanka, and due to his prowess as a guard his image is often found at the entrance to palaces and forts.

Ritual

Hindu worship (*puja*) is basically personal and private, although there are special ceremonies for birth, the naming of a child, marriage, the funeral cremation, etc. Most homes have a small shrine, which is usually tended by the women, and a few minutes every day will be devoted to the gods. Physical and spiritual purity are thought to go hand in hand, so even the morning wash is a religious act.

The temple priests have a series of daily ceremonies, but ordinary Hindus don't have to attend services and just pop in and out whenever it's convenient with baskets of fruit, strings of flowers and hard cash, which are presented to the gods in return for a blessing. There are also larger ceremonies, which include hymn singing and readings from the scriptures, but these are usually bound up with particular festivals. There are literally thousands of these, immensely colourful and noisy affairs with music, dance and processions.

Many people use their annual holiday to go on pilgrimage. Some will also choose to spend several months or years as a monk, taking to the road with saffron robes and begging bowl of the holy man or *saddhu*, or retreating to an *ashram* (refuge), to study under a particular *guru* (spiritual teacher).

Temple architecture

The image of the god is housed in a small sanctuary (*garbhagriha* or "womb-house"), topped by a spire (*shikhara*). The santuary is set in either a larger, rectangular hall or open courtyard with a porch at the front where the shoeminder sits. Larger temples have a number of sanctuaries, devoted to different gods, within the courtyard. The Dravidian temples in the south also have a *gopuram*, a highly decorated gateway tower, shaped like a pyramid. Some later temples, influenced by Muslim architecture, have a water tank for ritual bathing just outside the courtyard.

ISLAM

Origins

The Prophet Muhammed was born c.570 AD in Mecca, a town that was already a centre for religious pilgrimage. At the age of around 40, he started seeing visions, much to the alarm of the local dignitaries who feared he would damage the lucrative local pilgrim trade, and in 622 AD, he and his followers were thrown out. They trekked north to find a new home in a village called Yathrib, which later became known as Medina, or "the city of the Prophet". The Islamic calendar is calculated from the date of the *hijra* (trek).

In Medina, Muhammed gained followers and political power at an astounding rate, and in 628 AD he conquered Mecca. By the time he died in 632 AD, he was political and spiritual ruler of most of Arabia.

His place was taken by a series of caliphs (deputies), and the Islamic empire continued to grow. By the early-eighth century, it spread from Spain to north India. But political in-fighting began and when the fourth caliph, Ali, Muhammed's cousin and son-in-law, died in 661 AD, there was a massive split.

Sunnis

Most Muslims stuck with the new Caliph, Hasan, who believed in making decisions by consensus. These *Sunni* Muslims regarded *imams* simply as teachers or guides, and while the Caliph was the head of church and state, his authority was never absolute.

Hindu time

Time (*kalpa*) is a cycle of 4,320 million earth years, but was worked out by the teachers in god years (each god year being 360 earth years long). The kalpa is divided into 14 stages, with the universe and mankind being recreated at the beginning of each. We are in the seventh period. Each period is divided into 71 Great Intervals, each of which is divided into four *yugas*. The first yuga is 4,800 god years, the second 3,600, the third 2,400 and the 4th 1,200. We are currently in the fourth, or *Kaliyuga*, a time of great wickedness.

The title of caliph was abolished in 1924, shortly after Attaturk overthrew the last of the Ottoman emperors.

Shi'ites

The breakaway group believed that one *imam* should have absolute authority and that this leader should be a direct descendant of Muhammed through the line of Ali's daughter, Fatima. The group called themselves the *shi'at Ali*, or "the party of Ali". This was later shortened to *Shi'ite*.

A line of 12 Shi'ite *imams* continued until 878, when the last disappeared and his authority was taken over by a council of *ayatollahs* (literally meaning "signs of God"). The ayatollahs see themselves as a caretaker government until the return of the next *imam*, whom they call *al-Mahdi*, or "the rightly guided one".

Differences between the two groups have grown more ferocious than ever over the centuries, accounting for several incredibly bloody wars. Most Indian Muslims are Sunni.

There are two main holy texts in Islam, the most important of which is the *Qur'an*, the direct teachings of Muhammed. This is considered to be an absolute authority on every aspect of life. According to orthodox Muslims, you are not allowed to add or leave out anything, or even to interpret the words except exactly as they are written. The *Hadith* is a collection of stories about the life of Muhammed, written by his friends.

Beliefs

There is one eternal, all-powerful, and omniscient god (*Allah* means "god" in Arabic). A series of prophets or messengers has been used to lay down His law, including Abraham,

Moses, David, and Jesus. Muhammed is considered to be the last and greatest of the prophets.

Four things in a person's life are predetermined – their sex, whether their life will be happy or miserable, what food they will eat and the date of their death. Beyond these, everyone has free will. They are tested by Allah throughout their lives, and it is up to them to choose heaven or hell. *Islam* means "submission to God" in Arabic. A good Muslim hands all control of his life over to Allah.

Islam is the one true faith, and it is a Muslim duty to convert non-believers, by whatever means possible, including force. To die during a holy war or *jihad* is to die doing the will of Allah.

Women are bound by the same religious duties as the men, although they worship in a separate area of the mosque. The *Qur'an* favours modesty, but does not order them to wear a veil or live a sheltered, backroom life. Under *qur'anic* law, women are equal to men, with the same right of education. The only way that they lose out, in theory, is that the men, who are meant to support their wives and children, will get the lion's share of any inheritance.

Ritual

There are five essential duties, known as the Pillars of Islam, which map out not only what prayers to say, but when and how to say them. The first, the *Shahada*, is a simple creed, "There is no god but God, and Muhammed is the messenger of God", which is repeated during all prayers.

Muslims are called to prayer five times a day, starting at dawn and ending at sunset, must attend a service at the mosque at noon on Fridays, and must give part of their income to charity.

They must also observe the fast of Ramadan, a month long fast named after the victory at the battle of Badr, Ramadan, in 624 AD. For 30 days, adult Muslims are not permitted to eat, drink, smoke or have sex during daylight hours. Because the Islamic year is around 11 days shorter than the Gregorian one, Ramadan gets progressively earlier each year.

Finally, everyone who can should make the *Haj* or pilgrimage to Mecca. It is possible to visit Mecca at any time on the *umra* or Lesser Pilgrimage, but the *Haj* itself takes place over ten days, starting on the eighth day of Dhu-l-Hijja, the twelfth month in the Islamic calendar. Over a million people make the journey every year.

Mosque architecture

At the heart of the mosque is the *mirab*, a niche which points the way to Mecca. To one side, the *minbar* is a short staircase which leads to a pulpit. The main body of the mosque is an open hall or courtyard, with either a balcony or a section closed off for the women. Just outside is a water tank or fountain for ritual washing. At one corner is the *minaret* from which the prayers are called. It is forbidden to worship a human or animal image, so all decoration within the mosques is floral, geometric or, most commonly, based on writings from the *Qu'ran*. You must take off your shoes before you enter the courtyard.

BUDDHISM

Origins

Buddhism means "the path to enlightenment". Buddha means "one who has woken up". It is a title given to any truly holy man and, to distinguish him from others, Buddhism's founder is always known as The Buddha.

Born in about 566 BC, The Buddha, Prince Siddhatta Gautama of the Shakya tribe on the India/Nepal border, became unhappy with his luxurious lifestyle and turned first to spiritual studies, then left home to live as an ascetic. After six years he was still not content and sat down under a tree in Boddh-gaya to meditate. Forty-nine days later, he found his solution and the answer to the sufferings of the world. He then moved to a deer park called Sarnath, about four miles from Varanasi, where he preached his first sermon and gathered his first five disciples. The Tree of Enlightenment, or more strictly speaking the grandson of the tree, and the monastery at Sarnath, are both major pilgrimage sites.

Since then, Buddhism has spread across almost all of Asia. It also evolved and split into three main branches: southern or Theravada Buddhism, which is most common in South-East Asia; eastern Buddhism, with the largest number of followers, in China and the Far East; and northern or Tibetan Buddhism.

There are several important written works, including the *Patimokkha*, a core of 150 training rules set down by the Buddha himself, and the *Tipitaka* – a three part "basket" of the Buddha's teachings.

Beliefs

Buddhism believes that all creation is part of one vast whole and although religious worship is really considered irrelevant, gods, like men, are part of the whole and local gods are happily absorbed. Over the years, the Buddha himself has been raised to the status of a god.

The ultimate goal is to achieve enlightenment, an understanding of the absolute truth. Once you get there, you reach *Nirvana*, the state of bliss that marks the end of suffering, and leaves your mind free of doubts or prejudice, and full of joy. Those who make it become Buddhas, who are seen as teachers of both man and god.

The journey takes an incredibly long time, lasts over hundreds of lives, and involves great self-discipline and sacrifice. There are five main rules to be obeyed: do not destroy life; do not steal; do not misuse sensual pleasures; do not lie; and avoid all forms of intoxication. Charity is also extremely important, as is meditation. In order to get rid of anything that clutters or distracts the mind, you have to subdue the senses, dreams and imagination, give up material possessions and adopt a celibate lifestyle.

Ritual

Worship is meant to be unimportant but, in practice, it plays a big role, usually based around images or relics of a Buddha. Any thought or action made in the right frame of mind will help you gain merit, and even being there when someone else is making an act of merit will let some of it rub off on you. As a result, almost all Buddhist worship is public and communal.

To gain merit, you can clean or decorate the image or relic, chant prayers and make offerings. Charity is also often public as it benefits the onlooker as much as the giver and receiver. There are also services with readings, sermons and prayer chants, while at moments of change or danger, such as illness, death, or even moving to a new house, *paritta* or "protection" discourses are chanted.

There are four *uposatha* or holy days in each lunar month. Of these, the most important is the full moon. The main festival of the year is the Buddhist New Year, in spring. Other festivals vary from area to area and celebrate the seasons, such as the rains or the harvest, or episodes in the life of the Buddha. They are usually thoroughly jolly affairs full of noise and music, colour and dance.

Pilgrimage is increasingly popular, and does count as an act of merit, but is in no way essential. Little is!

Temple architecture

Buddhist shrines can be of any size – even portable. The most familiar name is the one used in the Far East – "pagoda", but in India, the shrine, which usually contains a relic, is known as a *stupa*. Traditional *stupa* design is a dome surrounded by a railed path with elaborately decorated gateways at the four compass points.

Images of Buddha were only added to the religion from about the first century AD onwards. Indian images are often beautiful but never reached the heights of opulence of those in South-East Asia, where giant, solid gold Buddhas seem almost common.

The shrine or statue can stand alone, or at the top of a worshipping hall or *chaitya*. There may also be an attached monastery or *vihara*.

JAINISM

Origins

Jainism began in the sixth century BC, as an ascetic, monastic order. Lay Jainism, which is seen as second-best by everyone, began in the fifth century AD.

Jains regard time in a cycle of 600 million years, divided into two sections, each of these subdivided into a further six. Within each cycle, there are 24 great teachers, known as *Tirthankaras* or *Jinas* (conquerors). These great teachers reintroduce the beliefs of Jain into each life cycle. Mahavira, the founder of Jainism, is believed by the Jains to be the last of the Tirthankaras of the current cycle.

"Mahavira" is an honorary title meaning "great hero". His real name was Vardhamana Jnatputra. He was born in about 540 BC near Patna in north-east India into a wealthy *kshatriya* family. At about the age of 30, he left home to become a wandering ascetic, and led this life for 12 years before he began to teach. He died in about 478 BC.

Shortly after his death, the religion split in two. Mahavira said that you had to renounce absolutely everything. The *Digambara* ("sky-clad" or naked) sect, believed that this meant giving up all clothes, while the *Shvetambaras* ("white-clad") felt that it was unnecessary to go quite so far, and that simple white robes were fine. Other disagreements followed. Women are allowed full status by the *Shvetambaras*, while the *Digambaras* exclude them, saying that they must await rebirth as men.

There is no common definitive scripture. The *Shvetambaras* use the *Siddhanta*, a series of sermons and dialogues by Mahavira written down in about 500 AD. The *Digambaras* believe that the *Siddhanta* is not authentic and turn instead to the *Anuyoga*, a collection of much older treatises.

Beliefs

Jainism is atheistic. The Tirthankaras are worshipped, but as models and teachers, not as gods. The universe is divided into a vast number of levels, gathered into four main groups, the underworld, the earth, the celestial world, and the *Siddha-loka*, or paradise.

All livings things are divided into two parts – the *jiva* (soul) and the *ajiva* (body). The *jiva* is complete in itself, immortal and omniscient, but is bound to the impure *ajiva* by *karma*. The aim is to break the tie and allow the *jiva* to discover its true nature and reach *siddha-loka*.

The only way to do this is by renouncing everything physical. The old may even be given permission to starve themselves to death as the ultimate renunciation of the flesh. There are no short cuts and the journey takes many lives.

Jains are most famous for wearing a mask to avoid swallowing small creatures and carrying a small brush to clear them aside before they sit. This is because of *ahimsa* or "non-injury", which forbids you to kill or harm any living creature – not out of pity, but to detach yourself from greed, materialism and aggression.

Ritual
Monastic
Would-be monks must prove they are physically and morally fit and must study for some time before being allowed to take their vows. They are to observe *ahimsa*, and a celibate lifestyle, renounce all ownership of possessions and avoid lying and stealing. Monks and nuns travel for around eight months of the year, gathering to study and meditate during the monsoon months.

Lay Jainism
There are eleven increasingly difficult stages in the life of a lay Jain, and 20 vows to live by. Daily *puja* (worship) begins early in the morning, after bathing but before eating. They draw a diagram which represents the universe in grains of rice; give homage to the Tirthankara; give the image a symbolic bath; make offerings of eight substances – representing the religious virtues; recite the names of all 24 Tirthankaras; and wave lighted lamps before the image.

Temple worship, pilgrimage, and birth, death and marriage ceremonies are all outside orthodox Jainism. The monks have little to do with the temples which even have lay staff.

Pilgrimage is considered important. There are also a great many festivals, the most important of which is *Paryushana*, in August/September, when people make their confessions, fast, or enter a monastery to live as an ascetic for a short while. It lasts eight days for *Shvetambaras*, and ten for the *Digambaras*.

KEY DATES IN HISTORY

First Century BC: First historic reports of South India. Although influenced to some degree by the northern Aryans, South Indians never formed part of the northern imperial

structure and were racially different, the descendants of the Dravidian peoples, the earliest known inhabitants of the subcontinent. South India at this time was split into four main kingdoms. The Cholas were predominant on the east coast, in what is now northern Tamil Nadu, with their kingdom centred on the Madras area. The Pandyas, a matrilineal society, occupied the southern tip of the subcontinent, with Madurai as their capital. The Keralaputras or Cheras held the land that is modern Kerala, while the Satiyaputras ruled an area roughly corresponding to modern Karnataka. The four seemed to be at perpetual war with each other – except when threatened from the north, when they all joined forces to defeat the common enemy.

During this time, the trading network with the rest of the world grew dramatically, both by land and sea, until India was at the centre of a web that stretched from Rome to Indonesia. This was helped by the discovery by Arab and Greek traders of the trade winds that blew across the Arabian sea, greatly cutting down on the tedious coastal journeys that had previously been required.

First century AD: Refugees from Roman Palestine arrive in South India. Christianity was theoretically brought by the apostle St Thomas, who is said to have arrived in Malabar in 52 AD. He was killed in 68 AD at Mylapore. At roughly the same time, the first Jewish community in India was set up at Cochin in Kerala.

c.550–900 AD: The political structure of the South continued to evolve, with Aryan ideas being adopted and **Hinduism** gradually taking over from Buddhism and Jainism as the major religious influence in society. In the early eighth century, a large group of Zoroastrians (Parsis), fleeing from religious persecution in their home country of Persia, settled on the west coast around Bombay.

1229–1301:   Mongols making a series of bloody raids south from central Asia, reached Madurai before the Southern Hindu kingdoms began to turn the tide and win back some of their lands. The retreat of the Sultanate created a power vacuum which left the local kings in a state of almost constant warfare and ever-changing patterns of alliances.

1498:   The Portuguese under Vasco de Gama arrived in India. By 1510, they had annexed Diu in Gujarat, and Goa, on the west coast, the first of the European powers to colonise the sub-continent.

1556–1605: Mughul king Akbar consolidated and expanded Mughul influence, extending it into South India. By his death in 1605, the Mughul Empire was firmly established.

1600: In England, Elizabeth I granted a Royal Charter to the **East India Company**.

1612–74: The British gradually asserted themselves in India. In 1618, they signed an agreement with the Mughuls, obtaining privileges in exchange for protecting the empire's trade routes from the Portuguese. In 1639, they established their first trading post at Madras. In 1661, Portuguese-held Bombay passed to Charles II as part of his marriage settlement. In 1674, Bombay became the East India Company's headquarters.

1712: Following the death of Bahadur Shah, the Mughul Empire began to decline. After the defeat of the Marathas by Afghans in 1761 at the Battle of Panipat, most of India crumbled into small principalities with no central control.

1773: The Regulating Act was passed, appointing Warren Hastings as the first Governor-General of all the British Indian territories, forcing Madras, Bombay and Calcutta to act together for the first time. He made a series of agreements with various Indian rulers, offering military assistance, enabling them to retain their local control.

1784: British Prime Minister Pitt passed the India Act, setting up official government control of the East India Company, with a London-based minister, the President of the Board, and a Calcutta-based Governor-General.

1799: Governor-General Lord **Wellesley** began the real territorial advance of British India, with an attack on the ruler of Mysore, Tipu Sultan, who was killed during the battle. Wellesley seized half his land and gave the rest back to the child head of the old Hindu ruling family. He then went on the rampage, acquiring huge tracts of land, either seizing or buying them, and insisting on stationing British troops "to guarantee the state's independence and protect it from outside attack". Wellesley was recalled in 1805 and went on to win Britain's highest honours and the title of the Duke of Wellington in his legendary defeat of Napoleon.

1818:   Almost the whole sub-continent was either directly or indirectly under British rule.

10 May, 1857:   Indian Mutiny began with the Uprising at Meerut. Indian society was split down the middle, fighting was ferocious, famous battles and seiges led to ghastly atrocities on both sides. It took the British until June 1958 to regain control.

As a result of the Mutiny, British India was again revamped. The Company's powers to govern were abolished and its army disbanded. The Governor-General, now called the Viceroy, headed an Indian Council responsible to the British Crown, while the Indian Army was reformed into the version that survived until Independence.

1877:   Queen Victoria was proclaimed Empress of India.

Late-nineteenth century: A new middle class of Anglicised Indians was born, freely borrowing lifestyle and ideas from the West. The traditionalists, Hindu and Muslim, were being left behind. For those in control, life became sweet, with peace, stability and wealth.

The same period, however, saw the emergence of the modern **Nationalist** movement. This was essentially a middle-class affair, born out of the Western thinking that had replaced tribal affiliations and, to a certain extent, religion by ardent patriotism.

December 1885:   The Indian National Congress held its first meeting in Bombay. Tariff changes that protected the British textile trade at the expense of the Indian, and the 1892 Indian Councils Act which gave the Indian legislature a purely advisory role, led to greater discontent. By 1900, the Congress had spread right across India.

1914–18:   Indian troops were poured into Europe to assist the British war effort. In 1917 the British Government publicly adopted a policy of gradual change towards self-governing, Dominion status for India.

1919: The war over, British administrators passed the Rowlatt Bills allowing for trials without juries and internment without trial in political cases. Grassroots discontent was given a new focus and charismatic leader, **Mahatma Gandhi**. A campaign of non-violent protest spread rapidly across India and, in a few places, led to riots. On 13 April 1919, in the Punjab, General Dyer lost his nerve and fired into a peaceful meeting in an enclosed space, killing 379 and injuring over 1,200. Indians everywhere became bitterly opposed to British rule.

1920: Gandhi announced a policy of Non-Cooperation which was enormously popular with the Indians as a whole.

1921: A new act passed devolving power to the provinces and giving Indians ministerial roles; the hated textile tariffs repealed.

1922: Gandhi arrested.

1924: Rowland Bills repealed; India given separate membership of the new League of Nations. Congress won significant support in local elections. Gandhi released from prison.

1927: Congress started demanding outright independence. Gandhi orchestrated a massive campaign of non-violent protest, making his famous march to the sea to make salt. Over the following year, over 100,000 people went to prison.

1929: Non-Congress Indian leaders made an agreement accepting a new federal constitution. The Viceroy began talks with Gandhi.

1932–4: Gandhi's campaign to secure political rights for the *Harijans* (untouchables) split Congress.

1935: Government of India Act passed, with the aim of creating a federal system with Dominion status.

This produced a number of autonomous states that would be ruled by elected governments while leaving the power of the Maharajahs intact in their lands. The idea of majority rule within each state, regardless of cultural differences, led however to further grievances between Hindus and Muslims.

1937: The first state elections, Congress obtained a clear majority across the country.

1938: Under the leadership of a Bombay lawyer, Muhammed Ali Jinnah, the Muslim community began to demand a nation of their own.

1939–45: India involved in Second World War without consultation. Dominion Status postponed.

1940: Muslim League officially stated their aim of a separate state of Pakistan (The name, first coined by Chaudhari Rahmat Ali in Cambridge in 1930s, was a conglomerate of the strongly Muslim territories of the sub-continent – P for Punjab, A for Afghans (Pathans), K for Kashmir, S for Sind and "stan", the Persian suffix, meaning country.)

1942: Gandhi devised another famous campaign of civil disobedience under the "Quit India" slogan. It lasted a year, during which 1,000 people were killed and 60,000 arrested.

1946: Provincial elections resulted in a clear split along religious lines. With a Labour Government now in control in Britain, the concept of independence was accepted.

Partition became the one crucial issue, sparking an increasing number of riots and attacks across the country. Gandhi, dedicated to the idea of a single state, travelled tirelessly and embarked on a number of hunger strikes in an effort to stop the violence.

June 1947: Viceroy Lord Mountbatten published a partition plan that was finally accepted by all parties.

14 August 1947: Independence Day. Two states, India and Pakistan, were created. Within days, Hindus, Sikhs and Muslims were all involved in bitter fighting – including the 50,000 troops who had been sent in to keep the peace. No one knows how many died, but it has been estimated as high as half a million, while over 12 million people left their homes to switch countries.

January 1948: Gandhi assassinated by a Hindu fanatic. Both countries were stunned, and the extremists discredited. Nehru, as Gandhi's chosen successor, finally gained a workable control of India.

1948 onwards: Since independence, India has been dominated by the Congress Party, and in particular by the Nehru
dynasty who have held the office of Prime Minister for 38
of the last forty-five years. Pandit Nehru remained as Prime
Minister until his death in 1964. In 1966, his daughter,
Indira Gandhi (no relation to the Mahatma), became Prime
Minister and, with one three-year gap, continued in office
until 1984. Her son Rajiv then took over until 1989. Both
were assassinated: Indira in 1984 by her Sikh bodyguard;
Rajiv in 1991 by Tamil extremists, during an election rally
in Madras.

For the moment, there are no family members in a position
to take office, but the younger generation is already grooming
itself and looks set to make a bid for power in the next five
to ten years. The current government is still led by Congress,
with B.V. Narasimha Rao as Prime Minister.

In global terms, India has become one of the leading
members of the Non-Aligned Movement. Only on its borders
has it been forced into confrontation. In 1948, 1965 and 1971,
it went to war with Pakistan over territorial disputes and the
two are still currently nose to nose across the Kashmiri border.
The Dalai Lama's flight from Tibet to live in India in the
1950s cooled relations with China, already soured by border
disputes here too. In 1961, India forcibly ejected Portugal from
its Indian territories, including Goa. In the mid-80s, India sent
in a peace-keeping force to prevent outright civil war in Sri
Lanka.

Internally, there has been almost continuous, but sporadic,
violence in the north, between Sikhs and Muslims in the
Punjab, with Kashmiri nationalists on the India-Pakistan
border, between fundamentalist Hindus and Muslims, and
between upper and lower castes. In the predominantly Hindu
south, however, life has been remarkably peaceful, with only
those Tamils who are offering active support to Sri Lanka's
Tamil Tigers causing any trouble at all. For the traveller,
it is calm, peaceful and friendly. You would have to be
exceedingly unlucky to find even a hint of unrest in this
laid-back environment.

THE PRACTICAL SECTION
All you need to know

ARRIVING

There are three main international air gateways to South India. **Bombay** is by far the most convenient, with a dozen different airlines running regular direct flights from Europe. There's a wide range of fares, from £450 up for the round trip. It is also the furthest north, so you will still be leaving yourself with a longish journey on arrival. Next comes **Madras**, on the east coast. Only two airlines, Air India and British Airways, run direct flights from London at present and, as these are not open to the enormously varied range of discounted tickets available for either Bombay or Delhi, Madras is usually the most expensive option. Finally, in recent years, there has been a growing number of charter flights to **Goa**. Most are linked in with short package holidays, but there should be some cheap flight-only options if you look around, or you could just abandon your hotel room and head inland.

The other alternative is to fly into **Delhi** and head south in stages after spending some time exploring the north. This is really only possible on a trip of at least two months.

Western countries tend to be fussy about night flying over crowded airport approaches, but India has no such scruples, so you will often find that you will both arrive and depart in the small hours of the morning. Because of this, I would strongly recommend booking at least your first night's hotel in advance.

Immigration and customs are both fairly straightforward.

You will be asked to fill in a currency declaration form on arrival and departure, but not much notice seems to be taken of it unless the amount has several Os attached. Customs operates a red and green channel system with spot checks and theoretically you may be asked to declare all valuables such as cameras, radios, etc, although in practice, no one seems to bother. Customs allowances are limited to 200 cigarettes and 1 litre of spirits. There are duty free shops on arrival in the main international airports, but neither the range nor the prices are good. You are not allowed to import or export Indian rupees but there are 24-hour banks in all the major airports so you can change some money on arrival. Hold on to your baggage claim numbers as you will be expected to produce them in order to take your luggage out of the airport building.

You must reconfirm your onward flight at least 72 hours before you are due to travel or you could lose your seat. On departure, you will be asked to pay an airport tax. This was Rs300 at the time of writing, but increases seem to be both large and regular. Unlike most things, it must be paid in rupees, so check the current rate before you reconvert all your money. You need to pay the tax at the airport bank and get a stamp on your ticket before you check in. I have also been asked to pay it several times when travelling on a domestic flight from an international terminal. This is not required, so stick to your guns.

The main international airports all now operate a *pre-paid* **bus and taxi system** to help you avoid being flung straight into the chaos of bargaining your fare. There are stalls within the airport building for both taxis and the different bus companies. All of them offer a door to door service to your hotel. The buses are obviously much cheaper, but they can also take a long time as they will wait to fill up and will then often make a number of stops before they get to your stop. Taxis are more expensive, but are still very cheap by Western standards (even though they do cost about 30% more than you will pay going in the other direction). When you buy your ticket, it will have a taxi number on it and a forecourt supervisor will find your driver for you.

Driving yourself in India is not recommended – see p.101. In any case the constant flaring of trouble in different parts of

Asia has made the old overland routes virtually impassable. Those who still want to try it will need a customs carnet valid for 6 months. If you fail to remove the car when you leave you'll be liable for duty of 300% of its new value. You will also need an international driving licence and local Third Party insurance.

ACCOMMODATION

Many people assume that visiting India equates with discomfort. This just isn't true. In most places that you are likely to visit, you will have a wide choice of accommodation from the most luxurious to the most spartan. Which you choose depends only on your budget. The few exceptions are in the smaller towns that are off the main tourist or business track, where a tourist bungalow or one or two star hotel will be the best around. Prices are reviewed and raised every October, all over India.

UPMARKET

The majority of truly luxurious hotels in India are run by two Indian-owned hotel chains, the **Oberoi** and **Taj** groups. Both operate business hotels in the major cities, such as Bombay and Madras, but they have also built resort-style hotels in main tourist areas and have converted some of India's many magnificent palaces into hotels that rival some of the best in the world. These all provide a full range of facilities from air-conditioning and swimming pools to extravagant shopping arcades and beauty salons. Service and hygiene are impeccable. As the upmarket package tours all use these, you should book ahead in high season.

There are fewer **Centaur** Hotels, owned by Air India. These are designed as business and airport hotels, so they are often sited inconveniently far from town between the runway and a main road. The facilities however are good, and they are very useful if you have an awkward flight call.

Finally come the **Ashok** hotels, run by the Indian Tourist Development Corporation. Unfortunately, it is impossible to assume any given standard where you see the name, as they are built to a variety of standards, from two star to five star. The best equal anything run by Taj or Oberoi, but the quality of the management seems to vary to the point where there are Ashok hotels with running water down the walls, but not in the shower!

In Bombay and Madras, you will find a wider variety of upmarket hotels, while the southern part of Goa is rapidly being lined by a variety of resort hotels representing virtually every major chain in the world. There is no shortage of good accommodation there now, but once Goa has become just another international strip, will anyone want to stay in them?

Prices are cheap by international standards, at anything from £20–50 a night, but this can still make a severe dent in your travelling budget if you never venture lower down the social scale. I prefer to make occasional forays when I need access to a telephone that works, am desperate for hot water, or want to escape for a short while from the bustle and heat of the country. Morale gets a much needed boost in surroundings of relaxation and efficiency, while prices further down the hotel scale are so low that you can afford to pamper yourself once in a while without feeling guilty.

The very best hotels are classified as five star luxury, as opposed to ordinary five star. This means that on top of the normal 10% hotel tax, added to all hotel bills, there is an extra 6% luxury tax.

MID-RANGE

Once outside the five star range, standards and prices drop rapidly. The comfortable, cheap, mid-range hotel that is the backbone of European tourism just does not exist, apart from one or two extremely rare exceptions. Prices range from around £4–15 a night for a double room.

What you can normally expect for this is a room with rather hard, lumpy twin beds, with a bottom sheet and probably some sort of light covering, lino floors, a fan and light that work and a private shower/toilet. The toilet might be Western-style, although the flush rarely works and a bucket and baler is provided instead. The shower probably will work, but with hot water only for a couple of hours a day or on request. There will normally be a simple restaurant and some sort of room service set-up for soft drinks and sandwiches. It will usually be perfectly clean and hygienic, often friendly and helpful.

At the top of the mid-range are the **minor palace hotels**. Sadly, there are not as many left in the south as remain further north, but there are still a few around, and where you can find one, go there, if only for a drink. They are often still owned and managed by the maharajah's family. A motley collection of small palaces, hunting lodges and some rather larger properties purpose-built as hotels by the British, most look as if they haven't been touched since independence. Stuffed animals adorn the walls and floors while faded photos of hunting parties stand gathering dust in libraries of yellowing leather-bound books. Old family retainers, resplendent in gold braid, creak their way across the dining room to serve you from the maharajah's teapot. If they have time, it is easy to get them talking about life pre-1948, or persuade them to give you the guided tour. To me, these are the very best of India's hotels, making up in atmosphere what they lack in comfort.

Another option in this range is the **tourist bungalows**. These are usually owned and operated by the state tourist boards. Few are as aesthetically pleasing as the small palaces, but you can rely on a certain degree of cleanliness and efficiency and can usually be sure that if there is a tourist bungalow in town, it will provide the best value in its class. Most have a choice of rooms, from dormitory beds to doubles with private bathrooms, ranging in price from around Rs30 to Rs250 a night. There will usually be a dining hall and, where possible, they have pleasant gardens. They are a good place to meet other travellers, and some operate a book exchange in a variety of European languages.

At the bottom of this price bracket are a wide selection of privately run hotels of all shapes and sizes. Some are good, some dreadful. The only way to judge is either by recommendation or inspection.

CHEAP

Cheap accommodation costs about £4 for a double room at the very most and works its way right down the scale.

The cheapest I was ever offered was Rs5 a night in a pilgrim hostel.

At the top of this price range come a variety of hotels, some just as good or better than those in the mid-range, and much cheaper. They are divided by locals into "Western" or "Indian", and they will be reluctant to point you towards an Indian one. The differences are minimal, however, based almost exclusively on what type of toilet they have, and there are good or bad examples of both. Most have a working ceiling fan (probably the most important consideration) and many will offer you a private toilet and shower. It is unlikely that either will work properly, however, and you will be reliant on the bucket and baler. Hot water is a distant fantasy. Many either offer triple rooms or will add in an extra bed for a minimal increase in the room price. Few have restaurants, although if you are determined not to go out, you can usually pay one of the staff to go and get you a take-away, anything from a drink to a full meal.

Amongst the best cheap accommodation are the **railway retiring rooms**, again anything from dormitories to private rooms with facilities. With prices as low as Rs10 a day (you hire by the 24 hours), they are exceptionally good value, extremely convenient and, unfortunately, exceedingly popular.

There are also a number of Youth Hostels, YMCAs and YWCAs, all of which give good, clean if basic dormitory accommodation. You don't have to be a YHA member to stay in them, although you will get preference and a cheaper rate, nor are there any of the many irritating rules you find in some European hostels.

If you want something cheaper still, it is sometimes possible to stay at the pilgrim hostels which are run by the monks to provide accommodation at a nominal cost. These obviously have fairly strict house rules, so don't stay there unless you are prepared to observe them.

Finally, it is often possible to do a deal with a **local family**, especially if you are planning to stay there for some time.

TOUTS

Every bus and train station is swarming with touts, some of them rickshaw drivers, who will promise you the earth to get you to go with them. They operate on a commission basis, so will take you to those places that pay up. Hotels that refuse can find themselves half empty as arriving travellers are told that it has burnt down, the roof has collapsed or the manager vanished. If you have somewhere definite in mind, insist on being taken there first. If not, give them your price bracket and let them take you around. Don't be afraid to inspect the room before agreeing and to say no if you don't like it.

FOOD

To Indians, Western food is bland and drab; amongst Westerners, one of the most frequent complaints is that whatever the combination of spices, it is usually so powerful and over-the-top that you can't taste individual flavours, so all dishes end up tasting the same! A number of foreigners get ill, not because of some fell disease, but simply because their stomachs can't cope with the spices and the amount of oil in Indian cooking.

You can get superb meals in India but, as ever, you do have to know where to look. On the whole, while you will be given something filling, nutritious and cheap, the quality will not be good, especially if you eat meat. Menus are famous for two things. One is the eccentricity of their spelling. It can be a game as good as a crossword trying to work out exactly what is on offer, from scrumpled egs to hororlixx. If in doubt, try out loud with an Indian accent – it's all phonetic. The other is their length, often running to some ten pages. At even the smallest restaurants, this will often be split into Indian, Chinese and Continental (Western).

WESTERN FOOD

Western food, of sorts, is available in most places, but even so after a couple of weeks most tourists find themselves craving simple, well-cooked, clean flavours like sharp apples, plain boiled vegetables or mashed potato. Unless you take a camping gas stove with you, these will be unobtainable, but a handful of muesli bars or other packaged treats of the sort that won't melt or crush can be great morale boosters.

The breakfast menu is the most comprehensive. Cornflakes and porridge are both usually grey, are made from millet rather than wheat, and are served with hot milk. Next come the eggs, in any form – boiled, poached, scrambled, fried or omelettes – also often grey. To finish up, there is toast and jam. The bread (also grey) is sweet and slightly elastic. The jam is highly coloured but seems to have little to do with fruit.

Later in the day, the menu seems to consist almost entirely of omelettes, in various guises, and chips, although some of the more adventurous will add spaghetti with a rather metallic, glutinous sauce. The chips however (ask for finger chips to distinguish them from crisps, also called chips) are usually quite good.

In the major cities these days there is usually at least one wonderfully hedonistic ice cream shop serving vast and varied sundaes, which are catching on in a big way with Indian teenagers. Little Americas, one and all, they are squeaky clean, neon and chrome establishments, pumping out rock music and chantilly cream in equal proportions. Some will also serve good burgers or pizza and, best of all, they are safe and hygienic.

If you are truly desperate for good Western food, the final solution is to head, once again, for the five star luxury hotels which will offer a full selection from croissants to steak, salad bar to sponge pudding.

CHINESE FOOD

Here again, you will find a familiar menu, with everything from chop suey and chow mein to sweet and sour. There will be few surprises and little in the way of haute cuisine. As methods of cooking Chinese food are far closer to Indian than Western methods, however, the quality is usually OK.

INDIAN COOKING

The word "curry" does not exist in India. There are several different theories as to where the word comes from: the

---

Southern Spice

Some two dozen different spices are commonly used, including chilli, cloves, turmeric, cardamom, fenugreek, cinnamon, cumin, garlic, mace, nutmeg, coriander, tamarind, poppy seeds, caraway, ginger, peppercorns, asafoetida, mustard and kari. These are blended by hand into various different combinations, known collectively as *masalas*, the precise mix often a jealously guarded secret. The "hot" is almost always provided by chillies, which are small, either red or green, come fresh, dried or ground, and are all ferocious.

Tamil word *kari*, which simply means "sauce"; the *kari* leaf, a commonly used spice, or *karhi*, a north Indian dish made from chickpea flour and buttermilk. Whichever is correct, the Indians would never dream of using it in the same blanket way we do.

Most Indian meals, including breakfast, involve highly spiced vegetables, meat or fish, served with rice and/or one of the many breads on offer, with side dishes of pickles or chutneys and *dahi* (curd or yoghurt). Mutton (either sheep or goat) and chicken are the most common meats, although you will find some pork in the far south, where Muslims are few, while in Kerala and Goa, which have large Christian populations, you will occasionally even find beef. However, the majority throughout South India are vegetarians.

By far the most common meal is the *thali*, which takes its name from the large round metal tray on which it is served. More frequently, however, it is simply called a "meal", and you will see the signs in front of every restaurant saying "meals ready". This is fast food, Indian-style. For a price that can be as little as Rs8, you will be given a huge heap of rice, some bread, three or four little bowls of different curries and at least one sort of chutney or pickle. The more upmarket outlets will also give you a bowl of curd and a pudding; in others, you will have to pay a little extra for these.

Some restaurants are strictly vegetarian. In the others you will be given a choice of "veg or non-veg". Non-veg usually costs a couple of rupees more. In many restaurants these days you will be given a perfectly normal plate, fork and spoon with which to eat. The traditional way of doing things is rather different, however, and you will still meet it. In the south, instead of the *thali* tray, you will be given a large piece of banana or palm leaf to use as a plate. You eat with your right hand, never the left, which is used for ablutions. (To use your left hand for eating is a grave social error, while to offer food to anyone else with your left hand is a major league insult.) The restaurant will have a sink in one corner for washing hands, before and after the meal, but it is a good idea to carry a small cake of soap with you and, if you are really worried, take a pack of antiseptic wipes. Don't worry about being dainty, just roll up your sleeves and dig in. If you look around you, most people will be covered up to their elbow.

Men with huge buckets of food circulate the restaurant giving more of anything and everything until you manage to convince them that you can't eat another thing, which you do by folding your leaf in half. The meals vary in quality, but are nutritious, come in quantities sufficient to satisfy the

---

Paan

At the end of a meal, or just for fun any time, comes a *paan*. The *paan* leaf itself is around four or five inches long and is heart-shaped. It is used mainly as an edible holder for a wide range of ingredients which will be mixed, to your specification, by the many *paan* sellers on the streets. The main ingredient is chopped betel nut, a mild intoxicant which can be addictive and will blacken the teeth if taken too often. Trying it while on holiday should do no harm, however. On its own, the nut is fairly tasteless, so to this will be added spices such as cloves, cardamom or fennel, lime paste or *catechu* – a red paste made from the bark of a tree. Once the *paan* is well chewed, you spit it out. This accounts for the many red splotches you see all over the pavements, floors, and even walls!

---

most gargantuan appetite, and as value for money, cannot be beaten.

Indian puddings are incredibly sweet, using, at their best, four times as much sugar as any other ingredient. Most are based on milk, rice, semolina or sago, flour dough and syrup, or any combination of these ingredients. For many, the milk is boiled right down until it forms a dough-like substance called *khoya*, which is then flavoured, set or fried. For those, like me, who find Indian sweets too much of a good thing, there is happily a wide range of fresh fruit available year round, all of which is safe as long as you peel or wash it yourself.

SOUTHERN DISHES

Breads and pancakes

Probably the most famous southern dishes are the wide variety of breads and pancakes that are usually eaten either for breakfast or as snacks. The most famous are:

Idlis

Dumplings made of ground, fermented rice flour, bound by a lentil *dal* and steamed. Usually eaten for breakfast, and to my mind, tasteless and boring.

Southern Specialities

Most of the dishes popularised by Indian restaurants in the West, such as biriyanis and tandooris, come from northern India. South Indian food is only now beginning to be known outside the area, chiefly due to the efforts of returning tourists. To make some generalisations, South Indian food is usually hotter, more often vegetarian, and less rich, using fewer cream sauces than in the north. One of the most obvious differences is in the extensive use of coconut and lime in the south, as flavourings and ingredients, in both savoury and sweet dishes. Coconut oil is also used as one of the most common cooking oils in the area. Among the highlights of southern food are the wonderful array of fresh fish available around the coast and the wide choice of fresh fruit on offer everywhere in the region.

Dosas

Very large (up to a metre diameter), very thin pancakes, make of the same fermented rice flour and dal, this time fried on a large griddle. They can be eaten with any sauce or syrup, but are most commonly found wrapped round a highly spiced potato filling as a *masala dosa*, probably the most common snack food in South India.

Appam

Thick pancakes made of rice flour and coconut and fried, crisp on the outside, soft in the middle, can come with a variety of flavourings baked in.

Puris

Very small wholewheat pancakes, twice fried so they puff up in the centre. Should be eaten hot while still fresh and crispy.

There are also **poppads** (like the northern poppadoms), **murka, vadas** and **uppamas**, as well as the **chappatis** and **paratha** that are common all over India.

Main meals

As elsewhere in India, the meal will consist of the staple rice, plain boiled or flavoured with coconut or lime, together with a variety of different spicy meat or vegetable dishes based on chicken or mutton, potato, cabbage, aubergine, okra, chickpeas and other pulses. Various fish are on offer, such as pomfret, shark, mackerel and sardines, or shell fish such as lobster, prawns, crabs, mussels and oysters. A number of dishes are cooked with **coconut milk, ginger** or **lime** as well as the more common spices.

Rasam is the local version of *dhal*, the ubiquitous lentil dish. Made in the south from a yellow lentil, the *arhar*, this is much more liquid than in the north, being used as a soup that accompanies almost every meal. Known in Tamil Nadu as *milagu tannir* or pepper water, it was later anglicised in name and style to become mulligatawny soup.

Sambhar is a good, all-purpose name for the vegetable stew that forms the basis of two meals a day, combining various pulses and vegetables, dependent upon what is in season, and flavoured with chili, coconut and tamarind.

Puddings and sweets

Most popular puddings occur in a roughly similar form all over India, although often under different names. In the south, there are only two major differences. One is, yet again, the addition of coconut; the other a substance called **jaggery**, a dark brown, molasses style sugar syrup that comes straight from sugar cane, which is grown all over the south. Look out also for the bananas, of which there are a number of varieties, including pink ones.

Payasam

A rich pudding made from *khoya*, with rice, sago or semolina and either *jaggery* or a normal sugar syrup and flavoured with raisins and nuts, cashew, pistachio or almond.

Barfi

Made from *khoya* and with flavours from rose to chocolate – and, of course, coconut.

Kulfi
Probably the only Indian pudding most Westerners have heard
of. Ice cream made from *khoya*, with sugar, cardamom and
pistachio.

Firnee
Rice pudding with milk, almonds, raisins and pistachios.

Gulab jamun
Khoya and flour dough balls, flavoured with rosewater and
cardamom, deep fried and served in syrup.

Bida
The South Indian version of *paan*, shaped like a pyramid and
containing coconut (what else?), as well as the more common
ingredients.

WHERE TO EAT

Standard advice says that you should never eat at **market
stalls**. This is not necessarily true and, if you are on a
low budget, they can provide a wide variety of options
at extremely low prices, although almost everything will of
necessity be snacks rather than full meals. There are a couple
of basic rules that should ensure your continued survival. If
your eye alights on something uncooked, such as the mounds
of cucumbers which look so tempting to the hot and thirsty,
make sure you buy one that has not been peeled or cut in
any way. If you are after something cooked, make sure that
you get the one that is in the pan when you arrive, so you
can watch it being cooked and eat it before either fresh air,
extra fingers or flies get a chance to go near it. The damage
is done when things are allowed to sit around.

There are a huge number of **cheap restaurants** around, all
serving pretty much the same menu with varying degrees of
success. A meal at any of them will cost you between Rs10
and Rs50, dependent on which menu you choose and how
many extras, such as soft drinks, you have. Unless you have
a recommendation, choose by degree of cleanliness and, that
age old standby, how many locals seem to be eating there.

It is quite OK to wander in, have a look around and read the menu before making up your mind. In many, the cooking is done out front as a draw to customers, so if you can stand the heat, you can get a table nearby and supervise your meal as it is prepared. If you can't find anywhere else inspiring, the **railway station** again comes into its own. All but the very smallest stations have separate veg and non-veg restaurants, serving *thalis* and a small range of Western food. Don't expect a gastronomic experience, but the surroundings are clean and the prices low. The **India Coffee Houses** are a nationwide chain of cheap cafés/restaurants, which are also very good value, with quite pleasant meals in relatively clean surroundings. For women travelling on their own, these usually have a ladies' dining room, if you want to relax your guard a little while eating.

There are some, although not many, **mid-range restaurants**, with more interesting menus, good food and some attempt at interesting decor. In the south, these are almost all either in the major cities or on the coast. Many are attached to hotels. Expect to pay from Rs100 to Rs300 a head, so if you are on a very tight budget you won't be able to afford these every day, but don't ignore them as these are where you find some of the best food in India, particularly in fishing ports such as Cochin where the fish is fabulous.

Finally, for the truly upmarket experience, we are back yet again at the **five-star luxury hotels** which are almost the only places which combine good food with grand settings, silver service and, usually, either a live band or cabaret. They are not exclusively tourist preserves in the evenings as the Indian upper classes will also come here to dine and dance. If you want good Western food, they are the only place to go. You will notice the difference to your wallet, but by Western standards they are still very cheap, unless you start on the cocktails. It is fairly difficult to spend more than about £10 on the meal itself – less than you would probably spend in your local High Street Indian restaurant at home.

If you want the experience at an even lower price, go at lunchtime, as almost all the big hotels run a fixed price lunch buffet, with prices from Rs150 to Rs300. Three or four curries, three or four Western hot dishes, a full range of side dishes and salads and a selection of multi-coloured puddings, usually of the nursery variety, are ranged along a groaning table. Eager waiters press you to go back again and again until you have tried every dish on offer and feel so bloated that all you can do is stagger on to the terrace or to the lounge and collapse there, blissfully air-conditioned, for the rest of the afternoon. As a morale-boosting treat, this can't be beaten.

DRINK

ALCOHOL

On the whole, India is a non-alcoholic country, so alcoholic drinks can be hard to come by. Some states are completely dry, giving drink licences only to the major hotels; others run dry days. Few restaurants serve alcohol, and where there are bars they tend to be hidden discreetly from view, their windows painted black to stop passers-by seeing in. Indian women would never dream of going near a bar and I have brought one to instant silence just by walking through the door, even though I was in the company of several men. We were hustled through and into the garden before anyone moved and when we left were shown out of a side door so that I couldn't disturb proceedings again! The exceptions are the five star hotels, which are designed almost exclusively for foreigners and run what we would consider a normal bar service.

India, wherever possible, believes in making things for itself rather than importing, so you will rarely get any familiar brand name spirits. Where you can find them, they are exorbitantly expensive. What is normally on offer is a local copy. These are known collectively as Indian-Made Foreign Liquor, either made from scratch or by adding imported concentrates to the local brew. The gin and rum can be good, although still best if drowned. The rest should be avoided.

There are a great many local spirits. The two main ones are *feni*, a powerful distilled liquor which comes from Goa and is made from either cashew trees or coconut palms, and *toddy*, which is much less alcoholic, and is made all over the south – from coconuts!

Imported wines are again rare, tend to suffer en route,

and fetch astronomic prices. There is some wine made in India, mainly in the south-western states of Goa, Karnataka and Maharashtra. I approached the Goanese red with some caution to find, to my surprise, a rather pleasant, smoky, sweet wine not unlike port.

In theory, there is an amazing variety of local beers and you will often be presented with an impressive drinks menu listing some two dozen. In practice, if you try ordering them, the choice will rapidly come down to one or two. They are all lagers with plenty of gas and varying degrees of alcohol, and all come in litre bottles. The most common is Kingfisher. A beer will cost anything from Rs10 to Rs50, dependent on which state you are in, the quality of the establishment, or how much they think they can get away with.

NON-ALCOHOLIC DRINKS

Tap water is, of course, extremely dangerous and should never be drunk unless thoroughly boiled, or otherwise treated. In the best hotels, the water in the restaurants is treated and I have normally drunk it without damage, but you still should not use the tap water. Thankfully, these days, **mineral water** seems to be available almost everywhere in the country and you rarely have to resort to the chlorine tablets unless you are trying to save money. The most common brand is Bisleri, but a number of others are now making an appearance. There is little to choose between them and any will do as long as the seal round the top of the bottle is intact. I have been asked anything from Rs6 to Rs35 a litre, but the norm from the street stalls seems to be around Rs10–12.

A major breakthrough in the **soft drinks** market came recently when India finally allowed Pepsi to manufacture under licence in the country. Until then, there were no familiar brand names, and even now Pepsi is rarely found. The local versions are freely available, however, and are perfectly acceptable. The most popular are Thums Up, a cola equivalent; Gold Spot, a Fanta-style orange; and Limca, which is lemonade. The drawbacks are that they are extremely sweet and sticky, and, rather too frequently, taste of soap. They cost from Rs3–6 on the street stalls, as long as you return the bottle.

Most people get heartily sick of these sugary drinks fairly fast and start looking longingly towards the many stalls offering **fresh fruit juices**, from sugar cane to mango or apple. Don't be tempted. Quite apart from being served in glasses that are suspect at best, most are diluted with ordinary tap water. You will almost certainly regret it if you succumb. The one exception in the south is **coconut water**. The coconuts are picked very young, before the husk has a chance to set, so the fruit is still full of liquid. The street sellers will just hack the top off with a machete and give it to you to drink with a straw. Once you have finished, hand it back and they will scoop loose any young pulp that is forming for you to eat. Delicious, refreshing and absolutely safe.

Once you are in a place with clean glasses, one of the most refreshing drinks around is **fresh lime soda**, ordinary soda water with fresh lime or lemon juice, served either plain, salted or with sugar, according to your taste (specify or it will come sweetened). Another option is a **lassi**, a curd drink like very thin yoghurt, which comes either plain, sweet or salt, or with a variety of flavours from fruit to masala (chilli). These are not only refreshing on their own, but have the added advantage, with a meal, that they are excellent at counterbalancing over-hot spices.

Although India is a major producer of **tea**, it can be surprisingly difficult to get a good cup. The traditional Indian way of making it is to put the tea leaves in with half milk, half water, and enormous quantities of sugar, and boil it all up together. All the *chai* you are offered on the stations, from street stalls or in the cheaper restaurants, will be made like this. It is cheap and some people like it. Once you go a little upmarket, you will be able to ask for "tray tea", which comes on a tray, with tea, milk and sugar separately, British-style. It can still be a disgusting, luke-warm, stewed mess.

Coffee, traditionally, is made the same way, with everything boiled up together. It is far more common in the south than it is further north, but even here, it is quite a bit more expensive than tea. The concept of black coffee with no sugar (or combining things for yourself) is spreading slowly and seemed far easier on my last trips than on previous ones, but it is still relatively rare and the resulting hot brown water bears little resemblance to coffee. Mysore coffee is considered to be a gourmet treat and will generally be served with suitable fanfares at the best restaurants and hotels. I find it so mild as to be almost tasteless. One odd relic of the Raj is that you will frequently find Horlicks on the menu if you feel in need of a little home comfort and a good night's sleep.

WHERE TO GO

Travellers in India often set themselves impossible targets, trying to "do" the whole country, without ever stopping to think that it is nearly as large as Western Europe and getting around is infinitely slower and more difficult. India is also one of the most exhausting countries in the world, so unless you have months to spare, limit the area you plan to visit. There will be plenty to see and do and you won't crawl home on your knees. Having said that, it's surprising how much ground you can cover in a three to four week trip if you are prepared to keep moving and **plan your route before you go**.

Wherever you go in South India, you can be sure of several things. The scenery will be stunning, the vegetation lush, the people friendly, the food and the weather hot, and there will be plenty of things for culture vultures to latch on to. The pace of life is generally slower than in the north and, as there are far fewer Western tourists in most places, you will truly be able to step into a different way of life.

Indians seem never really to have caught on to the idea of **beach** holidays, so although they have several thousand miles of some of the most beautiful coast in the world, only a few fragments of it are designated as swimming beaches. The rest act as toilets, so don't be clever and try to find yourself a deserted cove. There are three main beach resorts in the area. **Goa** is the largest and most famous, with some dozen different beaches stretched along a 120-kilometre sea front (see pages 57–186). In the far south is the much smaller **Kovalam Beach**, while in the east, just south of Madras, is another cluster of small resorts, based on the town of **Mamallapuram**. There are also one or two beaches just south of Bombay, used by locals for days out, but these have virtually no accommodation. Those who want a degree of sophistication and Western-style luxury in their hotel should look first to Goa, where the choice of international hotels is growing rapidly. Mamallapuram has a couple, and Kovalam only one. Those looking for the simple life will be able to find it in all three places, with a good range of small hotels and beach-front houses to let.

People hoping to do some heavy-duty **sightseeing** will be able to find enough to keep them happy in virtually any area. There are two main places to head for, however. The first is **Mysore**, a small city by Indian standards, which not only has a feast of treasures within its boundaries, but is well placed for visiting a great many more. The other is **eastern Tamil Nadu**, from Madurai in the south up to Madras. The whole area is littered with vast, extravagant and artistically stunning temples, most of them extremely ancient and incredibly well preserved.

Those looking for *wildlife* or *walking* should head inland to the **Nilgiri and Cardamom Hills** that start near Mysore and roughly follow the border between Kerala and Tamil Nadu down to the southern tip of India at Kanniyakumari. Throughout these hills are scattered some eight national parks, of which the best and most famous are perhaps Bandipur, Nagarahole and Periyar. All have elephants and tigers (although sadly you are unlikely to see these), as well as a host of other species, bird and mammal. **Ootacamund** and **Kodaikanal** are the two main hill stations for the south and both are excellent bases or starting points for trekking trips through the tea and coffee plantations and jungle of these stunning mountains.

THE WEATHER

Old India hands used to boast that they could forecast the exact day, and even hour, that the **monsoon** would hit. Well, since then, something's gone wrong. My last two trips to India were both carefully timed, I thought, to start just after the monsoon. Instead, as I left the airport, the rain was sheeting down and for the next two weeks I paddled round India as, in town after town, people looked at me and said: "Oh, no, the monsoon is late this year. It is only just starting!"

Whether it is yet another manifestation of the greenhouse effect or not, who can say? But the monsoon has definitely become erratic in recent years and as it is the one major climatic influence in South India, this can make planning a trip in the mid part of the year somewhat of a lottery.

For most of the year, the prevailing wind across India is from the north-east. The monsoon surges across the sub-continent from the south-west. Officially it begins in the south in late May/early June, sweeping north-east to hit Delhi some six weeks later. The amount of rain varies both from season to season and area to area, but when it comes, it falls in short, sharp bursts, often accompanied by strobe-like electric storms. Between them, the evaporating water steams skywards creating a pressure cooker-like atmosphere of high temperatures and higher humidity. The normally arid landscape turns to a

---

Indian Tourist offices abroad.

UK – 7 Cork Street, London W1X 2AB. Tel: 071 437 3677/8
USA – Suite 15, North Mezzanine, 30 Rockerfeller Plaza, New York, NY 10112. Tel: (212) 586 4901/2/3
   230 North Michigan Avenue, Chicago, IL 60601.
   3550 Wilshire Boulevard, Suite 204, Los Angeles, CA 90010. Tel: (213) 380 8855.
Australia – Carlton Centre, 65 Elizabeth Street, Sydney, NSW 2006. Tel: (02) 232 1600/1796
Canada – 60 Bloor Street, West Suite No 1003, Toronto, Ontario M4W 3S8. Tel: (416) 962 3787/8.

---

jewel-bright emerald as the vegetation thrusts up so fast you can almost watch it grow, twining its way round anything foolish enough to remain stationary. For those who don't mind getting wet it can be incredibly exciting, but with it inevitably come floods, disrupted power and a generally higher level of chaos than normal.

Winter **temperatures** right across the south are warm, ranging from a minimum of around 18°C at night, to between 27–33°C during the day. Humidity is around 50 – 60%. From March to May, the weather remains dry, but the temperatures soar and a parching sun beats down, leaving you too sapped of energy to do anything but sit in the shade and complain. During the monsoon (mid-summer), temperatures range from 28° to a horrible 41°C during the day, staying at between 20° and 22°C overnight. The humidity climbs at times to a stifling 95%. The only exception to this rule is in the Western Ghats, the collective name for the central mountain ranges that run from north to south, where the temperature is always pleasantly cool, often with dank, European-style mist in the mornings, and cold enough for quilts and log fires from October onwards. Sitting at home, you might decide this sounds horrible, but as a relief from the heat of the plains, it is marvellously refreshing.

The best time to visit is between late October and March, when temperatures are low enough to make life pleasant and, although there is some year-round rain in the south, you are almost guaranteed sunny skies.

FESTIVALS AND FAIRS

Festivals abound throughout India, varying from small, introverted celebrations behind closed doors, to major production numbers, with processions, music, feasts and dance. Almost all have a religious base, so dates vary. The Tourist Office should be able to provide you with a calendar of fixed dates for the coming year. The main ones to watch out for are:

January
Tiruchirapalli and Madurai (Tamil Nadu) and all over Karnataka. Known as **Pongal** in Tamil Nadu and **Sankranti** in Karnataka. Three-day harvest festival with highly decorated cows being processed through the streets.

January/February
Madurai (Tamil Nadu). **Float Festival**, a river procession, with temple deities on board a sacred barge.

February/March
Goa. **Mardi Gras**, the massive pre-Lenten carnival made famous throughout the world by the Portuguese and Spanish, has made its home here also, in week-long festivities unlike anything else in India.

April/May
Trichur (Kerala). **Pooram**, temple festival with processional elephants, music and fireworks.

April/May
Madurai (Tamil Nadu). **Meenakshi Kalyanam,** ten day festival culminating in chariot procession.

August/September
Aranmula, Kottayam, Alleppey (Kerala). **Onam**, the main festival in Kerala, officially a harvest festival, but the main

Weather chart

Temperature in °C　　Rainfall in mm

		Jan	Feb	Mar	Apr	May	Jun	Jul	Aug	Sep	Oct	Nov	Dec
Bangalore													
Temp	max	28	31	33	34	33	30	28	29	28	28	27	27
	min	15	16	19	21	21	20	19	19	19	19	17	15
Rain	avg	4	14	6	37	119	65	93	95	129	195	46	16
Bombay													
Temp	max	31	32	33	33	33	32	30	29	30	32	33	32
	min	16	17	20	24	26	26	25	24	24	23	20	18
Rain	avg	0	1	0	0	20	647	945	660	309	117	7	1
Cochin													
Temp	max	31	31	31	31	31	29	28	28	28	29	30	30
	min	23	24	26	26	26	24	24	24	24	24	24	23
Rain	avg	9	34	50	139	364	756	572	386	235	333	184	37
Coimbatore													
Temp	max	30	33	35	35	34	31	30	31	32	31	29	29
	min	19	19	21	23	23	22	22	22	22	22	21	19
Rain	avg	7	4	5	70	76	35	37	18	42	127	127	25
Madras													
Temp	max	29	31	33	35	38	37	35	35	34	32	29	28
	min	20	21	23	26	28	28	26	26	25	24	23	21
Rain	avg	24	7	15	25	52	53	83	124	118	267	309	139
Madurai													
Temp	max	30	32	35	36	37	37	36	35	35	33	31	30
	min	21	22	23	25	26	26	26	25	25	24	23	22
Rain	avg	26	16	21	81	59	31	48	117	123	179	161	43
Panaji (Goa)													
Temp	max	31	32	32	33	33	31	29	29	29	31	33	33
	min	19	20	23	25	27	25	24	24	24	23	22	21
Rain	avg	2	0	4	17	18	580	892	341	277	122	20	37
Pune													
Temp	max	31	33	36	38	37	32	28	28	29	32	31	30
	min	12	13	17	21	23	23	22	21	21	19	15	12
Rain	avg	2	0	3	18	35	103	187	106	127	92	37	5
Trivandrum													
Temp	max	31	32	33	32	31	29	29	29	30	30	30	31
	min	22	23	24	25	25	24	23	23	23	23	23	23
Rain	avg	20	20	43	122	249	331	215	164	123	271	207	73

attraction is a huge and decorative snake-boat race through the lagoons amongst the rice paddies.

August/September
Bombay, Pune (Maharashtra), Madras (Tamil Nadu). **Ganesh Chaturthi**, festival of the elephant god, Ganesh, with clay models of the god being processed through the streets then taken down to the water and submerged.

September/October
Mysore (Karnataka). **Dussehra**, the ten-day festival, is one of the most important in India and is celebrated all over the country. In Mysore, however, it is a major production number, still using pageantry that dates back to the middle ages.

October/November
Diwali, the festival of lights, is the most important in the Hindu calendar, their equivalent of Christmas, and is celebrated right across the country.

PAPERWORK

VISAS

Visas are required by citizens of all EEC countries, as well of the USA, Canada, New Zealand, and Australia – and almost everyone else. If you are unsure, you should check with your nearest Embassy or High Commission. The cost has recently come down, and the system has been simplified, so, as a tourist, you are automatically given either a 30-day six-month visa. This will run from the date of *issue*, not from your date of travel. If you wish to stay longer, you must apply for an extension to the District Superintendent of Police, and each case is judged on its own merit.

If you submit your application in person, you will be able to collect it in 48 hours. If you post it in, it will take about four weeks. You will need two passport photos and – it's surprising how many people forget – a current passport, with at least six

---

Visas – where to apply

UK – Visa Department, Indian High Commission, India House, Aldwych, London WC2B 4NA. Telephone enquiries: 071 240 2084/071 836 0990 from 09.30 – 13.00 and 14.00 – 17.30, Monday to Friday.

USA – Indian Embassy, 2107 Massachusetts Ave, NW, Washington DC 20008. Tel: (202) 265 6653.

Australia – Indian High Commission, 3–5 Moonah Place, Yarralumla, Canberra ACT 2600. Tel: 733 999/774.

Canada – Indian High Commission, 325 Howe St, 1st Floor, Vancouver, British Columbia.

New Zealand – Indian High Commission, Princes Towers, 10th Floor, 180 Molesworth St, Wellington. Tel: 736 390/1.

---

months' validity remaining. The only restricted areas in South India are the Andaman and Nicobar Islands, and you will need to apply separately for permission to visit them. This can, however, be given in London and at no extra cost. It should take about a week.

The cost of a six-month visa is currently £16, whether you want single, double or multiple entry, or £3 for 30 days. This should be paid either in cash or by postal order. Cheques and credit cards are not accepted.

SECURITY

Keep all important documents in a money belt, which you should wear night and day. Also take **photocopies** of the front pages of your passport, your visa, and any other important papers, as well as half a dozen passport photos. Keep these in a separate safe place, in case you lose the originals. It will speed up the process of replacement considerably and, because you still have some form of ID, make life much less complicated.

INSURANCE

Proper *insurance* is an essential if you are travelling in India. In a country where even the poorest Westerner is infinitely richer than the majority of the inhabitants, it is incredibly easy for your belongings to stray. More of a problem, however, are the risks to health, which are numerous and varied, from the appalling driving through to a wide and interesting collection of diseases. Your insurance should give you medical cover of at least £1 million, and must include Medivac facilities (a flight home, or even air ambulance) should you be ill enough to warrant it.

JABS AND PILLS

The Institute of Hygiene and Tropical Medicine in London classifies India as one of only a few "very dangerous" countries in which to travel. This not only means that you should be extremely careful while there (see page 59 for more detail), but that you should take every possible precaution before you go.

ADVICE

Before you start, get up to date advice from a specialist tropical diseases expert as the situation can change rapidly if, for instance, an epidemic breaks out. A normal GP is unlikely to keep up with the news. The Hospital for Tropical Diseases, 4 St Pancras Way, London NW1 0PE, runs a travel health hotline which should answer all the normal queries. Tel: (0898) 345 081.

For a more detailed breakdown, personalised to your own particular requirements, contact MASTA, Ross Institute of Tropical Hygiene, Keppel Street, (Gower Street), London WC1E 7HT. Tel: (071) 631 4408. Application forms should be available at the pharmacist's counter in all branches of Boots.

PREVENTION

Inoculations are the most important form of preventative health care. A full course can take several weeks, so consult a doctor as soon as you know when you are going. There are no statutory requirements for entry to India, but it is strongly recommended that you are covered for **typhoid, tetanus, polio, cholera, yellow fever, meningitis, tuberculosis and hepatitis A**. Some are available on the National Health, but you will have to pay for others. You can get them all from your GP or from a vaccination clinic such as those run by British Airways or Thomas Cook. Gamma globulin, the only form of protection against hepatitis A, is not a vaccine but a blood-based product which helps to build up natural immunity. Its effects are short-lived, so you should leave it until the last possible moment before you go. Be wary about having booster shots while abroad unless you are completely satisfied that the serum available has been properly treated against Aids. There is a vaccination against **hepatitis B** (the blood and sexually transmitted version of the disease), but this is extremely expensive and is not normally on offer. If you feel that you will be at particular risk, ask for it. If you are planning to take to the bush or will be working with animals, it is also worth considering immunisation against **rabies**.

The risk of catching **malaria** is also great and it is essential that you take prophylactics. Unfortunately, as super-mosquitoes develop resistance, these are not always sufficient to stop you developing the disease, and the only answer seems to be to keep increasing dosages while the scientists work to develop either a new drug or a vaccine. Meantime, you will normally expect to take a combination of **paludrine** and **chloroquin**, available over the counter from chemists. For those who can't take chloroquin, there is an alternative, malaprim, available only on prescription. You will need to start two weeks before you go, and continue for four weeks after your return home.

Get your teeth and eyes seen to before you go, and take a spare copy of your glasses prescription. If you are on long-term medication, make sure you have an adequate supply and get a letter from your doctor explaining why you are carrying large quantities of drugs, in case the Customs officials get too interested. If you have problems such as allergies, diabetes, etc, consider getting a **Medic Alert** bracelet or necklace and wear it at all times. The symbol is internationally recognised and there is a central number which any doctor can call to get details of your problem should you be unable to tell them yourself. Details from your doctor or any good pharmacist.

FIRST AID

Finally, although you should be able to get most things in India, it is worth putting together a reasonably comprehensive **medical kit**. I've listed the basics below. If you think you might need injections along the way, it is probably worth adding a pack of sterile hypodermics, while if you are going trekking or on an expedition, where you could find yourself a long way from assistance, add an IV drip, sutures and dressings, a basic antibiotic, and splints. If necessary, also add a general snake bite serum. MASTA will be able to advise and make up a kit for you. Then make sure you learn how to use it all! The Red Cross and St John's both run short First Aid courses that will teach you how to cope until you can get help.

Suggested basic kit
Analgesics (e.g. Aspirin, Paracetemol, etc)
Diarrhoea treatment (Immodium or Kaolin Morphine)
Constipation treatment
Indigestion tablets
Water purifiers
Malaria tablets
Mosquito repellant
Antihistamine cream for insect bites
Plasters
Elastic bandage
Scissors
Safety pins
Antiseptic spray (eg Savlon Dry)
Antiseptic wetwipes (which also double as the ordinary sort on journeys or when eating)
Sun block
After-sun cream
Lypsyl or vaseline for chapped lips
Eye drops
Oil of cloves or cream for anaesthetising toothache
Cough sweets

HEALTH HAZARDS

Taking good care of your health is perhaps the single most important aspect of survival in India. It is difficult. Not only are the food and water both suspect but the country serves up a cocktail of almost every lethal disease known to man. Before you start running scared and decide not to go, it is important to try and keep things in perspective. Few travellers come home with anything more than a minor tummy upset and a large number manage to escape even that. Plan sensibly (see Jabs and Pills, on page 57), don't relax your guard, and you should be fine.

WATER

Bad water is by far the largest single cause of disease in India, responsible for a wide range of ills from simple tummy bugs to cholera and dysentery. *Never* drink water straight from the tap, no matter how safe they tell you it is, remember not to use it even for cleaning your teeth, and try not to swallow any when in the shower. The water served in the dining rooms at the best hotels is usually safe, but it is still better not to risk it. Remember to ask for all your drinks without ice. Bottled mineral water is freely available, so use this instead. Always check the seal when you buy it, as you do hear stories of bottles being refilled with impure water. It is also worth taking a water bottle of your own, which you can treat and use as an emergency supply. Iodine is probably the best all-purpose purifier, although it shouldn't be used by anyone pregnant or suffering from thyroid problems. As long as you fill your bottle with tap water, which has nominally been treated already, ordinary chlorine tablets should be quite sufficient. Remember to leave them long enough before you take a drink, don't leave the bottle open once it has been treated and don't fill it up again without adding another dose.

Apart from coconut milk, steer clear of those enticing looking fruit juice stands. They are almost all diluted with ordinary water and are usually served in thoroughly unhygienic glasses. When buying fizzy soft drinks, make sure that the bottle is properly full and that it is opened in front of you. Again you hear about people siphoning some off the top and making up the difference with water. If you want tea or coffee from street or station vendors, take your own mug and use that.

Don't swim in natural water unless you are literally feet from the source. Everything, from the washing to sewage to dead bodies goes into the rivers.

FOOD

Be sensible but don't be paranoid or you will miss out on half the fun of travelling. Half the minor upsets that dog travellers are simply a reaction to too much highly spiced, oily food and are nothing to do with germs. Stick where possible to hot (as in temperature), freshly cooked foods. Most of the damage is done when things are allowed to sit around in the open air after they have been cooked. If you eat something straight from the pot or fire, it is as safe in a market stall as in the best restaurants. It is also safer to eat Indian than Western food – the cooks know what they are doing with something familiar. The meat markets are enough to make the most hardened carnivore throw up, so if you want to be really safe, eat vegetarian. India is one of the few countries in the world where it is easy to find good vegetarian food. Avoid fish inland, but it is absolutely fresh and quite delicious on the coast.

Salads and ice cream are two of the most notorious disaster areas, so avoid both, although they should be safe in the best hotels. Only eat fruit that you can either peel yourself or wash in treated water.

Be scrupulous about your own hygiene, as many germs are passed on to the food when you touch it. Carry a small cake of soap with you always, wash before every meal and, if necessary, use antiseptic wipes.

TREATING STOMACH UPSETS

Surprisingly, it is just as easy to get constipated as to get diarrhoea. If you do, be thankful. It makes life a lot easier! If it gets too bad, take a mild laxative. The best way to cope with diarrhoea is to leave it to work itself out. Stay close to the toilet for 24 hours, eat as little as possible, and drink lots. The chief danger is from dehydration. If necessary, use rehydration powders or add salt and sugar to your drinks to replace those salts you are losing. Try and eat something, but keep it simple and the quantities small. Dry toast or chappatis and yoghurt are both good, easily available options, but if you find yourself craving something else, give in to the craving. Your body normally finds a way of telling you what it needs. If you have to keep moving, take "cement" tablets, but these should not be used unless necessary. They plug you up, but they don't cure you and can actually slow down your recovery as the fastest cure is to flush out the system. If you show no sign of improvement within two to three days, seek medical help. You could be suffering from something more serious.

BUGS AND BEASTIES

Malaria is prevalent throughout South India, so you must remember to take your prophylactic tablets. These are not 100% efficient, so avoid bites where possible. Wear long sleeves and trousers after dusk, keep applying mosquito repellent to any patches of bare skin, and use a net or coils over night.

Don't walk around barefoot or you can pick up a variety of different worms or parasites, and use high-ankled boots out in the bush to help guard against the possibility of snake bites. Don't pet any animals, however cute. Rabies is endemic to the country. If you do get bitten, head for the nearest doctor immediately and start a course of treatment. Rabies can only be cured if caught in its very earliest stages.

EXHAUSTION

South India is very hot, very humid, and the sun is far stronger than most Westerners are used to. Tropical peoples the world over have developed a more leisurely lifestyle to cope with the climate. We, of course, rush in, spend all day out in the glare of the sun, and every night on a train, not daring to stop in case we miss something and convinced, subconsciously, of the superiority of our own frenetic activity. Then we fall over from sheer exhaustion!

There are a few simple rules. Don't try to do too much. You don't need to cover the entire subcontinent in two weeks. Even if you don't stop completely, slow down during the midday heat. Wear loose cotton clothes. Tightly fitting, skimpy synthetics are the worst of all worlds. Look at what the Arabs or the Indians themselves wear – long, flowing robes or loose pyjama suits that shield your skin from the sun and allow a flow of cool air. Get a wide-brimmed hat and wear it. If the glare hurts your eyes, use sun glasses. Use a sun block cream on exposed skin or you are in danger of painful sunburn now and skin cancer in later life. If you want to tan, do it slowly and cover up between sessions. Use plenty of moisturiser to stop your skin drying out and cracking. Use a lip salve regularly or your lips will also crack painfully.

In this sort of climate, you will sweat a great deal more than normal. Don't try to stop it, it's the body's way of lowering its temperature. However, you will have to replace not only the fluids, but the salts you are losing. Drink far more than you would normally, don't wait until you feel thirsty. If you find you are not urinating as often as usual, or that it is a much darker colour, drink even more. If you feel yourself becoming exhausted too easily, make sure you also step up your salt and sugar intake, with salt tablets or rehydration powders if required. You could also find that you will suffer from vitamin deficiency. Either take vitamin pills or eat as much fresh fruit as possible to guard against this. Fresh limes, which are plentiful and cheap as well as refreshing, are an excellent source of Vitamin C.

If things go too far and you or someone near you tips over into heat exhaustion, act immediately. Take a cold bath or shower, drink lots, take some aspirin for the headache and rest until fully recovered. If you continue to ignore the symptoms, there is a danger that the body's own regulatory system will break down and your temperature will soar out of control. This can be fatal and if it happens, you must seek immediate medical attention.

MEDICAL TREATMENT

India's hospitals vary wildly from small, ill-equipped village clinics with undertrained staff to great, sophisticated teaching hospitals equivalent to the best in the world. If you do need hospital treatment, ask the locals for advice and go, if possible, to a private clinic. The quality of treatment may be as good in the state hospitals, but standards of comfort will certainly not match up.

Try to avoid being given any sort of transfusion if at all possible. Aids is endemic and there is no guarantee that the blood banks have been properly treated. If you have to have one, supply your own needles and, if there's time, contact the High Commission. British embassies the world over are meant to be compiling lists of "clean" donors. They will also help you steer through the red tape if you or your companion needs to be sent home. The insurance company will pick up the bill for everything, but only as long as they are informed of anything very expensive and are included in the decision making process. All policies should supply you with a 24-hour hotline number.

WHAT TO TAKE

CLOTHES

The joy of choosing clothes to take to South India is that if you don't have enough, or have forgotten something vital, it is easy to find a local tailor to run it up for you – in silk, if you prefer, and for a fraction of the price you would pay in a European shop. A number of experienced travellers to India literally take only what they wear on the plane, find a tailor on arrival to run them up some suits of cheap cotton which they then ditch as they wear out or when they leave the country. The Punjabi suit or *shalwar kamiz* is one of the most practical and comfortable forms of dress, for both sexes.

The one thing you should *not* take is all those shorts, mini skirts and skimpy t-shirts that you would normally pack for a holiday in the sun. India is an intensely religious and very traditional country and such garments cause great offense. Men can get away with wearing baggy shorts, but should always wear long trousers when going sightseeing. One man we met ended up using a floral scarf of mine as a skirt before he was allowed into a temple, and both felt and looked pretty stupid! Trousers are fine for women, but shorts are not. Skirts should be below the knee, or as a good compromise wear culottes. The shoulders should always be covered, so buy shirts with sleeves. Short sleeves will do. It is quite acceptable for women to show their stomachs, but cleavage is out. One-piece swimming costumes for women and baggy trunks for men will be more acceptable than briefer versions on the beach, although, as the beaches are mainly for foreigners, there is more leeway here. Indian women often swim in their saris!

Keep your clothes loose. This is not only more acceptable socially, but far more sensible for the climate. Use cotton or a poly-cotton mix where possible. It is light, comfortable, and absorbs the sweat without smelling. If you can, get things that are drip-dry and don't require ironing, so that you can give them a quick wash if necessary. If you are spending time in the mountains, you will need a light jumper or jacket for the evenings. Smart casual is the norm for most occasions, so it is unlikely that you will need a suit or the little black number.

Sandals are the best footwear for the climate. You can buy a wide variety of very cheap, very comfortable leather sandals in India, again at throwaway prices. You are asked to remove your shoes before going into any temple or mosque, so something that slips on and off will save a lot of time and aggravation. If you are going trekking, you will obviously need proper boots, and for any trips into the bush you should wear at least high-sided trainers that will give a little ankle support and some protection against snakes.

USEFUL ITEMS

A wide-brimmed hat, sunglasses and, if you are travelling during the monsoon, an umbrella are also useful. Toiletries are all available, but the choice and quality are often poor, so take enough with you. A generous supply of toilet paper is essential, as few places provide, and women should remember to take enough tampons to survive. If you think you will need condoms, take them too. Few places have plugs in the basins, so take one with you (the universal, suction kind). Unless you plan to send all your laundry out, take a couple of tubes of Travelwash and a length of nylon line.

There are a number of general items that should also go in. They may not be essentials, but can make life much easier. Frequent power blackouts make a torch very handy. A water bottle with a carrying strap will ensure that you can always carry a supply of treated or mineral water with you, while a sheet sleeping bag and an inflatable pillow are useful, not only on trains, but in hotels where the bedclothes seem less than hygienic. I have a small penknife with spoon and fork attachments and a bottle opener which I use constantly. You can buy batteries, but the quality is lousy, so take spares. Film is also on sale, but only in major centres. The choice is limited and the sell-by date often ancient history, so take at least twice as much as you think you'll need. There can be few places in the world as photogenic as India.

Don't subject posh luggage to the battering it will inevitably receive. A rucksack or canvas duffel is much easier to cope with and will weather misuse more readily.

BAKSHEESH

Those who don't ask you for money are likely to ask for pens, stamps, coins of your country, or sweets, so fill up the gaps with a collection of small change, old stamps, cheap biros and boiled sweets. Then throw in a few brightly coloured postcards of home and some photos of your family to satisfy the endless curiosity you will face. More about **baksheesh** on p.85.

MONEY

The Indian currency is the *rupee*, split into 100 *paise*. At the time of going to press there were 47 rupees to £1 sterling, but the *rupee* is a soft currency and the situation changes rapidly. *Rupees* come in 1, 2, 5, 10, 20, 50 and 100 notes and 1 and 2 *rupee* coins. *Paise* coins are in denominations of 5, 10, 20, 25 and 50.

It is illegal to import or export *rupees*. If you want to take in a few to tide you over the first hours, it is usually possible to buy them at the independent bureaux de change in major cities around the world, but do bear in mind that you will be breaking the law and if you are caught, they will be confiscated.

CASH

It is usually difficult to get change, and small denomination notes are often in short supply, so if changing at a bank, get as much as possible in notes of Rs20 or less. Don't accept torn or damaged notes, even if they have been taped back together, as you won't be able to use them. Most are disgustingly dirty, but this seems to be OK.

Paise are of little practical value, almost never being used in day to day transactions, but it is helpful to keep a pocketful for giving to beggars. In fact, at many religious sites, money changers set up stalls to change the *rupees* of the faithful into these small coins. The many beggars who line the approaches to the temple or shrine will collect them until they have a sufficient number to turn back into *rupees*, releasing the coins for use by the next batch of pilgrims. And so the economy of the *paise* continues.

There is a black market for currency in all the major cities and tourist areas. It is illegal, but policing doesn't appear to be too ferocious. I found, however, that the rates being offered were not good enough to tempt me to run the greater risk of being ripped off if I let anyone know how much I was carrying on me. More useful is the prospect of heavy discounting for hard currency when shopping for the more expensive souvenirs and even for travel tickets.

PAPER AND PLASTIC

Major credit cards – Amex, Visa, Barclaycard, Mastercard and Diner's Club – are usually accepted by the most upmarket hotels and souvenir shops, but these are relatively thin on the ground. Take one with you as a useful back-up, but don't rely on it for funding and make sure you have plenty of other options.

Travellers' cheques are the easiest and safest way to carry large sums, but they are not infallible. You have to be licensed to handle foreign exchange in India and not all hotels, including some catering mainly to foreign tourists, or even banks will do so. When buying travellers' cheques, stick to US dollars or sterling. Other currencies are more difficult to change and, once you have found someone willing to buy, you will be very delayed while they try to find the exchange rate. Thomas Cook and American Express have offices in the major cities, where you can change their brand cheques easily and reasonably fast. There is some degree of suspicion about Amex cheques elsewhere however, owing to past fraud, and a number of banks refuse to handle them.

MORE BUREAUCRACY

Changing money is a time-consuming business. It involves filling in several lots of forms and at least two queues and can, in smaller towns, take several hours. It is not a process you will want to indulge in every second day, so make sure you change enough to last.

The rate you will be given at the hotels is slightly higher than that in the banks, but you don't pay commission. It is also a much faster, less arduous procedure.

Wherever you change your money, be sure that they give you a completed **currency exchange form**, and hang on to it. If you want to make any major purchases, such as international air tickets, in *rupees*, or if you wish to reconvert any leftover *rupees* into hard currency at the end of the trip, you will have to prove you changed the money legally. Nor will it work if you have exchange forms for £200 and want to reconvert £180 of them. The authorities have been known to make you sit down and account for every penny you have spent since you've been in the country.

If you are in India for more than three months, you will need **tax clearance** before you leave, basically as a way of proving that you haven't been earning. To get this, take your passport, currency exchange forms and any other paperwork you can think of to the nearest Income Tax office. They will give you a form to fill in, check it all and issue you a certificate.

Banks are open from 10am – 2pm Monday to Friday, and 10am – 12 noon on Saturdays.

PRICES

The cost of living is one of the main perks for the traveller to India. It is incredibly cheap. Once you realise that the majority of the population earns less than £15 a month on which to support an entire family, you begin to realise that the Indians are right when they say that even the most poverty-stricken Westerner is rich.

There is a certain maximum you can spend. It would be very difficult to find a hotel room for more than £50 a night and almost impossible to pay more than £15 for a meal. At the other end of the scale, you can get a spartan but comfortable room with a private shower and toilet for around £3–4 a night, and a filling, nourishing meal for 20p. It is possible to spend considerably less if you are happy with concrete floors and cockroaches, but it doesn't seem worth it unless you are into misery.

The inflation rate is high, but seems to be cancelled out by the *rupee* exchange rate, so that prices to Westerners remain roughly the same. The only thing to watch out for is price rises way above inflation in places that have become popular amongst travellers.

I would suggest that unless you are planning to wallow in five star luxury for the whole trip, a budget of £10–15 a day will give you a comfortable lifestyle with room for occasional splurges. Absolute rock bottom would be around £4 a day. Take extra for shopping. The souvenirs are stupendous and you will regret it if you can't afford them.

NIGHTLIFE AND ENTERTAINMENT

If you are looking for the bright lights, this is the wrong place to come. In a country where alcohol is a rarity and only the most decadent, Westernised women would dream of dancing with a man, there are few clubs or discos. The few that do exist are all in the major hotels and aimed almost exclusively at tourists. Even then, most tend to be restaurants with a cabaret. Some of these are based on local music and dance and are very good indeed. Some try to be Western and trendy and you will spend most of the evening in a kind of guessing game as you try to work out what tune the band is playing. The big resort hotels on the coast also run entertainments during the season, with such Indian displays as limbo dancers strutting their stuff to the Lambeth Walk. However, they also provide some good displays of local dance and music, puppetry and mime.

If you want to learn more about Indian theatre, music and dance, you will usually be able to find a concert in the larger cities. Make a special effort to see the Kathkali dancers in Kerala, an ancient, highly stylised and brilliantly coloured dance-drama. There are regular performances aimed at tourists in both Cochin and Trivandrum, which allow you to watch as the dancers don their elaborate make-up, give you a brief history of the dance, an explanation of its movements and the legends which inspire the dances.

It is also worth going to at least one movie, the Indians' own most popular form of entertainment. Cinemas are plentiful and always crowded and noisy with over-enthusiastic audiences as entertaining to watch as the films themselves. The major Western films all get a showing if you are in need of a little touch of home, but India outstrips even Hollywood in the number of films it produces each year. Most of them are extremely bad and, as a result, extremely funny, a dire mix of medallion man heroes, demure heroines, chase sequences and 60s-style song and dance. You won't understand a word, but you don't really need to. Go and see for yourself.

Some of the best evenings, however, are those spent wandering the streets, sitting in the small cafés or *chai* houses, chatting to the locals and watching the street entertainers.

Many Indians get up before dawn, so evenings tend to end early. Whatever you decide to do, don't expect to stay up to the small hours.

TIPPING

Tipping is not an absolute requirement, and only seems to be expected at all in those hotels and restaurants which cater for large numbers of tourists. At the most expensive end, a service charge of around 10% is beginning to creep in for the first time. Porters, doormen, etc, should only be given a couple of *rupees*. At cheaper restaurants and hotels, few people tip at all. Railway porters will normally get a small tip, but don't tip for other transport as you will have fixed a price before you start your journey. The expectation of a tip can and has, led to passengers being held to ransom in the midst of ugly scenes. If you have run up against the system and are banging your head against the nearest wall in frustration, a small tip ahead of time will buy you the willing services of someone who can find their way through the red tape.

If you are going to tip, don't make the mistake of converting back into Western currency and leaving too much. The tip should be in line with both what you paid for the service and with local salaries.

The far more complicated issue of *baksheesh* in its widest sense is dealt with on page 85.

ELECTRICITY

230–240 volts, 50 cycles, alternating current. There are frequent, if fairly short-lived, blackouts so take a torch.

TIME ZONE

GMT + 5½ hours. There is only one time zone, covering the whole of India. There is no change to summer time.

COMMUNICATIONS

TELEPHONES

Since the introduction of the satellite, it has become easier to phone overseas than to the next town. You should, theoretically, be able to dial direct from major Indian cities to almost anywhere in the world, but don't get too excited at the prospect. You will probably spend an extremely irritating hour before you give up and realise that the system has beaten you once again. It is much easier to book the call in advance through the operator. Things can get eccentric – my parents were thoroughly alarmed when alerted to a call by someone speaking fluent Russian – but you should finally get through on a reasonably clear line. If you are phoning from a public booth, you will have to leave a deposit (returnable if you don't get through), when you book the call. Overseas calls are expensive – upwards of £2 a minute to phone the UK.

Local and long distance domestic calls are a rather hit and miss affair. Again, you should be able to dial direct between major cities, although in practice, this rarely works and it is easier to use the operator. A standard call will go to the back of the queue, so you may have to wait some time. If it is more urgent ask for a Demand Call, which will take priority and cost more. If you have to get through straight away ask for a Lightning Call and be prepared to pay eight times the standard rate. Whichever rate you choose, the quality of the line is a lottery.

The easiest way to get through is from the better hotels. Their operators seem to be able to push calls through faster, and you can at least wait in comfort. They do charge a hefty surplus, however, ranging from 25 to 100 percent of the standard cost. There are manned public booths in most of the larger airports and train stations as well as at post offices. They are crowded and chaotic and many close for lunch and overnight, so if you are placing a call over several time zones, you will have to plan things carefully and book well in advance.

POST

The postal system is, on the whole, efficient, although it can be slow, taking up to a month for an airmail letter from London to reach Delhi. One travelling the other way reached me six months later! Queues at post offices are, as ever, long, so for simple letters and postcards, buy your stamps from hotels, where possible.

Poste restante facilities are good, but make sure that letters are marked "poste restante" and that you specify which post office to use, as the larger towns will have several and it would be easy for a packet without a firm address to be sent to any one of them. Also be careful with the labelling. Tell people to put your surname first, and underline it. All too many missing letters are eventually found filed under M for Mr or B for Betty. If in doubt, ask to go through all the letters in store

yourself. Where there are American Express offices, these are
a good alternative.

Be careful about allowing shops to post your purchases
home for you. In general, it is worth taking the time to do
it yourself. Pack the parcel carefully, then take it to a tailor
or one of the street vendors you will find outside the larger
post offices to have them wrap it in cloth, sew it in and wax
the seams, which you should then seal. Label it clearly and
indelibly and firmly attach two customs declaration forms
before taking it to be weighed and stamped. Always get a
receipt.

Post offices are open from 10am–5pm, Mondays to Fridays,
and 10am–1pm on Saturdays. Some of the larger city offices
will open earlier and stay open later in the evenings.

SIGHTSEEING

ENTRANCE CHARGES

Most museums, palaces and art galleries charge a small
entrance fee of a few *rupees*. This will be a fixed price, with
a ticket, and there is no differential pricing for foreigners.
If you want to escape even this small charge, many sights
have free entry on Fridays. The disadvantage is that Fridays
are very crowded and very noisy. Most places stay open all
day on Sundays, but will close on one other day in the week,
often but not always Mondays.

Temples make up a very large percentage of the sightseeing
round. Some of the largest and most famous will charge an
entry fee, but on the whole they rely solely on contributions,
which will be solicited eagerly by all priests, monks and guides,
as well as the beggars that line the courtyards. Take fistfuls of
very small change with you for distribution or you will find
yourself having to put notes in the plate and that can get
expensive, although you will be thoroughly blessed for your
generosity. Some of the holiest sites bar non-Hindus from
the inner temples, but on the whole you will be welcomed
everywhere, encouraged to watch or take part in ceremonies,
and the priest will lead you around the temple showing you
the best places to take your photos. There are clear notices

everywhere saying if you are allowed in, so keep an eye open, and if in doubt, ask.

WHAT TO WEAR

Make sure that you are wearing long trousers, or skirts below the knee, and that your shoulders are covered, if visiting temples. You will have to remove your shoes before entering any religious site, so wear something easy to get in and out and don't bother with socks, unless you want them to end up filthy and in holes. There is always an official shoeminder by the door or gateway who charges about 50 *paise* to 1 *rupee* per pair. If you go into a Jain temple, you should not have any leather on you (including watch straps, camera cases, etc), so you may have to leave valuables outside and visit in relays.

GUIDES

If you are looking for a guided tour, most towns offer good, if hurried, coach tours. These will usually be organised either by the state tourist office or the ITDC (India Tourist Development Corporation), or both. The cost is high by Indian standards, you will have to pay any entrance fees yourself, and the guide will expect a healthy tip.

An alternative is to get a private guide. There is a good system of government-trained and licensed guides who know their subject inside and out, speak good English, and work for a fixed scale (plus, of course, whatever large tip they can wring out of you). Ask at the tourist office again. At every sight, you will be bombarded by offers to guide you. At the larger ones, there will be some government guides. Elsewhere, you will have to decide first if you want one (you do, of course, sometimes get one whether you want him or not). Separate out one who speaks good English and negotiate a deal with him before you start. He will then fend off the rest. Some of the best I have found have been students supplementing their income.

If you just want to be taken around without a detailed commentary, one of the best ways to do it is to hire a rickshaw for the day. Many of the drivers speak good English and are surprisingly knowledgeable. Choose carefully and fix the price for the day.

PHOTOGRAPHY

Decide how much film you want to take, then double it, think about it and double it again. India has to be the most photogenic country in the world. Moreover, most of its people, male and female, are so keen for you to take their picture that they will form queues or, more frequently, almost trample you underfoot in their eagerness to get into the frame. In a very few places, you will find people asking for money, but this is highly unusual. More often, they will ask for a copy. If you agree to send one and take their name and address, do remember to send it. Alternatively, carry a polaroid with you as well. If you do, learn to say no, or you can go through a fortune in film in your first couple of days. You may also find yourself playing model in an unusual turnaround as Indian tourists ask if they can take your picture. It feels strange, but it's only polite to say yes.

Technically, taking photos of anything to do with the military is forbidden, so tread a little warily. Having said that, I have been approached by a company of soldiers waiting for their train and asked to photograph them. Theoretically, too, you need permission to take photos in the stations. Most of the time it is unnecessary, but if you do get stopped, go and ask the station master for a permit. You will get one without any difficulty. Some of the larger sights will make you buy a photo permit (one per camera) before you can take pictures inside.

Film is usually available at about the same price as you would pay at home, but the range is fairly limited and you should check the sell-by date carefully as much of it is old stock. The midday light is bright, but rarely harsh in the south, and to my mind isn't quite strong enough to justify some of the very slow films such as Kodachrome 25. I find that a mix of 100, 200 and 400 ISO covers most eventualities. If I had to choose one, it would be 200 ISO. However, that is a personal opinion and you will get different answers from different photographers.

SHOPPING

One of the best aspects of India from the tourist's point of view
is the range, quality and price of the souvenirs. The danger is
that you can get so carried away that your luggage will triple
in weight and your sitting room will look like an ethnic junk
shop once you unpack it all. Of course, some of what is on
sale really is junk, but it is very easy to ignore this and buy
things that are beautiful, well crafted and cheap. For those
with more extravagant tastes, there are also some real works
of art, whether carpets, jewellery or textiles, equal in quality
and price to the best the world has to offer.

WHAT TO BUY

Every area has its specialities and you may decide, for
sentiment's sake, to buy only those things that come from
the locality. In all but the smallest towns, however, you
will find a range of goods from all over the country – and
probably want to buy them all. **Southern specialities** include
spices, intricately carved sandalwood furniture, perfumes and
incense from Mysore; tea and coffee from the Nilgiri Hills;
cotton from Madras; and bronze and stone sculptures from
Mamallapuram. From the far north, from Kashmir and Tibet,
come the most famous carpets which range from traditional
mughul designs, beautifully crafted from wool and silk and
very expensive, to peasant-style *numdas* or *durries*. Know
what you are doing here, or at least take someone who does,
as the potential for being ripped off is huge. This area also
produces wonderfully warm and soft embroidered shawls and
bedspreads. Rajasthan and Gujarat are most famed for their
jewel-bright, richly embroidered textiles, including those that
use tiny pieces of mirror in the design, while the best silk in
the country is thought to come from Varanasi.

Leatherwork, including sandals and bags, is found everywhere, as are textiles for wearing, such as saris, cotton and
silk. If you take your own pattern, or even just a picture, the
tailors will run you up the garment of your dreams within 24
hours and at a nominal cost. Engraved or inlaid metalwork is

also produced in most areas, as are copies of silk paintings. These are particularly popular a souvenirs as they are not only attractive and reasonably priced, but also weigh virtually nothing. Take time to hunt around before you buy, however, as the quality of workmanship varies wildly. Surprisingly, the smaller paintings are often more expensive than the larger ones, as the amount of detail is greater and they therefore take longer to do.

India is still a country where the women traditionally wear the family wealth. My lack of adornment has won me many a pitying glance or comment. Jewellery ranges from ultra-cheap bangles and beads on sale in market stalls for a couple of *rupees*, via chunky traditional silver bracelets to dazzling confections of gold and diamonds, sapphires and rubies that weigh down the shoulders and blind the eyes. Many dealers will also bring out a tatty tin which, when opened, produces a technicolour heap of unset stones, for a fraction of the price you would pay for them at home. Great caution and some degree of expertise are again needed unless you are buying from hotel shops.

WHERE TO SHOP

In all the major towns, you will find a **Government Emporium**. These are fixed price shops, with a wide range of stock to choose from and fair prices that are only a little higher than those in the markets. If you can't face the hassle of bargaining (a game that wears very thin after a while), they are a good place for one stop shopping. They take major credit cards, and if you want to have something sent home, it will be done and has a good chance of arriving safely. If you prefer to do things the difficult way, a trip here will at least give you some idea of what is on offer and how much you might expect to pay.

Unlike most Western hotel shops, those in India charge reasonable prices and will also give you some assurance of authenticity.

Once away from these carefully monitored establishments, the crucial point, especially when buying anything of value, is to do your homework first and then bargain hard. However much of a bargain you think you have, be certain that in Indian terms, you are paying over the odds. Allow time for shopping and, once you have found something you like, price it at several places before you make up your mind. On my last trip, I found a tablecloth I liked but at Rs2,300 it seemed exorbitantly expensive. After some bargaining, I got the price down to just over Rs1,000 before deciding to go for a walk and make up my mind. I was very glad I did, because I ended up in another shop just round the corner, where I was offered an identical cloth at a starting price of Rs800. I eventually bought it for Rs300 and the man who sold it to me still seemed happy with his deal.

Your guide or driver will almost certainly try to steer you into those shops which give him a commission. I've had a couple of wonderful afternoons when I have allowed myself to be persuaded, ending up in workshops or small factories learning an immense amount about the traditions and skills that go into the crafts. However, don't allow yourself to be pressured into buying just for the sake of it. You have a perfect right to say no.

Also make sure that you are getting what you paid for. One friend spent an hour bargaining for a length of silk which she finally brought back to the hotel in triumph, only to discover the words "100% polyester" woven into the edge. Special care is needed with anything that claims to be old or original as there is a whole industry devoted to faking antiques, whether they be carvings or paintings. The workmanship will often be as good as the original, but chances are it was made last week. If you do find the real thing, it is forbidden to export anything over 100 years old. If in doubt, take it for an expert appraisal before you try and leave the country. In Bombay ask the Superintending Archaeologist, Antiquities, Archaeological Survey of India, Sion Fort. In Madras ask the Superintending Archaeologist, Archaeological Survey of India, Southern Circle, Fort St George.

DON'T BUY IVORY

Ivory is still on sale in a great many shops in India. Before you are tempted, remember that ivory is banned by almost every country in the world, and if you are caught trying to take it home, it will not only be confiscated, but you will be liable to a hefty fine or imprisonment.

TRADING

Many are tempted by visions of a quick profit to buy things to sell at home. Be very careful before you start on this. First, you will be liable to pay duty when importing them, which can dramatically bump up the price. Second, the professional importers often get such a good price that your precious carpet will cost less in London than you paid for it in India.

SELLING YOUR OWN THINGS

If you want to sell things yourself, you will have plenty of opportunities. Fashion trends provide a healthy market for well made, obviously foreign goods, in spite of the fact that there are usually perfectly satisfactory local equivalents. This is the country that prizes nylon above silk and where one soft drink used as an advertising slogan "Guaranteed 100% artificial"! However, unless you are running short of funds, it hardly seems worthwhile as the black market rate isn't sufficiently high to make the profit outweigh the risk. Those who do benefit are the increasing number of Russian tourists who cannot bring enough money with them, so bring trade goods to finance their trips. If you want to try, the best options are cameras, watches, and small electric or electronic goods, preferably still in their boxes and with the instructions. Don't take in several of the same item as Customs could get very suspicious. You will also run into trouble if you take anything for sale so valuable that you have to declare it on entry.

SEX AND DRUGS

In spite of India's deeply religious background, there are, sadly, unlimited options for casual sex in every permutation. Women, if they so desire, can have their pick for free; men will usually have to pay, although very little. It is obviously up to the individual as to whether they wish to indulge, but do realise the dangers. Aids, along with a host of other unpleasant diseases, is rampant and the risks to your health and even life are enormous. If you can't or won't refrain, take with you a large supply of the sturdiest condoms you can buy, and use them. Also steer clear of respectable Indian women. They take virginity and adultery far more seriously than we do and what you may regard as a casual fling can literally ruin a life.

Both hard and soft drugs are also widely available. Marijuana, known locally as *ganja*, grows wild and is smoked openly by many people. It is, however, still illegal and the authorities are attempting to crack down on the drugs trade, particularly in places like Goa which have earned themselves international notoriety. The police may turn a blind eye to the locals; they will step in if they see foreigners getting involved. The penalties for dealing are severe and while you will get assistance, you are likely to get little sympathy from your embassy.

CRIME

The crime rate in general in India is not high, but tourists, with their conspicuous wealth, are prime targets. The real danger is from sneak theft from hotel rooms or unattended luggage, or by pickpockets who are amongst the most skilled in the world.

Keep all your valuable papers, credit cards, etc, in a securely fastened moneybelt, which you should wear at all times, even at night, unless your hotel has a safe in which to deposit it. (An extra tip here is to wrap documents in plastic before they go in the belt. The combination of heat, humidity and sweat is a disastrous one and passports and travellers' cheques alike may go mouldy if unprotected. Try explaining that to a suspicious immigration man!) Take a photocopy of the front pages of your passport and your visa and keep them, together with the official numbered receipt for your travellers' cheques, in a separate safe place. It is also worth keeping a separate emergency supply of cash in case your papers go for a walk and you have to survive for long enough to get them replaced.

If you are carrying any sort of handbag, get one with a stout zip and a long strap, so that you can sling it diagonally. It won't always help, but it may deter more casual theft. Personally, I feel that there is little to be gained by using a lockable case as a lock is of little consequence to a professional thief, more expensive luggage can actually be more attractive, with the promise of better pickings, and the other advantages of a rucksack far outweigh the security risk.

If you are staying in cheaper hotels, take your own padlock with you and use it as well as or instead of the hotel's own lock. Lock your door securely at night. Left luggage offices at the stations are usually secure, but never leave your luggage unsupervised in public. Stations, trains and airports are notoriously bad spots and your entire rucksack can disappear in seconds. One of the main advantages of travelling first class is that you are in a cabin with a lockable door. Also be wary of leaving your possessions with fellow travellers you have only met casually. There are far too many reports of things being stolen by other Westerners.

Another favourite trick is sleight of hand, particularly common when dealing on the black market. The pile of notes that you saw the man counting carefully will, once back at your hotel, prove to be half the size, or include a number of folded notes. As the black market is illegal, and you are liable to be prosecuted if you admit to dealing, there isn't any way to complain.

There is less violent crime in India than in the West, although it does still occur occasionally. A few years ago, there was also a spate of druggings, where something was slipped into a drink or meal and the victim woke up hours later stripped of all his or her possessions. Thankfully, this seems to have died down again.

Finally, also beware of additions to your luggage, particularly when about to take an international flight. A common trick for drug dealers is to use an unsuspecting mule. A friend of mine, a solicitor by profession, was thoroughly shaken on his return from his last trip to find a completely strange bum bag in his luggage. It didn't have drugs in it, but it could easily have done and he would have been liable for a long prison sentence and the total destruction of his career. If he had been going the other way, to Thailand or Malaysia, he could even have found himself facing the death sentence.

GETTING OUT OF TROUBLE

If you lose your travellers' cheques and/or credit cards, you must report it to the company immediately and get some sort of proof that you have done so. You continue to be liable for any payments made until the report has gone through and the cheques or card can be cancelled. You will need proof of the cheques you had with you, together with a list of those you cashed yourself in order to get replacements. American Express and one or two other companies claim to replace all cheques within 48 hours, and on the whole they will do so. However, it can take up to a week, particularly if there are large sums involved.

If you are robbed, or even lose something, you will need a police report before you can claim from your insurance company. You will also need to go to them if you suffer any form of attack and, of course, if you get yourself arrested for any reason, you won't have a choice.

In general, the police are thought to be reasonable, if as bureaucratic as the rest of the country. In the last couple of years, however, there have been some disturbing reports, particularly from women, of harrassment, violence, and in one or two cases, even attempted rape, when they went in to report a crime. To be on the safe side, find a friendly face – your hotel manager, another traveller, or even someone from the crowd – and ask them to come with you as a witness and deterrent.

Also contact your nearest embassy or consulate at the first whiff of serious trouble. Even if it is too far away for them to get there immediately, they will tell you what to do, arrange legal representation if required and, if the situation merits, send someone to help as soon as possible. At the very least, they will then know where you are and that you may need help.

Be prepared to stand up for your rights. The police are required by law to let you have representation and if the embassy seems reluctant at times, they too have a duty to help.

If your air ticket goes, contact the airline office and explain the situation. If a new ticket needs to be issued, it has to be requested via the travel agency you bought it from. This is a relatively simple operation, and once they give the go ahead, it can be issued for you in India. However, you will either have to phone yourself or get someone at home to handle it for you. In some instances, dependent on the type of ticket, you will have to pay again and wait for a refund. This can take some months to come through.

If your passport goes missing, again contact the embassy at the first possible opportunity. With an ever increasing number of travellers selling their passports on the black market, they are often reluctant to provide you with a new one on the spot, but they will, at least, give you a temporary travel document, either to enable you to fly straight home or to cover the remainder of your trip. If you are left without any money or your return ticket, they may also be prepared to loan you enough to survive long enough to get home. This is a loan, however, and you will be expected to pay it back. If you need legal help, they will arrange it for you, but you will have to foot the bill yourself. For this, as much as any other reason, proper travel insurance is essential.

CULTURE SHOCK

India is a difficult country to travel in, with enough bureaucracy to make a civil servant curse, depths of poverty and squalor that few of us could imagine, a harsh climate and cultures and traditions that bear little resemblance to our own. A trip to India is never going to be relaxing, but even if you are prepared to come home more tired than when you left, it is easy to find yourself exhausted, confused, ill and utterly miserable. A little knowledge and a lot of common sense will help soften the blow.

PEOPLE AND PRIVACY

One of the hardest things to acclimatise to, amongst all the different types of culture shock you will face, is the sheer quantity of people surrounding you. Bangalore, with over 4 million inhabitants, is considered a relatively minor city in the national league – which gives you some idea of the others. However far you go into the bush, you are never

---

Embassies and High Commissions in India

UK
Bombay – Hong Kong Bank Building, M.G. Rd. Tel: 274 874.
Delhi – Shantipath, Chanakyapuri. Tel: 601 371.
Madras – 24 Anderson Rd. Tel: 473 136.

USA
Bombay – Lincoln House, 78 Bhulabhai Desai Rd. Tel: 822 3611.
Delhi – Shantipath, Chanakyapuri. Tel: 600 651.
Madras – 220 Anna Salai. Tel: 83041.

Australia
Bombay – Maker Tower "E", 16th Floor, Cuffe Parade, Colaba. Tel: 211 071.
Delhi – 1/50 G Shantipath, Chanakyapuri. Tel: 601 112/601 238.

Canada
Bombay – 1 Walchand Hirachand Marg. Tel: 265 219.
Delhi – 7/8 Shantipath, Chanakyapuri. Tel: 608 161.

---

going to be out of reach of human contact and for much of your trip you will be surrounded by crowds to equal Oxford Street on Christmas Eve.

In most places, you will also be an object of intense curiosity. I have found myself embroiled in mind-bending philosophical discussions with academics and businessmen, most of whom seem to have at least one PhD; surrounded by flocks of chattering women wanting to know about husband and babies (and commiserating loudly when I deny having either); trailed by three schools' worth of children who abandoned their teachers to watch me taking notes; and invited in for tea by a transvestite prostitute in Bombay. Every time the train stops, a crowd gathers opposite the window, many of them giggling disconcertingly. The Indians all want to meet you and talk to you, eager to hear your ideas or just to practise their few words of English. They are also immensely hospitable. It is exciting, rewarding and, for the most part, fun, but it is also very tiring. You need to scrap any idea of privacy and dig deep for endless resources of patience. By the time the six hundredth person has asked "What is your name?" and the seven hundredth has queried "Where are you coming from?", the charm of this limited contact has worn decidedly thin. Those who speak a bit more English can also be very disconcerting as they will ask what we would consider to be the most personal questions, from "How much do you earn?" to "Why are you so fat?" without blinking an eye. Most of us want to travel to meet people of other cultures, but there will be times when you think longingly of the blind anonymity that is the lot of travellers in Europe.

Savour those few moments of peace and quiet you manage to snatch, but don't cut yourself off or, despite the irritations, you will miss some of the best that India has to offer. If you feel like a zoo exhibit at times, you are, after all, only getting a taste of the same treatment that tourists through the ages have given to their hosts.

BAKSHEESH

One of the most irritating and upsetting aspects of India is baksheesh (as opposed to tipping, which is dealt with on page 70). However poor you may consider yourself, you will be regarded by almost everyone you meet as considerably richer than they are. On the whole, they will be right. You are therefore regarded as a legitimate target. They feel perfectly justified in trying to charge you outrageously high prices, or expecting you to pay for their food or entertainment, give away most of your cash and, if possible, all your worldly goods. None of us would begrudge a few pens, cigarettes or sweets, but when every conversation inevitably leads to a request for something, be it foreign coins or stamps for a collection or hard cash, it becomes difficult to remain civil. My lowest point came in Goa when, during a conversation about St Francis Xavier, the nun I was talking to asked me for a bottle of perfume.

Far more upsetting, however, are the hundreds of thousands of beggars who cram the streets of every town and city, many of them ill or crippled, many of them children, and all in rags. Most of India's wealth is in the hands of a few very rich people and its population explosion is running out of control. As a result, literally millions live on the streets, some as beggars, some with such a pitifully small income that they can't afford a house. Your immediate reaction will be one of intense guilt for your own good fortune, followed by a desperate desire to tuck each and every one of them under your wing. Finally will come irritation at the constant hassle and yet more guilt the first time you brush a beggar aside.

Before you try and give to everyone who asks, start hardening your heart. Your generosity can be a double-edged sword. Many beggars are hardened professionals, with their own beat. Some of those pitiful, adorable children are deliberately kept from school, or even maimed, because they can make more in a day with their begging bowl than their father will earn in a week. One mother in Bombay deliberately sent her naked toddler out into busy traffic, knowing that I would stop to yank it back to safety. I was promptly surrounded by the rest of the family who became almost threatening before I finally gave in, paid, and was allowed to go.

By all means give, but keep it under a *rupee* a time and be careful if you are visiting the same place regularly or word will get round and the crowds surrounding you will swell. Don't beggar yourself in your efforts to appease your conscience. You will never have enough to make any real difference and it is futile to try. If you really want to help, your money would be more valuable going to one of the many charities trying to make some longterm improvements. Meanwhile, for the sake of your sanity, learn to say no without feeling guilty.

LANGUAGE

English is still an official language of India and, given the complexities of the country, seems likely to remain so. In the whole country there are some 65 officially recognised languages and about 550 dialects. Of these, the most widely spoken, and the other language of government, is Hindi. In the south, however, Hindi will do you little good, as only the most highly educated speak it – and they all speak English as well. It can even do you harm, as the ascendancy of Hindi is bitterly resented and your carefully memorised phrases are as likely to offend as impress. If you want to learn something of another language. Tamil is probably the most widely spoken in the south, although outside Tamil Nadu, this won't get you far either. Other major languages in the area are Malayalam, Kannada and Telegu. I normally like to learn at least the basic civilities in the language of the country I am visiting, but in South India, it was so complicated, I gave up in despair. No one thought less of me and I rarely had trouble making myself understood.

WOMEN TRAVELLERS

If all Western travellers are objects of curiosity in India, women travelling on their own are even more interesting. It is almost inconceivable to most Indians, male or female, that you would be brave enough to set off across the globe without a chaperon, and totally unbelievable that you might reach the grand old age of 25 or over without a husband and children. The good news is that most of it is simple curiosity. You will, of course, face some hassle, from extravagant gestures of passionate love and even proposals of marriage, to the more normal attempts at a quick screw. Most are extremely polite however and a firm but smiling no is usually quite sufficient to shake them off. Only once has anyone ever attempted to grope me and that was a sailor in the very cosmopolitan port of Cochin.

Reasonably modest dress (shoulders and knees covered, nothing too low-cut or clinging) helps to establish you as someone respectable, even if you seem somewhat eccentric by local standards. Shorts should be confined to those beaches by the resort hotels, and even there leave the bikini at home and wear a one-piece costume. Topless or nude sunbathing is a real insult to local culture, so don't do it.

If worried, you can of course buy yourself a wedding ring and borrow or invent a husband and even children. Most women seem to find, however, that it just leads to a host more questions as people struggle to understand how you could abandon your children and how your husband would permit you to leave home without him. I have fallen back on fabrication only twice, when very hard pressed, inventing a fiancé who was to meet me in the next town. It worked a treat. If you are travelling with a man who is just a friend, give up any idea of explanations and turn him into a boyfriend, husband or brother. You will find that people like to pigeonhole you and that a simple platonic friendship between the sexes is something completely outside the comprehension of most.

Local custom dictates that there should be no physical contact between men and women in public, even if they are husband and wife. Unless you are with the most sophisticated people, don't shake hands. Some will try as a courtesy to you, but many others will use it as an excuse to say they've touched you. The usual form of greeting is to put your hands together in a prayer gesture and bow slightly. Unless you are in one of the top hotels, which work for the most part to Western rules, don't go into a bar on your own. Indian women don't drink and you will immediately be marked out as a whore. Also be careful about where you go on your own and which restaurants you frequent after dark. Some coffee houses have a women's room, which allow men in only if accompanied by a woman. Some trains have a ladies' carriage, all stations have segregated waiting rooms and some even have separate ticket queues for women.

A major plus point of travelling on your own is that you will get to meet and talk to women who would be unlikely to approach you if you had a man around. Another is that the Indians take the safety and respectability of their women far more seriously than we do. The amount of violence against women is far lower than in the West, penalties are more severe, and if you do run into real trouble, people are far more likely to come to your rescue. As long as you don't flout every convention, you will have a safe and rewarding trip.

TRAVELLING AROUND
Trains, boats and planes
– and rickshaws

TRAINS

Trains are the most widespread and efficient system of transport in India. They and the stations are also fascinating – small, perpetually bustling worlds that offer some of the best possible opportunities to come to grips with Indian life. If you never left the stations, you could come home with almost as good an insight into the country as someone who had conscientiously worked their way round every sight listed in the books. If you plan to travel independently, go by rail wherever possible.

The only disadvantages of the railways are that the trains can be exceedingly slow – 24 hours to do one memorable 500-kilometre journey on my last trip – and the system is incredibly complicated, like everything in India that involves bureaucracy. So how do you go about it?

INDRAIL PASS
The first stop, before you leave home, is to buy yourself an Indrail Pass. (If you don't have time, they are also on sale in Delhi, Bombay and Madras, and at a number of other major stations across India.) This is a season ticket designed specifically for foreigners and available for 7, 15, 21, 30, 60 or 90 days. There are versions for 2nd class (very cheap, but somewhat uncomfortable on long journeys or overnight), 1st class (the best bet, and still very cheap by Western standards) and 1st class air-conditioned (not worth it,

as it costs considerably more and the class exists only on a tiny number of superfast express trains). The prices are calculated in US dollars and the ticket must be paid for in hard currency. No credit cards allowed. At the time of publication, a 15 day 1st class pass cost US$135. You can buy your pass and even make all your train reservations up to 360 days before you start your journey.

Benefits of the pass are numerous. You have unlimited mileage for the duration of the ticket, on any train in India, with no time restrictions and no supplements for berths or express services. This can save you both the cost of the ticket and a lot of time as you can do almost all long journeys overnight, cutting out many hotel bills. With a 1st class pass, you will be slotted into the highest class available, will be given preferential booking treatment and will be eligible for the tourist quota on any train (for explanations, keep reading.)

BUYING YOUR TICKET

For those buying their tickets in Britain, there is an added advantage in the person of Dr Dandapani, who runs SDEL, an extraordinarily enthusiastic man who is rapidly achieving legendary status. He sees himself more as an ambassador for India than a salesperson and is determined to make sure his clients enjoy their trip with the minimum of hassle, to the point where he gets positively upset if he can't help you arrange your whole itinerary. He will suggest routes, make all your bookings, do his utmost to cater for any special requests and tenderly follow your progress round the country. He really is a fount of knowledge and the more use you make of him, the happier he will be.

S.D. Enterprises Ltd, 103 Wembley Park Drive, Wembley, Middx HA9 8HG. Tel: (081) 903 3411 or (081) 200 9549. Fax: (081) 903 0392.

USA: Hariworld Travels Inc, 30 Rockefeller Plaza, Shop 21, North Mezzanine, New York, NY 10112. Tel: (212) 957 3000. Fax: 495 2383.

Canada: Hariworld Travels Inc., Royal York Hotel, 100 Front Street West, Arcade Level, Toronto, Ontario M5J 1E3. Tel: 366 2000. Fax: 062 3918.

Australia: Adventure World, 37 York Street, Sydney, NSW.
Tel: 290 3222. Fax: 22680.
Penthouse Travel, 5th Level, 72 Pitt Street, Sydney NSW. Tel:
23311455. Fax: 10718892.

TYPES OF TRAIN

Indian railways, confusingly, have been built to two different
standards, **broad** and **metre gauge**. Unfortunately, there are
relatively few lines in the south on the wider, faster, broad
gauge, so almost all journeys are incredibly slow. Where the
two meet, they usually do so in different parts of the same
station, but you will occasionally be in for a badly sign-posted
hike of several hundred yards. As your ticket information will
not tell you that you are switching from one system to the
other, you can find yourself very short of time as well as
breath! There are also a couple of "toy trains" in the south.
These are the famous miniature trains that wind their way
up to the hill stations. The best is the one that runs down the

south face of the Nilgiri Hills, from Ootacamund to join the main line at Coimbatore. If you get a chance to go on it, do so. The views are spectacular and the train itself great fun.

Passenger trains are the very slowest, theoretically local trains, although they often cover a surprising distance. They stop everywhere, including a great many halts so small as to be invisible. They are often 2nd class only, although some have one 1st class carriage. None have sleeping accommodation. Prior reservation is not required. Interesting as an experience, they should be avoided if you actually hope to get anywhere.

Express/mail trains are what you will probably spend most of your time on. Just don't be fooled into thinking that express trains actually travel fast. They still meander their way across country at a leisurely pace, with numerous stops. They do, however, have a wider variety of accommodation, including sleeping cars. Advance reservations are essential for overnight journeys, and advisable, whatever you might be told at the station, for all but the shortest journeys during the day.

There are a very few **superfast** express trains, which really do travel fast, usually covering incredibly long distances, such as New Delhi to Madras, and stopping only at major stations en route. They will have a full range of classes and even a food service in 1st class (see below). Use them when you can find them, but this isn't always easy. Prior reservation is essential.

Finding your train is also complicated. The expresses are all given names, so there is no easy, instant way of knowing where they are going. They also prefer to use Up and Down to a simple north-south type system, so if you are halfway down the line, it is relatively simple to get on a train going in the wrong direction – and you may have to wait twelve hours for the next one! A simple rule of thumb is that Up will be towards the major station, while Down is towards the smaller terminal. However, don't take this as gospel. Ask, keep asking, and if necessary use a porter. They are far more valuable for getting you on to the right train than they are for carrying your bags.

CLASSES

In addition to 1st and 2nd class designations, there is a proliferation of sub-classes and name-changes designed to bewilder the most seasoned traveller. The list below is, believe it or not, a simplified version of the full range, giving only those classes you are most likely to come across.

2nd Class Ordinary

Equivalent to the now defunct 3rd class, the older 2nd class carriages have wooden slatted benches, while the newer ones have such uncomfortable padding that you think with longing of the wooden slats! Often very overcrowded, the overhead luggage racks are, more often than not, used as extra seating. There are no sleeper berths. Overhead fans may or may not work. No reservations possible and it's first come, first served if you want a seat.

2nd Class Sleeper

Also known as II 3-tier sleepers, these are carriages designed to provide sleeper accommodation for 72, split into groups of six with three tiers of padded berths and some extra, single seats for daytime travel. Overhead fans and individual lights, which usually work. These carriages are quite comfortable during the day, but can be extremely stuffy and noisy overnight. Reservations needed overnight.

AC Sleeper (2 tier) Class

This is the air-conditioned version of the 2nd class sleeper, with space for 46 berths, in two tiers instead of three. Some four berth sections have curtains across the aisle openings to allow some privacy, though do nothing to dim the noise level, while the singles on the other side of the aisle have no protection at all from the endless comings and goings. The newer carriages have separate compartments virtually indistinguishable from 1st Class (AC) Sleeper, but without the frills. There are reading lights by each berth. The windows have curtains, but don't open. Three Indian-style and one Western-style toilet to each carriage. Reservations are required overnight.

1st Class (Non-AC) Sleeper

Although these are supposedly being phased out, there still seem to be plenty of these carriages around. They are not super-luxurious, but are perfectly comfortable and are my personal favourites for overnight journeys. They are split into a mix of two- and four-berth compartments, with plenty of fans and separate reading lights for all berths. The windows are barred and have lockable louvred shutters to allow in extra air at night, and there are also windows if you want to look out without the outside getting in. Each compartment also has a lockable door, while the carriages are furnished with both Indian and Western-style toilets, basins, and occasionally a shower. During the day, six will be allowed into four-berth compartments. Reservations required at night and suggested during the day.

1st Class (AC) Sleeper

The newest, poshest, and most expensive carriages on Indian Railways, these are generally available only on the major inter-city express trains. They are also the only carriages you will not be able to use with an ordinary 1st class rail pass. Fully air-conditioned, compartments are four-berth, with lockable doors, sealed windows with curtains, carpets, a table, ashtrays, and other such undreamed of luxuries. There are both Western and Indian-style toilets with showers, and there are small washbasins in some compartments. Bedding, a towel and soap are provided within the ticket price. Advance booking is essential.

Chair Class

Various different versions of Chair Class exist, mostly designed for daytime journeys, so often to be found on shorter routes only. They are all open carriages without compartments or partitions. At the top is AC Chair Class, with full air-conditioning, aeroplane-style reclining seats and drop-down tables. There are Western and Indian-style toilets. 1st Class non-AC has all the same comforts, except that there are fans instead of air-conditioning. This has the added advantage, in my view, that you can open the windows. Advance booking is advisable, though not essential.

There is also a rarely seen 2nd Class (non-AC) version of Chair Class, which has wooden benches, and is really almost indistinguishable in terms of comfort from the humble 2nd Class Ordinary carriage.

MAKING A RESERVATION

Even if you have been terribly well organised and bought your rail pass and made all your reservations before you set foot in India, you are still not off the hook. You now have to reconfirm everything. If you don't have your reservations, you have to start from scratch. Buying a train ticket in India is a form of masochism, mixing the worst aspects of bedlam and bureaucracy that the country has to offer. To be fair, the authorities have realised how daunting it can be and have, where possible, instituted a number of measures specifically designed to help tourists, but even with these, make sure you have a strong constitution and plenty of time to spare.

Where possible, ignore the main ticket hall, which, in large stations, is generally designed for immediate sales of 2nd class tickets. There will, at the very least, be a separate reservations office, often set slightly apart from the main body of the station.

In Delhi, Bombay and Madras, and in a few other major tourist centres, there is a separate haven of relative tranquillity – the **International Tourist Bureau** or ITB – designed specifically to help foreign tourists buck the system. Even here queues can be impressively long so you will need to decide on your basic itinerary before you enter the fray. Most useful are the information people with a copy of the all-India timetable who can help you plot your journey, giving you the names, numbers and times of all the possible trains (these will be needed later, so write everything down).

If there is no tourist office, one of the windows in the reservations hall is often set aside for tourist use only. These are usually well-marked, but there are occasional hiccups in the system. I hunted round Bangalore for the tourist counter, only to assume, in the end, that it didn't exist. After an hour spent in a general queue, I finally reached the counter, where the man refused to serve me, pointing me instead to another window that said, confusingly, "disabled and freedom fighters only"!

In all major cities there is at last a **computerised booking system,** so they can give your reservations and even berth numbers on the spot for routes that are computerised. Be warned that the computer doesn't seem to speed things up, and only major routes are on the system. For the rest, they have to use the quota they have been given to sell, then telex down to the station where you will start your journey. If they have used up their quota, it doesn't necessarily mean that there are no seats on the train, merely that you will have to try again from somewhere else.

In order to make, reconfirm, alter or cancel a booking, you will have to fill in a **requisition slip.** You get nowhere without it. This piece of paper is usually available from the very same window at which you make the booking, so, at this stage, don't even try to queue politely but follow the general stampede. You will need a separate form for each journey, so make sure you get enough if you are doing multiple bookings. On it, you will need to put your name(s) and passport number(s), sex, age, the name and number and time of the train and the date of your journey, and the type of seat/berth you require. Your name, age and sex are later posted on the station and plastered to the side of the train for all comers to read and digest. Get the train details at least right, because if you have to make alterations, the queue behind sweeps forward and it is difficult to get your place back.

If the train is full, or you are making a late booking, you will be sent to see the Reservations Superintendent or the Station Master who will, if possible, use some of the **foreign tourist quota,** the few places always held back for distraught and bewildered travellers. Priority is given to those with rail passes. It doesn't always work, but you have a better chance than any Indian trying to get a ticket. Any places still unsold an hour or so before the train is due to go are on offer either on the platform or in the Ticket Superintendent's office, dependent on the size of the station.

It is worthwhile either booking or re-reconfirming your

onward ticket as soon as you arrive anywhere as peculiar things can still happen. On one memorable occasion, two of us arrived with confirmed 1st class tickets, only to find on checking that mine was fine, while my companion, for some reason, was on the stand-by 2nd class list!

STATIONS

Indian stations are amazing. Many of the larger ones were built during the Raj in the Victorian oriental style, monumental piles designed to daunt and impress, and succeed admirably in both aims. Architectural splendour aside, they are also immensely useful places. Many people travelling either on a strict budget or with limited time forget about hotels completely and live in them. All but the smallest have **retiring rooms**, a mix of dormitory and more private rooms, that range from simple beds to positively luxurious suites with air-conditioning, private bathrooms and room service. They cost only a few *rupees*, so although you have to take one for 24 hours, it can even be worth checking in for a few hours while waiting for an awkwardly timed train. The only problem is that they won't always let you book ahead, so you might not be able to get in. The 1st class waiting rooms are also equipped with hygienic showers and toilets and offer somewhere relatively peaceful to wait. If you are travelling every night, most stations have a cheap, secure 24-hour **left luggage office**, so you can dump your rucksack for the day instead of have to tote it around with you.

You will always find plenty to eat and drink at the stations, with both veg and non-veg **restaurants** as well as innumerable stalls selling tea, soft drinks, mineral water, masala dosas, fruit, biscuits and cake, etc. The quality is rarely good, but it is cheap and there is lots of it.

The stations are always swarming with **porters**, distinguished by their red shirts and turbans. Their rate is fixed, so many *rupees* per piece of baggage, and there will be a sign somewhere in the main ticket hall telling you what the rate is. If you arrive before the train, however, they will also charge you waiting time, which seems to be open ended, according to how much they think they can screw out of you. Unless you have huge quantities of luggage, they are most useful for delivering you to the right platform and carriage.

ON BOARD

Once on the train, all Upper Class carriages have their own **attendant** who will find your berth for you and settle you in. They will also provide you with **refreshments** – if they are available. Only the most upmarket express trains have a small pantry on board, from which you can get tea, coffee, soup and sandwiches. On other long journeys by express, the attendant will come round before mealtimes and take orders for omelettes or *thalis* which are then phoned ahead and picked up at the next station.

Of course, this does not always happen, in which case you will be thrown on your own resources. You won't be offered anything in 2nd class or on passenger trains. **Stops** at major stations can be lengthy and it is possible to slip off and get something to eat. At every station small boys swarm round with baskets of snacks and tea – though be warned. Every time I have bought something from one of them, I have bitterly regretted it. Not only did it taste dreadful, but it made me ill. The tea is probably safe enough, but take your own mug and ask them to fill that. Having watched the beggars collecting the so-called disposable cups from the tracks, after the rats have run around all over them, there is no way I would like to touch, let alone drink from, one of them. The safest option is to stock up with plenty of water and the materials for a picnic before you join your train.

Except in 1st class (AC) **bedding** must be ordered in advance and costs a bit extra. It is much easier to take a sheet sleeping bag and inflatable pillow. Ask the attendant to wake you up in time for your stop. I have set my alarm clock for five a couple of times, only to discover, once awake, that the train was running late and I could have had two more hours in bed. Keep the shutters down and locked at night, as otherwise you will not only be woken up by the lights at every station but will become a floor show for everybody on the platform. If you have difficulty sleeping through the general level of noise and lights, take an eye mask and stuff your ears with toilet paper. It works wonders.

During the day, especially in an open carriage, you will find that you are a magnet for anyone around, either on the platform or on the train. Get used to it, there is nothing you can do to prevent their interest or preserve your privacy. Everyone will want to talk to you, and if you get out your camera, be prepared for the rush as they struggle to have their photos taken. It does get wearing at times, but it is also fascinating. Once you have been through the stock questions, you can turn it round and start asking about their lives. I have met an extraordinary range of people on trains, from brigadiers and cabinet ministers to local milkmen and gipsy farm labourers. Without this contact, the India I have come to know would have been an immeasurably poorer place.

PLANES

(**Domestic**) **air transport** in India is plentiful. Few cities of any size are without an airport and the network is generally good, although you might have to go round the houses to get from one point to the next. Air India flies some of the major domestic routes, but almost all are served by either Indian Airlines, the state domestic airline, or Vayudoot. This newer, smaller company was originally set up to fly the minor routes, but is now expanding to cover some of the more popular ones as well.

Problems for would-be air travellers begin almost immediately on their arrival in the country. Indian Airlines, whether or not it is justified, has one of the most appalling reputations of any airline in the world, both in terms of its safety record and its efficiency. Many European travel agents will refuse even to try making a booking with them because it is so difficult to get a straight answer. Mine allowed me to make the booking and pay in the UK, but I had to sign a disclaimer saying I would not hold them responsible if I arrived to find the flight, or booking, did not exist. I was lucky, but I met a number of people with horror stories to tell.

Actually, as long as you appear in person, **booking** is relatively easy as the system has finally been computerised. As long, that is, as the computer isn't down – which it frequently

Trains

India boasts the second largest rail system in the world, with 70,000 kms of tracks and 7,000 stations. Some 10,500 trains run every day, carrying 13 million passengers. In the Bombay area alone, 4 million passengers a day commute to and from the city. In spite of the low ticket prices, Indian Railways also prides itself on being the only national rail system in the world to survive without government subsidies – and does, in fact, contribute heavily to state revenues.

India has long been famed for being one of the few countries left in the world to use steam. Sadly for tourists, if not for efficiency and the ozone layer, the pace of conversion to diesel, or in a few rare instances electrification, is picking up and I noticed far fewer steam trains on my last trip than on the previous one. If you are a steam fanatic and its trains would be a major reason for your trip to India, go soon.

If you want to visit locomotive sheds, you need to get prior permission via the High Commission or Embassy. Do your research well and list those you would like to visit. Give yourself plenty of time, as it can take up to three months for the permission to come through. You will also officially need permission to take photographs of trains or in the station, although many authorities turn a blind eye. If you are stopped, go and see the Station Superintendent.

is. Prices for foreigners are calculated in US dollars and you have to pay in hard currency. They refused to accept my *rupees* even though I had a sheaf of exchange forms to prove I had converted legally. The dollar price is higher than the *rupee* price paid by locals, but is still not expensive. Children under two only pay 10% of the full fare, and those from two to 12 pay 50%.

The best news for young travellers is that there is an automatic 25% **Youth discount** for everyone under the age of 30. They also offer 14-day "Tour India" and 21-day "Discover India" **air passes** which allow unlimited access to the network. At the time of writing, the cost was US$400 for 21 days, so if you want to cover a lot of miles in a short time, they can be very good value.

The catch is that you could spend a large part of your holiday sitting around in less-than-exciting airport lounges.

A plane that leaves on time seems to be a real rarity. One seasoned traveller I met suggested that you should never consider flying unless the alternative journey would take at least 12 hours. It's wise advice.

Airport **security** is fierce, if a little haphazard. As you enter the terminal building, you should take your main luggage to the X-ray machine and have it checked and security sealed before you take it to check-in. The terminals are all plastered with large labels telling you that all batteries, including items with batteries in them (i.e. cameras), should be checked into the hold as it is illegal to carry them in the cabin. However, no one even queried me when I carried my cameras through. Nor were there any problems about them hand checking film.

ROAD

If you are planning to drive yourself round India – don't! Traffic in India is by far the most lunatic I have ever encountered, and that includes such notorious countries as Egypt and Turkey. A stock car champion might have a hope of survival, but even the best driver would be reduced to a gibbering wreck after a fortnight. To try and follow some theoretical rule that makes perfect sense at home would be positively lethal.

Driving is theoretically on the left, but in practice is wherever there's a gap. Roads are, on the whole, narrow, overcrowded with an amazing assortment of motley vehicles from gaudily painted lorries to ox-carts, and usually have more holes than surface. The way to cope with them seems to be to drive, as fast as possible, up the wrong side of the road until you see something coming in the other direction. You wait until the last possible moment, then stick your hand firmly on the horn and swerve back to the left, straight into the path of the lorry coming up behind you, narrowly missing the peasant woman who is drying her clothes on the verge. Once this is successfully negotiated, you look round to see if you managed to put anyone into the ditch or if your passenger is throwing up yet before grinning broadly and starting again. The number of deaths in road accidents a year runs at over

20,000, a figure most astonishing for the fact that it isn't a great deal higher.

No self-drive *car hire* is available in the country. Presumably on the basis that someone who has grown up in this madness is more likely to survive it, **hiring a car with a driver** still costs less than a self-drive car would cost you in Europe. Prices start at around Rs400 a day, plus a kilometre rate and, of course, the cost of petrol, the driver's accommodation and food. Ask the hotels or tourist information offices to arrange one for you. There are also numerous travel agents in the major cities who will put together a specially tailored package for you, including private transport with a chauffeur/guide, but this is, needless to say, about the most expensive way you could find of doing things.

Buses are cheap and plentiful, but they make the railways seem like havens of peace and civilisation. Unfortunately, there are some places where they are the only option, especially if you are heading up into the mountains. The bus stations are marginally more chaotic than the rest of India, with no discernible gates or bays. Even the ticket office is often unmarked, while few signs are written in English or even in Western script. Unless you speak and read the local language, therefore, you can expect no official help in finding the right bus. The only way I have found to circumvent this problem is to hire one of the many small boys who hang around eager to help. For a couple of *rupees*, they will find your bus, take care of your luggage and even grab a seat for you.

Although the main bus companies are state owned, there are some private buses operating on long or exceptionally busy routes. Among these are the dreaded **luxury coaches**. Although these might sound, at first, like a good thing, the luxury comes with the provision of a video or sound system. After several hours of hairpin bends and potholes to the accompaniment of Hindi films or pop music, both as shrill and noisy as each other, you will be desperate for even some Indian-style silence – the sort of noise level you might expect to find, say, at Oxford Circus during rush hour. To my mind, the best of the buses are the tattiest, those which have given up trying to keep their windows intact and have removed them altogether. In these you do at least get plenty of fresh air and none of the normal array of interesting smells from manure to stale sweat.

There are two important considerations while boarding your bus. The first is that the luggage generally travels on the roof. Unless you are travelling very light, there will be an uproar if you try to take yours inside with you. You therefore have to see it safely stowed, so that it won't fall off, preferably without any tin trunks, baskets of chickens or sacks of feed on top of it. On arrival, incidentally, you must make sure that the bus is not going to take off again before you have a chance to get your bags down!

The second is to get a seat, preferably at the front of the bus. The general bounce as the bus roars blindly across the potholes is far worse at the back. I have nearly knocked myself out a couple of times when I have connected particularly fast with the ceiling. Getting any seat is an art, however, as there is no system of reservation, nothing so orderly as a queue, and all buses carry at least twice the legal number of passengers. Any dirty trick will do. If there are two of you, one can supervise the luggage while the other joins the mob. Otherwise, rely on the expertise of the small boy who will swarm in through the window to hold a place for you. If you don't get a seat at first, don't despair. The innate politeness of the Indians towards foreigners usually leads them to offer you the first place that becomes available later, even if it is the engine housing – very hot, but in other ways the most comfortable place on board.

Once underway, life settles into the usual routine of intense curiosity, barter of sweets for fruit, etc. As the buses also act as mail vans and general haulage for anything from livestock onwards, the first few hours can be fun. The novelty wears off with the onset of backache and the creeping numbness induced by terror. You can then keep yourself occupied for a while longer by praying for your safe delivery from the hands of the demon driver. In the end, however, there is nothing but boredom and cramp. Buses are more frequent, and marginally faster, than the trains, but use them sparingly and only when absolutely essential.

Hitch hiking is possible, although not always easy. It is generally rather pointless, however, as public transport is so cheap and you will probably be asked to pay the equivalent of the bus fare anyway. If you do decide to hitch, the bad driving is probably more of a risk than violence, but the threat still exists, so take the usual precautions.

More popular are **motorbikes and bicycles**. Many travellers hire these by the day or week for pottering around the area they are staying in. There are numerous hire shops for bikes and mopeds in the main tourist centres. They do give you a degree of freedom otherwise impossible, and once off the major highways, you can find plenty of quieter roads that needn't stretch the nerves too far. If you hire a pedal bike, you will need to be reasonably fit to cope with the heat and, inland, with the mountains, as the bikes are usually the old, sturdy, unbendable kind with no gears.

If you are planning a longer journey, it probably makes sense to buy a larger motorbike or better bicycle and sell it again at the end of your trip. As these are the main forms of private transport in India, there is no shortage of supply, although there isn't a great deal of choice. If you want a super upmarket bike with 95 gears and all the trimmings, take it with you from home, but do realise that it could be stolen or damaged and that it will almost certainly return home far more battered than it left. For the Indian version, motorised or pedal, just ask around. You will have to cope with the laws regarding ownership papers, different in each state. If you are buying from an agency, they should be willing to handle things for you. If not, pay the clerk at the Motor Vehicles Office to help you. Don't part with your money until everything is signed and sealed and legally in your name.

The good news is the huge number of cheap and useful repair shops around. You can get almost anything fixed or replaced on the spot, particularly if your machine is a common one in India. You probably won't even have to mend a puncture yourself.

BOATS

There are few options for boat travel anywhere in India. The most famous is the Bombay-Goa steamer, which is meant to travel down the coast out of monsoon season. It has, however, been totally out of commission for several years now, and, although everyone talks of its imminent revival, nothing seems to happen. Don't hold your breath. There is also talk, though no action as yet, of hydrofoil services along the Goa coast and the Tamil Nadu coast just south of Madras.

Otherwise there are small ferries to some of the islands, particularly in Bombay, and across the rivers in Goa. The best of all, however, is the water bus that provides the local transport through the rice paddies just south of Cochin in Kerala. This provides a lovely lazy day out for no more than a few rupees, and is well worth doing.

LOCAL TRANSPORT

Once in town, you are faced by a wide range of options as
to how to get around, at a variety of prices. Top of the range
are **taxis**, usually the sturdy cream-coloured Ambassadors that
were the only cars in India until very recently. Still cheap by
European standards, these are by far the most expensive form
of transport around. They are, however, clean, fast and safe,
with windows that close and doors that lock, if you are
worried about travelling at night. With several of you, of
course, the price per head comes right down. Taxis can be
ordered in advance, or found at ranks or at the grander hotels,
but can rarely be picked up in the street.

All taxis are licensed and fitted with meters, and by law
have to use these at rates set by the government. The meter
usually works and, with a little persuasion, or if there is a
policeman nearby and you make a lot of noise, you can get the
driver to switch it on. This isn't the end of the story, however.
The meters were all fitted a long time ago and haven't been
adjusted as prices rose. Instead, each taxi is given a card of
comparative charges which you should be allowed to consult
if you ask. It shows 9 *rupees* on the meter, but the card price
is 36, for instance. This usually works on a simple scale,
but is different in every city, from "4½ times the meter"
in Bombay to "meter plus 20%" in Madras, last time I was
there. It changes so frequently however that no book could
keep up, so ask someone without an axe to grind what the
rate is as soon as you arrive in the city and stick to it.

Next on the social scale come the little black and yellow
auto-rickshaws, three-wheeler scooters with a soft canopy and
open sides. Licensed to carry up to three passengers, they are
by far the most popular form of public transport (and my
personal favourite) – cheap, convenient and numerous. There
are ranks dotted all over town, but the drivers also cruise
the streets and you are unlikely to have walked a couple of
hundred yards without at least one driver drawing up beside
you. Auto-rickshaws are also licensed and are all fitted with
meters that are meant to be used, but finding one with a meter

in working condition and a driver who is prepared to switch it on is a rare occurrence.

Further down the pecking order come the **cycle-rickshaws**. Generally, the larger the town, the fewer you will see around. These carry two comfortably, although you do occasionally see them piled high with a family of six. A little cheaper than the auto-rickshaws, they are of necessity very slow and are really only suitable for short journeys. There is, of course, no meter, but I find that the drivers are usually pleasant and willing and far easier to deal with than auto-rickshaw drivers.

At the lowest end of the scale come the horse-drawn **tongas** (except in Bombay, where there are a number of rather grand Victorias, decorated to the hilt and used mainly for tourist joy rides). These are usually a pitiful sight, with a small, flea-bitten nag, more rib than flesh, stumbling its way along the road, lashed ferociously by its driver. I avoid them as much as possible. The **tonga** itself will normally seat up to six, some facing forwards, some backwards. They have only two wheels, so balance is all important. It's easy to get thrown out if you get it wrong.

FARES

To get around without being ripped off too badly, you'll have to hone your haggling skills. As a newcomer to any town, the first problem is knowing how far your destination is and what the real fare should be. If possible, ask at the hotel or tourist office for some sort of price guide. Otherwise, you have to use your own instincts. Assume all the time that however well you haggle, you are still not going to pay the same price as a local. Regard the extra as a tourist tax. The trick is to avoid paying too much over the odds, and never to get into any vehicle without agreeing the price in advance. It always leads to grief at the other end of the journey. I normally start at around quarter of the price they originally suggest and settle for between a third and half. You can usually tell when the absolute bottom line has been reached. If there are a number of drivers around, let them do your work for you. They will often bargain each other down in their eagerness to get your custom as long as you stand firm and say no occasionally.

And don't be afraid to walk away. Nine times out of ten, they will follow and capitulate. On the tenth, there are other drivers further on.

GUIDED TOURS

If you want to spend the day **sightseeing**, there are two ways to go about it. The first is to take one of the bus tours organised by almost all the tourist offices. These offer a good introduction to the city or area and cost relatively little, but are almost always hurried and ultimately exhausting. I prefer, where possible, to find a good rickshaw driver with a reasonable command of English and do a deal for the day. They all know the major tourist sights and will take you on the standard tour, which you can then take at your own pace. Occasionally I have even found one with a real interest in and knowledge of the subject who has acted as a guide as well. With them, I have been taken to other wonderful places that are not on the general route, or even fetched up at their homes, meeting their wives and families. Almost all the drivers will try to take you shopping or to a restaurant of their choice, where they will, of course, get commission. A firm no will put you back on track, but when I have agreed to their suggestions, I find that they have rarely steered me wrong.

MAHARASHTRA

Maharashtra means "Great Land", or possibly "Land of the Great". The origin of the name is obscure, but is generally thought to have derived from the Sanskrit word *maharathi*. These were the drivers and builders of great war chariots, *rathi*, used during the conquest of the local Naga people. Whatever its derivation, the name is apt. The state is the third largest in India, with a coastline 720 kilometres long, while its borders drive a wedge 800 kilometres long through the centre of the country. It also has one of the largest populations of any state (around 85 million) and, with Bombay at its centre, is today the economic heartland of the country. Only the south-west corner of Maharashtra is within the area covered by this book.

The majority of the state is on the huge, scenically uninteresting Deccan plateau, but in the west the high hills of the Western Ghats block these agricultural plains from the sea. The heavily wooded mountains near the state capital Bombay are dotted by small, attractive hill stations that are popular weekend resorts for city dwellers. They are also now being developed by the Maharashtra Tourist Development Corporation as centres for trekking, rock climbing and other adventure sports. The MTDC is also beginning to develop various beaches in this area, although as yet, they are still small and more or less deserted once the daytrippers have gone home.

The main language in the area is Marathi. Although based on *Sanskrit*, it derives from the popular variation, *Prakril* that was very different to the classical form. Marathi developed early and became acceptable after its adoption by various local saints in the thirteenth and fourteenth centuries, who left behind them a large body of devotional literature. In spite of this, Maharashtra and, in particular, Pune, is also seen as the spiritual home of *Sanskrit*.

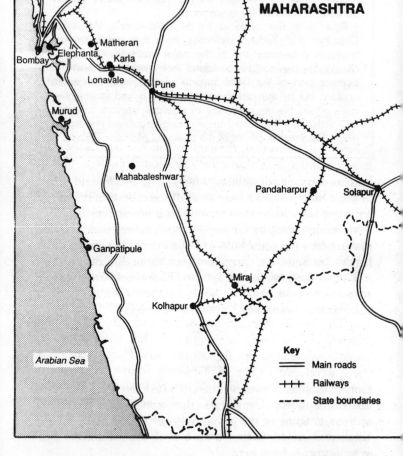

Dotted across the state are the ruins of 175 forts, 111 of them built by the great Maratha emperor, Chhatrapati Shivaji Maharaj, who was crowned at Raigad in 1674. Of these, the most famous are Torna, Raigad, Sinhagad, Purandor, Pratapgad, Vishalgad, Sajjangad, Ahmednagar,

---

A state of war

Maharashtra has a bloody history. The first mention of the state in foreign texts is in the writings of the Chinese traveller, Hsuan-Tsang, in the seventh century BC. As the effective frontier between North and South India, control of the region constantly changed as the southern states battled between themselves for supremacy.

Ruled over the centuries by the Satavahana, Vakataka, Chalukya and Yadava dynasties, from the eighth century onwards, it became one of the major battlegrounds as the Muslim Empires sought to extend their boundaries south. It became part of the Delhi Sultanate in the early-fourteenth century, but by the mid-sixteenth century it had fragmented once again. Nearly a century of constant warfare followed until victory by the early Maratha kings stabilised the region and it became the centre of the powerful Maratha Empire.

Bassein, Sindhudurg, Janjira, Alibag, and Daulatabad. Most of them however are a long way off the tourist beat and are not sufficiently interesting to warrant a major detour.

More important by far are the much earlier rock temples. Maharashtra has some 80% of India's rock cut temples, both Hindu and Buddhist, carved between about 300 BC and 800 AD. The most famous, at Ajanta and Ellora, near Aurangabad, are outside the scope of this book, but there are fine examples at Elephanta Island and Karla, near Bombay.

BOMBAY

Bombay positively sweats money. It has skyscrapers, streets of luxury shops and elegant cafés that would grace the streets of Vienna. Some of the property prices would make a New Yorker blanch. More than a third of all the income tax paid in India comes from here.

More than anywhere else on the sub-continent, however, India's second largest city is also a place of extremes. Just around the corner, those drawn unthinkingly to the bright lights live in conditions of the most appalling squalor. Every small patch of bare ground is filled by lean-tos made from old plastic and flour sacks. Take a suburban train, and only a couple of minutes from the station, you will be travelling for literally miles through smelly shanty towns that squat malevolently in a sea of mud, oozing typhoid and cholera. Washing is laid out on the lines to dry; children play under the wheels of the express trains; some 30 people a day are killed on the tracks. There is no clean water, and not even the most rudimentary toilets. Food is scarce and jobs are rarer still. The slums are some of the worst in the world and there seems little hope of any improvement. Even if the authorities could afford to rehouse the people, there is little land for development. Meanwhile literally thousands more people pour into the city every day. Right now, the population is 11 million.

Tourists usually avert their eyes, or don't even notice, this side of the city. For them, Bombay can be a gentle introduction to the sub-continent, a sophisticated, cosmopolitan centre that offers every convenience and even works somewhat more efficiently than other cities.

At one time, the area covered by this sprawling metropolis consisted of seven low-lying, marshy, malarial islands (called Colaba, Fort, Byculla, Parel, Worli, Matunga and Mahim). As the city has grown, however, it has spread to encompass two others – Mulund and Dahisar – while land reclamation projects have joined all the islands together and to the mainland, with bridges only over the swampiest areas. Effectively, Bombay is now a peninsula.

Unlike other cities in India, it was originally a European creation. The sheltered bay has drawn travellers and traders from the West for thousands of years. Roman, Assyrian and Persian ships all anchored here, and Ptolemy visited the islands, which he christened "Heptanasia", in 150 AD. They also formed part of various great empires, including those of the Mauryans and the Silharas, while in 1348 they came under Muslim rule for the first time as part of the state of Gujarat. The area was notoriously unhealthy however and, for the most part, the Kolis, the simple fishermen who lived in the marshes, were left pretty much to their own devices.

In 1534 the territory was ceded to Portugal, which already possessed nearby Goa, by Sultan Bahadurshah of Gujarat as part of the Treaty of Bassein. Strangely, the Portuguese didn't seem too impressed by their new acquisition and it received little of the attention given to Goa. In 1661 the island settlement was transferred to British rule when Charles II married Catherine of Braganza, receiving the territory as part of her dowry. In 1668, a Royal Charter gave it to the fledgling East India Company, in exchange for an annual rent of £10 in gold.

Almost immediately, Bombay began to grow as a trading centre and port. In 1687, the presidency of the East India Company was transferred here from Surat, and in 1708 it became the headquarters for all the Company's west coast operations. Nevertheless, it remained a small city and an unpopular posting with company officials.

Bombay's great boom started with the transport revolution of the nineteenth century. From 1813 onwards, passenger steamers began to arrive, bringing with them the so-called "Fishing Fleet", flocks of women in search of husbands. Bombay was often their first port of call and the settlement's men got the pick of the bunch. In 1854, the first railway line east of Suez was laid from Bombay, making it far more accessible to the rest of the country. Just twelve years later Sir Bartle Frere began the first great land reclamation project, creating whole new areas for development, as well as starting to build the vast dock complex and putting up many of the city's most impressive public buildings. The telegraph service began in 1865. In 1869, the opening of the Suez Canal turned the old trade routes on their heads. Bombay was now unquestionably the most convenient port for trade with Europe.

By the turn of the century, Bombay was the economic heart of India – a position it has never lost. It's the centre of India's thriving textiles trade, there is oil and gas production just off its coast, it has the third largest stock exchange in the world, and is its largest film-producing city. It has the busiest airport in India; and the docks handle half of all foreign shipping trade.

Mumbai

Officially, Bombay is called Mumbai — although few have ever heard the name and no one ever uses it, even in the most official of publications. There are various different theories about how the city got its name. The most likely is that it was named after Mumba Ai (also known as Maha Amba or Mumba Devi), an incarnation of Parvati and the patron goddess of the local fishermen, the Kolis. Others claim it derives from the Portuguese *bom bahia* or "beautiful bay". My favourite theory, however, is that it was called after the little local fish, the *bombelli*, which is known to the rest of us, once it's been dried and salted, as the pungent "Bombay duck".

GETTING THERE

Bombay airport is the busiest in India. Almost all the **major international airlines** which fly into the country have services to Bombay — usually at the same price as the Delhi flight, although, for some reason there, are not as many good discount deals. There is an excellent **domestic network** with connections almost everywhere, and several flights a day to the other major cities. There are two terminals, some distance apart. The older of the two, **Santa Cruz**, now handles all domestic flights, while the newer **Sahar** terminal copes with the international traffic. Both are on the mainland, about 26 kilometres from the city. There are shuttles between the two every 15 minutes. Airport buses run every half-hour from the Air India building at Nariman Point. Taxis into the city centre operate on fixed fares. Allow plenty of time as the journey can take up to two hours in rush hour.

Bombay is exceptionally well connected to the hinterland with regular express and mail **trains** to almost every large city in India and connecting services to absolutely everywhere. The shortest journey time from Delhi is 17 hours; from Madras 24 hours. There are also huge numbers of regional trains and even a busy and sophisticated network of suburban and city trains, many of them electrified.

The fun and games start when you have to work out which station you are travelling from. Bombay is also the border between the Central and Western Railway regions and while theoretically they work together, the practice is, as always, somewhat deficient.

By far the largest and busiest station, and the best place to start your enquiries, is **Bombay VT (Victoria Terminus)**, in the centre of the city. Standing on the site of the Kolis' temple to Mumba Devi, it is a vast, neo-Gothic pile, itself like a cathedral, complete with stained glass and stone animals, built by Frederick William Stevens over a ten-year period. Opened in 1888, it is considered to be one of the finest stations in the world. It's worth a visit as a tourist sight, even if you have no intention of ever getting on a train. VT is the headquarters of

Central Railways and the starting point for almost all journeys to the south (and some to the north – northerly Rajasthan is within the Central jurisdiction, and Delhi trains also leave from here). Tickets for surburban services are bought in the echoing main ticket hall and can't be reserved.

There is an excellent Foreign Tourist Bureau, which you must visit if you hope to get tickets from the foreign tourist quota, but which is also immensely helpful with information when plotting an itinerary. Reservations for all but suburban services are handled by the separate Computerised Reservations System Building next-door to the main station, where there is also a tourist counter. Get a chit from the FTB authorising you to a reservation from the quota before you head down there. In theory, the computer is linked to the other main Bombay stations, so you can make reservations for all trains in and out of the city. You can also buy Indrail passes here.

The other major long-distance station, **Bombay Central**, is headquarters of the Western Railways. In spite of its name, it has nothing to do with Central Railways – nor is it in the centre! In the surburbs, a few kilometres north of the city centre, the easiest way to get here is via a shuttle service from Churchgate Station. Trains from Central head north to Gujurat, as well as to Rajasthan and Delhi (see where the confusion creeps in?).

Churchgate Station, in the city centre is, first and foremost, a suburban commuter station, feeding over 2 million people a day into the city centre. Unless you want to get knocked over, avoid it like the plague during rush hour. More importantly, Churchgate handles all foreign travellers for Central Station and this is where you should come for information and tickets for travel on Western Railways. The Foreign Tourist Bureau and foreign reservations counter are both in the CRS building beside the station proper.

Since 1968, the small suburban station of **Dadar** has been developed to cope with the overflow from VT and Central. Both Central and Western Regions run some services from here and have suburban links to it. There are also plans to develop another suburban station, **Kurlar**, for the same purpose.

Enquiries: Central Region (Tel: 204 3535); Western Region (Tel: 493 7575/3535).

As might be expected, the city is connected to almost everywhere by frequent **bus** services. The **Long Distance Bus Station** is on the corner of Dr Anadroa Nair Road and J Boman Behram Road, next to Bombay Central Station. The State bus companies from Maharashtra, Gujarat, Karnataka and Madya Pradesh all have offices here. Computerised advance bookings are only available for the luxury services. The booking office is open from 8am–11pm (Tel: 374 272). If you want to get any sense out of them, your only real option is to go in person. Allow several hours, and also allow plenty of time before catching the bus. The place is chaotic and few signs are written in English.

GETTING AROUND

Because the central area is not large, the best possible way to see the city is to put on your most comfortable walking shoes and spend the day **walking** the streets.

With a network of 28 stations, Bombay is the only city in India to provide a sensible, usable system of local transport by **train**. The electric trains are frequent and, if anything, too fast – you have to learn to leap on and off while they are still moving or you might miss your chance and end up at the other end of the city before you get another one. They are also exceptionally crowded at rush hour and busy the rest of the time. Most have Ladies' Only and 1st Class compartments, but if you are too picky about where to get on, you'll miss the train. Churchgate Street Station is the main starting point for suburban services to the western suburbs, while those to the eastern suburbs start from VT. Ask for details at Churchgate FTB.

Unusually, Bombay also has a good network of **buses** across the city and suburbs, operated by BEST (the Bombay Electric Supply and Transport). They are very cheap, very frequent, very crowded and very slow – Bombay's traffic is extraordinarily congested. Those marked CBD operate within the Central Business District, those marked Ltd make limited stops only. The tourist office should be able to provide a list of routes.

Tiffin

Forget buying sandwiches from the café on the corner. If you want to see a food delivery service at its most impressive, hang around Bombay's main stations at about mid-day.

Indians believe in the benefits of a proper mid-day meal and, in Bombay at least, prefer home-cooked food. Enter the small army of around 2,000 *dabbahwallahs* who make their living providing just that. (A *dabbah* is a metal "tiffin" or lunch container containing a stacking set of small metal dishes.)

Once the wives have waved good bye to their husbands in the morning, they set to work to cook his lunch — a full meal of rice and several different dishes. At about 11am, the *dabbahwallah* gets on his bike and does the rounds of his patch, collecting the *dabbahs* from houses over a wide area. He takes them to the second man in the chain, who acts as a sort of wholesaler, packing them on trays, taking them to the station and sending them into town. Once they arrive, a third band sorts them all out and off they go, carried in small hand carts, on bicycles, and even yokes. By about one o'clock, some 100,000 office workers are sitting down to a fresh, home-cooked meal. At the end of it, the *dabbahs* are collected and taken home ready to be used again next day.

Those without wives to provide the meals are catered for by specialist kitchens. Almost none are wrongly delivered — an amazing feat, given that most of the *dabbahwallahs* are illiterate and have to sort the tins by a complicated series of coloured marks on the lid. And the whole service costs only a couple of *rupees*.

There are plentiful supplies of **taxis** and **auto-rickshaws** both absolutely everywhere. With a little bit of urging, they can even be persuaded to use their meters, although remember that the fare shown will then have to be converted using the official conversion chart which they carry. If they refuse point blank to turn on the meter, find someone else. Late at night, the system breaks down and unless you are within earshot of a policeman, you will almost certainly have to negotiate a fare before you set off.

Elderly but still elegant horse-drawn **Victorias** are a world apart from the tatty *tongas* you find elsewhere. The horses, for the most part, even look well fed and well groomed. Mostly designed for tourist trips rather than as serious transport, they

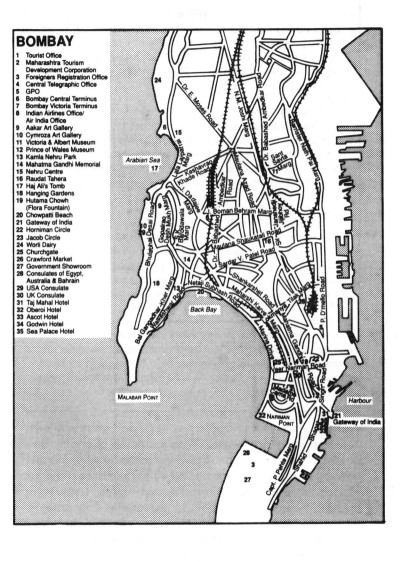

BOMBAY

1 Tourist Office
2 Maharashtra Tourism
  Development Corporation
3 Foreigners Registration Office
4 Central Telegraphic Office
5 GPO
6 Bombay Central Terminus
7 Bombay Victoria Terminus
8 Indian Airlines Office/
  Air India Office
9 Aakar Art Gallery
10 Cymroza Art Gallery
11 Victoria & Albert Museum
12 Prince of Wales Museum
13 Kamla Nehru Park
14 Mahatma Gandhi Memorial
15 Nehru Centre
16 Raudat Tahera
17 Haj Ali's Tomb
18 Hanging Gardens
19 Hutama Chowh
  (Flora Fountain)
20 Chowpatti Beach
21 Gateway of India
22 Horniman Circle
23 Jacob Circle
24 Worli Dairy
25 Churchgate
26 Crawford Market
27 Government Showroom
28 Consulates of Egypt,
  Australia & Bahrain
29 USA Consulate
30 UK Consulate
31 Taj Mahal Hotel
32 Oberoi Hotel
33 Ascot Hotel
34 Godwin Hotel
35 Sea Palace Hotel

are more expensive than auto-rickshaws, but they can be a fun way of having a quick tour of Bombay by night. There are Victoria stands at VT, Central and Chowpatty.

The Maharashtra Tourist Development Corporation runs

regular **tours** of the city, the suburbs, and longer trips to other major tourist sights in the state. Details and booking at their office in the CDO Hutments, Madame Cama Road (see **Fact File**, pp. 134–139).

There are also regular **boat** tours around the bay and to Elephanta Island, leaving every 30 minutes or so – whenever the boats are full, as well as daily trips to some of the nearby beaches. These all leave from the Gateway of India. There is a ticket booth on the quay.

GETTING YOUR BEARINGS

Some years ago, the city decided to Indianise all street names. Some have been accepted, some have stubbornly resisted change. The result is that some listings and maps use one name, some another. Where the official version and the one commonly used differ, I have put the one to use in brackets.

Although Bombay is sprawling ever further outwards, the centre is actually fairly compact and manageable. The city is built on a long, thin island, connected to the mainland by bridges over marshy ground. At its widest, the island is only about 6 kilometres wide. The heart of the city is built at its narrowest point, in the south. From the highest buildings, you can actually see the sea on both sides. For the energetic, most places are in walking distance.

The oldest part of the city is in the south-east, around the **Gateway of India**. This is the site of the original fort and harbour. Known today as Colaba (but also known as Fort Bombay), this is where you will find the cheap hotels and restaurants, the small shops and street markets. Here also is **Victoria Terminus** (known to all as Bombay VT – Bombay loves initials), the city's main railway station. The main marker points in the district are the Gateway of India, VT Station, Horniman Circle, Hutatma Chowk (more commonly known as Flora Fountain) and Mahatma Gandhi Road (known to most as MG Road). Along the coast to the north of Colaba are the main docks.

The western edge of Colaba is marked by a series of long, thin **parks**, known as Oval Maidan, Cross Maidan and Azad Maidan, which run almost exactly up the centre of the island. To the west of them is the area known collectively as **Back**

Bay. At the southern end of this huge, sweeping bay is **Nariman Point**. This is the modern business centre of Bombay, with ever-more skyscrapers adding to a mini-Manhattan style skyline. Many of the airline offices, banks and consulates are to be found here.

From Nariman Point, Netaji Subhash Road (known to all as Marine Drive) follows the line of the bay. **Veer Nariman Road** (or Churchgate Street), which leads off it a couple of kilometres north of Nariman Point, is at the centre of one of Bombay's main upmarket shopping centres. A little way inland, Churchgate Station provides another useful landmark. Meanwhile, Marine Drive continues on, past the Sports Clubs to **Chowpatti Beach**, the only long stretch of sandy beach in the city. It is well used and very lively, particularly in the early evenings, but swimming is not advised.

As the north end of the bay curves over, the Malabar Hill area, which has a large park, the Hanging Gardens at its centre, and fabulous views over the city, becomes one of Bombay's most exclusive residential suburbs. If you need convincing that there is money in India, this is where to come.

DON'T MISS . . .

Although Bombay has plenty of museums, galleries, temples, churches, etc, it **has surprisingly little unmissable, heavy-duty sight-seeing**. What it does have is a great many impressive Victorian buildings and a lot of atmosphere.

The Gateway of India

The city's most famous landmark, this massive arch stands on its own beside the sea in impressive splendour. When George V and Queen Mary visited India for the Delhi Durbar of 1911, a huge, highly decorative plaster arch was built here to greet their arrival. It seemed like a good idea and the arch was replaced, and their visit permanently commemorated, by the current monument, designed by George Wittet, the Bombay City Architect and completed in 1927. A fairly traditional European triumphal arch, it has also borrowed detail from Gujarat. The best time to see it is at dawn or dusk when the low light makes its basalt stone glow like gold.

The **Apollo Bunder**, the vast, open space which surrounds the Gateway, is great fun in its own right. It is a busy, bustling, vividly coloured concourse thronged with street sellers and entertainers as well as holidaymakers from all over India and the world. It is also Bombay's small boat harbour, jostling with brightly painted fishing boats and tourist ferries.

Elephanta Island

If you only have time to see only one thing in Bombay, this is the trip to take, although it is officially outside the city.

Boats leave every 30 minutes or so from the Gateway of India until 2pm. Buy your ticket from the booth on the quay. There are two Classes – economy and luxury boats. Both get you to the same place in roughly the same time, and the luxury boats cost about double. However, as the price is still so reasonable, and the luxury boats have a guide on board, it is worth paying the extra. Services are sometimes suspended in rough weather during the Monsoon.

The 10 kilometres journey takes about an hour and also, incidentally, provides a fascinating tour of the harbour area as the little tourist launches chug their way through the queues of tankers, freighters, and even naval vessels waiting to enter the port. It also passes through the eerie docks graveyard with its huge, rusting hulks.

On arriving at the island, you will be greeted by a positive army of would-be guides. Ignore them all, and take the official tour you will find at the top of the hill. The official guides know their subject inside and out, speak excellent English, and the tour actually costs less than the private guides demand. The caves are reached by a steep stairway up the hill. For anyone who can't manage the climb, the service economy has provided palanquins and you can be carried up! For the rest, it is a pleasant, shaded walk with plentiful drinks stalls and huge numbers of souvenir sellers to provide a good excuse for a stop. The monkeys put on a wonderful sideshow while you are waiting for the tour to begin.

The island was originally called Gharapuri or Fortress Island. During the Mauryan Dynasty, this changed to Sripuri or City of Wealth. It was given the name of Elephanta Island by the Portuguese, because of the giant stone elephant that once stood at the entrance to the temple. This collapsed in 1814, but was rescued and now stands in the Victoria Gardens in Bombay.

There are four rock cut temples on the island, thought to have been carved out between 450 and 750 AD in the classic Brahmanic style. They are some of the finest temples of their type in India. Sadly they were damaged by Portuguese soldiers stationed here in the sixteenth century, who used the temples as store rooms and for target practice.

The largest temple has a columned verandah 30 foot wide, behind which a massive hall digs deep into the mountainside. All the walls are decorated by nine sculptured panels depicting scenes from the life of Shiva. At the back of the cave is a 16 foot, three-headed figure, the *mashemurti*, representing Brahma the Creator, Vishnu the Preserver and Shiva the Destroyer. Other panels show the wedding of Shiva and Parvati; Shiva dancing the Tandava, the dance that is said to shake the world, watched by Parvati and Ganesh; and Shiva's battle against Ravana, the demon king of Lanka. There is also a separate shrine with a *shivalingam*.

The Hindi Hollywood

It might be wealthy in other ways, but Bombay derives most of its glamour from its film industry. It is the great, unsung film capital of the world – there are more films made here, around 400 a year (mainly in Hindi, but also in a dozen other languages), than ever see the light of day in Hollywood. And while the Bengalis might make the serious, high quality dramas that reach European cinema screens, this is where the blockbusters come from, where the great stars of the Indian screen are to be found.

The first feature film to be made in India, *Raja Harishchandra*, directed by Dhundiraj Palke, was shot in Bombay in 1912. The city was also home to the first sound picture, *Alam Ara* (1931), and the first colour film, *Kisan Kanya* (1937), both directed by Ardeshir Irani. Development followed on familiar lines – at first the studios had total control, with long-term contracting of players and directors, but this has slowly given way to control by the stars, who not only command huge fees, but have the final say on script, cast and director. For a long while, too, the themes mimicked those from the West, with Indian-style cowboys and Indians – nicknamed "curry Westerns" – swashbucklers, and romances.

Today, the popular blockbusters have a little bit of everything. Some are based on episodes from the great epics, such as the *Ramayana*. Others are all-singing, all-dancing romantic comedy thrillers (commonly known as "*masala*"

Prince of Wales Museum

Bombay brings a whole new meaning to the phrase monumental architecture – the Victorians and Edwardians, not noted for taking a modest approach, went haywire when building here. The marble-domed Prince of Wales Museum is another of their vast, formidable constructions. Built between 1904–14, it was pressed into service as a hospital during the First World War and only opened as a museum in 1923. Today, it is the finest museum in India, with a magnificent array of exhibits all properly housed and labelled. There are archaeology, natural history, fine and applied arts sections. Look out in particular for the smaller sculptures, paintings and bas reliefs from Elephanta Island, and for the magnificent collections of china, silver and films, after the all-spice flavouring). Good guys wear white with gold medallions, baddies are in black, dutiful wives in saris and loose women in Western dress. There is revenge and bloodshed, some extremely demure sex interest, plenty of melodrama and a good dose of slapstick. The good guys always win, usually in a final dramatic punch-up. Dance routines hop around a 1960s-style fantasy land and feel vaguely like the after-effects of an acid trip. The songs, which can make or break a film's box office, are the basis of the whole pop music industry in India.

Stars make up to 30 films a year, so they will often work on several at once. Yet remarkably few of the films (around 10%) break even and only 2% make a profit. Endless series of producers go bust, but there are always plenty of new hopefuls ready to take their place.

Most of the studios are in the eastern suburbs and can be visited (contact Tourist Office). Film City is owned by the government; others such as RK Studios, Rooptara and Mehboob are in private hands.

With a largely illiterate population, most of whom are too poor to afford a television, film is the most popular form of entertainment in India. Luridly coloured billboard posters beckon in enthusiastic audiences who cheer on the hero, boo the villain, and talk energetically most of the way through the show.

You won't understand a word of the dialogue, but it really doesn't matter — it's easy to follow the plot — and a trip to the cinema is one of the great Indian experiences.

---

crystal. There is also a scale model of a Parsee **Tower of Silence**.

In the elegant grounds of the museum stands the *Jehangir Art Museum*, Bombay's most important art gallery, opened in 1952, which houses exhibitions of modern Indian art and tourist exhibitions from around the world.

Both museums are open from 9am–6pm, Tuesdays to Sundays, and are closed on Mondays. They are free on Tuesdays and have a nominal entrance fee on other days.

Victoria and Albert Museum and Gardens
Officially these are now called the **Veermata Jijabai Bhonsle Udyan**, but no one ever uses that name. The 48-acre botanical

gardens were first laid out in 1862 and were opened to the public by Lady Frere in 1872. The gardens themselves, well stocked with species from around the globe, and by now mature, are the stars of the show in a city with little spare space for greenery.

The small museum has an interesting section on Bombay's own history, and several fine sculptures in the grounds, amongst them the elephant from Elephanta Island. Open Monday, Tuesday, Friday and Saturday, 10.30am–5pm; Sunday, 8.30am–4.45pm. Closed Wednesday.

The gardens are also home to Bombay Zoo. Open Thursday to Tuesday, 8am–6pm.

Malabar Hill

Laid out in 1880 and renovated in 1921, the **Pherozesash Mehta Gardens** at the top of the hill are commonly known as the **Hanging Gardens**. They're not actually hanging at all, but are suspended over the top of three huge reservoirs which contain Bombay's main fresh water supply. They have some rather endearing topiary animals which provide hours of fun while you try to decide what they are. Behind a huge curtain wall next to the gardens, out of sight and strictly forbidden to visitors, are the Parsee **Towers of Silence**. On the opposite side of the road is the **Kamala Nehru Park** with a popular children's playground.

The best time to visit here is in the early evening when the local people turn out for a walk and the whole place is a hive of activity. There are superb views over Back Bay from both parks and a copper map showing the main landmarks from a viewing point in the Kamala Nehru Park.

At the end of the peninsula is the **Walkeshwar temple**, an important Hindu pilgramage site. According to legend, Rama stopped here on his way to rescue Sita from the demon Ravana and built a *lingam* of sand. There has been a temple on the spot for a thousand years, but the current building was only put up in 1715. Walkeshwar is the Hindu god of sand.

Chowpatti Beach

Created from reclaimed land, the great, sweeping curve of Chowpatti Beach and Marine Drive are also amongst the

The Parsees

The Parsees were the original Pathian peoples who inhabited Persia before the arrival of the Iranian peoples. They first came to India from Persia with the Muslims in the eighth century. Legend has it that they sent representatives to the King of Surat, asking for land to settle. They returned, bearing a brimming cup of milk as a symbol that while the land was fertile, it was also full. The Parsees added a spoonful of sugar as a token of the sweetness they would add to the life of the kingdom and sent it back again. The king was convinced and they settled in Gujarat.

In 1670, attracted by the gathering wealth of Bombay, they moved south and immediately became an important part of the economic life of the city. As ship-builders, bankers and traders, they have built vast economic empires and many have become leading professionals, lawyers, doctors and academics. Jamshetji Jeejeebhoy became the first Indian to be made a baronet in the mid-nineteenth century. The Tata family founded an airline in 1932, that later became Air India.

The Parsees are a small, tightknit community, who generally live a somewhat introverted life. They speak Gujurati, rarely marry outsiders, and follow a different religion to those around them. It is for this that they are probably best known.

As Zoroastrians, they believe in one god with seven facets, all of which are worshipped separately. The duality of nature is represented by a powerful figure of evil, with whom God is constantly battling. The aim of man is the salvation of the world and he is judged by his actions at his death, when he is sent to either heaven or hell. At the end of the world a saviour born of a virgin mother will be born, the dead shall be brought back to life, and there will be a huge battle, followed by the Last Judgement.

The religion is elemental, based on the concept of the absolute cleanliness of earth and water. Parsees also follow rigid disciplines to ensure their own physical and mental purity. Fire is seen as the symbol of God and temple ritual revolves around fire-worship. When someone dies, neither the earth nor the fire can be polluted by their body, so bodies are laid in Towers of Silence, stone towers topped by iron biers. Flesh is stripped away by vultures, and the bones are purified by the sun and the wind.

most popular spots in the city for an evening stroll. The middle classes of Bombay are considerably more Westernised than in most other cities and here, unlike anywhere else in India, you will see young Indian couples strolling arm in arm along the sand. In the evenings, the air is filled by the smell of wood smoke and spice as the food sellers who line the back of the beach open up their stalls. Between them, the entertainers claim their patch, with jugglers and conjurers, snake charmers and musicians all adding to the festive feeling.

The best possible time to come here is in September, for the festival of Ganesh. This fat little god with an elephant's head is probably the most popular in India, being associated with wisdom and prosperity. Each year literally thousands of clay models of him are made, while on the beach the sand images are so huge that the sculptors need elaborate scaffolding. At the full moon, on the tenth day of the festivities, the models and sculptures are all brought down to the water shore, immersed in water, and eventually wend their way out to sea.

A little further along, on Marine Drive, there is the **Taraporewalla Aquarium**. Open Tuesday to Sunday, 11am–8pm.

Flora Fountain Area
Now officially renamed **Hutatma Chowk**, the Flora Fountain monument and the circle in which it stands are to Bombay what Piccadilly Circus and Eros are to London. It was erected in 1869 as a tribute to Sir Bartle Frere who, as Governor of Bombay from 1862–7, was responsible for many of the city's grandest landmarks.

This is a good starting point for a walk around many of the finest buildings of Bombay. Nearby, on KB Patil Marg, is the **Cathedral of St Thomas**, started in 1672 by Gerald Aungier and consecrated in 1718. Further along KB Patil Marg is the neo-High Gothic extravagance of **Bombay University**. This is totally dominated by the 79-metre high **Rajabai Clock Tower**, designed by Sir Gilbert Scott, and commissioned by nineteenth century banker Seth Prechand as a memorial to his mother, Rajabai. It cost 300,000 *rupees* to build. Beyond this is the vast bulk of the Early English **High Court** building, designed by Fuller and built between 1871–9. It is topped by statues of Justice and Mercy.

From the top of KB Patil Marg, Veer Nariman Road and MG Road are two of the busiest shopping streets in the district. Veer Nariman Road leads towards the Horniman Circle (originally called the Elphinstone Circle, but now named after a newspaper editor who championed the Nationalist cause). Just off this are the **Town Hall**, the **Mint**, and the remains of **Bombay Castle**. The Town Hall was largely funded by public lottery both as a centre of local government and as a home for the Asiatic Society Library. Designed by Colonel Thomas Cowper, it took 15 years to build and was eventually opened in 1833. It is open to the public and has statues of many of Bombay's most famous citizens, including Sir Bartle Frere, Sir Jamsetjee Jeejeebhoy and Lord Elphinstone. The facade is pure Doric in style. Next-door, the Mint, which was completed in 1829, has an Ionic façade. This too is open to the public, but arrangements must be made in advance. The Castle is now used as army barracks.

A little further north still, and you reach the 1,500-foot façade of Bombay VT.

Crawford Market
Properly called **Mahatma Jyotiba Phule Market**, this vast complex is just round the corner from VT, on Dr Dadabhai Naoroji Road. To the right, the fish market contains almost every sort of fish you have ever heard of and quite a few others. In the back is a large area devoted to the salting and drying of *bombelli* (Bombay duck). On the left, the main body of the market contains everything you could possibly think of from baskets to caged birds, fruit and flowers, fortune tellers and jewellery. Take a large bottle of perfume and a scarf if you plan to go into the meat market, as you will find that you and the local dog population will be paddling your way through huge piles of fly-blown entrails sufficient to make the most hardened carnivore into an instant vegetarian.

ALSO WORTH VISITING
Afghan Church
On Cuffe Parade, behind the World Trade Centre. Construction

of this church, dedicated to St John the Evangelist, began in 1847. It was consecrated in 1858. It is a memorial to the soldiers who died during the Sind Campaign of 1838 and the First Afghan War of 1843.

Mani Bhavan

19 Laburnum Road, near August Kranti Maidan. Mahatma Gandhi stayed in this house on his frequent visits to Bombay between 1917 and 1934. It now houses a small museum and library dedicated to his life and work. Open 9.30am–6pm daily. Token entrance fee.

Mahalahshmi Temple

On the shore, near Haji Ali's tomb, this is the most popular of Bombay's Hindu temples, dedicated to the goddess of wealth. Legend tells that three temples, dedicated to Lakshmi, Saraswati and Kali, once stood on Malabar Hill, but were destroyed by invaders. Lakshmi felt so persecuted that she leapt into the sea. Some time later the British were trying to reclaim this land, but all their efforts were frustrated by fierce tides. The goddess appeared in a dream to a Hindu contractor, Ramji Shivji, and told him to bid for the contract. She further promised that if he would rescue her and her sisters from the sea and build them a new shrine, she would remove all obstacles from his path. He built the temple and went on to complete the land reclamation project successfully.

Haji Ali Mosque

This mosque is built on a small island 500 metres out to sea and can only be reached by a narrow rock causeway at low tide. It contains the mausoleum of a Muslim saint who died while on pilgrimage to Mecca. The casket containing his body floated out and lodged on this small rocky island. The mosque was built around the spot and is an important pilgrimage place for Muslims.

At low tide, the causeway is lined by hundreds of beggars, who know that charity is a holy act of great benefit to the giver, and are only too willing to help the souls of the faithful. At the beginning of the causeway, moneychangers do a brisk trade turning *rupees* into heaps of *paise* pieces, to ensure that the visitors can be greatly blessed by giving to many, without having to give too much. At high tide, the beggars convert the coins back to *rupees*, ensuring that the paise coins can go back into circulation.

Nehru Planetarium and Science Museum

On Dr Annie Besant Rd, near the Haji Ali Mosque. There are planetarium shows in English at 3 pm and 6 pm daily, except Mondays. The science museum has a transport gallery with everything from old railway engines to a supersonic plane, as well as a gallery and audio-visual display on life science and a children's science park. Open 9.30am–6pm daily, except Mondays. Token entry fee.

Falkland Street

Fascinating for those with strong stomachs, this short street, commonly known as "the Cages", is the heart of Bombay's red light district. Heavily made up prostitutes of many nationalities, both sexes and all ages (from nine or ten upwards) display their goods behind barred doorways (hence the name), as well as actively prowling the pavements in search of custom.

Sanjay Gandhi National Park

Popular with Bombay residents for a day out, the Park is in an area called **Borivli**, about 20 miles north-east of the city centre.

The **Sanjay Gandhi National Park**, also called the *Krishan-viri Upavan National Park* and usually known simply as the Lion Safari Park(!), covers a huge area, only a small part of which is actually the safari park. This has special safari vehicles which drive visitors through the lions' enclosure. You are free to wander elsewhere and there is other wild-life in more remote areas, including antelope, moose deer, and even bears and panthers, but you are unlikely to see them. There is also a small lake, *Tulsi Lake*, where you can hire pedalos, and a toy train which runs right round the park.

Also within the park are the **Kanheri Caves**. There are a total of 109 of these rock cut temples, carved by Buddhists in the second century AD. Only a few of the caves are worth a visit; many are so crudely carved that they are little more than a hole. A few are impressive, however, in particular the first three, the unfinished Cave 1, with massive pillars, Cave 2 with a large hall and a number of sculptures, and Cave 3, the **Great Chaitya Cave**, which has a long colonnade of pillars and two massive *stupas*. There are no images of the Buddha in the complex.

The park is open from 9am–5pm daily, except Mondays. The easiest way to reach it is by train to Borivli Station. The Safari Park is within walking distance from here; the caves are some 10 kilometres away. Buses run on Sundays and holidays; at other times, you will have to take a taxi.

Reached by a special BEST bus service is **Vihar Lake**, at the southern end of the National Park, a large, attractive lake with a landscaped parkland, gardens, and picnic sites.

SHOPPING

Needless to say, Bombay is a really good place to shop. As you are likely to end your trip here, it is also convenient. Serious shopping can take a long time. Not only are most shops tiny, so you have to do a lot of investigating before you find what you are looking for, but once you find it, the bargaining starts.

For the quick version, one-stop shopping, there are three good, easy places to go. Most of the **state emporia** are in the arcade at the World Trade Centre, Cuffe Parade. You will find a wide range of high quality souvenirs at fair prices, from all over India. If you are looking for something really upmarket, both the *Oberoi* and the *Taj Mahal* have excellent shopping malls, with a large number of boutiques selling clothes, shoes, jewellery, and other souvenirs. Both also have good bookshops. Credit cards are welcomed with open arms.

For those of you who are braver, or have more time, most of central Bombay behaves like one big market. There are some 70 separate named markets that also act as nationwide wholesalers. The largest of them is **Crawford Market** near VT (see p. 129).

The **Colaba Causeway** area has a great many textiles, but its speciality is leatherwork, with shoes, belts, and handbags. There is also a fair amount of costume jewellery and a thriving trade in art and antique reproduction. Anything you find here is unlikely to be genuine. If you like it, and it doesn't matter that it was made yesterday, you can find some good buys. If you think you bought an antique, you have probably been ripped off.

The streets round **Flora Fountain** are lined with stalls selling all sorts of "dry goods" – anything from paper and biros to cameras and computers. If you need some extra cash in a hurry, it's a good place to come. I had five offers for my camera in as many minutes. Check things work, the sell-by date on film, etc, before you buy them. There's an awful lot of junk on offer. There's a brilliant second-hand bookstall just in front of the Central Telegraph Office.

Nearby, opposite Bombay Gymkhana, **Fashion Street** lives up to its name, with loads of second hand and surplus clothes, including t-shirts and jeans, at bargain basement prices.

Mohamedali Road is a predominantly Muslim bazaar, with food, but also furniture, rugs and carpets. The lanes near here include the **Mangaldas, Mohtaa** and **Mulji Jetha Markets,** which are good places to look for fabrics, from high quality silks and saris to cotton.

Two blocks away is the enchanting **Jhaveri Bazaar** or Jewellers' Market, off Mumbadevi Road, with rows of tiny shops glowing with gold and diamonds. Around the corner from this are the silver market, **Pydhoni,** and the brass market on **Kalbadevi Road.** These are wonderful places for a wander, and for getting rid of serious amounts of money on both antique and modern pieces. Obviously you need to be very wary about prices and authenticity.

Bhuleshwar caters to the Gujurati and Jain populations. As well as food stalls, it has a wide array of copper and brass utensils.

Chor Bazaar, the "thieves' market", off Maulana Shaukatali Road (Grant Road) is the Indian version of a flea market, with every conceivable type of second hand goods – anything from antique porcelain to chandeliers if you are lucky, or enormous quantities of tat if you are not.

FACT FILE

AIRLINE OFFICES

Air Canada: Oberoi Towers, Shopping Arcade, Nariman Point. Tel: 202 7512/7632.

Air France: Taj Mahal Hotel, Apollo Bunder, Tel: 202 4818 (information); 202 5021 (reservations).

Air India: Air India Building, Nariman Point. Tel: 202 3747.

Air Lanka: Mittal Towers, C-Block, Ground Floor, Nariman Point. Tel: 223 288/299.

Alitalia: Industrial Assurance Building, opp. Churchgate Station. Tel: 222 112/144 (reservations); 220 646 (office).

British Airways: Vulcan Insurance Building, 202/B Veer Nariman Road, Churchgate. Tel: 221 362 (information); 220 888 (reservations).

Cathay Pacific: Taj Mahal Hotel, Apollo Bunder. Tel: 202 3366, exts 388, 389, 390.

Indian Airlines: Air India Building, Nariman Point. Tel: 202 3131 (information); 202 3131/202 7154 (reservations).

KLM: 198 Jamshedji Tata Rd, Churchgate. Tel: 221 185/013.

Lufthansa: Express Towers, Ground Floor, Nariman Point. Tel: 202 0887/3430.

Pan Am: Taj Mahal Hotel, Apollo Bunder. Tel: 202 9048/4024.

Qantas: Hotel Oberoi Towers, Nariman Point. Tel: 202 0410/9297/9288/6373.

Sabena: Nirmal, Ground Floor, Nariman Point. Tel: 202 3817/3240/3284/2724.

Swissair: Maker Chambers VI, Ground Floor, 220 Nariman Point. Tel: 222 559/402.

The following airlines also have offices in Bombay: Air Lanka, Air Mauritius, Air Tanzania, Yemen Airlines, Aeroflot, Biman Bangladeshi Airlines, Czechoslovak Airlines, Egypt Air, Ethiopian Airlines, Garuda Indonesian Airlines, Gulf Air, Iran National Airlines, Philippine Airlines, Japan Airlines, Kenya Airways, Pakistan International Airlines, Polish Airways, Saudi Arabian Airlines, Singapore Airlines, SAS, Thai Air, Syrian Arab Airlines, TWA and Zambia Airways.

BANKS

There are obviously literally hundreds of banks in a city of this size, and almost all the larger branches will deal with routine transactions.

However, some of the larger foreign banks also have branches or representative offices here.

American Express: Oriental Building, Dadabhoy Naoroji Rd, Fountain. Tel: 259 421. (Will also handle *poste restante*).

Bank of America: Express Towers, Nariman Point. Tel: 202 3431.

Barclays Bank: 67 Maker Towers, (FPO Box 6071), Cuffe Parade. Tel: 212 797.

Chartered Bank: 25 Mahatma Gandhi Rd, Fountain. Tel: 258 451.

Chase Manhattan: New India Assurance Building, 3rd Floor, MG Rd. Tel: 274 518/516.

Midland Bank: Maker Chambers IV, 14th Floor, Nariman Point. Tel: 240 303/607.

National and Grindlays: 90 Mahatma Gandhi Rd, Fountain. Tel: 275 002.

Thomas Cooks: Cooks Building, Dadabhoy Naoroji Rd. Tel: 258 556.

COMMUNICATIONS

GPO: Nagar Chowk, nr VT Station. **Poste restante** service open from 8am–6pm, Monday-Friday. The parcel office at the back of the building is open from 10.00am–4.30pm, Monday-Friday.

Central Telegraph Office: Veer Nariman Rd, nr Flora Fountain. Open 24 hours. Public telephone service, including all international calls (mostly direct dial), plus public telex and telegram service.

CONSULATES

Australia: Maker Tower E, 16th Floor, Cuffe Parade. Tel: 216 114/211 071.

Canada: Malhotra House, opp. GPO. Tel: 261 240/265 219.

UK: Hong Kong Bank Building, M.G. Rd. Tel: 274 874.

USA: Lincoln House, 78 Bhulabhai Desai Rd. Tel: 822 3611–8.

TOURIST INFORMATION AND TOURS

Maharashtra Tourist Development Corporation: 9th Floor, Express Towers, Nariman Point. Tel: 202 4482/4584/4522. Telex: 011–3980 MTDC IN.

Tours and reservations office – CDO Hutments, opp. LIC Building, Madame Cama Rd. Tel: 202 6713/7762/7784. You can also hire tents, climbing, and other camping and adventure sports equipment from here.

Government of India Tourist Office: 123 Maharishi Karve Rd, opp. Churchgate Station. Tel: 293144. Open 8.30am–6pm, Monday-Friday; 8.30am–2pm, Saturday and holidays; closed Sundays.

Indian Tourist Development Corporation: Nirmal Building, Nariman Point. Tel: 202 6679/3343.

BEST Buses: Transport House, S. Bhagat Singh Rd, Colaba Causeway. Tel: 240 601.

ACCOMMODATION IN CENTRAL BOMBAY

This is an expensive city by Indian standards, so expect to pay a bit more for accommodation than you would elsewhere in the country. It is also very busy, so phone ahead and secure yourself a room if at all possible.

CHEAP

Railway retiring rooms: VT (Tel: 264 503); Central (Tel: 377 292). Some of the grandest in the country, but obviously extremely popular and only suitable for short stays.

YWCA International Centre: 18 Madame Cama Rd. Tel: 202 0445. Women only. Men can stay if part of a family or couple, but not on their own.

YMCA International Guest House: 18 YMCA Rd, Central Tel: 890 219. And 12 Wodehouse Rd, Colaba. Tel: 202 0079.

Salvation Army Redshield Hostel: 30 Mereweather Rd. Tel: 241 824. Dormitory accommodation plus a few double rooms for married couples (who really do have to be married).

Three others worth trying are **Whalley's Guest House:**   41 Mereweather Rd. Tel: 221 802; **Rupam Hotel:**   239 P. D'Mello Rd. Tel: 266 225; **Bentley's Hotel:**   17 Oliver Rd. Tel: 241 733.

Medium

Hotel Apollo: 22 Landsdowne Rd, Apollo Bunder, Colaba. Tel: 202 0223. Telex: 11–5959 BLKM IN.

Ascot Hotel: 38 Garden Rd, Colaba. Tel: 240 020. Telex: 11–71361.

Astoria Hotel: 4 JT Rd, Churchgate. Tel: 221 514–7.

Sea Green South Hotel: 145A Marine Drive. Tel: 221 613/662.

Sea Palace Hotel: 26 PJ Ramchandani Marg. Tel: 241 828. Telex: 11–3252 LXRY IN.

Hotel Godwin: 41 Garden Rd, Colaba. Tel: 241 226/287 2050. Telex: 11–5929 BKLM IN.

Garden Hotel: 42 Garden Rd, Colaba. Tel: 241 476/700. Telex: 11–5929 HKLM IN.

Luxury

The Oberoi Towers: Nariman Point. Tel: 202 4343 or 202 4440 (reservations). Telex: 4153/4154 OBBY IN. Fax: 204 3282. Skyscraper block on Nariman Point with wonderful views over Back Bay and every possible luxury and brilliant service. The **Oberoi** next door caters to the business trade. Have a look at the lobby, go up to the top to have a look at the view, and ask, if possible, for at least a glimpse of the Shamiana and Kohinoor suites.

The Taj Mahal: Apollo Bunder. Tel: 202 3366. Telex: 11–3837/6176/6175/2442 TAJB IN.

Flagship of the Taj Group, built in 1903 by Jamshetji Tata. This is to Bombay what Raffles used to be to Singapore. It is also meant to be the best hotel in India. It is an excellent hotel in a superb location, overlooking the Gateway to India – but with the modern skyscraper **Taj Mahal Inter-Continental** built next-door, and sharing common public rooms, to my mind it has lost much of the old atmosphere and become just another very good international-style hotel.

ACCOMMODATION NEAR THE AIRPORT

All is relative. There is almost nothing really cheap around the airport, and what classes as a medium hotel here would cost the equivalent of an expensive one in town – be warned. If you really are on a tight budget, you will probably have to forfeit convenience and stay some way from the airport.

Cheap
Airport retiring rooms: Santa Cruz domestic terminal. Ask at the Airport Manager's Office. One night only.

Medium
Hotel Airport Plaza: 70-C Nehru Road, Vile Parle. Tel: 612 3390–3/9420/8235/613 0565–8. Telex: 11–71365 PLZA IN. Right beside Santa Cruz domestic airport.
Hotel Ajanta: 8 Juhu Rd. Tel: 612 4890–1. Telex: 78302 RBEX IN. 6kms from the airport, near Juhu Beach.
Hotel Airport Kohinoor, JB Nagar, Andheri-Kurla Rd, Andheri. Tel: 634 8548/9; telex: 11–79279.
2 kms from Sahar; 4 kms from Santa Cruz.
Kumaria Presidency Hotel: Andheri-Kurla Rd, Marol Naka, Andheri-East. Tel: 604 2025/6.
1 km from Sahar terminal.

Expensive
Centaur Hotel: Santa Cruz. Tel: 612 6660. Telex: 11–71171 CHTL IN.
One of a nationwide chain of airport hotels, right beside the domestic airport. Large, efficient, in a useful location, and utterly without character.
Leela Kempinski: Sahar. Tel: 636 3636. Telex: 11–79236 KEMP IN. Fax: 636 0606.
Literally only 1 km from the international terminal, this is probably the most accessible of all the posh airport hotels.
Searock Sheraton Hotel: Land's End, Bandra. Tel: 642 5454. Telex: 11–71230/71140.
This Welcomgroup hotel is actually on the coast about 8 kms from the airport. Nevertheless it can be classed as one of the airport hotels. It is an extremely comfortable hotel in a fabulous location, right on the sea shore, with a choice of six different (good) restaurants.

Also within easy reach of the airport are the resort hotels of Juhu Beach. Amongst the best of these are: the **Ramada Inn Palm Grove**

(Tel: 614 9361/43. Telex: 11–71419 PALM IN. Fax: 9122–614 2105);
the **Hotel Sea Princess** (Tel: 612 2661. Telex: 11–78160); and the
Sun-n-Sand Hotel (Tel: 620 1811. Telex: 11–71282).

RESTAURANTS

Bombay behaves like a truly cosmopolitan city when it comes to food.
There are enormous quantities of restaurants of every price range and
cuisine. There are obviously all sorts of Indian restaurants and the
usual high number of Chinese, but there are also such exotic variation
as Polynesian. For desperate travellers yearning for Western food, it is
even easy to get top quality hamburgers, milk shakes, ice cream and
pizza. You can eat very cheaply, but it is one of the few places in India
where you truly can find food of a gourmet standard and, as food is
generally so cheap in India, why penny-pinch? It is worth making up
for all those third rate Rs10 *thalis* when you get here and splashing
out on some really wonderful food.

Cheap
Rangoli Restaurant: Performing Arts Complex, Nariman Point.
New India Coffee Shop: Kittridge Rd, Sassoon Dock.
South Indian food.
Kwality House: Kemps Corner
One of the best places in town for an ice cream, but it also has good
Indian and Chinese restaurants.
City Kitchen: Fort Market
Lunchtimes only. Good Goanese food with plenty of fish. Go early.
Leopold's Restaurant: Wodehouse Rd, Colaba
Open all day, with reasonable food and prices. Popular travellers'
hangout.
Open House: Veer Nariman Rd
Hamburgers and pizzas for the desperate.

More expensive
Gaylord: Veer Nariman Rd (Marine Drive end).
  Indian food in the evenings, with live entertainment from classical
Indian dancers and musicians. During the day, it feels like a rather
elegant tea room, with pavement tables and wonderful milkshakes.
Copper Chimney: branches on Dr Annie Besant Rd, Worli, and at 18
Rampart Row, Kalaghoda.
North Indian and Mughlai food.
Nanking: Shivaji Marg, Colaba.
Excellent Chinese food. It's been written up by a number of people,
so is getting more crowded and more expensive than before, but still
good value.
Delhi Durbar: Holland House, nr Regal Cinema, Colaba. Good
Punjabi, Mughlai and Chinese food, no liquor licence.

Hotels

Many of Bombay's best restaurants are attached to the big hotels, so it is rarely worth turning up your nose and going to find the little place round the corner, the way you might in London or New York.

The **Oberoi** and the **Taj Mahal** both have several restaurants, catering for all budgets, including 24-hour coffee shops that serve excellent snacks and simple meals that won't hurt anybody's pocket. The Oberoi also has a good pastry shop for those longing for edible bread.

If you want a real blow-out at a reasonable rate, look for the lunch-time buffets. For the equivalent of about £5, you can eat as much as you like. With a huge salad bar, a choice of half a dozen hot dishes, all the side dishes to accompany them, and three or four puddings, often of the spongy kind with pink icing, you can do some really serious eating. The best food is at the **Oberoi**, the best atmosphere is at the **Taj** (rooftop restaurant with great views and the very worst live band in India).

The **President**, and **Ambassador** hotels also serve excellent food with cabaret. **The Top**, at the Ambassador, Veer Nariman Rd, is a revolving restaurant with the best views in town.

HILL STATIONS NEAR BOMBAY

MATHERAN

This tiny village hill station 100 kilometres east of Bombay, perched on the slopes of the Western Ghats at an altitude of about 800 metres, was "discovered" by Hugh Mallet in 1850, and soon became a popular retreat from the humidity of Bombay. Its name literally means "jungle-topped hill", and even today it is popular more for its shady woodlands and relatively cool temperatures than for any particular tourist sights. Spread out along the crest of a hill, it is literally ringed by superb viewpoints as the cliffs plunge down hundreds of feet on to the plains. It is said that on a clear day you can see Bombay (or at least the fog of pollution that marks the spot).

Most of the time, Matheran is extremely quiet and peaceful, a perfect place to spend a few days recovering from the rigours of India's cities and the heat and dust of the plains. Best of all, with nothing that absolutely has to be visited, it's a good way to take a break from sightseeing without feeling guilty.

If possible, avoid the weekends and festivals, unless you want to take a look at the Bombay trendies who arrive in noisy packs, complete with loud pop music, and totally ruin the atmosphere.

GETTING THERE

From Bombay, take a train or bus to Nerala and transfer on to the **toy train**. This famous narrow guage railway was opened in 1907 and has become one of the most famous of India's trains. It takes two hours to wind its way up the 21 kilometres to Matheran. The journey is wonderful, with spectacular views, entertainment provided by the local monkeys, and sustenance courtesy of the hordes of vendors who cling to the sides of the carriages. There are four trains a day each way, some of which connect with express services to Bombay and Pune.

The schedule is cut right back during the monsoon, and in bad weather the train doesn't run at all. The only way to get there then is either by shared taxi from Nerala (an uncomfortable experience, as the Indian concept of a full taxi is very different from ours) or to walk up. There is a beautiful 11-kilometre path through the forest. It's very steep and should only be attempted by the reasonably fit.

Everyone who enters the town has to pay a small tax on arrival at either the railway or taxi stations.

GETTING YOUR BEARINGS

The town is long and thin, spread over about 12 kilometres along the top of a roughly north-south ridge. The **railway station** is in the centre of town, along with some of the cheapest hotels and restaurants. The better hotels tend to be spread, resort-style, around the edges of the town. The taxi stop is to the north of the town, about 2 kilometres from the centre. Turn left and follow **MG (Mahatma Gandhi) Road** to reach the centre. The **tourist office** opposite the railway station can provide a map.

All **motor vehicles** are banned in the town. Most people just walk, and everything is within comfortable walking distance. For those who prefer to ride, there are plenty of ponies for hire. The only public transport is by rickshaw, pulled (and pushed) by men on foot.

A **torch** is essential if you wish to go out after dark, as there are no street lamps.

DON'T MISS ...

Of the many **viewing points**, the best are considered to be those to the north and west. From **Hart Point** and **Panorama Point** you are meant to be able to see Bombay, particularly at night. **Porcupine Point**, near the centre, along a stretch known as Cathedral Rocks, is considered the best for watching the sunset.

Charlotte Lake, on the south-east edge of town, is also a popular picnic site, while the market is good for a browse. If you want to shop, cane and leather work are the local specialities. Look out also for *chikki*, a local sweet made from nuts, ultra-chewy and ultra-sweet.

FACT FILE

WHERE TO STAY
Because this is a resort area, there are a surprisingly large number of hotels for the size of the town. Many of them are very small, however, and there are no luxury hotels. Almost all the hotels expect you to eat in their own dining rooms as it is not so easy to stumble your way across town in the pitch dark, and base their prices on full or half-board options. Many of the hotels close during the monsoon, those that do remain open drop their prices by as much as 50% in the low season.

Cheap
MTDC Holiday Camp: Tel: 77/88.
Near the taxi stand, about 2 kms north of the town centre. Dormitory accommodation, double and triple rooms. Government run, so even if it's spartan, it is at least clean.

Mid-range
Hotel Tourist Towers: 187 MG Rd. Tel: 71.
Near the railway station.
Sylvan Hotel: Acharya Atre Marg. Tel: 1.
About 1 km south of the town centre, near Charlotte Lake.
Brightlands Resort: Maulana Azad Rd. Tel: 44/144.

About 1/2 km from the station. Open throughout the year, with room only and full board options. Gujurati, Mughlai, Parsee, Chinese and vegetarian menus on offer.

Royal Hotel: Nr station. Tel: 47/75.

50 rooms, a bar, coffee shop, travel agency, bank, etc. It also arranges dance and puppet displays if you are looking for some evening entertainment.

Smarter options

Lord's Central: Nr station. Tel: 28.

Near the station. It does have a beer bar and video games!

Hotel Regal: Kasturba Rd. Tel: 42/87

Near the station. 75 rooms and a menu offering Gujarati, Punjabi and Chinese food.

LONAVALA AND KHANDALA

Although technically two separate towns, these stations are only about 5 kilometres apart, and with the development of new resorts and holiday homes, have almost run together. They are set in gentler surroundings than Matheran, in rolling green hills, about 625 metres above sea level. They are about 100 kilometres from Bombay, and 60 kilometres from Pune.

The area is being developed as a centre for hiking and adventure sports, and is also a health centre with several sanitoria around. There are a number of attractive lakes and waterfalls, and a couple of forts within striking distance. The reason most tourists come here however is to visit the cave temples at nearby **Karla, Bhaja** and **Bedsa**. The towns are quite pleasant, but have little of any interest. Lonavala is the larger, and more convenient, Khandala is the prettiest.

GETTING THERE

Both Khandala and Lonavala are on the main **rail** and **road** routes from Bombay to Pune. Most express trains on the route stop here and there are also a number of slow passenger trains and frequent bus services.

GETTING AROUND

The towns themselves are tiny and everything is within easy walking distance. There are stations at Khandala, Lonavala,

Malavali (the nearest to the Karla and Bhaja Caves) and
Kamshet (the nearest to the Bedsa Caves), and it is possible
to get within striking distance of most places on the local
train services. There are also local bus services, but these
tend to be overfull and erratic. The easiest way to visit the
nearby sights is to hire a rickshaw for the day. There are
stands beside the railway stations. Wear comfortable shoes,
as, even with a rickshaw, you will have to do a fair amount
of walking. A torch is essential at night, even in the centre
of town.

DON'T MISS . . .

Karla Caves

This fine set of Buddhist temples, carved out in the first
century BC, includes some of the best – and best preserved
– examples of the period in India. They are about 11
kilometres from Lonavala, off the Pune road. The car park
is about 1½ kilometres from the main road and there is a
steep walk of about ½ kilometre from the car park up to
the caves.

The main *Chaitya* (hall of worship) belongs to the classic
phase of Himayana architecture. It's the largest cave temple
in existence, 124 ft long, 47 ft wide and 45 ft high. Inside,
it is lined by 37 columns with humans, elephants and lions
on the capitals. At the far end there's a large *stupa*. The
roof is vaulted by vast teak beams that are said to be
2,000 years old. Just inside the mouth of the cave is an
inner façade, with a finely carved "sun window" and some
sculpted panels, including figures of the Buddha, that were
added in the Mahayana Period, around the fifth or sixth
century AD. The elephant motif is continued in the porch.
Inside, inscriptions in Brahmi characters give the names of
those who donated towards the building costs. Unfortunately, a rather ugly modern temple has been built right in
front of the main *Chaitya*, blocking the best views of the
façade.

Also in front of the main *Chaitya* is a pillar topped by
four lions, a symbol commonly associated with the emperor
Ashoka. Next to this is a monastic living area, also carved
from the rock, with a narrow staircase that winds its way
up onto a series of balconied floors. A number of other

temples, some of them now used as Hindu shrines, surround
the crest of the hill, but while the path that connects them
is a pleasant walk, none of them is worth much architecturally.

Bhaja Caves
The opposite side of the main road to the Karla Caves, there
is a walk of about 3 kilometres from Bhaja Village to reach
the caves. There are 18, slightly older than the Karla Caves,
dating from around 200 BC. The best of them is Cave 12,
but Cave 1, the home of the master architect, is also of
interest. There are some fine sculptures in several of the
other caves, a group of 14 *stupas*, and several monastic
viharas. Seven of the caves have inscriptions commemorating
their donors.

Continue past the caves and there is an attractive view
over nearby Lohagen and Visapur Forts and a waterfall that
is suitable for swimming at some times of year.

ALSO WORTH VISITING
Bedsa Caves
About 12 kilometres further on towards Pune (about 23
kilometres from Lonavala), this is another hilltop group
of Buddhist cave temples. They are thought to be slightly
newer than Karla, probably built in the first or second
century AD, and are less well constructed. Nevertheless
they do have some fine sculptures. Their chief problem
is that they are difficult to get at. The nearest station is
Kamshet, but there is a 6-kilometre walk from there to reach
the caves.

Lakes
There are several attractive lakes in the area, including
Lonavala and **Bhushu Lakes**, either side of the road from
Lonavala to Shivaji Camp, about 4 kilometres out of town.
Just to the north of Lonavala, off the Rajmachi Road, is
Tungauli Lake, while halfway between Lonavala and Karla
is the **Walvan Dam**.

FACT FILE

WHERE TO STAY

Cheap
Hotel Swiss Cottage: Lonavala. Tel: 2561. Pleasant location on the edge of town.
Hotel Adarsh: Shivaji Rd, Lonavala. Tel: 2353/3741–4. In the centre of town. Large, impersonal, spartan and clean. Vegetarian only and strictly no alcohol.
MTDC Holiday Camp: Karla. Tel: 30. A mix of accommodation, from simple four-bed rooms to de luxe suites, all at reasonable prices. The only drawback is that it is completely isolated, about 8 kilometres from Lonavala.

Smarter
Hotel Duke's Retreat: About halfway between Khandala and Lonavala on the main Bombay-Pune road. Tel: 2336/2189/2187.
Resort-style with tennis court, swimming pool and golf course.

Top of the range
Fariyas Holiday Resort, Frichley Hills, Tungarli. Tel: 2701/5, 2107. Telex: 11–3272 ABAN IN. Full luxury treatment with all the trimmings, including 2 restaurants, a 24-hour coffee shop, and swimming pool.

WHERE TO EAT
On the whole, stick to the hotels for meals. There are a number of small restaurants in both towns, but most are dingy, dirty and thoroughly uninspiring. The best that can be said of them is that they are cheap. The exception that proves the rule is the popular Sagar's Snack Bar, opposite the Hotel Adarsh, Lonavala.

PUNE

With a population of over 2 million, Pune (also known by its old spelling of **Poona**) is the second largest city in Maharashtra. At a height of 580 metres above sea level, on the inland edge of the Western Ghats, it prides itself on being cooler and healthier than Bombay — something not immediately noticeable while I was there — and, with easy access to the hill stations and the coast, was always a popular posting with the civil servants of the Raj.

Nowadays though Pune is a sprawling, slightly dislocated

city, with narrow streets of old houses leading off highways shrouded in a thick layer of carbon monoxide, and attractive garden suburbs sandwiched between industrial estates.

Until the sixteenth century, Pune played little part in the sub-continent's history, but all this was to change when the great Maratha Emperor, Shivaji, was born and brought up here. The city became the heart of his empire and later the capital of the Peshwa kings. With the growth of Maharashtra's textile industry, Pune grew rapidly into an industrial centre, and although its mills no longer play such an important role in India's economy, other industries have also come here to make it a thriving industrial city.

Pune's main claim to fame, however, and with some justification, is as the intellectual capital of India. It has an extraordinarily high concentration of educational establishments – about 500 schools and 100 universities and colleges, each with up to 2,000 students. Locals announce proudly that some 90% of all the politicians in India come from the region, and most of the rest have studied here. Exaggeration, no doubt, but probably not too over-the-top. It is the centre for the study of Sanskrit and in 1961, the Film Institute was founded here, to fund art and experimental cinema.

GETTING THERE

By far the easiest way to get here is via Bombay, 170 kilometres west. There are daily **flights** from Bombay and Delhi. The flight from Bombay takes 30 minutes. There are also some flights every week from Bangalore, Hyderabad and Ahmedabad. The airport is about 15 kilometres to the north-east of the city centre.

Pune has excellent **train** connections, as it is the first major stop on the Bombay-Madras line, and the junction with the southern line to Miraj. There are several trains every day from Bombay, ranging from passenger trains which take up to 5 hours (or 9 after I had waited on Bombay station for 4 hours in the vain hope that the train might move) to express services which take 3$\frac{1}{2}$ hours. Booking is essential on these services, as some people even commute daily into Bombay from Pune and the trains are always crammed. There are through-services to Madras, Bangalore, Kanniya Kumari, Kolhapur, Nagpur, Delhi, Secunderabad, Trivandrum and Vasco da Gama. The main railway station, another Edwardian-style extravaganza, built in the 1920s, complete with black marble pillars at the entrance, is in the city centre near the Sangam Bridge. There are also several suburban stations along the main line.

By **road**, Pune is also connected to Bombay by a national highway and there are regular buses and shared taxis operating between the two. There are also MTDC bus services to Panaji, while other operators run services to Aurangabad, Bangalore, and Mangalore. In addition, there are services to most large towns within Maharashtra.

The shared **taxis** operate from outside the main railway station, but there are three bus stations. The largest of them is the **Swargate bus station** near the Nehru Stadium to the south of the city centre. The private luxury services to Mangalore and Bangalore leave from here. Many other southern destinations, including Goa, use the terminal beside the main railway station. Buses to Aurangabad, and other northern and eastern destinations use the **Shivaji Nagar bus station**. Check carefully as to which you will need, as there are few signs in English at any of them.

GETTING YOUR BEARINGS

Pune is centred on the confluence of two large rivers, the Mula, which loops down from the north-west, and the Mutha, which comes up to join it from the south-west. They join beside the Sangam Bridge (formerly the Wellesley Bridge, built in 1875) and head off due east together, as the Mula-Mutha River. The confluence marks the northern edge of the city centre, while the southern boundary is formed by the Mutha Right Bank Canal, which flows eastwards from the Mutha, about 10 kilometres south, and roughly parallel with the Mula-Mutha River. Most of the hotels and restaurants are in the streets surrounding the main **railway station** and along the **Connaught Road** (the main road just to the left of the station as you leave the concourse). The main shopping street is **Mahatma Gandhi Road** (MG Road), which continues on from the southern end of Connaught Road.

There is a **tourist office** in the Central Buildings, Manekji Menta Road, but ignore this and go to the **tourist information counter** at the main railway station. It's much better. This

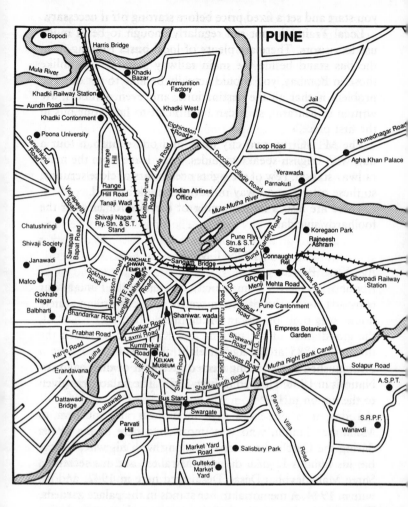

PUNE

is also where the **tours** leave from, and where you can book MTDC bus tickets. The Indian Airline offices are on Connaught Rd, next to the Hotel Amir (tel: 64189).

Everything's fairly spread out and not really within sensible walking range.

Auto-rickshaws are plentiful and easily the best way of getting around. Metres should work (with a card of current charges, don't go by the price on the meter), but check before you start and set a fixed price before starting off if necessary.

Local Trains do not run regularly enough to be of much use to visitors. There are plenty of local **buses** running from the bus stand beside the main railway station, and unlike those in Bombay, you should actually be able to get on. The problem is that all the destinations, and even numbers, are written in Marathi, so it can be difficult to find your bus in the first place.

The MTDC run two **city tours** and one **suburban tour** a day, with English-speaking guides. They leave from the main railway station. Few of the sights need hours of close scrutiny, so these offer a good way of having a look around.

There are also a large number of **bicycles** for hire for the foolhardy/suicidal.

DON'T MISS . . .

Aga Khan Palace

About 5 kilometres from the city centre, on the Pune-Nagar (Airport) road. The palace, more like an Edwardian stately home, was built by Sultan Muhammed Shah Aga Khan III, the grandfather of the present Aga Khan. He ascended the throne in 1885 at the age of eight and went on to have a distinguished career, being elected President of the League of Nations in 1938. He died in July, 1957. The palace was given to the nation in 1969.

Today, it is preserved as a monument and museum to Mahatma Gandhi, who was imprisoned here in the 1940s during the Quit India campaign along with his wife, Kastur Ba, his famous English disciple, Miraben, and his secretary, Shree Mahadevbhai Desai. Desai died here in 1942, and his wife in 1944. A memorial to her stands in the palace gardens. The museum has retained their rooms as they were during their imprisonment and also has an excellent photographic display and history of Gandhi's life.

Open from 9 am-4.45 pm daily. Small admission charge.

Shaniwar-wada

On the Shivaji road, next to the Mutha River, in the city centre. The vast enclosure of this Peshwa fortress stands in open space carved from a network of tiny bustling shopping streets. It was built between 1730–2 by Peshwa king Bajirao I, and became the centre of his empire. Over the next century, the walls were more heavily fortified, bastions and gates were added, while pavilions, court houses and fountains were created within the walls. In 1828, however, the complex was gutted by fire, and only the massive surrounding walls and gates remain today. The interior of the fort is now a pleasant, two-hectare park. There are five gates and nine bastions. Look out for the heavily studded gates designed to fend off elephants.

Raja Kelkar Museum

On the Sri Thorle Raji Roa Road about 1 kilometre from the Nehru Stadium, at the southern end of the city centre. This small, eccentric, but utterly fascinating museum is housed in an entirely appropriate, Rajasthani-style house, brightly painted in colours from purple to green. It was originally a private collection, donated to the government about ten years ago. Raja Kelkar himself only died in 1990, at the age of 95. There is an extraordinary range of exhibits, from artistic masterpieces to the frankly bizarre: carved and painted doorways of Gujarati homes to a collection of foot scrubbers from all over India; collections of icons, fans and toys to musical instruments, noodle makers and betel-nut crackers. Look out for the suit of armour made of fish scales and the nineteenth-century Keralan hairdryers that look more like barbecue forks.

Open 8am-12.30pm and 3–6pm

Tribal Museum

Just south of the railway, near the centre of town. This small museum, attached to an academic institute, shows a fascinating glimpse of a totally different side of India. Eastern Maharashtra still has a large number of tiny minority tribes who live utterly outside the mainstream of Indian culture. Some even still follow the ancient, pre-Aryan animist religions. The museum is little more than a bare introduction, but the staff are eager to talk to those who express a greater interest.

Open 10.00am-5pm daily. Free admission.

Rajneeshdham
About 2 kilometres west of the main railway station, between the railway line and the Mula-Mutha River, is the *ashram* of the **Bhagwan Rajneesh**, whose followers in the 70s and 80s were seen the world over in their orange-coloured clothes (their Westernised version of traditional saffron robes). For a long time the *ashram* was a place of intense curiosity amongst Indian tourists who came to Pune to gaze in bewilderment at the thousands of Westerners who flocked to sit at the feet of the guru, wander the *ashram* in the nude and practise group sex. Since the Bhagwan's death in 1990, the cult and the *ashram* have survived but the whole place is far more low-key. The faithful no longer wear orange and locals just shrug and endure their presence. If you wish to stay here, you will need a certificate to prove that you are not HIV positive (see also pages 154–155).

ALSO WORTH VISITING

Parvati Hill
Just south of the Mutha Right Bank Canal, the colourful **Parvati temple** is set on top of a moated hill, with good views over the city. At the foot of the hill is a temple to Ganesh and there are also temples to Vishnu and Kartikeya.

Panchaleshwar Temple
Near the centre of town is a small rock cut temple dating from the eighteenth century AD and similar in style to those at Ellora. Legend claims that it was completed in a single night.

Parks
Just north of the Mutha Right Bank Canal, on the eastern edge of the city centre, is the large, well-laid out **Empress Botanical Gardens** which also houses the small **Peshwe Udyan Zoo**, which boasts a toy train and elephant rides as well as a small variety of animals. On Bund Garden Road, beside the Mula-Mutha River, the smaller **Bund Gardens** are popular in the evenings, and offer boat rides in the river's quieter backwaters.

Gandhi

Mohandas Karamchand Gandhi was born in 1869 in Porbandar, son of the hereditary Prime Minister of this small state in Kathiawar, Gujarat. He was married as a child to his wife, Kastur Ba, and trained as a barrister in London. Returning to India, he practised as a lawyer for some time before heading off to South Africa in search of new opportunities. He had already been strongly influenced by the teachings of the large Jain community in his home district, and he now soaked up Christian and humanitarian, liberal and Marxist thought. Borrowing freely from these very different philosophies, he began to weld together his own system of beliefs. His first successful attempts at non-violent protest came in South Africa, where he became, almost by accident, leader of the growing Indian community.

He returned to India in 1915, at the age of 46, and was awarded the title of *Mahatma* or "great soul" by Rabindranath Tagore, an honour quickly accorded by the whole country. Soon involved in the political struggle for independence, he became one of the leading figures of the Nationalist movement, a position he held for the next 28 years, and for which he spent several years in prison.

His vision extended far further than political independence, however, towards a true social revolution. One of his main ambitions was to break down the traditional caste system and create a truly classless society in India. In 1921, he adopted the peasant's dress of homespun *dhoti* and shawl, partly as a symbol of India's independence from the textile mills of England, but mainly as a gesture of solidarity with the untouchable castes, whom he rechristened the *Harijan* or "Children of God". At the same time, he removed his Hindu sacred thread which the untouchables were forbidden to wear and, at his *ashram*, instituted a fair division of all labour, including the most menial jobs, something that made him unpopular for a time even with his own followers. He succeeded, however, and the *Harijan* became part of the political and social decision-making process for the first time in India's history.

His philosophy centred on belief in the power of love as a force for change. As violence was a product of hate, the product of love was *ahimsa*, or non-violence, the ability to accept suffering cheerfully and by suffering and self-discipline to reach the truth and strike a chord in those surrounding you.

Gandhi's intelligence, skill and vast personal charisma were such that while his ideals struck at the heart of Hindu orthodoxy, the industrial economy and the Raj, all levels of Indian society and even the British were united in acknowledging his greatness, however uncomfortable he made them.

Through a series of flamboyant gestures, such as his famous march to the sea to make salt and break the British monopoly, he brought India to the brink of independence. Through a series of hunger strikes, he managed for a time to hold the tortured society together as violence flared between Muslims and Hindus. In the end, however, he could not halt the deep religious and political divide that led to partition and its attendant violence.

Gandhi was assassinated in January, 1948 by a young Hindu extremist, but his influence lives on and today he is still given the stature of a prophet throughout the entire world.

OUT OF TOWN

Sinhagad Fort
25 kilometres south-west of Pune, the fort is one of the many
built by the Marathas in the seventeenth century and was the
scene of a famous battle. In 1670, Shivaji's general, Tanaji
Malusre, led his army up the steep slopes in the dark, using
lizards, according to legend, to take the ropes to the top and
secure them. Unlikely as this sounds, the army completely
surprised and crushed the Bijapur forces camped in the fort.
During the battle, however, Tanaji lost first his left hand and
then his life. Monuments still mark both spots.

Today the fort itself is little more than a ruin, standing
near a telecommunications tower nearly 1,300 metres above
sea level. The views are superb, though, and there are
a number of nineteenth-century bungalows to look at on
the way.

To get to **Sinhagad village,** take one of the regular buses that
leave from Swargate bus station. From the village, you have
to walk. The climb takes a couple of hours, and while there
is a drinks stall at the top, it's worth taking supplies for the
journey.

FACT FILE

WHERE TO STAY

Cheap
National Hotel: Station Rd. Tel: 68054.
Directly opposite the main railway station. A tatty but charming old
mansion, which has had a series of bungalow rooms built around the
courtyard garden at the back. Friendly, helpful and pleasant staff.
Hotel Woodland: Sadhu Vaswani Circle. Tel: 661 111. Telex:
0145–454 WOOD IN. Fax: 2121–660688.
Popular large hotel a few minutes' walk from the station, with a pleasant
courtyard and some air-conditioned rooms.
There are also a number of places with dormitory rooms. These include
the **railway retiring rooms** at Pune Station; the *Youth Hostel*, Fergusson
College Hostel; the **YMCA**, 6 Arjun Marg, Tel: 665 004; and the
YWCA, 5 Gurudwara Rd, Tel: 660330.

Bhagwan Rajneesh

One of the earliest, and certainly the most notorious, of India's "export", gurus, **Rajneesh** created a blend of Indian mysticism, pop psychology and free love perfectly designed to appeal to the mood of the late hippy period. His basic philosophy was of cattantic breathing, movement, self-expression and physical pleasure, and he taught that spirituality and the body are one. Thousands of Westerners flocked to his *ashram*, building it into a business with a turnover of more than £2 million a year, while even more came pouring in from sales of the guru's 336 books and 4,000 hours of taped wisdom.

Flushed by success, the guru and his inner circle packed up and moved to Oregon, USA. They wandered the area in a fleet of Rolls-Royces paid for by the faithful pilgrims, who were encouraged to part with everything they owned. Devotees, reduced to penury, stayed on as virtual slave labour to build a new, *vast ashram*. Stories of brainwashing, fraud and sexual orgies (sex, however, being part of the Guru's creed) began to leak out and gradually relations with the local people soured. When things deteriorated to the point of physical violence, with bands of the Bhagwan's followers roaming the streets and threatening anyone who dared complain about them, the authorities were forced to act. The Bhagwan was deported, four and a half years after his arrival in America. He died in Pune, in January 1990, aged 58. His cult lives on.

Mid-range

Hotel Amir: 15 Connaught Rd. Tel: 212–661 840. Telex: 145–292 AMIR IN.
A little faded, but comfortable, with good facilities and in an extremely convenient location.

Hotel Sagar Plaza: 1 Bund Garden Rd. Tel: 661 880. Telex: 145–645.
Near the river and the Bund Gardens, with a swimming pool, 24-hour coffee shop, etc.

Expensive

Blue Diamond: 11 Koregaon Rd. Tel: 663 775. Telex: 0145–369. Fax: 212–666 101.
Large, international-style hotel with swimming pool, air-conditioning, a 24-hour coffee shop and comfort. 2.5 kilometres from the main railway station, near the Mula-Mutha River.

Hotel Executive Ashok: 5 University Rd, Shivajinagar. Tel: 57391, 50463. Telex: 0145–565 HEAP IN.

Another large international business hotel with all the trimmings, but a few kilometres from the city centre, near Shivajinagar station.

WHERE TO EAT

Kwality: 6 East Street. Tel: 664 629.
Like all others in this chain, large, cheerful, relatively cheap, and with a good range of Indian food.

Savera Restaurant: Station Rd.
One of the best of a large number of small vegetarian restaurants along this road.

Coffee House: 2 Moledina Rd. Tel: 667 716.
A popular hang-out with locals and tourists alike, with vegetarian Chinese, continental, Mughlai and South Indian food.

Venky's: 2 Wellesley Rd. Tel: 27924; and opp. Ferguson College, FC Rd. Tel: 53484.
Paradise for those who are dreaming of home, with pizzas, burgers, fried chicken and milk shakes.

Hotel Amir: Connaught Rd.
A good choice of food with a coffee shop that serves hamburgers, a good Indian restaurant, and a Chinese garden barbecue.

The other large hotels, the **Blue Diamond**, the **Regency**, and the **Executive Ashok**, each have several different restaurants and cater for most pockets with a range of good Western, Indian and Chinese food.

GOA

This tiny state on India's west coast has been described as many things – "Pearl of the Orient", "Paradise" and "the hippies' Mecca", to name but a few. According to Hindu legend, the sea god Parasurama, an incarnation of Vishnu, waged a great war during which he killed 21 kings. Filled with remorse, he looked for a place in which to rest and do penance. Finding none, he shot an arrow into the air, which fell into the Arabian Sea. Where it fell, the god reclaimed the land and created Goa.

His handiwork is a patch of coast, 105 kilometres long and 60 kilometres wide, with about a dozen picture book beaches of silver sand, where fishermen lay out their nets between heavy dugout canoes and ramshackle villages hide in the dense groves of coconut palms. Inland, a network of rivers carves its way through the lower slopes of the Western Ghats to create a patchwork of rampant woodland, cashewnut groves, mangrove swamps and paddy fields. With the end of the monsoon, the greens are so vivid they almost hurt, and growth is so fast that you fear to stand still unless you too are caught in the web.

Unlike almost any other part of India, Goa has no huge cities. There are only four towns of any size – **Panaji** (the capital), **Margao**, **Mormugoa**, and **Mapusa**. With a population of about one and a quarter million, there is little of the massive overcrowding that characterises the rest of India, and there are relatively few signs of desperate poverty. The pace, even in the towns, is extremely laid-back. It's easy to see what attracted the hippies.

"The people here are not lazy," explained one man, "but their needs are simple. They have plenty of rice, plenty of fish and plenty of coconut. Why should they work hard when all their needs are met by God?"

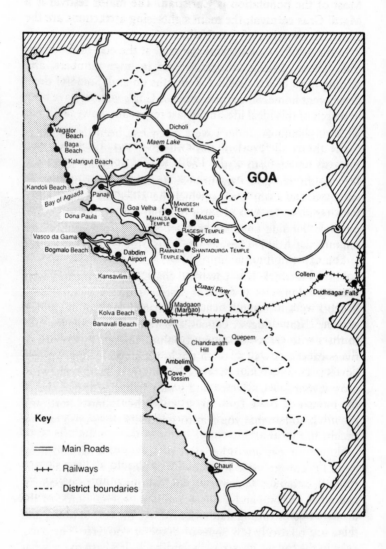

Nearly 500 years of **Portuguese** rule has left its mark. Brightly painted bungalows peer on to the roads from beneath a fringe of vegetation. You still hear Portuguese being spoken in the streets. Goanese food owes as much to Portugal as it does to India, and Goa, unusually, is a wine producing region. Most of the population is Christian. The major festival is a **Mardi Gras carnival**; the main sightseeing attractions are the **Christian churches of Goa Velha.**

In the 1960s, Goa became the goal at the end of the hippy trail. These off-beat tourists arrived in huge numbers, and settling in to beach shacks for months on end. Some of them never went home. Since then, most of Goa's visitors have been in search of this ideal life. In the last few years, however, it has all been changing.

For a start, the overland route closed down. Then the swing towards materialism of the 1980s led Europeans to regard a Five star hotel, not a beach shack, as the ideal destination. In Goa itself the airport was opened to international flights and the charter companies arrived, followed closely by the developers. Finally, the Goanese had enough and there has been an ongoing and heavy crackdown on nudity and the sale of drugs.

You can still find the hippy lifestyle in Goa, if that is what you are looking for, but most of the long-term residents are moving out of state in search of a less well-publicised paradise. When I went to Anjuna Beach at the start of the main tourist season, I found about two hippies, and two coachloads of tourists with cameras trying to photograph them. Meantime, the southern stretch of coast is being given over to the big developers. Near **Covelossim**, four upmarket resort hotels were under construction and a total of 16 are planned along the stretch of coast from here to **Bogmalo**. There are some planning constraints in an effort to keep these new giants within the local architectural framework – nothing is to be built within 200 metres of the sea; no building should be more than two storeys high; and they should all have sloping roofs. Nevertheless, development will inevitably change the character of the place. Goa is well on its way to becoming a mainstream, top of the range tourist destination for those who want a two-week package beside a tropical sea.

GETTING THERE

There are numerous **charter flights** from major European cities over the high season, often at excellent rates. Air India,

History

Goa was colonised by the Aryan peoples towards the end of the second millennium BC. From then until the thirteenth century AD, it was ruled by a series of Hindu dynasties. From the thirteenth century until 1510, the province was ruled by Muslim dynasties.

1510–37: The Portuguese arrived on 25 November, 1510, led by Alfonso de Albuquerque. With the help of the Vijayanagar family, he defeated the Adil-Shahi rulers then in power and drove them from Old Goa. Over the next 30 years, the Portuguese gradually expanded their territory to include all of current Goa, as well as taking over the other territories of Daman, Diu and Nagar Haveli.

1537–1961: The Portuguese managed to hold their own in the face of attack by both the Marathas and Mughuls. Under their rule, Goa was, initially, a stable and prosperous trading base, but the Inquisition terrorised the local people and with the subsequent loss of confidence came a slump in trade. The Portuguese remained in control, however, until 1961, when they were forcibly evicted from India by the newly-independent Congress government.

Indian Airlines and Vayadoot all fly to Goa, with regular services from Bombay, Bangalore, Cochin, Delhi, Trivandrum, Hyderabad and Pune.

The airport is at **Dabolim**, about 6 kilometres from Mormugoa and 29 kilometres from Panaji. The journey to Panaji takes about 40 minutes by car. **Taxis** are plentiful and operate a fixed rate fare on the airport run. The **Kadamba bus company** runs an airport bus from the Indian Airline offices in Panaji. Check the timetable carefully as it is inclined to be erratic. If you try to do it by local bus, it can take anything up to five hours – once you have done the trek from the airport to the main road.

There is a single, metre gauge **railway** line into Goa, which connects up with the main South Central network at Hubli. The journey from Hubli is relatively short, but takes around eight hours. It is best to do it overnight. There are through services to Bombay and Bangalore (both taking around 24 hours), but you will almost certainly have to change trains to get anywhere else.

Vasco da Gama railway station, the only large station in Goa, is 3 kilometres from the centre of Mormugoa, and 30 kilometres from Panaji. You can also get trains from Margao, but bookings have to be made either at Vasco da Gama or at the Railway Out Agency at the Panaji Bus Terminal. If you are travelling on an Indrail Pass, you have to go to the Tourist Counter at Vasco da Gama.

The main coastal highway south from Bombay follows the full length of Goa's coast before heading down towards Mangalore and Cochin. Another highway branches off the main road from Pune to Bangalore at Belgaum and crosses Goa to Panaji. Before you get too excited, however, the highways have pretensions above their station. They are, in fact, winding two-lane **roads,** severely potholed in places and always jammed by every sort of conveyance from belching juggernauts to ox carts. The 600-kilometre journey from Bombay takes about 13 hours, non-stop.

A wide selection of **long-distance buses** – luxury, deluxe, super deluxe, etc, including the dreaded video buses – connect Mapusa, Panaji and Margao with a number of nearby major cities. The **Kadamba Transportation Corporation,** the Government of Goa state-run bus service, runs regular services to Bangalore, Belgaum, Bombay, Gokarna, Hubli, Karwar, Malwan, Mangalore, Miraj, Mysore, Pune, Ratnagiri and Vengurla. Some private companies also operate on major routes, such as Goa to Bombay or Bangalore.

There is, in theory, a coastal steamer which operates between Goa and Bombay from October to May, taking about 24 hours to do the voyage. In practice, this hasn't been running for several years, although everyone is keen to assure you that it is due to be reinstated any moment. There are even rumours of a much faster service that will continue down the coast as far as Cochin. Don't get your hopes up.

GETTING AROUND IN GOA

Goa's main **rivers** – the Tiracol, Chapora, Mandovi, Zuari, Sal and Taponi – divide the state up far more efficiently than its 11 district boundaries. In particular, the Zuari divides the north from the south.

There is a reasonable network of small **roads**, many of them still dirt-surfaced, across most of the state. Only in the south-east is there a severe shortage. The main resorts here are strung out along the coast and are not linked by any regular transport service, so it can be difficult to go out for an evening unless you have private transport.

The Kadamba Transportation Corporation runs a good network of **local buses**, which will, eventually, get you to anywhere you want to go, for rockbottom prices. Destination boards are written in English and you pay on the bus. The problems are that they are almost always overcrowded, they are not terribly frequent, and they are exceedingly slow. If you have limited time, look for another option.

One of the good things about Goa is that it is perfectly possible to hire a taxi for the day without being overly extravagant. The **tourist taxis**, which are usually newer than most Indian cars, and can be extremely smart, are operated both by the Goa Tourist Development Corporation and by a few private companies. You can book them through the Corporation or through most hotels. There is a fixed fee for a day or half-day. This is based on an eight-hour day and 100 kilometres. If you exceed either, you go on to either a kilometrage or hourly charge. Even with this, my most expensive bill for a day worked out at about £15. Many of the drivers speak good English and are knowledgeable enough about the state to act as tour guides.

Yellow-top taxis and auto-rickshaws are available from ranks, or they can be flagged down within the main towns. Fares are based on a minimum plus distance charge and should be on a meter. As always, the meter is more myth than reality so check on the current rate and fix a fare before boarding. If you leave the municipal boundaries, you will be expected to pay for the return journey. They are also entitled to a small surcharge for luggage or for waiting time.

Motorcycle taxis are a Goanese speciality and can be found in all the towns and anywhere there are likely to be tourists. One passenger only (not quite as obvious in India as it sounds), and there are no such luxuries as crash helmets. Fix a price for the journey before you start.

Motorbikes and bicycles are freely available for hire in most of the towns and tourist centres. To hire a motorbike, you will need your passport and a hefty deposit, but no one seems to worry too much about a driver's licence. The machines are usually elderly Enfields or slightly less battered Rajdoots (the local Indian make). Hire costs are around Rs150 a day. Bicycles are much cheaper, and can be hired by the hour, the day or the week. They are hard work, however, with heavy frames and no luxuries like gears – and most of Goa is very hilly, as well as being hot and humid.

Main road bridges are few and far between and much of the time you will have to cross the rivers by **ferry**. Since the Mandovi Bridge collapsed shortly after it was built, even the heavy traffic of the coastal highway from Panaji to Betim or to Malim has to cross by ferry, or trek miles inland on tiny by-roads. A new bridge is being built but is taking its time. Meantime, there are round the clock ferries across

the Mandovi River. These are free for foot passengers and bicycles, and have a nominal charge for motorised vehicles.

The landing place for journeys to Mapusa is opposite the Tourist Hotel; for Aguada and points north, up the coast, it is opposite the Mandovi Hotel. Buy your ticket before you board. There are also passenger-only launches from Panaji to Malim.

There are also services from Dona Paula to Mormugao (September to May and foot passengers only); Aldona to Corjuem; Amona to Khandola; Carona to Calvim; Colvale to Macasana; Cortalim to Marcaim; Keri to Tiracol; Naroa to Divar; Old Goa to Divar/Piedade; Pomburpa to Chorao; Ribandar to Chorao; and Siolim to Chopdem. The frequency of services varies greatly from constant crossings to service on demand, or one a day. Check before you leave.

The Tourist Development Corporation runs a series of **sightseeing tours** by bus, including daily tours of North and South Goa, pilgrim tours of the churches of Old Goa and the Ponda temples, and tours of the more famous beaches on request. They also run holiday specials to the wildlife santuaries and Dudhsagar Falls. Most of the tours leave from the Tourist Hotel in Panaji, but a few leave from Margao, Vasco da Gama and Mapusa.

The Corporation also runs two one-hour launch cruises, with live entertainment, up the Mandovi River each evening. They leave at 6 and 7.15 pm from the landing place opposite the Tourist Hotel in Panaji. On full moon nights, these are joined by a third, two-hour cruise leaving at 8.30 pm, with the option of dining on board.

In the high season, they also run occasional village culture evenings with traditional dinner.

PANAJI AND NORTH GOA

A small, friendly town with unmistakably Portuguese roots, **Panaji** only officially became the state capital in 1843. It's situated on the south bank of the Mandovi River. The shift downstream from Old Goa had begun a long time before however, when in 1759 the Viceroy moved his residence from Old Goa to the sixteenth-century palace of the Adil-Shahis, in what was then called Panjim. Today, narrow streets are lined

Goa festivals

The Goans love to party and make the most of any occasion, celebrating both Hindu and *Christian* festivals to the full.

Hindu celebrations

All the temples hold *jatras*, feasts of the temple deity, with celebrations that can last up to a week and night-time chariot processions honouring the gods which draw huge crowds.

January: the *jatra of Shantadurga Prasann* in the village of Fatorpa, near Margao, and the *Bodgeshwar jatra* in Mapusa.

February: the *Hunuman jatra* in Panaji, the *Kavalem jatra* at the Shri Shanta Durga Temple, Ponda, and the *Manguesh jatra* in Mangueshi.

March: the spring festival of *Shigmotsav* or *Holi*, celebrated all over Goa. People throw packets of coloured powder, representing flowers. In Cuncolim, a Procession of Umbrellas escorts the solid silver image of Shantadurga to the site of a ruined temple, from which it was taken and hidden just before the Inquisition destroyed the temple in 1580.

May: the *Siridao jatra* in Bicholim, one of the largest, with fire walks, processions and fairs.

August: the *Ganesh Chaturthi*, the birthday of Lord Ganesh, when statues of the deity are processed to water and immersed at the end of a month-long celebration.

October: *Navratri*, a nine-day celebration at the Ponda temples.

The major Hindu festivals, including *Dessara* and *Diwali*, are all celebrated here, as in other parts of India (see page 153).

by whitewashed houses festively adorned by red-tiled roofs and wooden balconies. An occasional open doorway will give a glimpse of an overgrown courtyard beyond. The busy river front opens out into a wide tree-lined avenue perfectly designed for strolling in the evenings.

GETTING YOUR BEARINGS

Panaji's **Tourist Hotel,** opposite the ferry landing point, seems generally to be regarded as the centre of town. A few blocks to the right, the Pato Bridge leads over the Ourem Creek to a rather marshy extension of the town. Turn left from the hotel and follow the road round and you will eventually find

Christian celebrations

January: the *New Year* starts with a bang. The celebrations then continue for the next ten days. At Cansaulim, epiphany is marked by a procession dedicated to the three kings as well as a fair and a ball.

February/March: *Carnival*, a three-day riot of colour and noise borrowed from the traditional Portuguese Mardi Gras and given a peculiarly local twist. The highlight is the arrival on Fat Saturday of King Momo at the head of a magnificent costume procession. In the country, peasants go door to door, performing satirical playlets or *Khells*.

August: the *Festival of Novidades*, or harvest festival, when the first sheaves of the year's rice crop are taken to be blessed. There are bullfights at Taliego and Santa Cruz and a float procession at Divar Island.

Easter, Christmas, and a host of saints' days also give reason for celebration. Of these, the most important are the Feast of St Francis Xavier on 3 December (with a procession at the Basilica of Bom Jesus, Old Goa), and the Feast of Our Lady of the Immaculate Conception on 8 December, with a procession and fair at the church in Panaji.

The Goa Tourist Office will supply a list of all the main festivals, their dates for the coming year, and which town is the best in which to see them.

yourself beside the open sea of **Aguada Bay**, at the north end of the **Miramar Beach**. Turn inland from here, and you will find yourself at the foot of the **Altinho** (or Hill), which marks the southern boundary of the town centre. The area really is very small, and it is difficult to get lost.

DON'T MISS ...

In the case of Panaji, it is not so much don't miss, as go and see if you really can't think of anything better to do. Panaji is the centre of all administration, so if you need to deal with any business, this is where you will have to come. It is also a pleasant place to wander round for an afternoon. Apart from its general ambience however, there are few sights of any importance here. If you feel a real urge, take a look at the **Church of the Immaculate Conception** in the Municipal

Gardens near the corner of Dr Dada Vaidya Road (turn inland beside the Tourist Hotel) and Emidio Gracias Road. The **Mahalaxmi temple** is further along Dr Dada Vaidya Road. There is a good view over the town, the river and the bay from the top of the **Altinho** if you feel like taking a longer walk. **Miramar Beach,** in the suburbs about three miles from the town centre, is the nearest to the town. To get there, follow the coast road.

FACT FILE

TOURIST INFORMATION

Directorate of Tourism: Tourist Home, Patto. Tel: 5583/5715/4757. There are also tourist information counters at the Tourist Hostel, the Interstate Bus Terminus, and Dabolim Airport.
Goa Tourism Development Corporation: Trionora Apartments. Tel: 6515. Telex: 194–334 TDC IN.
Government of India Tourist Office: Communidade Building, Church Square. Tel: 3412.

TRANSPORT

Indian Airlines: Dempo Building, D Bandodkar Marg. Tel: 3826/3831 4067. Telex: 0194–219. Or Dabolim Airport. Tel: 2788. Telex: 01910–280.
Air India: Hotel Fidalgo, 18th June Rd. Tel: 4081/5172.
Vayudoot: Alcon International, Hotel Delmon, Caetano Albuquerque Rd. Tel: 5197. Telex: 0194–252 ALCO IN.
Bus station: Merces Road, Patto.

COMMUNICATIONS

Central Telegraph Office: Dr Atmaram Borkar Rd. Tel: 3742. Telegrams and public telephones.
Post Office: Jao de Castro Rd. Tel: 3706. Postage and *poste restante.*

WHERE TO STAY

There are huge numbers of tiny hotels and guest houses sprinkled across Goa. The Directorate of Tourism publishes an excellent brochure listing them all, with telephone numbers, prices, etc.

Cheap
Youth Hostel: Miramar Beach. Tel: 5433.
Dormitory-style accommodation with brilliant beachfront location.
Tourist Home: Patto. Tel: 5715.
Dormitory-style accommodation run by the tourist office, just the other side of the Ourem Creek.

Just behind the Tourist Hotel on José Falca Rd are a number of good, small hotels including the **Mandovi Pearl Guest House** (Tel: 3928) and the **Republica** (Tel: 4630), while Ourem Rd, which leads back through the old town along the creek contains several others, including the **Tourist Home** (a different one), the **Hotel Avanti**, the **Hotel Flamingo** and the **Hotel Dunhill Palace**.

Moderate

Tourist Hostel: on the river front. Tel: 7103/3396. Run by the tourist office. Clean, cheerful and good value, right at the centre of everything, but also very popular, so it's often full.

Hotel Aroma: Municipal Garden Square. Tel: 3519/4811. Good service and an excellent tandoori restaurant.

Panaji Inn: E-212, 31st January Rd. Tel: 4273. Attractive old balconied mansion with shady garden.

Keni's Hotel: 18th June Rd. Tel: 4581–3. Positive luxury with a restaurant, bar, rooftop garden and hot water.

Hotel Palácio de Goa: Dr Gama Pinto Rd. Tel: 4289. All rooms have balconies, but it is strictly vegetarian and non-alcoholic.

Hotel Nova Goa: Dr Atmaram Rd. Tel: 6231/9. Newish hotel with swimming pool.

Smarter Options

Hotel Mandovi: D.B. Bandodkar Marg. Tel: 6270–9. Telex: 0194–226 SHOME IN. Reckoned by locals to be far and away the best hotel in the centre of town.

Hotel Fidalgo: 18 June Rd. Tel: 6291–9. Telex: 0194–213 REST IN.

Real Luxury

There are no luxury hotels in Panaji itself, but these are within easy reach.

Fort Aguada Hermitage and Beach Resort: Sinquerim. Tel: 7501–9. Telex: 0194–291 TAJ IN.

Two separate complexes, a more formal hotel and an attractive resort with thatched bungalows, both run by the Taj Group, with all mod-cons. Just across the Mandovi River from Panaji.

Cidade de Goa: Vainguinim Beach, Dona Paula. Tel: 3301–7. Telex: 0194–257 DONA IN.

The Welcomgroup's luxury Goanese resort at Dona Paula, the other side of the peninsula from Panaji, 10 to 15 minutes drive away.

RESTAURANTS

Hotel Venite: Dr Cunha Gonsalves Rd. Tel: 5537. Pretty surroundings, excellent seafood and Goanese cuisine, a buzzing, friendly atmosphere and reasonable prices.

Hotel Mandovi: D.B. Bandodkar Marg. Tel: 6270–9.
A bit pricey, but the rooftop restaurant, which specialises in Goanese food, is the best in town.
O'Coquiero: a few kilometres from Panaji on the Mapusa Rd.
Again wonderful Goanese food – at a price.

OLD GOA

All that remains today of the state's former capital is a tiny village surrounded by an extraordinary number of vast Baroque churches. About 9 kilometres east of Panaji, still on the Mandovi River, Old Goa became the capital of the state in 1052, when it was moved here from Chandor by the Silahara dynasty. A thriving city and trading centre, by the time of the Bahmani dynasty it had a large moated fortress and was sufficiently important to be the second city (after Bijapur) of the Bahmani Empire. Under the Portuguese, it grew still larger and more glamorous, coming, some said, to rival Lisbon itself. Numerous religious orders rushed in to establish monasteries and convents. The Franciscans arrived first, in 1517, closely followed by the Carmelites, Augustinians, Dominicans, Jesuits and others. Using mainly Italian architects, and with a degree of professional rivalry to spur them on, they built a series of increasingly large and magnificent churches. Almost all are built from laterite blocks and lime plaster and require constant upkeep to protect them from the elements.

From the end of the sixteenth century, Portugal's naval supremacy began to fade, while the ravages of several severe epidemics, together with the activities of the Inquisition, led the city into ever deeper decline. Once the capital moved to Panaji, Old Goa lost all importance. The churches have collectively been declared a World Heritage Site and have been handed over to the Archaeological Survey of India to maintain – a job that they could do infinitely better than they are doing at present. The churches are open from 9am–6.30pm, except during services.

GETTING YOUR BEARINGS

Getting to Old Goa is fairly easy, with every bus between Panaji and Ponda passing through. The journey takes about

20 minutes. Alternatively, hire a rickshaw or taxi. During festivals, a ferry offers a pleasant alternative, taking 45 minutes from Panaji.

Once in the village, almost everything is visible and the route from one site to the next is clearly signposted. The main churches are all within easy walking distance. The outlying ones are also within walking distance, but require more energy. It takes several hours to see everything, drinks are few and far between and there is no food on sale, so take plenty of supplies with you.

DON'T MISS ...

The Convent and Church of St Francis of Assissi

This complex is a good place to start the tour of Old Goa, as the Convent now houses Goa's **Archaeological Museum**, founded in 1964. The current buildings date back to the 1660s, but this was the site of the first monastic house in Goa, created by the Franciscan monks who arrived in 1517.

The Key Gallery contains an eclectic selection of exhibits, from a suttee stone to a bronze statue of Alfonso de Albuquerque, and serves as an introduction to the museum. The Sculpture Galleries around the courtyard have a fine collection of Hindu bronzes, hero stones, suttee stones and architectural friezes. Adjoining rooms have a collection of Indo-Portuguese coins, a model ship and fortress, while the Portrait Gallery on the first floor contains the portraits of 60 different Portuguese governors of Goa.

The Museum is open from 10am–midday and 1–5pm daily, except Fridays. Entrance is free. The Archaeological Survey of India publishes an excellent small guide to Old Goa, available from the museum.

The Church of St Francis of Assissi replaced an earlier chapel in 1661, only keeping the chapel entrance. It is a rectangular building with a Tuscan exterior and Manuline main entrance. Side chapels line the nave, while interior buttress walls are decorated with a series of intricate floral frescoes. The gilded high altar includes a large crucifix and equally large statue of St Francis, together with the saints' three vows of poverty, humility and obedience. In the nave, a series of paintings on wood tell the life of the saint.

Chapel of St Catherine

Just to the left of the Church of St Francis of Assissi, this little chapel was rebuilt in 1952 on the site of a chapel built by Alfonso de Albuquerque in 1510 to commemmorate his entry to the city on St Catherine's Day. That was itself built on the site of the gates of the Muslim city. The chapel was given the status of a cathedral by Pope Paul III in 1534, and enlarged in 1550 by Governor George Cabral. It remained as the cathedral of Goa until the dedication of Sé Cathedral.

Sé Cathedral

Joined to the east end of the convent by the Bishop's Palace, this is the largest of Old Goa's churches, built by the Portuguese Government for the Dominicans with the profits made on the sale of Crown Land. It was begun in 1562 and the main body of the church was completed by 1619, although the altars were only finished in 1652. Its lopsided appearance

was caused by the collapse of the north tower in 1776. The surviving south tower houses a bell known as the "Golden

Bell" because of its rich sound. The cathedral is basically Portuguese-Gothic in style, Tuscan outside and Corinthian inside. The rectangular building is given a cruciform shape inside by the eight side chapels that line the nave. The magnificent, gilded main altar is dedicated to St Catherine of Alexandria and depicts her martyrdom.

Church of St Cajetan

Follow the road to the left, past the Cathedral and you reach the Church of St Cajetan. This large, elegant church is built, again, from plastered laterite, this time in the form of a Greek cross with a central dome. Built by Italian friars of the Order of Theatines, in the second half of the seventeenth century, it was modelled on St Peter's, Rome. The columns, inside and out, are Corinthian, while the altarpieces – great heavy monuments flanked by barley sugar columns, ornately carved, painted and gilded – are pure baroque. The main altar is dedicated to Our Lady of Divine Providence.

In the grounds of the church stands the **gate of the palace of Adil Shah**. It is all that now remains of a once magnificent building that was finally demolished in 1820. On the road to the left, leading down to the river, is the **Viceroy's Arch**. A niche at the top holds a statue of Vasco da Gama. Originally built just after the Portuguese conquest, it was altered many times and finally entirely rebuilt in 1954.

The Basilica of Bom Jesus and the Professed House

Across the road from the convent is the **Basilica**. Again built of laterite, its lime plaster was removed, leaving it as a sombre, dark red building with heavy buttresses and small windows. Built by the Jesuits, it was completed in 1605. It was upgraded to a basilica in 1946. The basic cruciform building has a three-storey facade with Ionic, Doric and Corinthian columns. Inside the structure itself is simple, but the effect is lost behind the richness of the various altar pieces.

In a chapel on the southern side of the transept is the **mausoleum of St Francis Xavier**. A gift of Cosmas III, Duke of Tuscany, the mausoleum was created by Florentine sculptor, Giovanni Batista Foggini. It took him ten years to make and was assembled in Goa in 1698. The base of the tomb is of reddish and purple jasper, decorated with carvings in white marble. The next layer is another rectangular plinth set with bronze plaques depicting the life of the saint. On this stands a silver statue of the saint and the silver and glass reliquary containing his remains. The chapel is further decorated by other paintings and wood carvings depicting the life of the saint.

The **Professed House** next door was first completed in 1585, but part of it burnt down in 1663 and was re-built in 1783.

Holy Hill

Just off the road back to Panaji are the churches of Holy Hill. First, on the left, is the **Convent and Church of St John of God**, a plain-looking building constructed in the eighteenth century. It is now run as an old people's home by Franciscan Hospitaller Sisters.

The **Convent of St Monica**, on the right, was originally plastered with lime, but is now rendered with cement. Built around a central courtyard, it was begun in 1606 and completed in 1627, burnt down in 1636 and rebuilt in 1637. It is now a Theological Centre used by some 62 orders of nuns from around the world. The church was originally divided by a screen to cut off the enclosed order of nuns. The large central cross originally stood in the nuns' section, but was moved to make it accessible after it miraculously wept twice in the nineteenth century.

A little further up the hill on the left is the **Tower of the Church of St Augustine**. This colossal, ruined bell tower is all that now remains of the church which was built by the Augustinians in 1602. With religious suppression in 1835, the church and adjoining convent were deserted, and it has been left to crumble since.

Opposite the tower is the **Royal Chapel of St Anthony**, dedicated to St Anthony, Patron Saint of Portugal. Built in the early–seventeenth century, is was closed in 1835, but reopened and renovated in 1894. It was reinaugurated after another complete renovation in 1961.

At the top of the hill is the **Church of Our Lady of the**

St Francis Xavier

Born in 1506, Francis Xavier came from an aristocratic Spanish family. A notable scholar, he studied in Paris before meeting Ignatius Loyola in 1531. In 1534 he became one of the founder members of the Jesuit order. After ordination in 1537, he was sent to Rome and then Portugal, where, in 1541, he was appointed Apostolic Nuncio for the East.

He arrived in Goa in May, 1542, and over the next ten years, preached all over southern India before turning his attention to Japan. He died in November, 1552, just off the coast of Canton, while trying to arrange for permission to preach in China. It is claimed that he was personally responsible for converting 300,000 people and performing a number of miracles. He was canonised in 1622. He has since been declared Chief Patron and Protector of the Orient, Patron of the Propagation of the Faith, Patron of all Missions, Patron of the Works of the Holy Infancy, and Patron of Navigators. He is also Patron Saint of Goa.

When his body was exhumed, two months after his death, it was said to be in perfect condition (this, however, is a common "saintly" claim). It was brought back to Goa in 1554, and in 1613 was transferred to its current home, a glass coffin in the Basilica of Bom Jesus. Since 1553, the body has been somewhat mutilated. Various bits have been cut, and even bitten, off by over-enthusiastic pilgrims, while sheer old age is finally causing it to dry and crumble. It is nevertheless still in an extraodinarily good state of repair. He is brought down from his mausoleum for five days every ten years for exhibition to the pilgrims. The next time should be in 1994.

Rosary. This was a votive chapel built in fulfilment of a vow taken by Alfonso de Albuquerque during the battle with the Bahmani Sultans. It was however only built after his death, between 1544–9.

There are also several other churches in the vicinity, including the **Church of Our Lady of the Angels**, behind the Professed House, the **Church of the Cross of Miracles** on the Pilar road, the **Chapel of St Francis Xavier** and the **Gate of St Paul's College** on the Ponda road, the **Church of Our Lady of the Mount** on a hilltop overlooking the village, accessible from the Ponda road, and the **Church of the Carmelites**, on the Kumbarjuva road, behind St Cajetan's.

THE PONDA TEMPLES

When the zealous Christian Portuguese arrived, they set to with a will to stamp out Hinduism, banning Hindu ceremonies and destroying most of the temples in Goa. When the Hindus began to rebuild, it was in isolated, wooded valleys hidden from the prying eyes of the Inquisition. Those most worth visiting are in a relatively small area, clustered round the town of **Ponda**, 20 kilometres inland from Panaji, along the Zuari River.

These are very different from the magnificent classic temples to be seen in Tamil Nadu, and if you are visiting other parts of South India, will come as a disappointment. They are however worth a quick look. They have a distinct architectural style, having borrowed freely from Christian and Muslim architecture as well as from neighbouring Maharashtra. Many of them have Christian-style domed roofs, and a Maharatha-style *stambh* or lamp tower in the courtyard. They are also generally very gaudy, with brightly painted walls covered by decorations and paintings of the various gods and goddesses. Those most worth visiting are:

Shantadurga: at Kavalem, about 2 kilometres south of Ponda, just off the Durbhar road. This domed, red-painted temple is remarkably similar in basic layout to a Christian church. Amidst the garish decorations is a beautiful silver screen and shrine, containing the images of the Goddess of Peace, Vishnu and Shiva. It is a place of pilgrimage for the Saraswat Brahmins.

Shri Ramanath: about 1 kilometre further on, near Bandara. The rectangular temple is **split in three**, with a barrel-vaulted ceiling with decorative painted plasterwork of birds and fruit in green, blue, pink and purple. The shrine is silver.

Shri Ragesh: across the valley, at Farmagudi, this is outwardly the prettiest of the Ponda temples, with yellow and white walls, onion domes and a lamp tower in the courtyard. A Nandi bull stands at the entrance. Inside, the single-storey

Music and dance

Goa has developed a distinct tradition in music and dance, borrowing equally from east and west, Hindu and Christian. Even the instruments have been blended, with Indian *ghumats* and *dhols* (drums) and cymbals alongside flutes, harmoniums, violins and guitars in the typical Goanese orchestra. Many of the most famous dances belong specifically to one festival. These days, however, there are also plenty of displays in the main hotels. Amongst the most common dances are:

Mando: sad, sweet songs and dances performed by young men and women. The dance is similar to the minuet, the accompaniment is drums and violins, and the theme, usually, unrequited love.

Fugdi and dhalo: common dances, performed by the women, at times such as the harvest or the birth of a child.

Jagar: folk drama dealing with traditional village life. A different version, the *perani*, concerns itself with metaphysical themes.

Goff, Talgadi and Shigmo: folk dances associated with the spring festival. *Goff* involves weaving multi-coloured ribbons, similar to a May Pole, and is mostly danced by the people of Canacona taluka. *Talgadi* uses sticks and hand movements. *Shigmo*, a lively colourful dance, is the highlight of the *Shigmo* festival.

Ghode-Modni: warlike dance celebrating the warriors of ancient Goa. The dancers wear elaborate costumes with horse effigies attached to their waists, and brandish swords.

Dekhni: a popular folk song and dance about a young woman. Performed by the women to drum beats, it blends Indian melody with Western rhythm.

Mussal Khell: the Pestle dance. Introduced by the Kadambas, it is kept alive by the Christian community of Chandor (Salcete). Some dancers carry pestles to symbolise the *shivalingam*, while others carry lighted torches. With the addition of a man disguised as a bear, it is performed on the second day of Carnival.

building has a brightly coloured bas relief round the painted ceiling, and images of the dancing Shiva on either side of the silver main shrine. A shrine to Ganesh stands to the right.

Shri Mahalsa: about 3 kilometres away, near Mardol, this temple is dedicated to Vishnu. Two *stambhs*, one red and white, one brass, stand in the courtyard. Closer to classic temple architecture than the others, it has impressive carved wood pillars and ceiling.

Shri Manguesh: 1 kilometre further on, at 400 years old this is the oldest of the Ponda temples. Set in a traditional courtyard with water tank and lamp tower, the main temple is heavily influenced by Christian architecture, cruciform in shape, with a domed roof and carved detail round the roof edge. The shrine contains a gold statue of Shiva, to whom it is dedicated.

NORTH GOA'S BEACHES.

Harmal
The most northerly and primitive of Goa's beaches, with virtually no amenities at all. The nearest village is **Arambol**, which is accessible by bus. You can also rent basics such as cookers and mattresses here. The only accommodation, so far, is basic palm huts. There is a small Western population, mostly those still determined to keep alive the hippy ideal of the 60s.

Vagator
One of the most attractive beaches in northern Goa, this has a long, curving stretch of sand, backed by rocks, and overhung by coconut palms. On the hill at the far end of the beach is the well-preserved Portuguese *Chapora Fort*. It's quite a hike to get up there, but the view from the battlements is great. The village of *Chapora* serves both Vagator beach and the tiny sandy coves which stretch round the peninsula to the north of the fort. It is a popular place with long-term visitors, but the beach houses are spread out and there is rarely a feeling of being crowded by other Westerners. There is a post office and several small seafood restaurants, most of which are very pleasant. The *Vagator Beach Resort* has the most upmarket accommodation in the area, with comfortable cottages as well as a restaurant and bar, although even this is fairly basic. For something cheaper, just ask around. There are buses from Mapusa every two hours, and occasional buses from Panaji.

Anjuna
Continuing south, next in line is Anjuna, the most famous of the hippy hangouts. Strictly speaking, it isn't even a beach,

Food and drink

Goa prides itself on its superb food and drink. At the bottom end of the market, however, there is little difference to that found elsewhere in India. The good news is that if you are prepared to splash out a little on the price, you can eat wonderfully well here.

Most meals are slow baked or grilled in earthenware pots and are based on a combination of rice, fish, coconut and chilli. It's surprising what a range of dishes you can get. I had a lobster *masala* that I will never forget. Look out also for *prawn balchao*, a prawn pickle eaten as an entrée, *Apa de Camarao*, a prawn pie with coconut paste in a semolina and rice crust; or *Pomfret Recheiado*, a whole pomfret stuffed with sweet and sour red *masala* and grilled. If you want meat, because Goa is mainly Christian, there's plenty of it, including pork. Try the Goanese pork sausage — *chourisso, sarpotel* — a dish made from pigs' liver, or *Chicken cafrael* — chicken seasoned with *masala* and oven baked or pot roasted. Finally, for the brave, Goa is the home of the famous *Vindaloo*!

Bread is better here than in most of India, with rolls known as *undes* and *poyos. Saanas*, special cakes made of rice fermented in *feni*, are made for festivals. Puddings include *bebinca*, a baked dish of coconut milk and egg, which can take up to eight hours to make.

Goa is one of the few areas of India where alcohol is not only freely available, but is made on the spot. There is a wide range of wines from dry white and even a sparkling white to a heavy, sweet red that is far more like port. Some of them are palatable, none will cause the French to lose any sleep. The local spirit, *feni*, is distilled from coconut or cashew. It is also possible to get a much smoother, double-distilled version, sometimes flavoured with cumin, ginger or sasparilla. Feni is potent, easily available, and a bottle costs little more than a beer.

but a seaside village on top of a small, bright red cliff, with black volcanic rocks at the bottom. If you like sand, this is not the place to come. Most people come for the company, in search of a dream, or out of sheer curiosity. Part of that dream has died with the cleanup on the drugs and nudity, and a little more has gone as the charter tourists come rubbernecking, but if you like the off-beat, you are almost certain to find it here. Accommodation can be difficult.

There are a couple of small hotels next to the bus stand, but most of the accommodation is in basic bungalows and extremely primitive shacks on the beach, and people tend to hire these for several months at a time. If you want something a little more comfortable, try the **Granpas Inn**, Gaunwadi (Tel: Mapusa 2503/2031). There are plenty of little restaurants and bars scattered around, with little to choose between them. The Chapora bus, which leaves Mapusa every two hours, stops here.

Baga and Calangute

Calangute was the first stop of the hippy trail. They had a beach party for 20 years, but even though it's over, there are plenty of them still there. Slowly but surely, things have changed, though. It's still a noisy, lively busy place, but it's all becoming a bit more orthodox and you are more likely to be offered hand crafted souvenirs than *ganja*. The beach itself is not wonderful.

Until recently, **Baga** was treated pretty much as an extension of Calangute, but the beach is much prettier and it's now becoming more popular than its more famous neighbour.

The two are so close however that they really still behave as a single entity.

There are plenty of places to stay, and remarkably few of them are real duds. Among the best of the cheap ones are the tourist office's *Calungute Tourist Resort* (Tel: 24), *Coco Banana*, the *Miranda Beach Resort*, the *Sunshine Beach Resort* and the *Hotel Riverside*. A bit further upscale are *Estrela do Mar* (Tel: 14), the *Ronil Beach Resort* (Tel: 68), *Varma's Beach Resort* (Tel: 77), and the *Hotel Baia do Sol* (Tel: 84/5), and they're priced correspondingly higher. Many of the restaurants also have rooms attached and there are a number of small beach huts for private or long-term lettings.

To find somewhere to eat, just wander down to the beach. Probably the most famous place is *Tito's*.

There are frequent buses from both Panaji and Mapusa, but many of them stop in Calangute, so if you are trying to get to Baga, check first or prepare for a walk.

Aguada

The long, lovely Sinquerim beach is totally dominated by *Fort Aguada*, which stands at one end. This formidable Portuguese fort was built in 1612 to protect Aguada Bay and access to Old Goa. The first lighthouse in India was also built here. It has been superceded by a more modern one, but the old one still stands as a historic monument. The beach is open to the public at large, but behaves more like a private one, and there are no facilities other than the expensive kind. The fort has been converted into an extremely luxurious hotel, to which an elegant resort has since been added (both run by the Taj Group): the *Aguada Hermitage* and the *Fort Aguada Beach Resort* (Tel: 7501–9. Telex: 0194–291 TAJ IN).

Bogmalo

Small pretty beach tucked in under the cliffs, a couple of kilometres from Dabolim Airport. A tiny village in the river valley contains a few souvenir shops and drinks stands, but no cheap accommodation. Effectively, this is more or less a private beach for the **Oberoi Bogmalo Beach Resort**, one of the first luxury resorts to be built in Goa. For reservations, Tel: 2191/3311–5. Telex: 0191–297.

Majorda

A vast stretch of gleaming silver-white sand, broken only by a gurgling stream. In the background behind, the palms groan under their weight of fruit, at the waterline turquoise waves uncurl gently on the sand. Clichés apart, this has to be the most beautiful of Goa's beaches. It is also about the most deserted, with no cheap accommodation and virtually no drinks stands. If you want to stay here, the only option is to splash out on the **Majorda Beach Resort**. (Tel: 20751/20203/20025. Telex: 196–234 MBR IN.)

Colva and Benaulim

This is where all the people who can't afford Majorda go. The southern equivalent of Calangute, this was once hippy territory; now it must be one of the most highly developed stretches of coast in the whole sub-continent. Colva village has become a bustling seaside town with a whole array of hotels, guest houses and cottages, as well as souvenir stands and ice-cream sellers.

The beach itself is as beautiful as ever, the wide white sand stretching for several kilometres in either direction. Those who don't like too much sun be warned – there's little shade to be found. It is also still a fishing centre, with plenty to watch. The larger, motorised trawlers anchor out to sea, but there are still a number of smaller fishermen who haul their heavy canoes up on to the beach and and lay out their nets on the sand. In the centre of town, the women wash the fish in the nearby creek and pile it on the pavements for sale. The smell can get a bit too interesting around midday.

For cheap accommodation, try the tourist office-run **Colva Tourist Cottages** (Tel: Margao 22287); **Vailankanni Cottages**; or **Summer Queen Cottage** in Colva. In Benaulim, try **Brito's Tourist Corner**; **Kenkre Tourist Cottages**; or **Palm Grove Cottages**.

For something a little further up the scale, try **Longuinhos**

Beach Resorts (Tel: 22918/9, 21038. Telex: 196–242 INTY IN); the Hotel Silver Sands (Tel: Margao 21645/51. Telex: 0196–239 SAND IN). Or, for something still smarter, the Penthouse Beach Resort (Tel: Margao 21030).

As with the more popular northern beaches, there are huge numbers of tiny beachfront restaurants, all pretty much the same standard. If you want to splash out on a really good meal, try the restaurants at the posher resorts.

Cavelossim to Canacona

Although the glorious sand continues right down through this southern stretch of Goa, for some reason until recently it has been all but ignored by the tourist trade. No more. This is the area that the Development Corporation has given to the multi-nationals and it now resembles a huge building site as they all rush to build competitively glamorous and upmarket five star resorts. Oberoi, Leela, Dalmia and a host of others are involved. The only one open as this went to press was the Ramada Renaissance Resort, Varca Village. (Tel: Margao 22178. Telex: 0916–211 RMDA IN.) Others will be following shortly.

As this stretch of coast is a little off the beaten track, there are also rumours that they might run a boat or hydrofoil service down the coast. It will probably be several decades before this turns into fact.

MORE TO SEE IN NORTH GOA

Mapusa

This is the main town in North Goa and you will have little choice about whether to go there if you are trying to get to the northern beaches or need supplies. The Friday market is worth a visit, a colourful affair where you can buy anything from chillies to antique silver. Don't bother to stay here. It's easy to get to the beach resorts and they are much more pleasant. Mapusa is connected by bus to most places in North Goa, as well as Panaji and even Bombay.

Lake Maem
Up in the mountains behind Bicholim, this largish lake is one of the most popular spots in Goa amongst the local community. It is pretty, with gardens, lakeside walks and pedalos for hire, but it felt rather as though I had gone some 5,000 miles to have a drink in an English park. If you want to stay up there, the tourist board run the cheap and cheerful *Maem Lake Resort* (Tel: Bicholim 344).

Bondla Forest Resort
The smallest, most accessible and best groomed of Goa's wildlife parks, this is not the great jungle experience, but it will at least assure you of seeing some game, as the animals are kept in large cages or enclosures. "It also offers rose gardens, fruit orchards and a jungle trail. To get there, you must find your

---

Mansions

A few of the mansions built by the Portuguese aristocracy still survive. Most of them are sprawling single or two-story buildings, set around a central courtyard. Huge windows and doors open on to a verandah with a sloping roof which runs right round the outside of the building. The houses were built from wood seasoned in salt water and plastered with mud from termites' nests, while the window panes were made from oyster shells. The woodwork was finely carved by Portuguese and Indian craftsmen to create ornate latticed patterns and highly decorated banisters and balconies. Many of them have exceptionally fine collections of antiques drawn from China and Japan as well as Europe and India.

They are all still lived in, but some can be visited if you make an appointment. Ask at your hotel, or at the tourist office. These are: **Luttolim Figeraldo's house**; **Mario Miranda's house**; **Judge Enrico D'Silva's house** in Margao; the **Menezes Braganza house** in Chandor; the **Deshprabhus' house and guest house** at Pernem; the **Gonsalves' house** at Guirim.

---

own transport, as the nearest bus station is Ponda. There are a few tourist cottages and some dormitory accommodation, bookable through the Chief Wildlife Warden, Junta House, Panaji (Tel: 4747/5926).

Mollem Wildlife Sanctuary

This is closer to the real thing for people who prefer their jungle thick and their animals wild. The downside, of course, is that Indian wildlife is pretty shy and it can take quite a time to see anything. The southern end of the sanctuary, centred on Collem, is known as the **Bhagwan Mahavir Sanctuary**. The Molem Tourist Resort at Collem (Tel: 38) is run by the tourist office and offers cheap, clean accommodation.

Dudhsagar Falls

These magnificent 200-metre waterfalls are right on Goa's border with Karnataka. Inaccessible by road, the only way to get there is by train. It is possible to take a day trip to the Falls from Collem.

MARGAO AND SOUTH GOA

The largest town in the area, **Margao** is pleasant if uninspiring, and acts as a useful shopping and transport centre for those staying at the southern beach resorts.

Like Panaji, it has some attractive streets and squares, with wooden balconies and flowering shrubs, and it also has a couple of grand Portuguese mansions which can be visited if you make arrangements in advance. The covered market is well worth a visit.

There are regular bus services to all the other main towns in Goa, and Margao is on the railway line.

GETTING YOUR BEARINGS

Margao's **railway station** is on the edge of town. Turn right as you leave the station. The Municipal Gardens mark the centre. The **tourist office** is in the Secretariat building at the bottom of the gardens, with a taxi and rickshaw stand behind it. The **post office** is at the other end of the gardens. The main **bus station** is about 11/2 kilometres from the centre of town on the Panaji road.

FACT FILE

FOOD & LODGING

Cheap
Tourist Hostel: Tel: 21966/20470. Run by the Tourist Office
Goa Woodlands Hotel: Miguel Loyola Furtado Rd (opposite the City Bus Station). Tel: 21121 Two bars, a restaurant and friendly service.
Hotel La Flor: Erasmo Carvalho St. Tel: 21591/3, 21381/2.

Medium
Hotel Metropole: Avenida Concessao. Tel: 21516/21169. Swimming pool, roof garden, bar and restaurant.

VASCO DA GAMA/MARMAGAO

These two small but busy towns have now linked up. This is the transport centre of Goa. Not only is Vasco the end of the railway line, but this is the nearest town to the airport at Dabolim, about 6 kilometres away.

Apart from convenience, Vasco has little to recommend it. The one thing of interest, although not a classic tourist attraction, is Marmagao's docks. **Marmagao Bay**, at the mouth of the Zuari River, claims to be one of the finest natural anchorages in the world – as well as one of the oldest harbours. It is certainly busy, with occasional tourist liners threading their way between oil tankers and coal carriers and even Indian Navy ships. It's a fascinating reminder that India is not just there for foreign visitors.

Don't bother to stay there unless you have to. If you do, try the *Maharaja Hotel*, Rua Leopoldo Flores, (Tel: 2559/2269/2748); the *Hotel Zuari*, Dattatria Deshpande Read (Tel: 2127–9); or, for something a little more upmarket, the *Hotel La Paz Gardens*, Swatantra Path (Tel: 2121). If you want luxury, try the *Oberoi Bogmalo Beach* which is about 15 minutes' drive away (see Goa's Beaches, below)

KARNATAKA

About 600 kilometres from end to end, and stretching halfway across the sub-continent, Karnataka covers a vast area, about 192,000 square kilometres in all. The current population is around 47 million, but is growing fast. The main local language is Kannada.

Like Maharashtra to the north, the bulk of Karnataka is on the high, rocky central plateau of the sub-continent, cut off from the sea by the Western Ghats, which continue their march south, clad in forests of rosewood and teak, patterned by vast, lush coffee plantations.

The humid and overgrown coastline of the Kanara province connects the two more famous coastal stretches of Goa and Kerala. Yet this area too, with **Mangalore** as its main port, has been a great trading centre, hosting ships from Greece and Rome, the Arabs, Portuguese and British. Fields of cardamom, pepper and turmeric nestle beside the rice paddies, earning Kanara a place on the so-called "Spice Coast" of South India.

The history of the state is immensely complex, and at almost every stage its local rulers were great builders. The main tourist areas of the state are in the north, around **Bijapur** and **Hampi,** and in the south, around **Bangalore, Mysore** and **Hassan.** This is not because the centre is a cultural desert, but because in a state with a positive embarassment of riches, sights that might be considered important elsewhere fade into relative insignificance against Karnataka's most spectacular offerings.

When Chandragupta Maurya converted to Jainism in the third century BC, he came to live in **Sravanabelagola,** which is still the centre for southern Jainism. The Chalukya kings

of Badami not only built magnificent temples themselves in
the sixth century AD, but created a model on which much of
South India's temple architecture was founded. The Hoysala

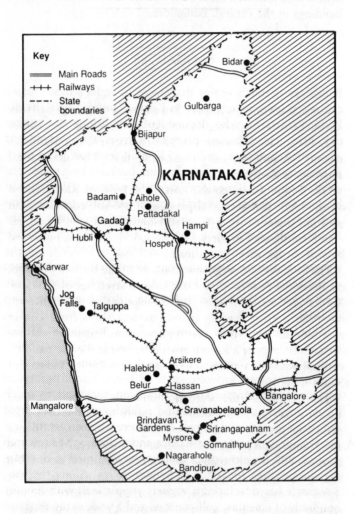

kings of the eleventh to fourteenth centuries created their
own masterpieces at Belur and Halebid, near Hassan, while
the Vijayanagar kings created the great buildings of Hampi
from the fourteenth to sixteenth centuries. Meanwhile, the

defeat of the Hoysalas in 1327 brought the Muslim builders of the Bijapur Sultanate to the area. Haider Ali and Tipu Sultan added their mark in the eighteenth century, while the British who followed them built a series of monumental public buildings in the capital, Bangalore.

BANGALORE

Bangalore is much newer than most of India's other major centres. It owes its existence to Kempa Gowda, a Yelahanka Prabhu chieftain, who dreamed of establishing the perfect city here. He obtained permission from the Vijayanagar emperor Achutaraya, and in 1537 built four towers to mark its boundaries. These remain, in ruins, but have long since been swallowed up by Bangalore's steady expansion. His city soon became a thriving commercial centre, specialising in the grain and cloth trades. It was annexed later that century by the Bijapur Sultanate who in turn lost it to the Mughals. They sold it to the Maharaja of Mysore for Rs500,000. In the eighteenth century it became one of the main fortress cities of the Muslim empire of Hyder Ali and Tipu Sultan, before their defeat by the British. It became a British garrison town in 1809.

Today the capital of Karnataka has a population of well over 4 million. On a plateau 1,000 metres above sea level, with a pleasant climate, and good communications, it is one of the fastest growing cities in India. For a provincial city, it is surprisingly cosmopolitan, priding itself as much on its academic institutions and publishing as on its rapid industrial growth and its role as a centre of government. It is fast becoming a centre for science and technology as research projects and the electronics industry have homed in to create the closest thing India has to Silicon Valley. Along the way, Bangalore has developed a vaguely yuppie feel, with literally hundreds of cinemas, golf courses, and a wide array of shops and restaurants, while horse racing is a positive passion.

It is a popular place with Indians for honeymoons. For tourists, it is a pleasant place for catching up and doing business, but there is little surviving from its chequered past

---

Benda-Kalu-Ooru

Once upon a time, or so the story goes, King Veera Ballala lost his way while out hunting. An old woman, living alone in a small hut in the forest, gave him shelter and a meal of baked beans (*benda kalu* in the local language, Kannada). The king was so grateful, he named the area *Benda Kalu Ooru* or "the place of baked beans". In time, this was became shortened to Bangalore, and so the city got its name.

---

and it has few major "sights". Now, it is mainly renowned as a garden city, with a surprising number of parks and gardens (102), landscaped circles (47), and broad avenues lined with jacaranda, laburnum, gulmohar and bougainvillaea. The greening process was begun by Hyder Ali, but is chiefly the responsibility of Krishnaraja Wodeyar IV. During the Silver Jubilee of his reign, in 1927, he urged the people of the city to improve its appearance. As a result, the avenues, parks and boulevards were laid out under the direction of Sir M. Visvesaraya and Sir Mirza Ismail, transforming the city centre into one of the most attractive in the country. It still is, although the massive, over-rapid expansion of the city is placing severe stress on their design, and already its pristine image is beginning to fray at the edges.

GETTING THERE

Air connections are excellent, with daily flights (and several a day on the main routes) from Bombay, Calcutta, Cochin, Coimbatore, Delhi, Hyderabad, Goa, Trivandrum and Madras, four flights a week from Pune, and three flights a week from Ahmadabad and Mysore. Most are with Indian Airlines, although Vayudoot fly to Hyderabad and Mysore.

The airport is about 7 kilometres south-east of the edge of the city. There is a fixed fee system for **taxis and buses** into town. On the way out to the airport you will need to negotiate a fee with your taxi or rickshaw as the meter is not valid outside the city limits.

The good news is that Bangalore is the meeting point of four main **rail** lines, so there are regular services to every part of India. The bad news is that three of these lines are metre guage, so that journeys can be somewhat leisurely. The broad guage line runs from Bangalore to Madras. Along the route, it connects with the broad guage line south to Coimbatore and the west coast railway, and in Madras it meets the east coast railway to Calcutta. The direct line north to Hyderabad, the north-western line to Miraj, and the south-western line to Mysore are all metre guage, and long journeys are not only very long but will rarely be direct, as you have to switch networks at some point along the way. There are daily services to most southern and central cities, many of them overnighters. With the exception of Mysore (minimum travelling time 3 hours) and Madras (minimum travelling time 7 hours), it seems to take over 18 hours to get anywhere. The fastest Bombay trains take 24 hours, while the fastest train to Delhi takes 42 hours. If you need to head north from Bangalore, and can't afford such leisurely progress, fly.

Both broad and metre guage lines run from **Bangalore City Railway Station**, on the western edge of the city centre. There is no tourist information bureau in the station, but there is a tourist booking counter in the modern computerised booking centre just outside the main station. On my last visit, the counter (the first to the left as you enter) showed no signs of being marked for tourists, but was instead clearly labelled for "the Disabled and Freedom Fighters Only". Ignore this, as other counters won't handle foreign bookings, as several of us discovered after queuing for well over an hour. The reservations centre is open from 7am–1pm, and 1.30–7pm, from Monday to Saturday, and on Sunday mornings. The city's other station, Bangalore Cantonment Station, is of little use to travellers, chiefly acting as being a halt for trains from the main station, and a freight yard.

For inquiries and reservations, Tel: 1st Class – 74172; 2nd Class – 76351. For inquiries about arrival and departure times, Tel: 258 465.

Bangalore's central position also means that it has good **road** connections, with National Highways to Madras, Madurai, Mysore, Mangalore, Bombay and Hyderabad. These in turn connect with every other major centre in India.

The majority of **buses** are operated by the **Karnataka Road Transport Corporation** (the KRTC), but a number are also run by the **Andra Pradesh State Road Transport Corporation** (the APSRTC), the **Thiruvalluvar Transport Corporation** (the state bus company for Tamil Nadu), and a number of private operators. Buses to Mysore run approximately every 15 minutes, and there are also very frequent services to Madras, Hassan, Mangalore and Madurai. Several services run each day to Bombay, Bijapur and Hyderabad and there are daily services to Hospet, Ooty, Goa and almost everywhere else in southern and central India.

The vast Central Bus Station, which is alarmingly well-organised for this part of the world, is directly opposite the City Railway Station. All long distance buses leave from here. For tel information on KRTC services, Tel: 74386.

GETTING AROUND

There is a good network of local **buses** across the city, which will take you almost anywhere you want to go. Many of them operate out of the main **Bangalore Bus Station**, beside the railway station, but others run from **City Market**, at the southern end of Avenue Road and **Shivajinagar Bus Station**, near Cantonment Railway Station, in the north-east corner of the city.

As ever, there are plentiful quantities of **auto-rickshaws** and a fair few **taxis**. Officially, they work on the meter, with a conversion card for up to date prices. In practice, it is extremely difficult to persuade them to do so, unless there happens to be a policeman nearby, when the drivers behave like angels in their hearing and promptly try to up the price as soon as they are out of sight.

The KSTDC runs two half-day and one full-day **sightseeing tours** of the city each day, all of which tend to dash round the sights to allow plenty of time for the shopping stop at the end. They also run very long one-day tours to (relatively) nearby places of interest, such as Mysore, Belur and Halebid, and three-day tours to those even further afield. You can book any of them at any State Tourist Office. The tours leave from Badami House, Narasimharaja Square.

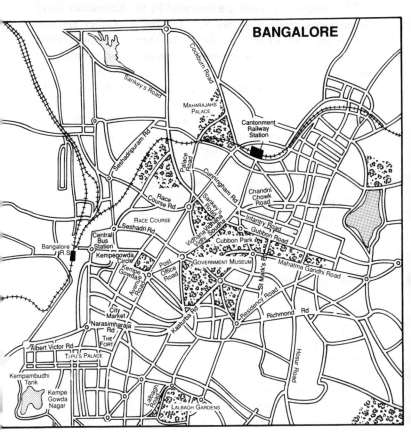

MAP TO GO HERE

GETTING YOUR BEARINGS

The geographic centre of Bangalore is the huge **Cubbon Park**.
The museums and state legislature buildings are in, or just
near, the park. About 5 kilometres due east from this, past the
race course, are the **City Railway and Bus Stations**. The area
between the park and the stations, centred on **Kempegowda
Circle**, is a busy shopping centre, with a large number of
cheap hotels, cinemas and restaurants. This is probably the
most convenient area to stay in.

Due west of the park is **Mahatma Gandi (MG) Road**. This is the business heart of the city, with useful offices, such as the airlines and tourist offices, as well as a number of better hotels, the government emporia, and several good restaurants and cafés.

To the south of the park is the old part of the city, with its winding streets and tiny shops and market stalls. Here also are the **fort**, **Tipu Sultan's palace**, and the **Lal Bagh Gardens**.

The city centre extends over a large area and distances between tourist sights are too far to walk.

DON'T MISS . . .

Cubbon Park

First laid out in 1864, on what was then the edge of town, this 300-acre park is now the heart of Bangalore in more ways than just its geographical location. It is a pleasant, shady place for a stroll or a picnic, with flowering trees, well laid lawns, bandstand, and the "Fairy Fountain", which is illuminated at night. There is a children's playground, the **Jawahar Bal Bhavan**, with a small boating lake, a toy train and fairground, and a children's educational centre which organises activities such as painting and craft sessions, film shows and theatre performances.

The **Government Aquarium** is also in the park, with some 75 species of fresh and saltwater fish. Open 10.00am–5pm, Friday to Wednesday. Closed Thursdays. Admission charge. There is a fish stall nearby for those who prefer their fish on a plate!

Many of Bangalore's finest buildings, including the Public Library, the *Attara Kacheri* or "Eighteen Courts" – the High Court, and Bangalore's two main museums are also either in, or just on the edge of the park.

Vidhana Soudha

This vast granite structure, built in 1954, in the neo-Dravidian style, must be one of the most imposing buildings in India – for its sheer size alone. Situated on the north edge of Cubbon Park, it houses the State Legislature and Secretariat. The Cabinet Room has a massive, famous sandalwood door. The public are allowed into the entrance hall only, after office hours, to

view the dome (Tel: 79401). It is floodlit from 7pm onwards
on Sundays and public holidays.

Government Museum

On the Kasturba Road side of Cubbon Park, established in
1886, this is one of India's oldest museums. It has 18 depart-
ments, with collections that include archaeology, sculpture,
painting, coins, ethnology and natural history. It also has
a collection of South Indian *virakals* or hero stones, and
finds from the Harappan site of Mohonjodaro, in the Sind,
dating back 5,000 years. Open 9.30am–4.30pm, Thursday
to Tuesday. Closed Wednesday. Token admission charge.

The Fort

Opposite City Market, on Krishnarajenda Road, about 4
kilometres south-west of Cubbon Park. This was the first
mud-built fort put up by Kempe Gowda in 1537, although
it was almost totally rebuilt in stone by Haider Ali and Tipu
Sultan in the eighteenth century. A number of British soldiers
were imprisoned here during the British campaign against
Tipu Sultan, at which time the fort was also severely damaged.
Open 6am–6pm daily (in theory).

Tipu's Palace

On Albert Victor Road, about 1 kilometre from City Market, 5 kilometres from Cubbon Park. This sadly neglected
monument was begun by Hyder Ali and finished by Tipu
Sultan in 1791. Used as the Summer Palace, it was known
at the time as *Rashk-e-Jannat* or "the Envy of Heaven".
Mainly constructed from wood, it is highly decorative, with
five elaborately carved arches topped by minarets, while the
walls and ceilings are painted with floral designs and trellises
in red, blue, yellow and gold. It is very similar in style to the
more famous Daria Daulat Palace in Srirngapatnam. Open
6am–6pm daily.

Lal Bagh

The prettiest of Bangalore's many parks, these 240-acre
botanical gardens were first laid out by Haider Ali in 1760.
Tipu Sultan continued to develop them, adding many rare

and exotic species obtained from Europe, the Middle East, and even Mauritius. Today the gardens house more than 1,000 species of flowers, shrubs and trees from around the world. A vast Glass House, modelled on the Crystal Palace in London, was built in about 1890. There is also a quartz flower clock, 7 metres in diameter. The Lal Bagh is home to the Mysore Horticultural Society, who run a sales room and organise twice yearly horticultural shows here, in February and August. Open 8am–8pm daily.

Basavanagudi (Bull) Temple

In the south-west corner of the city, on Bull Temple Road, near the corner with Bugle Rock Road, about 15 kilometres from Cubbon Park. This temple, built by Kempe Gowda, in the Dravidian style, is one of the oldest in Bangalore. It is chiefly famous for its vast Nandi bull, 15 foot high and 20 foot long, carved from a single stone. Legend has it that the temple was built to appease a bull that had been running rampant and eating all the groundnuts in the local fields. There is a Groundnut Festival here every November or December, at which the farmers offer the first groundnuts of their crops to the bull. It is believed that on the day of the festival you can eat unlimited quantities of groundnuts and *jaggery* without getting indigestion!

ALSO WORTH VISITING

K. Venkatappa Art Gallery

Just beside the Government Museum in Cubbon Park, this small art gallery has a permanent exhibition of court paintings from the turn of the century, but also houses temporary exhibitions by modern Indian artists. Open 9am–5pm, Thursday to Tuesday. Closed Wednesday.

Visveswaraya Industrial and Technological Museum

Also near the Government Museum, on Kasturba Road, this is a hands-on science museum with sections on the use of science and technology in industry, and on human welfare. Plenty to keep children happy, but not an essential stop for those wanting to see India. Open 10am–4.30pm. Tuesday to

Sunday. Closed Monday and public holidays. Small admission charge.

Karnataka Folk Museum
In Kumara Park West, between Sankey's Road and Seshadripuram Road, about 4 kilometres from Cubbon Park. This small museum run by the Karnataka Janapada Trust has an interesting collection of masks, costumes and artefacts relating to the folk history and tradition of Karnataka, as well as a collection of tapes of folk music and video tapes of folk dance. Open 10.30am–5pm daily.

Gavi Gangadareshwara Cave Temple
In the south-west corner of the city, near the Kempambhudi Tank. This cave temple, built by Kempe Gowda in the mid-sixteenth century, has four monolithic pillars with Shaivite emblems, and a statue of Agni, God of Fire. The best time to visit is a bit precise – on 14 January between 5 and 6 pm. This is the **Festival of Makara Sankranti** and the temple was built so that, as the sun sets on this one day of the year, its rays pass through a stone arch, a window, and the horns of Nandi to strike the *shivalingam.*

Kempegowda Towers
There are still two of the original marker towers laid out by Kempegowda which can be visited, although only from the outside. One is in the south-west corner of the city, near **Kempabhudi Tank**; the other is in the far north of the city, in the Rajamahal Vilas Extension, near **Sankey's Tank**.

OUT OF TOWN
Sai Baba Ashram
Sixteen kilometres from Bangalore, next to Whitefield Railway Station, is one of the largest and most famous of the *ashrams* in South India, attracting devotees from all corners of the subcontinent, as well as from abroad. When the Baba is in town, he holds *darshan* at 9am. For further information, contact the Information Centre, Brindavan, Kadugodi 560 067. Tel: Whitefield 842 233.

Ramohalli

This is the site of a 400-year-old **banyan tree** that has spread over the years until it covers an area of four acres. It is said that Sage Muneshwar did penance under the tree. Today, however, it is an attractive picnic site, with a restaurant for those who prefer someone else to provide the food, (28 kilometres from Bangalore, just off the Mysore Road).

Nandi Hills

The main hill station for Bangalore, surrounding the fortified hill village of Nandidurg, 60 kilometres from Bangalore, off the Bellary Road. There are good views in all directions but look out particularly for **Tipu's Drop**, a sheer 600-foot granite cliff. In the centre of the settlement is a large tank known as the *Amritha Sarovara* or "Lake of Nectar". Tipu Sultan kept yet another palace here, while Gandhi, Nehru, Queen Elizabeth II and a number of other dignitaries from around the world have also stayed here.

You can stay at the KSTDC-run **Hotel Mayura Pine-Top** (Tel: 1; advance reservations, Bangalore 578 901), or at the **Department of Horticulture Cottages** (Tel: 21; advance reservations, Bangalore 602 231).

FACT FILE

AIRLINE OFFICES

Air Canada: 131–2 Residency Rd. Tel: 215 416.
Air France: 68 St Mark's Rd. Tel: 214 060.
Air India: Unity Buildings, Jayachamaraja Rd. Tel: 224 143.
British Airways: c/o TT Travels, 33/1 Imperial Court, Cunningham Rd. Tel: 269 632.
Cathay Pacific: West End Hotel, Race Course Rd. Tel: 269 745.
Indian Airlines: Cauvery Bhavan, Kempegowda (KG) Rd. Tel: 211 211.
Lufthansa: 44/2 Dickenson Rd. Tel: 564 791.
Pan Am: 24/1 Race Course Rd.
Singapore Airlines: 51 Richmond Rd. Tel: 213 833.
Swiss Air: 51 Richmond Rd. Tel: 211 983.

BANKS

State Bank of India: St Mark's Rd. Tel: 53602.
Andhra Bank: Narasimharaja Rd. Tel: 28664.
Bank of Maharashtra: 16 SJP Rd. Tel: 72073.
Reserve Bank of India: 10/3/8 Nrupathunga Rd. Tel: 76810.
Indian Bank: MG Rd. Tel: 53309.
In addition, the Canara Bank, Allahabad Bank, Dena Bank, and Syndicate Bank all have branches on Kempe Gowda Rd.

COMMUNICATIONS

General Post Office: corner of Dr Ambedkar Veedhi Rd and Cubbon Rd. Tel: 266 772.
Poste restante office open from 10am–7pm, Monday to Saturday, and 10.30am–1.30pm, Sunday.
Central Telegraph Office: Cubbon Rd (next to the GPO). Tel: 264 762.
Open 24 hours a day.
Thomas Cook: 55 MG Rd. Tel: 571 066.

SHOPPING

Government Silk Emporium: Gupta Market, Kempe Gowda Rd.
Kaveri Art and Crafts Emporium: 23 MG Rd. Tel: 571 418.
Central Cottage Industries Emporium: MG Rd.

TOURIST OFFICES

Government of India Tourist Office: KFC Building, 48 Church St. Tel: 579 517.
Karnataka Department of Tourism: 9 St Mark's Rd. Tel: 597 139. This is the main state tourist office. Open 9am–7pm daily.
Karnataka State Tourist Development Corporation: 10/4 Kasturba Rd. Tel: 578 901.
Reservations office for KSTDC tours: Badami House, Narasimharaja Square. Tel: 221 299.
You can also book tours at any of the other tourist information counters.
There are also state **tourist information counters** in the Shrunagar Shopping Centre, MG Rd (Tel: 572 377); at City Railway Station (Tel: 70068); and at the airport (Tel: 571 467).

VISA RENEWALS

Commissioner of Police: Infantry Rd.

WHERE TO STAY
Cheap
Railway retiring rooms: Bangalore City Station.
Both dormitory accommodation and some rather upmarket double rooms.
YMCA: 57 Millers Rd. Tel: 575 885.
Families only.
Also, for men only, at Infantry Rd, and Nirupathanga Rd.
YWCA: 86 Infantry Rd (Tel: 570 997), families only; and 32 Mission Rd (Tel: 228 574).
Youth Hostel: 25 Gangadhara Chetty Rd. Tel: 611 292/569 943. Opposite the Ajanta-Lakshmi Theatres.
Hotel New Victoria: 47–8 Residency Rd. Tel: 570 336/7, 571 715. Telex: 0845–2298 Attn. N3. Fax: 91–81–213 281 Attn. N3.
Brindavan Hotel: 108 Mahatma Gandhi Rd. Tel: 573 271.

Medium
Woodlands Hotel: 5 Sampgani Tank Rd. Tel: 225 111. Telex: 0845–2399 WDLD IN.
Hotel Cauvery Continental: 11/37 Cunningham Rd. Tel: 29358–9. Telex: 0845–8112 HCC IN.
Hotel Bangalore International: 2a–2b Crescent Rd, High Grounds. Tel: 258 011–7. Telex: 0845–2340 HOBI IN.

Expensive
ITDC Hotel Ashok: Kumara Krupa, High Grounds. Tel: 79411. Telex: 0845–2433.
Good, but a little tired in comparison to the others in the same price range.
Windsor Manor Sheraton: 25 Sankey Rd. Tel: 79431/28031. Telex: 0845–8209 WIND IN. Fax: 0812–74941.
Run by the Welcomgroup. Built in the 1980s, but trying to pretend it's a century older.
Taj Residency: 14 Mahatma Gandhi Rd. Tel: 0812–568 888; Telex: 0845–8367 TBLR IN. Fax: 0812–563 548.
Well up to the usual standard of others in the Taj group.
West End Hotel: Race Course Rd. Tel: 0812–29281. Telex: 845–2337 WEND IN. Fax: 0812–27610.
This might only attract three stars, but is the oldest of Bangalore's good hotels, a genuine Raj hotel, with a fine garden, spacious rooms and a general air of unhurried elegance. Now run by the Taj Group.

WHERE TO EAT

Cheap to medium

Kwality: Brigade Rd. Tel: 572 331.
Part of the huge chain, with Indian and Chinese food, kebabs and an ice cream parlour.

The Indian Coffee House: MG Rd.
Also part of the nationwide chain, with cheap *thalis* and snacks. Indian food only.

Indiana's Fast Food: 9 St Patrick's Complex, Residency Rd. Tel: 566 176.
One of the best places in town to pig out on hamburgers and shakes.

Mac's Fast Food: Church St.
Another good place for fast food, including fish and chips.

RR Plantain Leaf Brigades: 55/1 Church St. Tel: 563 060.
Specialises in food from Andra Pradesh, served on a banana leaf plate.

Expensive

Blue Heaven: 36 Church St. Tel: 561 796.
Popular Chinese restaurant. Booking recommended.

Copper Bowl: 28 MG Rd. Tel: 565 397.
Tandoori, Chinese and Cantonese food, plus a licensed bar and dance floor.

Prince's, 9 Brigade Rd: Curzon Complex, 1st Flr. Tel: 578 787.
Good Indian, Chinese and Continental food, plus the Knock-Out Disco – the only disco in town.

There are also several good restaurants at the **Windsor Manor** and **West End** Hotels.

NORTHERN KARNATAKA

BIJAPUR

Wandering around the dusty roads of this small, sleepy city in northern Karnataka, it is hard to believe that it was once the capital of a great, if short-lived, Muslim empire. Only the litter of buildings, with more than 50 mosques, 20 mausoleums, and a sprinkling of palaces gives a clue to its illustrious past.

The city was first founded by the Chalukyan emperors of the tenth and eleventh century, who named it "*Vijayapura*" or the "City of Victory". This later became corrupted into Bijapur. At the end of the thirteenth century, Islam arrived when it was captured by the Delhi Sultanate. In 1347, it was taken over by the Bahamani sultans of Bidar, and in 1489 it became the capital of the Adil Shahi dynasty. In 1686, its territories were annexed by the Mughul emperor Aurangzeb, and on the collapse of the Mughul dynasty, the town was ruled briefly by the Marathas before being taken over by the British. Unusually for the south, it is still strongly Muslim.

For the visitor, although it has a population of around 250,000, Bijapur still has something of the atmosphere of a ghost town, its monuments out of proportion to its size and all in dire need of some tender loving care.

GETTING THERE

Getting to Bijapur is a lengthy process. The nearest airport is Belgaum, over 200 kilometres away, without a rail connection. Probably the most convenient air connection is via Pune, over 300 kilometres away.

Bijapur is on a metre guage **rail** line that runs between Solapur (on the main Bombay-Madras line) and Hubli (on the line from Goa to Bangalore). The only services on the line are extremely slow passenger services, stopping at every village halt, and an overnight sleeper, also very slow. The journey from Pune takes about 12 hours; the journey to Goa takes 24.

There are better **road** connections, as the town is on the national highway between Solapur and Bangalore, as well as being connected to most other nearby towns. The KSRTC runs **buses** to Badami, Bagalkot, Bangalore, Belgaum, Hubli and Solapur, and there are also services to Bidar, Hyderabad, Hospet, Pune, and Kolhapur.

GETTING AROUND

There is a local **bus** service that runs every quarter of an hour along Station Road from one side of town to the other, costs little and is rarely crowded.

There are a number of **auto-rickshaws**, but **no taxis**. Most people however travel by **tonga** or **cycle-rickshaw**. These are plentiful and the best way to see the sights is to hire one for a day or half-day.

There are no tours as such, but there are **government guides** available from the tourist information office. You will have to pay their fee, as well as for transport, but it doesn't come to much, and is well worthwhile. Numerous others will try and hire out as private guides, but as few of them speak English and even less know anything about their subject, don't bother.

GETTING YOUR BEARINGS

Finding your way around Bijapur is, for once, pretty easy, as it is not only small but its 14-kilometre long city wall is still mainly intact. The **railway station** is just outside the east gate of the city. From here, Station Road leads straight into the centre of town, clustered around the old citadel, and out to the west gate on the far side. Most of the hotels are in the centre, or along the west portion of Station Road, while the **bus station** is in the centre of town and hard to miss.

The **tourist information office** is in the Hotel Sanman, on Station Road, opposite the Gol-gumbaz (Tel: 58610). They can provide a useful sketch map of the town, complete with drawings of temples and steam trains.

DON'T MISS . . .

Gol-gumbaz

This vast mausoleum, just inside the east gate, is chiefly famous for its enormous size. Built in the 1650s, on the orders of Mohammed Adil Shah, the seventh of the Adil Shahi kings, it is 51 metres high, with a floor area of 1,700 square metres and walls 3 metres thick. The walls are plastered with a mixture of eggs, *jaggery*, cow-dung and grass. The dome, with a diameter of 37 metres, is the second largest in the world (St Peter's in Rome is the largest). *Gol-gumbaz* literally means "round dome".

Seven-storey towers at each corner lead to a rooftop terrace with superb views over the town and surrounding countryside. Inside, the dome is ringed by a Whispering Gallery with enough room to hold 1,000 people. The acoustics are superb, with up to 14 echoes – if you can ever quieten the din made by visiting school parties for long enough to hear them.

There are six tombs in the basement of the mausoleum. Those on display on the ground floor are copies of the originals. They belong to Mohammed Adil Shah himself, who died in 1656, his two wives, his daughter Bibi, and

---

The Adil Shahi Dynasty

Yusuf Adil Khan was a son of Sultan Muhammed II of Turkey, who fled from the country during a massive struggle for the succession that resulted in the massacre of much of the royal family. Bought as a slave by the Prime Minister of Bidar, Mahmud Gavan, he was presented to the Bahamani emperor, Muhammed II. In 1481 he was sent to Bijapur as governor of the province. Shortly afterwards, the Bahamani empire began to collapse, and in 1489 he declared independence, establishing the separate state of Bijapur. The rest of the empire split into four other separate states of Bidar, Golconda, Ahmednagar, and Bidar.

There were nine kings altogether in the Adil Shahi dynasty, the last only ten years old when the territory was invaded and conquered by the great Mughul emperor, Aurangzeb in 1686.

---

her son. The last belongs to Mohammed's favourite mistress, a Hindu dancing girl called Rambha.

The small building in front of the Gol-gumbaz is called the **Naga Kham**, which was the name given to the nine different types of drums and bugles played to honour a member of the royal family when they visited the mausoleum. This is now a government-run museum with exhibits on the history of Bijapur. There are also a small mosque, water tank and elaborate gateway within the complex.

Open from 6am–6pm daily. There is a small entrance fee to the mausoleum, except on Fridays, when it is free. It is floodlit from 6.30–7.30pm on Saturday and Sunday. The museum, which is always free, is open from 10am–5pm daily.

Ibrahim Rauza

The second of Bijapur's two main mausoleums, just outside the west gate of the town, this is a much smaller affair than the Gol-gumbaz, but is also infinitely more elegant, and is said to have been the inspiration behind the Taj Mahal.

Built between 1610 and 1626, on the orders of Taj Sultana, wife of the sixth king, Ibrahim Adil Shah II, and designed by architect, Malik Sandal, it houses six graves – those of Ibrahim Adil Shah II, his wife Taj Sultana, their only daughter Jeruhar Sultan, their two sons, Daraman and Suleiman, and Ibrahim's mother.

Delicate minarets rise 24 metres into the air, and as, unusually, local Hindu craftsmen were used in the construction, the pillars are sculpted with Hindu iconography, including lotus flowers, elephants, *kalasa* (used in Hindu marriage ceremonies) and *turan* (green mango leaves traditionally hung over the front door of a house, to bring good fortune). A mosque and water tank also stand within the well-kept gardens.

Jami-e-Masjid

This mosque, the largest and grandest in Bijapur, just across the road from the *Gol-gumbaz*, was begun by Ali Adil Shah I, and built between 1557 and 1686. It is the earliest of the dynasty's many monuments and is also the biggest mosque in South India, covering an area of 10,810 square metres. Basically a simple building, it has nine huge, elegant arches that lead towards five inner arches, creating 45 compartments. The domed roof is decorated to represent an opening bud. The courtyard also contains a fountain and tank. The inner area is painted with readings from the *Qu'ran* picked out in gold leaf. Aurangzeb extended the mosque to the east, added the north and south verandahs and built the eastern gate, as well as having the floor painted with individual spaces for 2,250 worshippers. It was never completely finished, and is still missing two minarets.

Malik-e-Maidan

Just next to the west gate stands the last of the city's 96 D-shaped bastions to remain in good condition. It is a good place to get a view over the town and the town walls. These were erected by Ali Adil Shah I in the late-sixteenth century, are 15 metres high, and are surrounded by a moat for their full 14-kilometre length. There were originally seven fortified gateways.

On top of the bastion stands the enormous **Malik-e-Maidan cannon**, still one of the largest bell metal guns in the world. The name means "Monarch of the Plains". It was cast in Amanagar in 1580 by Mohammed Hasan bin Rumi, a Turkestani officer, and given as war tribute to the Shaha kings. It took 10 elephants, 400 oxen, horses, and hundreds of soldiers to manoeuvre it into position, and it has not been moved since, although the British tried hard.

The cannon was cast in one piece from a five metal alloy of gold, silver, iron, tin and copper, and is now polished a deep green. It weighs 55 tons, is 4.45 metres long and 1.5 metres in diameter, and has a range of 15 kilometres. The muzzle is the head of a lion, crushing an elephant between its open jaws, and there are a number of inscriptions in Arabic and Persian.

It has only ever been used once, during the Talikoti Wars of the fifteenth to sixteenth centuries. The explosion was so loud that the pit behind the gun would be filled with water and the gunner would light the fuse, then submerge himself to deaden the sound as it went off.

Over the years, a number of legends have grown up around the gun. It is said that the metal remains cool, no matter how hot the sun, and that it gives off a clear bell-like tone when tapped. It is also said that if you touch it and make a wish, it will be granted.

ALSO WORTH VISITING

The Citadel

Once a fine fortress with a moat, fortified walls and a number of palaces and pavilions, little now remains of the **citadel** but a few stretches of broken wall and one or two of the pavilions. The vast *Gagan Mahal*, left open on the north side so that the public could watch the proceedings, was built in 1561 by Ali Adil Shah I as a Durbar hall, while the upper floor was a royal residence. The mainly ruinous *Sat Manzil* was a seven-storey residence built by Mohammed Adil Shah, while the *Jala Manzil* was a pavilion designed for relaxing near water on hot, sunny days.

Asar Mahal

Built in 1646 by Mohammed Ali Shah as a Hall of Justice, this two-storey building just to the east of the citadel is believed to house two hairs from the beard of the Prophet Mohammed. Inside, it is covered by a riot of frescoes with patterns of fruit, flowers and defaced human figures. Women are not allowed inside.

Upli Buruj

This 24-metre tall watchtower, near the western wall of the city, was built in 1584 at the same time as the city walls by the Bijapuri general, Hyder Khan. It can be climbed by a winding outside staircase, and offers an excellent view of the surrounding country. On the roof are two guns called the *Lambachari* or "long ones". They are 9 and 8$^{1}/_{2}$ metres in length, although as they are only 30 centimetres in diameter, they cannot come near to matching the massive *Malik-e-Maidan*.

Mehtar Mahal

Commonly known as "The Balcony", this tall, thin house, just behind the citadel, was built by Ali Adil Shah I in the sixteenth century as a place in which he could sit and watch his city. It is open to the public, but is best seen from the outside as its crowning glory is the intricately carved balcony, made entirely from stone. It now acts as the gateway to a small mosque.

Taj Bauri

This huge tank near the west gate was built in 1620 as the swimming pool of Taj Sultana, wife of the sixth king, Ibrahim Adil Shah II. An elegant arch, flanked by two octagonal towers, leads to the steps down to the water. This is more than 100 feet deep, and, as there is no outlet for it, is a rich, soupy green. Nowadays, it is used as the local laundry.

Bara Kaman

If it had been finished, this mausoleum, begun by the eighth king, Ali Adil Shah II, might have been the greatest of them all, a fairy tale confection of soaring arches perched high above the earth. Built on a 25 foot-high platform, flanked by a massive stairway, it was designed to have 12 storeys, each 25 foot high, with 12 arches, reaching a height of 325ft. If finished it would have cast a shadow at mid-day over the *Gol-gumbaz*. Only the first floor came anywhere near completion however, and only one arch was finished.

FACT FILE

FOOD AND LODGING

There are no luxury, or even particularly upmarket, hotels, although there are several that are cheap, cheerful and quite comfortable. There are a few small cafés in the centre of town, but if you want to be sure, eat at the hotels. You are not going to find gourmet food anywhere.

Hotel Mayura Adil Shahi: Anand Mahal Rd. Tel: 934.
Run by the KSTDC, this is the most pleasant of the hotels in the town, set around an attractive courtyard garden.

Hotel Mayura Adil Shahi Annexe: Station Rd. Tel: 401.
Also run by the KSTDC, originally as an overflow, this is now larger than the original hotel and more modern. However, it is also more expensive and less attractive, so while it is a good second choice, try the other one first.

Hotel Sanman: Station Rd. Tel: 21866.
The newest hotel in town, and good value.

There are also ultra-cheap, dormitory-style **retiring rooms** at the railway station.

BADAMI, AIHOLE AND PATTADAKAL

These three small villages, tucked out of the way in northern Karnataka, have an extraordinary history, and magnificent artistic heritage. Together, from the sixth to the ninth centuries AD, they formed the heartland of the Chalukya kings, one of the earliest of the great Hindu dynasties of South India. They left behind them a legacy of literally hundreds of temples, from simple caves to elaborately carved masterpieces, dedicated to Hinduism, Jainism and Buddhism, while the design of some is thought to have been the earliest inspiration for the great southern temples such as Madurai.

All three villages are strung along a rocky, sandstone stretch of the Malaprabha River valley. Each of the towns was first built as a capital city. **Aihole** was the earliest, founded in 450 AD by the first of the Chalukyan kings. Its original name was "Arya-Hole", or "City of the Aryans".

Next came **Badami**, 46 kilometres away. Known originally as "Vatapi" (after a demon swallowed by a particularly inventive local sage), this was founded by King Pulakesin I in about 550 AD. It was occupied between 640 and 653 AD by the Pallava king Nerasimhavarma.

Pattadakal, 29 kilometres from Badami, and 17 kilometres from Aihole, was the last of the three to be founded by Chalukyan king Vikramaditya II, in the early-eighth century, after his victory over the Pallavans. The dynasty finally collapsed in 753 AD, when they were conquered by the Rashtrakutas.

Today, of the three, Badami is the only town of any size, with a population of around 16,000. (Aihole has 3,000 and Pattadakal even fewer.) It is also the only place with any real facilities, so unless you plan to stay in Bagalkot, nearly 70 kilometres away, aim for here.

GETTING THERE

Forget about getting there quickly. The nearest airport, Belgaum, is nearly 200 kilometres away, and still leaves you with a long journey by road.

Badami is on the Solapur-Hubli metre guage railway line which connects with the main lines from Bombay to Madras and Goa to Bangalore. The only trains that stop here however are the ultra-slow, 2nd class only, passenger trains. The best way to get here by train is from Bijapur, the nearest town of any size (4 hours), or from Hospet/Hampi (one train a day, taking 6 hours).

By road, the journey is almost as slow. The KSRTC runs bus services to Bangalore, Bagalkot, Belgaum, Bijapur, Gadag, Hospet, and Hubli, as well as to other small towns and villages in the local area.

GETTING AROUND

A KSRTC "city" bus service runs from Badami railway station (5 kilometres out) into the centre of town. Otherwise, the only local transport in Badami consists of a very few private taxis or a tonga.

There are regular local buses, run by the KSRTC, between the three villages, and these, though slow, offer the best option for travelling between them. If you are happy to stick with the edited highlights, it is possible to do all three villages in one day, as long as you are prepared to start fairly early in the morning.

There is no public transport in either Aihole or Pattadakal, but once you have got there, both villages are easily small enough to walk around.

There are no organised tours, but the tourist information offices at the Hotel Mayura Chalukya in Badami and the Tourist Home, Aihole will be able to provide information and/or a trained guide.

BADAMI

Of the three villages, Badami, a little way from the main river, is not only the largest, but the most famous for its natural beauty, with red-gold sandstone cliffs overlooking the attractive Agastyatirtha tank, built in the fifth century. Like the others, it is littered with hundreds of temples, monuments and inscriptions, from all ages and cultures, including the

Chalukya, Yavada, Pallava, Vijayanagar, Adil Shahi and
Maratha dynasties.

DON'T MISS . . .

Cave Temples
There are five cave temples set into the side of the gorge,
of which one is natural. The other four were all carved out
during the reign of the Chalukyan king Mangalesa (598–610
AD). As they are partway up the cliff, a visit involves climbing
some 200 steps.

Cave I: dedicated to Shiva. There is a particularly fine sculpture of Nataraja, the Dancing Shiva, with 18 arms, suggesting
81 different dance positions. Other figures include a number
of *ganas*, the dwarves who attended Shiva; Vishnu with four
arms; Ardhanari (Shiva and Parvati as the male and female
halves of one god); a Nandi bull; and Ganesha.
Cave II: dedicated to Vishnu, in all his incarnations. Images
include the boar, Varaha, who rescued the world from the
great flood; Vamana, the dwarf who rescued the world from
a particularly malevolent demon; a four-armed Vishnu riding
the eagle, Garuda; and Krishna. There are also images of
Shiva, and various decorations including swastikas and fish
wheels.
Cave III: the largest and most magnificent of the temples, with
a carved façade. This seems to have been used to worship
both Vishnu and Shiva, and has, amongst its carvings, one
of Hari-Hara, a god who was half-Vishnu, half-Shiva. Other
carvings include Narasimha, the half-lion, half-man incarnation of Vishnu; and Vishnu-Narayana, sitting and reclining
on Ananta, the snake who represents eternity. There are also
several rather faded frescoes, and an inscription dating the
temple's creation to 578 AD.
Cave IV: this is the latest of the cave temples, and, unlike the
others, is Jain. There is a statue of Mahavira, as well as images
of some other Tirthankaras and Padmavati.
Cave V: this natural cave has been adapted for use as a
Buddhist temple.

Badami Fort

Reached by steep steps which lead up the cliff between Caves II and III. At the top, in the southern end of the fort, there is a gun placed in position by Tipu Sultan. There are excellent views over Badami from **Gun Point**. The fort also contains a number of granaries, a watchtower, a treasury building and a number of temples, including the **Malegetti Shivalaya**, the oldest in Badami, dedicated to Shiva as the garland maker.

Bhuthanatha Temples

Down near the banks of the Agastyatirtha Tank are two small groups of temples, with an image of the local serpent goddess, Nagamma; two temples dedicated to Shiva as Bhuthanatha, the god of souls; and, at the top of the cliff above them, a rock pool surrounded by a sculpted frieze showing the different incarnations of Vishnu.

Sculpture Gallery

There is a small archaeological museum, with an excellent collection of statues from Badami, Aihole and Pattadakal, as well as from various other sights in the nearby area, on the Bhuthanatha Temple Road. Open 9am-5pm except Fridays, entrance free.

AIHOLE

There are about 100 temples clustered in and around this tiny village, about half within the walls of the fort, the rest just outside. Together, they cover the architecture of several cultures – Dravidian, Chalukya, Hoysala, Buddhist, Jain, Nagara and Rekhanagara – and several centuries, showing clearly the artistic development of the region, from simple rock cut halls to extravagant sculptured fantasies.

DON'T MISS . . .

Temple of Durga

The finest of the many in Aihole, this seventh to eighth-century temple, dedicated to Vishnu, gets its name from the earlier "*durgadagadi*" or, simply, the "temple near the fort". The main body of the temple, a rectangular hall with a semi-circular apse, seems to have been copied from Buddhist *chaitya* design. It is elaborately carved with high relief panels telling episodes from the *Mahabaratha* and *Ramayana*; as well as images of Chamundi Devi trampling on the buffalo demon; the half-man, half-lion god, Narasimha (an incarnation of Vishnu); several images of Shiva, including the Dancing Shiva, Nataraja, and Ardhanari (Shiva and Parvati as the male and female aspects of one god).

Temple of Lad Khan

One of the earliest of the temples in the area, first built in the fifth century as a royal assembly hall and marriage *mandapa*, in the style of a Panchayat hall. It got its name when a Muslim prince, Lad Khan, converted it into a home. It is a simple,

square-built design, with latticed stone screens and windows.
While the inner sanctums house beautiful sculptures – including
a four-armed Vishnu, a *shivalingam*, a Nandi bull, and the
river goddess Yamuna riding a tortoise – a stone ladder leads
to the roof, where there is a second sanctuary, dedicated to
the sun god, Surya. There is also a good view over the whole
village from the roof.

Ravana-phadi Temple
A sixth-century cave temple, carved into a low outcrop
south-east of the Huchimalli Temple. The entrance vestibule,
with two square stone pillars between carved side panels,
appears simple, but inside there are a number of exceptionally
fine sculptures. These include Nataraja, the Dancing Shiva,
Ganesha, and Ardhanari. The ceiling is also decorated.

Meguti Temple
The only temple in Aihole to be dated – 634 AD – this small,
simple Jain temple was never completed and is now partly
ruined. An inscription on one of the outer walls shows that
it was built by Ravikeerti, a commander and minister of
Pulakesin II. The porch and hall are later extensions. Amongst
the images insides are a Jain saint, Jura, Ambika, the goddess
of cosmic power, and Mahavira, the founder of Jainism. There
is a good view over Aihole from the roof.

Buddhist Temple
A plain, two-storey temple just below the Meguti temple, this
has a relief on the ceiling of a smiling Buddha with a Bodhi
Tree growing from his head.

Konta Temple Complex
A group of four temples in the middle of the bazaar, the earliest
dating from the fifth century. The **Konti-Gudi** temple is a simple building topped by a tower with eight horizontal friezes.
Inside there are a number of beautiful sculptures, including
the goddess Lakshmi with some elephants; a three-headed
Brahma, the Creator; and Nataraja, the Dancing Shiva. In the
Uma Maheshvari there is a finely carved sculpture of Brahma
seated in a lotus flower.

Huchimalli Temple
One of an extremely early group of temples just behind the
Tourist Home, this has borrowed in style from the north, with
a *rekhanagara* tower over the sanctuary, and is also the first
of the temples in this area to add a vestibule. There is a fine
carving of Kartikeya, the god of war, riding a peacock, on the
porch ceiling.

PATTADAKAL

The smallest of the three villages, Pattadakal reached its peak
from the seventh to ninth centuries, as the place where the
Chalukyan kings were crowned. It was in existence long before
that, however, being mentioned by Ptolemy as "Petrigal". It
was also known as Raktapura ("Red Town") and Pattada
Kisuvolal at other stages in its past.

As well as about ten fine temples, there are also a great
many other inscriptions and monuments, and even a collection
of small-scale, experimental architectural models, the earliest
being a third to fourth-century brick-built *mandapa*.

DON'T MISS . . .

Temple Complex
Six of the most important temples in the village are grouped
together in one spectacular, enclosed complex. There is also a
small **sculpture gallery** here, run by the Archaeological Survey
of India. Open 10am-5pm on working days, entrance free.

The **Virupaksha temple** (originally known as the Loke-
shwara temple) is the largest of the temples in the village (76 × 36m, for those who need to know). It was
built in 740 AD by Queen Lokamahadevi, wife of King
Vikramaditya II, in honour of a victory by the Chalukyans
over the Pallavas. The hall is supported by 16 pillars with
sculpted capitals and there are four windows in each side
wall. Amongst the many sculpted panels are scenes from
the *Mahabharata* and *Ramayana*, and there is a sculpture
which looks like an elephant on one side, and a buffalo on
the other.

The **Mallikarjuna temple**, which is similar in style, if smaller, was built by King Vikramaditya II's other wife, Trailokyamahadevi, at much the same time. It was originally known as the Trailokeswara temple. Sculptures here include Gajalakshmi, Nataraja and Parvati, while the capitals of the pillars tell the epic story of the life of Krishna, the Bhagavata.

The **Galaganatha temple**, built in the northern "*rekhanagara*" style, with a highly ornate, curved tower above the sanctuary, was never completed, but is nevertheless beautiful, with a fine sculpture of Shiva killing the Andhakasura.

Other temples in the complex include the **Sanghameswara temple**, the oldest in the village, built by King Vijayaditya (696–733 AD). This is Dravidian in style, with a sanctuary, inner passage and worshipping hall. The small **Kada Siddeswara temple** is North Indian in style, with a sanctuary and worshipping hall, and has an image of Shiva holding a snake and trident, with Parvati beside him. The **Jambulinga temple** is also small, with a North Indian tower and a sculpture of Nataraja, the Dancing Shiva, accompanied by Parvati and Nandi.

OUTSIDE THE COMPLEX

Papanatha Temple
A richly decorated temple built in about 680 AD, it borrowed from both north and south in design and is a classic example of early Chalukyan architecture. The 16 pillars in the main hall are carved in human form, while the ceiling is decorated by images of Vishnu, Shiva and Parvati, as well as other gods, and the side panels portray episodes from the Mahabharata and Ramayana.

Jain Temple
Built in the ninth century, this is a classic Dravidian temple, and has a number of beautiful sculptures, including two wonderful stone elephants. About 1/2 kilometre from the enclosure on the Badami road.

FACT FILE
FOOD AND LODGING

There are two or three small, simple hotels in Badami, and one in Aihole, while both have a sprinkling of tiny cafés, which are all much of a muchness, serving *thalis* and *dosas*. You won't find luxury, or even, probably, a hot shower, but it will be cheap. There is no accommodation or food in Pattadakal, so take supplies.

Hotel Mayura Chalukya: PWD Complex, Ramdurg Rd, Badami. Tel: 46.

By far the best place to stay locally. About 1/2 kilometre from the centre of town, run by the KSTDC.

There are several small, rather scruffy, hotels in the main street, if you can't get in.

Tourist Home: Hungund Taluk, Aihole. Tel: 41. Run by the KSTDC. Small and simple, but adequate.

HAMPI

Look around these desolate, boulder-strewn hills on the edge of the Tungabhadra River, and it is hard to believe that you are standing at the heart of a city once considered greater than Rome. At its height, half a million people lived here in glittering splendour, supported by an army of over a million. Today, there are a village of just over 1,000 inhabitants and 26 square kilometres of ruins.

Hampi, the capital of the Vijayanagar empire, for a time one of the largest and most powerful in India's history, is one of the most magnificent of India's monuments, but, chiefly due to the effort required to get there, it is almost unknown and way off the beaten tourist track. If you can afford the time, make the effort. It is well worthwhile.

The city has a long and illustrious past, stretching back thousands of years into the mists of legend. It is said to be Kishkinda, the country of the monkey king, where Rama first met the monkey god, Hanuman. It also claims to be Pampatira, the spot where Parvati (known locally as Hampi) met and married Shiva.

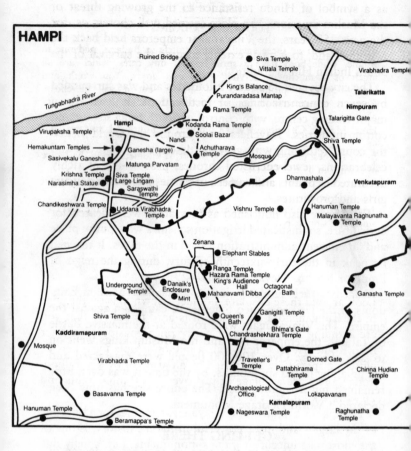

The city itself was founded in 1343 by the Telugu princes
Harihaka and Bukka. They had been captured by the Delhi
Sultanate during the Deccan wars, converted to Islam and sent
back to restore Muslim rule to the area. On their arrival, they
promptly reverted to Hinduism, and, in 1336, broke away
and set about founding a new empire. This, in time, came
to control vast areas of land from the Arabian Sea to the
Bay of Bengal, the Deccan plateau to the southern tip of the
sub-continent. They chose the site for their city, which they
named Vijayanagar or "the city of victory", on the advice

of a holy man, Vidyapuri, who selected this sacred spot as a symbol of Hindu resistance to the growing threat of the Muslim invasion. The place seemed well chosen, as, for the next 250 years, the Vijayanagar emperors held back the Muslims, and, to a great extent, ensured the survival of the South Indian Hindu tradition.

The city covered 33 square kilometres and was surrounded by seven concentric rings of fortifications. It was also a major trading centre, with control of South India's spice and cotton industries. Travellers from around the world visited the court, returning with glowing descriptions of feasts and celebrations, jewel-encrusted thrones, processions of richly decorated elephants and camels, of parties filled with dancing girls and prostitutes.

The empire also flourished as new areas were cleared for agriculture, sophisticated irrigation schemes were put in place and an efficient administration raked in the taxes. It reached its peak in the early-sixteenth century, during the reign of Emperor Krishna Devaraya (1509–29).

Tragedy struck suddenly in 1565, when the Muslim kingdoms of the Deccan joined together to campaign against the empire. The Vijayanagars were routed at the massive Battle of Talikot, the emperor fled and the Muslim kings went on to sack the city. Over 100,000 people were massacred and the pillaging lasted six months. By the time it was over, little remained but a ruinous shell. The entire site has now been declared a World Heritage Monument.

GETTING THERE

Like so many places in this area, it requires a degree of dedication to get to Hampi. The nearest **airport** is at Bellary, 74 kilometres to the east, but as the only flights in here are Vayudoot flights from Bangalore, it can be as easy to fly into Bangalore, Belgaum or Goa and go on by ground transport.

The nearest **railway station** is in **Hospet**, 13 kilometres from Hampi. This is also the only place nearby with anything approaching decent accommodation, so you would as well to make this your base and travel out to Hampi for the day. The best trains are the **express services** between Hubli and Bangalore (change at Hubli if you are going onto, or coming

from Goa). There are also some very slow passenger services
north to Badami and Bijapur.

For those who prefer to travel by **road**, Hospet is on the
National Highway from Solapur to Bangalore (which also
runs though Bijapur and Badami). There are hourly **bus**
services to Bellary, ten express services a day to Bangalore,
as well as three a day to Hubli (for access to Goa), and daily
services to Hyderabad, Belgaum, Badami, Bijapur, Hassan,
Mangalore and Mysore, as well as to a number of smaller
and more local destinations.

GETTING AROUND

Hospet

The **railway station** is on the north edge of the town, about
20-minutes walk to the centre. The **bus station** is in the centre,
also on Station Road, opposite the Hotel Vishwa. If you don't
feel like walking, the best way of getting around town is by
cycle rickshaw, of which there are plenty. Remember to fix a
price before you start off.

Hampi

The easiest way to get to Hampi is by bus from Hospet. These
run roughly every hour between 6am–8pm, and take about
30 minutes to do the journey. They will either drop you at
Kamalapur village, on the southern edge of the site, or will
take you through to Hampi Bazaar, beside the river.

If you prefer other methods of transport, you can hire a
tourist taxi. These are not too expensive, particularly if you
are not on your own, but arrange for it to come back for you,
rather than paying waiting time, as you will probably be at
the site all day. Alternatively, you can get a place in a **share
taxi**, which will leave as soon as it is full, or hire a **bicycle** for
the day.

Once at Hampi, unless you are prepared to give it only
the most cursory glance, the best, and often the only way,
to get around is on foot. Wear your most comfortable shoes,
stock up with a good supply of water and be prepared to do
a fair amount of walking. You can get around the sight in a
day if you start early, but if possible, it would be better to

avoid mental and physical exhaustion and give yourself two
or three days.

GETTING YOUR BEARINGS

Hospet
Although it is a fair-sized town, with a population of around
120,000, Hospet has little to offer the visitor, except as a base
for visiting Hampi. MG Road (Station Road) leads straight
from the **railway station** into the centre of town, past several
of the hotels and the **bus station**.

There is a fairly useless **tourist information office** in the Old
Fire Station Building, Taluk Office Complex (Tel: 8537). Very
short on information, but if you want to do a tour, or hire a
private guide, this is where to ask. The tours last all day, but
only the morning is spent in Hampi. Two hours are devoted
to lunch and the whole afternoon is spent at the Tungabhadra
Dam. For better information, ask the manager of the **Malligi
Tourist Home**. (See p.228)

Hampi
The Tungabhadra River forms the northern boundary of
Hampi, with the modern village and bazaar near the river
bank, roughly in the centre of the site, and a large number
of temples clustered along the water's edge. Behind them, the
fortress wall marks the start of the royal city, with palaces,
state apartments, the stables and, of course, more temples.
Other ruins are scattered over a wide area around these two
concentrations. To the south of the fort wall is the village of
Kamalapur.

There is another pretty useless state **tourist information
counter** in Hampi Bazaar. Better information comes from the
offices of the **Archaeological Survey of India** in Kamalapur
(Tel: 8744/8737), which publishes a good booklet of the site,
complete with a map, as well as running a small museum.
There is a good bookshop in Hampi Bazaar which will also
be able to supply a variety of site guides.

DON'T MISS ...

The most important of the sights at Hampi fall into three main areas. Along the banks of the river, surrounding Hampi Bazaar, are a number of the larger temples and other religious monuments. These fall into two separate groups, those to the left of the bazaar, clustered around the **Virupaksha temple**, and those to the right, of which the **Vittala temple** is the most important. On a hill to the south are the remnants of the Citadel, or walled city, together with the palace ruins. A great many other monuments, mainly temples, are scattered around the larger area, but these are of lesser importance. Excavations however have barely begun, and there is thought to be enough work to keep the archaeologists happy for the next 400 years, so watch this space!

Virupaksha Temple

To the east of Hampi Bazaar, this is the oldest, largest and most sacred of the Hindu temples, and, as a major pilgrimage site, is one of only a few in Hampi still in use. It is dedicated to Shiva, under the name of Virupaksha or Pampapati. Dating back to the nineth century, with a few late Chalukyan and Hoysala features, it was mainly built during the Vijayanagar period (15th – 16th centuries).

At the main entrance is a 10-storey, 165 foot (52m) tall *gopuram*, the **Bristappaiah Gopuram**. A second *gopuram*, the **Rayara Gopuram**, leads into the main courtyard. At the centre of this is the **Virupaksha temple** itself. A hall with mythological scenes painted on the ceiling and finely carved pillars leads to the inner sanctum. Also within the courtyard are the **Hampamma temple**, the **Goddess Bhuvaneswari temple**, with a sculpted Chalukyan doorway flanked by pierced windows, and the **Temple of Vidyaranya**. Behind the temple, there is an opening which acts as a pinhole camera to show an upsidedown picture of the main tower. Open from 6.30am–12.30pm and 2–8.30pm daily. Nominal entrance charge.

Ganesha monoliths
Just south of the Virupaksha temple complex are two large monolithic statues of the elephant god, Ganesha. The 10-foot-tall **Sasave Kalu Ganesh** stands in an open-pillared **mandapa**. The 16 foot-high **Kadale Kalu Ganesh** is in an east-facing hall with high columns on the slopes of Hermakunta Hill.

Krishna Temple
Now badly damaged, this was built in 1513 by the Vijayanagar King, Krishna Devaraya, to house an image of Krishna (now in Madras Museum) which he brought back as war loot after his victory at Udayagiri. There are stucco figures of the king and battle scenes on the entrance tower.

Statue of Yoga Lakshiminarasimha
A little further south, a 22 foot monolithic statue of Yoga Lakshminarasimha with a seven-headed snake above it stands in an open courtyard. Erected by Krishna Devaraya in 1528, the statue was badly damaged and has been restored to some extent, although restoration work has now ceased.

Badavalinga
Next to the Narasimha statue is a Shiva temple with a 10 foot tall monolithic *lingam*.

Also within this area are the **Uddana Veerabhadra**, with an 18 foot monolithic statue, and the **Akka Tangi Gundu** or Sister's Stone, where two vast boulders create a natural arch.

LEAVING THE BAZAAR
A large monolithic statue of **Nandi**, Shiva's bull, stands on the road that leaves the bazaar to the west. To the right (away from the river) a complex of **Jain temples** stand on the slopes of **Matunga Parvatham**, a hill from which there is an excellent view across much of the site. To the left, on the river bank, you come to the **Kodanda Rama temple,** built to comemmorate the place where Rama crowned Sugriva after killing Bali. The image of Rama is a focus for pilgrimage and the river below, which has some dangerous eddies, is

used, not without occasional tragedies, for sacred bathing. The temple often floods during the monsoon. The road that leads from here to the **Achyuta Raya temple** is known as the **Soolai Bazaar**. It is the last remnant of the market that brought Hampi most of its fame and fortune during the glory days.

Achyuta Raya Temple
Named after **King Achyuta Raya**, who built the temple in 1539, this is, more correctly, called the **Tirvengalanatha temple**. The temple itself is ruined, but the double enclosure contains a number of finely carved columns, including some with erotic sculptures.

King's Balance (Tula Purushadana)
This huge, rectangular, granite arch, 15 foot high and 12 across, was built as a massive scale. On certain feastdays, the king would have himself weighed and his weight in gold and jewels would be distributed amongst the Brahmans. The carved pillars include portraits of the king and his two wives.

Vittala Temple
Architecturally splendid, this is considered to represent the finest flowering of Vijayanagar art. Dedicated to Vitoba, a Marathi god who was worshipped locally as an incarnation of Krishna, legend has it that Vishnu found it too rich to live in, and this is why it was never consecrated or used. In reality, work began in 1513 under Krishna Deveraya and was continued under his successors, but was still not completed when the city was sacked in 1565.

Set in a rectangular courtyard, the main sanctuary is behind an elaborately carved hall, with 56 elegant pillars. Each is said to give off a different musical note when tapped. In front of the main temple is a **stone chariot**, built as a replica of the wooden chariots used during festivals. It is a magnificent work of art, so finely detailed that at one time the wheels could even turn. Sadly, the brick superstructure which held the image of the eagle, Garuda, no longer exists.

THE CITADEL

Zenana enclosure

This large walled enclosure contains a number of buildings including a watch tower, the quarters of the Queen's Guard, the ruined base of the Queen's Palace, a treasury or store house and a water pavilion. Most important however is the **Lotus Mahal**, an open, two-storey pavilion on an ornamental stone base. Built in the Indo-Saracenic style, the base, roof, cornice and stucco work are Hindu influenced, while the delicately arched windows and balconies of the upper storey, reached by a staircase on the north side, have borrowed from Islamic design. A large lotus bud at the centre of the domed and vaulted ceiling gave the building its name.

Elephant stables

Just behind the Zenana enclosure, this impressive row of eleven large, domed rooms, built on either side of a central two-storey pavilion, was built to house the emperor's elephants. It is strongly Islamic in design.

Hazara Rama Temple

Just south of the Zenana enclosure, this is thought to have been the emperors' private family temple. Built in the early-fifteenth century, it stands in a rectangular courtyard, the walls of which are decorated with friezes of elephants, horses, soldiers and dancing girls. The walls of the temple itself have three rows of sculpture depicting scenes from the *Ramayana*, while the finely carved, highly polished basalt pillars inside the hall show the different incarnations of Vishnu.

Mahavanavami Dibba

A little further south, this immense platform was originally the base of a 100-columned pavilion from which the king watched the Mahavanami celebrations. According to the Portuguese traveller, Paes, this festival, which took place annually in September or October, combined a durbar, with its royal audiences and the exchange of gifts and hon-ours, with a grand sacrifice to reconsecrate the emperor's armies, and processions, sporting events and even firework displays.

Built by Krishna Devaraya in 1513, after his victory over Udayagirl, the platform is 36 feet high and is decorated with processions of soldiers, horses, elephants, camels and dancing girls, as well as hunting and battle scenes. There are stairs on the north and south sides of the platform.

From it, there is an excellent view over the royal enclosure. Also within this area are a number of other buildings, includ-ing the **Underground temple**, officially called the **Prasanna Virpaksha**. Dedicated to Shiva, it was built between 10 and 12 foot below ground level. Near this are the **Danaik Enclosure**, home of the commander-in-chief of the emperor's army, and another enclosure popularly thought to have housed the **Royal Mint**. Near the Hazara Rama Temple are the remains of the **King's Audience Hall**, and a vast monolithic **stone trough**, 42 feet long, used for watering horses and elephants. Near the Mahanavami Dabbi, a stone aquaduct leads to the **Puskarani**, a decorated, stepped well made from black basalt. Also near here is vast **stone door** now set by itself beside the road. Made from a single piece of stone, the bolt sockets are part of the integral structure.

A little further south still, you come to the **Queen's Bath**, a walled, moated enclosure built in the Islamic style, with an arched, vaulted corridor and elaborately decorated balconies surrounding a small swimming tank. West from here is the **Octagonal Bath**, surrounded by an open colonnade.

Museum

The small museum at the south end of the site, in Kamalapuram, is run by the Archaeological Survey of India. It has a collection of coins, sculpture, paintings and copper plates. Open 10 am-5pm daily, except Fridays.

OUT OF TOWN

Tungabhadra Dam

This high, 2-kilometre long dam has backed up to form a huge lake. Along the shore, there is a **park** with topiary, espalier and Japanese gardens. The terraces are illuminated on Saturday, Sunday and festival evenings. It is an extremely popular picnic and weekend spot with the locals, so tends to be oversold by them, but it is a pleasant enough excursion if you need a break from ruins.

Regular buses run from the Hospet bus station, taking 15 minutes to do the journey.

FACT FILE

WHERE TO STAY

There are no upmarket or luxury hotels in the vicinity, but there are a number of good cheap places that will provide a clean if spartan room.

Hampi

There are one or two tiny lodging houses in Hampi village. About the only one worth any consideration is the **Hampi Power Station Guest House** which lets a couple of rooms out if they are not needed by officials. The **Virupaksha temple** has a number of unfurnished rooms and dormitory space for pilgrims that can be hired at a nominal price.

Hospet

Malligi Tourist Home: Jambunatha Rd. By the canal. Tel: 8101.
Hotel Vishwa: MG Rd. Opposite the bus station. Tel: 7171.

Hotel Priyadarshini: 45a MG Rd. Tel: 8838/8096.
Hotel Sandarshan: MG Rd. Tel: 8574/8451.

Tungabhadra Dam
Hotel Mayura Vijayanagar: Just below the dam. Tel: 8270. Run by
the KSTDC. Pleasant, reasonably cheap, but thoroughly inconvenient
if you are there to look at Hampi.

WHERE TO EAT

Hampi
Amongst the number of small restaurants in Hampi Bazaar, probably
the best are the Ramsingh Trishul Tea Shop, run by the Sri Aurobindo
Ashram, and the Hotel Mayura Lotus Mahal Restaurant run by the
KSTDC.

Hospet
Shanthi Restaurant: Hotel Vishwa.
Nirmal Garden: Malligi Tourist Home.
Eagle Garden Restaurant: opposite the Malligi Tourist Home.
Chalukya Restaurant and Manasa Bar and Restaurant: Hotel Priya-
darshini.

SOUTHERN KARNATAKA

MYSORE

The name Mysore is thought to derive from that of the
demon Mahishasura, but the first mention of the city is
in the *Mahabharata* under the name of Mahisamati. It also
appears as Mahisha Mandala in the records of King Ashoka,
who sent a missionary to convert the city to Buddhism in the
third century BC. Whatever the truth of it, the city was for
centuries capital of a powerful principality, ruled in turn by the
Cholas, Hoysalas, Vijayanagar, and Wodeyar dynasties. These
last ruled the state from the fourteenth century until they were
deposed by Hyder Ali in 1759. On Tipu Sultan's defeat in
1799, they were reinstated by the British, but from then on
were rulers in name only. Left with little to do, and a great
deal of money, they spent the nineteenth century in building
a vast number of extravagant palaces, five in Mysore alone,

as well as hosting a whole range of fabulous entertainments. Even this came to an end with Independence in 1947, but the Maharajah's son still lives in a small section of the City Palace, reliving his glory days just once a year during the Dussehra celebrations.

By Indian standards, the modern city, with a population of around 700,000, feels positively small and cosy. At a height of 770 metres, near the edge of the **Nilgiri Hills**, Mysore itself has relatively little in the way of tourist sights, but it is an excellent jumping off point for a number of places of interest in the nearby area. It also has a charming, laid-back atmosphere that has drawn tourists like a magnet.

Mysore is probably most famous, however, as a shopping centre. If you wish to take home any souvenirs of your time in South India, this is the place to find them. Even if you don't want to buy, window shopping is a delight. The streets are piled high with flowers, the local girls wear jasmine and marigolds in their hair, and the whole town is perfumed with the scent of jasmine and incense. The surrounding area supplies most of India's sandalwood and also produces silk (see box below), gold, incense and essential oils. Mysore is also one of India's main centres for ivory goods, but do remember that the sale and import/export of ivory is strictly forbidden and will be severely punished.

GETTING THERE

There are officially three flights a week to Mysore from Bangalore on Vayudoot, but these have been suspended recently, leaving Bangalore, 138 kilometres away, as the nearest airport.

By far the easiest way to get to Mysore is on the metre guage **railway** line from Bangalore. There are some half dozen express trains each day, taking about 3½ hours to do the journey, plus a number of slower passenger or mail services. This line is due (at some distant point in time) to be upgraded to broad guage, which will give Mysore much better connections with other parts of the country.

The only other link is to the north-west, also on metre guage, via Hassan to Arsikere or Mangalore. There are not many trains on this line and all travel at a snail's pace, but if you are planning to visit Belur and Halebid, this is the best way to go. This line will also take you through to Jog Falls and Goa. There are no lines going south, so you will have to take to the buses to cross the mountains, unless you want to do a very long loop around them.

The **City Railway Station** is close to the centre of the city, just off Irwin Road. Like many of the others in the area, it is a splendid Victorian creation with a domed clock tower, wide, breezy verandahs and positively luxurious retiring rooms. The Advance Reservations counters, which are in a separate area off the main lobby, will deal with tourist enquiries and bookings, and the Commercial Superintendent's Office across the road handles reservations on the tourist quota. (Tel: 20100)

Mysore is well connected by **road**, with national highways running to Bangalore in the east, Mangalore in the west, and Coimbatore to the south. They are all, however, still Indian-style roads with too many cars, and too many pot holes.

The area is particularly well served by **buses**. Non-stop services leave for Bangalore every half-hour, and there are also stopping services every hour for the masochistic. There are half a dozen daily departures each for Ooty and Belur; 12 a day for Arsikere, Mangalore and Calicut (some of which go through to Cochin); and around 24 for Hassan. There are also two to three departures a day for Bellary, Bandipur, Coimbatore (where you can meet up again with the broad guage railway), and Nagarhole, and an overnight service to Panaji.

The long-distance bus services all operate from the **Central Bus Station**, two blocks from the City Palace. (Tel: 20853/25819.)

For services to nearby place of interest, see below.

GETTING AROUND

The city centre is relatively small and most things are within **walking** distance. Alternatively, there are plenty of **tongas** and **auto-rickshaws** prowling the streets. Set a price before you go as you will almost never be able to persuade them to use a meter, and as there are a fair number of tourists around, expect them to be more adept at trying to fleece you (in an extremely good-humoured fashion) than in some of the other nearby centres.

For journeys into the suburbs, or to outlying tourist sights, the cheapest way is to travel by **local bus**. These all leave from the chaotic **City Bus Stand,** with its seemingly permanent queues of several hundred people. This is near the City Palace, on Albert Victor Road. Buses to Somnathpur leave from the other side of the New Statue Circle, opposite the Ritz Hotel. (Tel: 20853/25819.)

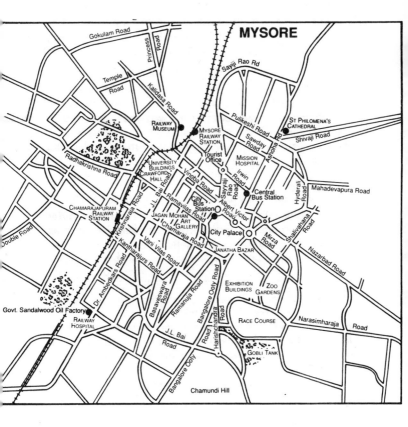

Taxis are available through a number of travel agents or through hotel reception desks, and can be booked on a flat

Silk

Although Westerners tend to regard silk as the ultimate luxury, in India it is worn by everyone from Maharajahs to the most humble *shudra*. White or natural-coloured silk was traditionally reserved for Brahmans, while the women wore bright colours and the *shudras* darker shades. It is considered to be a pure fabric, and as such, is suitable for ceremonial and religious use. It is worn for births and marriages, and lengths of cloth are offered as gifts to the gods. Those that can afford it wear it the rest of the year as well.

There has been a thriving silk industry in India for thousands of years, but early silks were all from indigenous, wild species of silkworm. The cultivated mulberry silkworm was smuggled in from China two or three hundred years ago (no one is sure exactly when it arrived). Until then, China had kept the production process a carefully guarded secret. Some say it was a Buddhist monk who brought in both the eggs of the silkworm and the seeds of the mulberry tree in hollow bamboo canes. Others say it was a Chinese princess who hid them in her elaborate hairdo when she arrived as the bride of an Indian prince. Whatever the case, for the last 3,000 years or so, India has been one of the great silk producers of the world.

The silk industry in Karnataka was set up under Tipu Sultan in the eighteenth century. Today, it is the single largest silk-producing state in India, producing plain and watered, printed and flowered silks and saris.

The production process is handled by a number of different people. The female moth produces between 400 and 600 eggs within 30 hours of mating, after which she is killed and checked for signs of disease before the eggs are allowed to hatch. This takes 10 days. The pupa are then sold to the mulberry bush owner who feeds them constantly on mulberry leaves for the next 28 days, until they are up to 15 centimetres long. At this point the pupa turn yellow and start spinning their cocoons, which takes another 4 days. Once this is complete, they are sold on to a reeler who destroys the unfortunate pupa and starts unreeling the cocoon. Each cocoon can give up to 1200 metres of fine thread. This is then twisted into yarn, and sold to the weavers at government-run silk auctions. The weavers contract out the dying process and weave the cloth.

There are numerous government and private workshops in the south of the state, which can be visited on request.

fee for a half or full-day sightseeing trip, which will also take in the surrounding area. Prices are reasonable, especially if there are several of you.

The KSTDC run daily mega-**tours** of Mysore and the surrounding sights, including Somnathpur, Srirangapatnam, Brindavan and Ranganathittu (in season, June to September). They also have tours to Ooty and Belur, Halebid and Sravanabelagola which run daily in season (April to June, and September to November), three times a week out of season. Information and bookings at the KSTDC Tourist Office in Irwin Road (Tel: 22096), or the Hotel Mayura Hoysala, from where they also leave.

GETTING YOUR BEARINGS

The **railway station** is in the north-west corner of the city centre. The **central bus station** is about 2 kilometres due east, in the north-east corner. The south-east corner, about 1 kilometre south of this, is taken up by the **city bus stand** and the **palace**, while the **botanical gardens**, due south of the railway station, make up the fourth corner of the square. Almost everything you might want to visit, including the smaller hotels, restaurants, best shops and the **market** are within this small area. The posh hotels are outside the city proper and you will need transport to reach them. St Philomena's Cathedral is due north of the city centre; the zoo and race course are to the south-east of the palace.

There are two **tourist offices**, both just round the corner from the railway station. The local Regional Tourist Office is in the Old Exhibition Building, Irwin Road. (Tel: 22096.) The KSTDC office is in the Hotel Mayura Hoysala, 2 Jhansi Lakshmi Bai Road. (Tel: 570 005/23652.)

Chamundi Hill is about 4 kilometres south-east of the city centre, but 13 kilometres if you go by bus. **Somnathpur** is 35 kilometres east of the city; **Srirangapatnam** is 19 kilometres north; and **Brindavan Gardens** are 19 kilometres north-west. The **Ranganathittoo Bird Sanctuary** is 3 kilometres from Srirangapatnam.

DON'T MISS . . .

The Amber Vilas (City Palace)

Built in 1897 at a cost of Rs4.2 million, to replace the original palace which had burnt down a short while before, this massive extravaganza was the brainchild of an Englishman, Henry Irwin. He borrowed inspiration freely to create a gigantic, Indo-Saracenic pile – one of the largest palaces in India, a country never known for building on a modest scale. Set in an open courtyard designed to give agoraphobia to the hardiest soul, the main building, the **Amba Vilas** durbar hall, is built of granite, its three storeys giving way to a dominating five-storey central tower topped by a massive gilded dome. The rest of the roofline is alive with smaller domes and cupolas while every façade is laced by delicate windows, arches and balconies.

Inside the extravagance goes even further. The ground-floor walls are painted with scenes from *Dussehra* processions, family portraits line one room and another houses a collection of silver and glass chairs. In the east courtyard the famous gold *howdah* (containing 40 kilograms of pure gold) is on display. On the first floor is the fantastic (in both its senses) durbar hall itself, with an intricately carved teak ceiling, a floor inlaid with precious stones, including jasper, cornelian and lapis lazuli, and doors of silver, teak and rosewood. Ivory panels depict the different incarnations of Vishnu, and on the west wall are paintings by one of India's most famous artists, Raja Ravi Varma, showing scenes from the *Ramayana* and *Mahabharata*. During *Dussehra*, the solid gold, jewel-encrusted throne of the Wodeyars is displayed in here, but during the rest of the year, the "second-class" solid silver throne goes some way towards making up for not seeing it. The rest of the building is almost as ornate, with panelled and painted walls and marble floors and magnificent stained glass (from Glasgow).

Other buildings in the grounds include the peacock (marriage) pavilion, the armoury, music and drawing rooms, and a temple. The family jewel collection is now also on permanent display. On Sunday evenings, from 7–8pm and festivals, the building is illuminated with some 50,000 bulbs, leading architectural historian Philip Davies to liken it, somewhat acidly to "an Oriental Harrods". The description is extremely apt.

Open 10.30am-5.30pm daily. Small admission charge, plus charge for shoeminder and the inevitable guide.

Devaraja Market

Just off Sayiji Rao Road, right in the centre of Mysore, this large market couldn't be more of a contrast to the palace – a teeming, muddy mass of tiny stalls piled high with chains of flowers, bananas, great heaps of multi-coloured spices, and everything else. Look out for the sandalwood incense sticks, one of the local specialities, turned out in their hundreds of thousands each day in homes throughout the city. The market is probably not the best place to try and buy your souvenirs, as you will be far more sure of getting good quality in the less exciting, but well run government emporium, but it is a wonderful place to wander and soak up the atmosphere of the town.

ALSO WORTH VISITING

Jaganmohan Palace

Just off Ramavilasa Road, near the City Bus Stand, this much smaller palace was converted into an art gallery in 1875, and now houses a fine collection of Indian miniature paintings, including a number done on gold leaf. The older, western pavilion has a display on Mysore history and a collection of the personal property of the Maharajahs. There is also a room dedicated to the work of Raja Ravi Varma, a number of paintings by international and modern Indian artists, and a collection of musical instruments.

Open 8.30am-5pm daily. Small admission charge.

St Philomena's Cathedral

Another extravagance, this time neo-Gothic, a soaring cathedral that is one of the largest Christian churches in India. There is a statue of St Philomena in the crypt.

Regional Railway Museum

Just behind the main railway station on KRS Road. The only rail museum in South India, this is a mecca for lovers of steam, but may seem rather neglected and disorganised to the less obsessive. There are a number of paintings and photographs charting the history of the railways in the area, the Maharani's saloon car and kitchen/dining car, a few steam engines and a toy train for the kids.

Open 10am-1pm, 3–7pm, Tuesday to Sunday. Admission charge and photographic permit.

Folklore Museum and Art and Archaeology Museum

Both run by the University of Mysore at Manasa Gangotri, just off Vinoba Rd, near the railway station. Two small collections which together cover everything from local antiquities, weapons and coins to jewellery and the carved wooden toys which are a speciality of nearby Channapatna.

Open 10.30am-5.30pm, except Sundays. Entry free.

Zoo Gardens

About 1 kilometre east of the palace on Lokaranjan Mahal Road, this was created by the nineteenth-century Maharajah Shri Chamaraja Wodeyar Bahadur. Small, but reasonably well maintained, the animals include, amongst others, elephants, lions, tigers, kangaroos and rhinos. There is also a snake park.

Open 8am-midday, 2–6pm weekdays, and 8am-6pm Sundays. Small admission charge.

OUT OF TOWN

Chamundi Hill

There are two ways to get to the top of Chamundi Hill, where, legend has it, the great battle between Chamundeswari and Mahishasura took place. The easy way is to go by bus or taxi up the winding, 13-kilometre road. Take Bus No 101 from the City Bus Stand. They leave about every 30 minutes. Alternatively, you can walk. It is 4 kilometres to the top, but it also involves 1,000 steps, cut into the side of the hill on the

Dussehra

One of the major festivals of the Hindu calendar, **Dussehra** celebrates the victory of good over evil, personified by the destruction of the buffalo-headed demon Mahishasura by the Goddess Chamundeswari (Durga). The origins of the festival date back to the days of the Puranas, but it grew to an almost unbelievable level of pomp and pageantry under the Vijayanagar kings, to whom it was known as *Mahavanavami* (see page 226). Today, the ten-day festival takes place each year in early October.

Chamundeswari is the patron goddess of the Wodeyar kings of Mysore, and the city celebrates the festival in grand style. The Palace comes back to life with exhibitions and entertainments, all the main buildings of the city are illuminated, and the streets are decorated and alive with music and dance. On the final spectacular day, the Maharajah's son leads a procession of richly decorated elephants, ceremonial troops, the image of the god Bharatmata in a golden howdah, state coaches, musicians and dancers through the streets. A temple float procession at the foot of Chamundi Hill and a temple car festival at the top add to the gaiety, while the evening brings a torchlight procession and massive firework display.

orders of a seventeenth-century Maharajah. Halfway up, you will meet a 4.8 metre high monolithic statue of Nandi, Shiva's bull. One of the largest monolithic statues in India, it is itself a draw to pilgrims and is almost permanently decorated with garlands of flowers. At the top, you will be greeted by a gaudy, ferocious statue of the demon Mahishasura and, thankfully, a number of very necessary drinks stalls.

The **Shri Chamundeswari temple** dates back to the twelfth century. It is most renowned for its seven-storey *gopuram*, which stands some 40 metres high, every centimetre of it covered with ornate carvings. Priests and pilgrims alike are anxious to show you around, and will arm you with sacrificial flowers so that you can receive a blessing.

Also on top of the hill is the **Rajendrah Vilas Palace**, built in 1939, but already crumbling. It is run as a hotel, but is worth a visit even if you don't plan to stay there, more for its eccentricities than its glory. Look out for the red velvet dining room, the elephant's head over the stairs, and if you ask, you will be taken to see the royal bed-rooms.

Chamundi Hill is nearly 1100 metres above sea level, and about 350 metres above Mysore. There are superb views over the city and the surrounding countryside from the top.

Brindavan Gardens
These amazing gardens beside the Krishnarajasagara Dam, 19 kilometres north-west of Mysore, are immensely popular with local people. Access is across a 2 kilometre dam wall, one of the longest in India, which has created a 130 square kilometre lake on the Cauvery River. The gardens have formal displays of flowers and trees, but more importantly, have a number of fountains, some of which are illuminated with multi-coloured lights and one of which is musical! During the day, you can wander, or take a boat ride on the lake. In the evenings, repair to the verandah of the restaurant, once a royal guest house. They do a mean line in cocktails and there is a good view of the light show.

Illumination times: summer – 7–7.55pm, weekdays, and

7–8.55pm on holidays; winter – 6.30–7.30pm weekdays, and 6.30–8.30pm on holidays. Admission charge expensive if you take a car over the dam, so leave it at the other end and walk. Camera permits also costly.

Somnathpur

A tiny village 35 kilometres from Mysore, Somnathpur is home to one of the most beautiful of South India's thousands of temples. The **Sri Channakeshara temple** was built in about 1268 AD by the Hoysala kings, who were also responsible for the temples at nearby Belur and Halebid. It is the latest and best preserved example of their work. Set within a rectangular courtyard, the temple itself is shaped like a 16-point star, and consists of a central *navagara* or dancing hall and three shrines. The south cell is dedicated to Venugopala, the west to Vishnu, and the north to Janardhana. The domed ceilings are wonderful, but best of all are the immaculately preserved friezes which literally cover the buildings. There is a 30 feet stone pillar just to the north of the temple.

Ranganathittu Bird Sanctuary

A few kilometres along the Cauvery River from Srirangapatnam, this small island sanctuary is best seen during the
monsoon months (June to October), when it is crowded with
an astonishing number of species including, amongst many
others, open bill storks, white ibis, pond herons, cormorants,
and wild ducks. There are also a few crocodiles and flying
foxes (fruit bats) in the area. It is possible to hire boats here.

Srirangapatnam

First settled in the tenth century, this island city on the Cauvery
River rose to prominence under the Hoysala kings when the
great philosopher, Ramanuja, fled here from Chola repression
in 1133. It was was turned into a fortress by a local chieftain
in 1454, during the period of Vijayanagar rule. In 1610, the
Wodeyar Maharajah of Mysore made it his capital. Its most
famous associations however are with Tipu Sultan. He used
the city as a base from which he fought battle after battle in
his territorial campaigns, and the fortress itself came under
siege on a number of occasions. In 1799 came the final battle
against the British, during which Tipu Sultan lost his life.
The British forces were commanded by one Colonel Arthur
Wellesley, better known as the Duke of Wellington. It was his
first great victory and the real beginning of his extraordinary
military career.

The town still has a population of around 20,000, most
of whom seem to be under the age of 12 and want to sell
you postcards, but they seem to rise up not from a living
community but from the shattered ruins that were left after the
looting and pillaging in that last great battle. The battlements
and gates still tower forbiddingly high, and you can visit the
dungeons where a number of British officers were imprisoned
by Tipu in hellish conditions.

The Hindu temple is dedicated to Sri Ranganatha, who
donated his name to the city. There is a massive statue of
Vishnu reclining on the coils of a snake, Ananta, in the inner
sanctum, but this cannot be visited by non-Hindus.

On the other side of the main road is Tipu's Summer Palace,
the **Daria Daulat Bagh** (the name, oddly for something so far

inland, means Splendour of the Sea). It is a brightly painted, sadly neglected, wooden pavilion set in attractive gardens. It now houses an exhibition on Tipu Sultan's life; together with paintings of his various campaigns. The palace was later used as a residence by Wellesley, who remained in the area as governor for five years, and also gave his name to the nearby bridge.

Next-door, the elegant, onion-domed **Gumbaz** houses the bodies of Hyder Ali, Tipu Sultan, his wife and various other members of the family. It has a high platform with a polished, black basalt floor and is set in well tended gardens.

The **bathing ghat** at nearby Sangam is a little off the beaten track, but is an attractive, peaceful place, with a small marble pavilion on the steps leading down to the river.

FACT FILE

TRAVEL
Indian Airlines: Hotel Mayura Hoysala Complex, JLB Rd. Tel: 21846. Open 10am–1.30pm, 2.15–5.15 pm, except Sunday.
Vayudoot: c/o MITA Travel Agency, 66a Chamaraja Rd. Tel: 20031.

BANKS
State Bank of Mysore: cnr Sayiji Rao Rd and Sardar Patel Rd.

COMMUNICATIONS
Central Telegraph Office: New Sayiji Rao Rd. Tel: 20900. Just east of the City Palace. Open 24 hrs.
Head Post Office: Mahavir Circle, Ashoka Rd. Tel: 22165.

SHOPPING
Books
Premier Book House: Anand Vihar, Makkaji Chowk.
Ashok Book Centre: Dhanvantri Rd.
Geetha Book House: KR Circle.

Souvenirs
Cauvery Arts and Crafts Emporium: cnr Sayiji Rao Rd and Irwin Rd.
Brilliant state-run shop that feels like walking into Aladdin's cave. Open 10am–2pm, 3.30–7.30pm, Friday to Wednesday. Not the cheapest place in town, but the quality is guaranteed, prices are fixed and fair, they

accept credit cards and will, if required, pack and send your purchases for you.

There are also a number of other good shops in Sayiji Rao Rd and Dhanwantri Rd, and a visit to the **Devaraja Market** (see page 235) is essential.

Karnataka Silk Industry has a shop on Visweswara Rd, but it is more fun to head out of the centre of town to their factory on Mananthody Rd (about 3 kilometres from the city centre), where you can go on a guided tour of the machine weaving works before settling down to some serious spending. Open 7.30–11.30am, 12.30–4.30pm, Monday to Saturday. Phone ahead for a tour. Tel: 21803.

Sandalwood Oil Factory, just off Ambedkar Rd, about 1 kilometre from the silk factory. This is where over half of India's sandalwood oil is produced. Phone ahead for a guided tour of the works, with details of how the oil is extracted and incense is made. There is also a sales counter. Open 9–11am, 2–4pm, Monday to Friday. Tel: 22856.

WHERE TO STAY

Luxury
Lalitha Mahal Palace: T. Narasipur Rd. Tel: 26316/27650. Telex: 0846–217.

About 8 kilometres from the railway station, on the eastern edge of Mysore. Built in 1931 as a guest house for those carnivores amongst the Maharajah's visitors (his own household being strictly vegetarian), this was designed by E.W. Fritchley. The dome is modelled on St Paul's in London. Well worth a visit, even if you can't afford to stay there. Now run by the ITDC, the facilities are still positively palatial. It also has wonderful gardens and a good view over Mysore.

Mid-range
Rajendra Vilas Palace: Chamundi Hill. Tel: 20690. Telex: 0846–230.

Out of town at the top of Chamundi Hill, this is faded and eccentric, but stuffed full of atmosphere and with superb views (see also page 237). Still owned and run by the royal family and staffed, in part, by creaking family retainers.

Hotel Metropole: 5 Jhansi Lakshmi Bai Rd. Tel: 20681/20871, Telex: 0846–214 RITZ IN.

Near the railway station, in its own gardens.

Quality Inn Southern Star: Vinobha Rd. Tel: 27217. Telex: 0846–256 QSSM IN.

Near the railway station and downtown area. Large, modern, and efficient.

Cheap
Hotel Mayura Hoysala: 2 JLB Rd. Tel: 25349.
 Very close to the railway station. Run by the KSTDC. Pleasant and friendly, with the tourist office on the premises.
Kings Court Hotel: JLB Rd. Tel: 25250/32684. Telex: 0846–263 KING IN.
 Close to the station and city centre. Modern.
Hotel Dasaprakash: Gandhi Square. Tel: 24444/22821.
 Huge, modern chain hotel in the city centre.
Hotel Siddhartha: 73/1 Guest House Rd, Nazarbad. Tel: 26869. Telex: 0846–312 HOTL IN.
 Near the City Palace and Central Bus Station. Good value and popular with travellers.
Railway retiring rooms: Central Railway Station. Both double rooms (one a/c) and dormitory accommodation of a high standard.

WHERE TO EAT

Lalitha Mahal Palace: T. Narasipur Rd. Tel: 27650/26316.
Excellent evening buffet, as well as *à la carte* Indian and Continental food and a coffee shop.
Shilpashri Restaurant and Bar: Gandhi Square.
 Rooftop restaurant and bar above a liquor store, with an amazing menu of beers, of which they usually have about two! The food, Indian and continental, is cheap and cheerful, but reasonably good, and it is a good place to meet other travellers.
Kwality Restaurant: Dhavantri Rd.
 Like others in the chain. Good Indian (veg and non-veg), continental and Chinese food at reasonable prices.
Shanghai Restaurant: Sivarampet Rd.
 Good, reasonably priced Chinese food.
Para's Restaurant: Sayiji Rao Rd.
 South Indian, North Indian, Continental and Chinese food.
Bombay Indra Bhavan: Sayiji Rao Rd.
 Run by the same people as Para's. South Indian snacks and sweets.
Gun House Imperial: Bangalore Nilgiri Hill Rd.
 Indian food. Live music in the evenings.
Parklane Hotel: Curzon Park Rd.
 Outdoor restaurant specialising in "sizzlers".

HASSAN

A supremely uninteresting town, with only one major virtue. It is the nearest railway station to Belur, Halebid and Sravanabelagola, and in addition, has a reasonable selection of hotels, to make it a convenient centre from which to visit the three sights.

GETTING THERE AND AROUND

Hassan is on a metre guage **railway** line between Mysore and Arsikere. There are three passenger trains a day along the line, taking around 4½ hours to do the 115-kilometre journey from Mysore. Journey time to Arsikere is 1½ hours. From here, you can connect through to Jog Falls, Goa or Bangalore. There are also several trains a day from Mangalore. The **railway station** is 2 kilometres from the centre of town, on the Bangalore road. (Tel: 8222)

Hassan is also situated on the national highway between Mangalore and Bangalore, with a reasonable **road** connection through to Mysore. There are about 20 **buses** a day each from Bangalore and Mysore, as well as regular buses to Arsikere and Mangalore, and connections, via Hubli, to Goa. The **bus station** is in the centre of town.

There is a **tourist information office** on the Bangalore-Mangalore (BM) Road (Tel: 8862), but it's probably a waste of effort to go there. The **Cauvery Tourist Centre** on Race Course Road (Tel: 8026) is a local tour operator, who should be able to arrange a round tour of the local sights for you.

FACT FILE

WHERE TO STAY AND EAT

There are no luxury or upmarket hotels or restaurants.

Mid-range
Hotel Hassan Ashok: Bangalore-Mangalore Rd. Tel: 8731–37. In the town centre. Run by the ITDC, with all the main facilities, including a bar, shopping arcade, etc. Also has the best restaurant in town.

Hotel Amblee Palika: Race Course Rd. Tel: 7145/6/7. In the town centre. Relatively new, with good facilities, including bar, coffee shop, and exchange, as well as the **Malanika Restaurant**.

Cheap

Vaishnavi Lodging: just north of the bus station. Tel: 7413.

Hotel Lakshmi Prasanna: about 300 metres south of the bus station. Tel: 8391.

Also has a good, basic and very cheap restaurant, serving vegetarian *thalis*.

Satyaprakash Lodge: Bus Stand Rd. Tel: 8391.

The **Shanthala Restaurant** downstairs serves South Indian food.

For Chinese food, try the **Abiruchi Restaurant** near the Hotel Lakshmi Prasanna.

HALEBID

The capital of the Hoysala kings, Halebid was founded in the eleventh century, and known then as Dvarasaumudra. At one time a rich, powerful city, it was sacked in 1311 and 1327 by the troops of the Delhi Sultanate and abandoned soon afterwards. The name of the city was later changed to Halebid, which means "old capital". Today, it is a small, insignificant village, with a large temple.

GETTING THERE

There are 10 buses a day from Hassan 32 kilometres away, taking about an hour to do the journey, and several buses a day run between Halebid and Belur (17 kilometres), so you can do a round trip. Alternatively, you can hire a **private taxi** for the day at a reasonable cost, or take a **tour** (see under **Hassan**). Once there, everything is within walking distance.

DON'T MISS . . .

Hoysaleswara Temple

Work began on this, the largest of the Hoysala temples, in about 1121. It continued for 86 years, and while it produced some of the greatest carving of the period, for some reason, now lost, the temple was never completed, and still lacks its *sikhara* (spire). Set in well-tended lawns, it is typical of Hoysala design, a low, multi-celled temple set on a star-shaped plinth. A Nandi bull stands outside, while a passage connected the temple to the palace (which once stood on the nearby hillock). The friezes around the lower walls are of elephants, lions, horsemen, flowers, and swans or geese, as well as incidents from the *Mahabharata* and *Ramayana*, with images of Krishna, Shiva, Parvati and Ravana, amongst others. Above is a series of statues of the Hindu deities, carved with the same loving detail. Inside are a number of figures carved from polished blackstone, including an image of Queen Shantala Devi.

ALSO WORTH VISITING

Next to the Hoysaleswara temple is a small **Archaeological Museum**, with a fairly insignificant collection of carvings, coins etc. Open 10am-5pm, Saturday to Thursday. Entrance free.

There are around a dozen other temples in the area, of which the best preserved is the **Kedareswara temple**, just behind the Dvarasamudra tank. This is thought to have been the royal family's private chapel. There are also a number of Jain *bastihalli*, about 1 kilometre from the centre of the village.

FACT FILE

FOOD AND LODGING

KSTDC Tourist Cottages and **Bungalow**: in the grounds of the Inspection Bungalow. Tel: 24.
Simple, but clean, with fans, mosquito nets, and cooking facilities and restaurant.

BELUR

The earliest of the Hoysala capitals, this remained an important centre after the capital moved to Halebid and only lost its status after its destruction by the Delhi Sultanate in the early fourteenth century. Today, it is a small town.

GETTING THERE

Belur is 40 kilometres from Hassan, 16 kilometres from Halebid. There are around 20 **buses** a day from Hassan,

The Hoysalas

According to legend, the Hoysala name was conjured into being by an ascetic monk. Threatened by a tiger, he called out for help to a local tribesman named Sala. ("*Hoy, Sala*" means "Strike, Sala"). Sala slew the tiger, and took the cry as his family name. A man killing a tiger was also adopted as the family emblem and can be seen in many of the temples commissioned by the dynasty.

The family are said at first to have been simple bandits, who rose through their misdeeds to a position of power. The first of them to break away from the Ganga empire and form an independent kingdom was Nripakama, who ruled from 1006–46 AD. The greatest of the dynasty was the fifth king, Vishnuvardhana, who ruled from 1108–42. He is also known as Bittadeva, and is thought to have changed his name when he converted from Jainism to Vaishnavism under the influence of Ramanuja. The dynasty came to an end in 1310, with the defeat and death of King Ballala at the hands of the Delhi Sultanate.

While the Hoysalas were powerful kings who came to rule a large area of southern India, they are most famous as patrons of the arts. Poetry and music flourished at their courts, but greatest of all were the temples they commissioned. There were, in all, some 700 of these, of which around 80 survive today, although most are in an extremely bad state of repair. Squat, star-shaped buildings on a plinth, unlike anything else to be found in India, they are architecturally magnificent, but are best known for the carvings which literally cover every available inch of space. Carved from steatite, a type of blue-grey soapstone that is soft when first quarried but hardens on exposure to the atmosphere, the stone allowed the sculptors to devote extraordinary attention to detail, with filigree work so fine that the jewels of the dancing girls trembled in the breeze. Equally importantly today, as the stone hardened it preserved the detail. To the modern visitor it seems extraordinary to think that these magical works were created some 800 years ago.

taking about 1¹/₂ hours to do the journey, and a reasonable number between Belur and Halebid. It is also possible to hire a **private taxi** in Hassan at a reasonable rate. Once in Belur, everything is within easy walking distance.

DON'T MISS . . .

Channekeshava Temple

This is the only one of the major Hoysala temples still to be in use for worship, but non-Hindus are nevertheless encouraged to go inside. Building began in around 1117 AD under King Vishnuvardhana, who commissioned the temple in honour of his victory over the Cholas at Talkad in 1116. It was the first of the great Hoysala temples, designed by the architect, Jakanachari. Like the others, it is a multi-celled temple, built on a star-shaped plinth. The *sikhara* (tower) was destroyed in the early-fourteenth century during the Islamic invasions. The temple was dedicated to Vishnu, and at the entrance are shrines to the god in his various forms, together with images of his vehicle, the eagle Garuda, who also represents the heavens, and the serpent Naga, who represents the earth.

The friezes on the lower part of the wall include 650 elephants (representing stability), as well as lions, birds, animals, dancing figures, and a row of women both dancing and dressing. Above these are a series of magnificent carvings, mainly of women, each set in a filigreed bracket. There are 42 in all and each is different – one looks into her mirror; another talks to her pet parrot; one struggles half-naked to wrest her dress back from a monkey; one is wringing the water from her wet hair, each drop so tenderly carved that you expect it to fall; and still another has a scorpion crawling at her feet. There are also scenes from the epics.

Inside, the carvings are as exuberant and numerous as on the outside, with even the ceiling covered in a riot of delicate detail; each finely chiselled pillar unique in design. The Narasimha pillar in the centre of the hall could be turned.

A small space has been left blank to be carved, so the story goes, by anyone who feels they have the talent to complete the work. So far it remains bare.

Nearby, there are two lesser temples, the **Viranarayana temple** and the **Channigariaya temple**.

FACT FILE

FOOD AND LODGING

Hotel Mayura Velapuri: near the bus stand. Tel: 9. Run by the KSTDC. Simple, cheap and clean, with meals if you order in advance.

There are a number of small cafés and restaurants in the centre of the town.

SRAVANABELAGOLA

Although only a small village, with a population of around 4,000, **Sravanabelagola** is one of the most important pilgrimage sites in India for Jains, with particular importance for the *Digambara* (skyclad) sect. The name derives from two words, *Sravana*, meaning "naked ascetic" and *belagola*, meaning "white pond". Its history stretches back to the third century BC, when Chandragupta Maurya came here after renouncing his kingdom, accompanied by his guru, Jain Muni Bhadrabahu. It was he and his disciples who went on to convert many South Indians to Jainism.

GETTING THERE

The best way to get here is from Hassan, 36 kilometres away (see page 243). There are three **buses** a day from here, taking 1^1/2 hours to do the journey. There are also a number of buses from Arsikere (also taking 1^1/2 hrs), and direct buses through to Mysore and Bangalore.

There is a **tourist information office** at the foot of Indragirl Hill. Open 10am-1pm and 3–5.30pm daily. Remember that it is forbidden to wear or carry any animal products within Jain shrines, so even leather watch straps or camera cases should be left outside. You can leave your luggage with the tourist office if you need to.

An Arm for Art's Sake

Jakanachari was an architect and sculptor who, swept along by ambition, abandoned his wife and son and set off in search of fame and fortune. By and by, he arrived at the court of the Hoysala king, Vishnuvardhana, who, struck by his mastery of his craft, hired him to build the temple at Belur. The years passed, and the temple grew. Finally, with the sculpting of the great image of Ganesha, the work was finished. The statue was so beautiful that its fame spread far and wide and people from across the country came to take part in the ceremonies that would turn the cold stone into the personification of the god.

Just as the ritual was about to begin, however, a voice piped up from the crowd and a boy came forward. The statue was flawed, he claimed, and therefore unfit for worship. Jakanachari was appalled and challenged the boy to point out the imperfection, vowing to cut off his right arm should any be found. The boy took up a hammer and struck the navel of the god, which shattered to reveal a frog. The distraught artist had to keep his vow, and cut off his arm before the crowds. Thus this statue was the last work that the great artist ever created. And the boy? He turned out to be Jakanachari's longlost son!

DON'T MISS . . .

Statue of Gomateswara

This massive statue of Lord Bahubali stands on the summit of **Indragiri Hill**, visible from 15 kilometres away.

Bahubali was the son of the first Tirthankara who fought a ferocious battle against his brother, Bharata. On winning, however, he recognised the futility of his actions, gave his brother the kingdom and took up the life of an ascetic – thus gaining enlightenment.

The statue was commissioned between 980–983 AD by Chamundaraya, a general of the Ganga king Ramachalla, and built by the sculptor Aristanemi. Chamundaraya was also known as Gomata, and Gomateswara means "master of Gomata". It stands nearly 17 metres (57 foot) high and is the second largest statue in the world (the largest being the Egyptian colossus of Ramases II). Prince Bahubali is depicted naked, standing on a lotus, with vines twining around his body.

Legend has it that flowers rained down on the statue while its hands shone with radiance and gave off perfume.

Every 12 years, it is the focus for the *Mastakabhisheka* festival, at which time scaffolding is erected around the figure, and literally thousands of pilgrims come to annoint it with everything from water to ghee or coconut milk and even gold dust. The next is due to take place in 1994.

Small admission charge. 500 granite steps lead up the hill to the entrance of the sacred enclosure. Here you have to leave your shoes before tackling another 189 steps. Be prepared to sacrifice a pair of socks as the steps can get excruciatingly hot.

ALSO WORTH VISITING

There are several small shrines on the way up Indragiri Hill – the **Odeagal Basti, Brahmadeva Mandapa,** the **Akhanda Bagilu,** and the **Siddhara Basti.** The Brahmadeva Mandapa dates back to the tenth century AD, the others were all constructed in the twelfth century. In the courtyard surrounding the statue are a number of tombs.

On the smaller hill opposite, **Chandragiri Hill,** are some 100 memorials, to Jains who chose to die, dating from the seventh to ninth centuries, together with another 15 shrines. King Chandragupta is also buried here. The **Chandragupta Basti** is thought to have been commissioned by the emperor Ashoka, while the **Akkana Basti** is of Hoysala style.

The **Bhandari Basti,** in the centre of the village, is also of Hoysala construction, and has images of all 24 Tirthankaras.

FACT FILE

FOOD AND LODGING

Tourist Canteen and Rest House: Tel: 54.
Run by the Department of Tourism. Basic and cheap.
Shriyans Prasad Guest House
This is the pilgrim hostel, but it has double rooms as well as dormitory accommodation.

There are a number of small coffee shops and restaurants scattered round the village, but you won't find anything but the most basic food. Alternatively, stay in Hassan and take a picnic.

JOG FALLS

High up in the forests near the Karnataka coast, the **Jog Falls**, on the Sharavati River, are the highest in India. They drop, in total, a spectacular 253 metres. There are four distinct falls: the **Raja**, which drops vertically over the full height, into a 40 metre-deep pool; the noisy **Roarer**; the **Rocket**, which seems to be trying to take off, as the water shoots out over the cliff in an attempt to defy gravity; and the gentler **Rani** (once known as the Dame Blanche or White Lady) which tumbles over the rocks in a cascade of foam.

The flow varies dramatically with the seasonal rains. The air around the falls is always damp with spray and alive with rainbows, but at the height of the monsoon, the spray is so thick that you can hardly see a thing, while the trees and buildings drip green with mildew and the damp seeps deep into your bones. By the New Year, however, the flow is already dwindling and the falls are at less than their impressive best. If possible, choose your timing carefully to coincide with the end of the monsoon.

GETTING THERE

Even by Indian standards, the Falls are remote, and there is absolutely no chance of being able to do a quick detour.

The nearest **railway station** is at Talguppa, at the end of a branch line a few kilometres from the falls. This is served by a couple of passenger trains a day from Birur, one of which continues through to Hassan, Arsikere and Bangalore, while one coach branches off to Mysore.

There is a long **bus** ride from Karwar (7 hours) each day, returning the following morning, or you can take a local bus from Sagar, 30 kilometres to the south-east.

Alternatively, if there are several of you and you are in a hurry, hire a **taxi** for the day from Hassan, 59 kilometre to the west.

FACT FILE

FOOD AND LODGING
Try not to stay here. The best accommodation on offer is the PWD Inspection Bungalows, but these are permanently booked up and very difficult to get into. If you wish to try, contact the District Commissioner's Office at Shimoga, 16 kilometre away. Other alternatives include the Hotel Woodland, and the state-run Jog Falls Guest House, both of which seem to come with teeming resident insect life, in bed and out. The Woodland has the only restaurant.

BANDIPUR AND NAGARAHOLE NATIONAL PARKS

Although officially two separate parks, these are in fact both part of one massive tract of land, together with Mudumalai in Tamil Nadu and Wynad in Kerala. Formed around the core of the Maharajah of Mysore's former hunting preserves, together they cover an area of more than 1,500 square kilometre (580 square miles). Of this, one-third is designated wilderness area and all human activity, including timber felling and tourism, is forbidden.

Bandipur covers 865 square kilometres (333 square miles) along the southern border of Karnataka, on the approaches to the Nilgiri Hills. This is more open landscape than much of that found at Nagarahole, slightly to the north, which is mainly covered by thick forest, including many valuable timber trees such as teak and rosewood, as well as giant bamboo. Bandipur was the first park in South India to be created by the Project Tiger scheme. However, the more forested Nagarahole is far more popular with the tigers themselves. It is unlikely however that you will get to see one even here.

What you should be able to find is elephants. Together, these parks hold the greatest concentration of wild elephants left in India, with more than 1,000 roaming the area. You could also see *gaur* (wild oxen), four species of deer including the *sambar, chital, muntjac* and *chevrotain* or mouse deer; the four-horned antelope; wild pigs, pangolins and

---

Project Tiger

The tiger is, without doubt, one of the most romantic creatures in the world. It is also one of the rarest. Walk into any palace or hunting lodge in India and it is easy to see why. In some, the walls are literally festooned with snarling heads and the floors awash with stripy skins. At the turn of the century, there were estimated to be some 40,000 in the country (there is no record of how many had already been shot out in the preceding 200 years). By the 1960s, the population was down to about 1,800, and two of the six species in the world were already extinct. An international appeal was set up to try and rescue the remainder. The result, in India, was Project Tiger, which began in 1972.

Tiger hunting was finally abolished and central government put up 50% of the finance to help the state governments set aside land for tiger sanctuaries. India now has 300 national parks, covering some 12% of the country's total land. Of these, 15 are official Project Tiger reserves. There has been a degree of success. Tiger numbers in the country are up to around 5,000, and as a bonus, a number of other endangered species, including elephants and rhinos, have also begun to multiply again. But there are still problems.

---

porcupines; and two species of monkey, the Hanuman langur and the macaque. There are also a number of predators including leopards, wild dogs, hyenas, jackals, civets and a variety of other smaller cats. These are however mainly nocturnal and very shy, so sighting them is extremely difficult.

Each of the two parks has a game viewing centre, and a third, **Karapura**, stands on the boundary between them. Bandipur is the most accessible, so is the best to visit during the monsoon, but during the dry season you are most likely to get good game viewing at Nagarahole, as the Bandipur animals all migrate into the wetter areas in nearby parks.

GETTING THERE

The nearest rail head and jumping off point for all three areas is Mysore, from where you will have to continue by bus or taxi, if you're feeling flush.

India's national parks are not people-free, but are scattered by villages and smallholdings. As the human population continues to grow, there is pressure to clear more land for agriculture, and to cut more wood for fuel. At the turn of the century, 40% of the sub-continent was forested; now trees cover less than 7% of the land. Tigers are solitary creatures and take up a lot of space. A single adult male needs a territory of around 25 square miles, and he will share that with only 3 to 5 females, all of which have their own sub-territory. As the squeeze on the forests continues, a few tigers have taken to raiding on the edge of the fields and the old spectre of man-eaters is raising its head again, amidst totally overblown reporting and mass hysteria. It seems that the only way to solve the problem completely would be to move out all the people, but that would mean displacing literally millions who have no source of support other than their tiny patches of land. Everyone is trying their best, but, as with everything in India, the solution seems to slip further away with every week that passes.

In the south, the largest area of national park is based on the old Maharajah of Mysore hunting preserves round Bandipur and Nagarhole in Karnataka, Mudumulai, just across the border, and even stretching into Kerala. Although there are tigers here, however, you will be lucky to see any. Not only are they rare and solitary, but they are nocturnal, shy and extremely well camouflaged.

Bandipur

The main road from Mysore to Ooty runs right through the park, so any of the many buses that do the journey each day will get you there. The 80 kilometre journey takes 2 to 3 hours.

Nagarahole

Two buses a day run here from Mysore. The journey takes about three hours. You must be there by 6pm as the road through the park is closed at night.

Karapura

Buses between Mysore and Manandawadi stop here. There are several extremely slow buses a day, and the journey can take up to 4 hours. If you are heading for the Kabini Lodge, you will have a 2-kilometre walk from the bus stop.

GETTING AROUND

All three areas offer guided game viewing drives in jeeps or vans. At Bandipur you can go out for hour-long rides on an elephant. There are boats for hire at Bandipur, or coracle (small buffalo-hide boats) trips at Karapura, where you can also go on walking trips, as long as you have permission and take a game guard with you. All three have a number of hides and viewing platforms. Game viewing trips are normally between 6–9am and 4.30–6.30pm.

FACTFILE

FOOD AND LODGING

Accommodation is limited in all three places, and as they are also popular with Indian tourists, advance booking is probably sensible.

Bandipur

Forest Lodges: A number of comfortable bungalows, together with a few more upmarket guest houses with baths, and a couple of 12-bed dormitories. Booking and information via the Assistant Director, Bandipur National Park (Tel: 21); Forest Officer, Forest Dept, Woodyard, Ashokpuram, Mysore; Field Director, Project Tiger, Government House Complex, Mysore (Tel: 20901).

Nagarahole

Forest Lodges: Three fairly simple government-run lodges. Booking and information: Range Forest Officer, Nagarahole National Park (Tel: Kutta 21); Chief Wildlife Warden, Aranya Bhavan, 18th Cross, Malleswaram, Bangalore (Tel: 341 993); Forest Officer, Forest Dept, Woodyard, Ashokpuram, Mysore.

Karapura

Kabini River Lodges: Distinctly upmarket in comparison to the other two, converted from the former Maharajah's Hunting Lodge and Viceroy's Bungalow. Westerners are charged more than Indians, but prices include full board, all game viewing trips and evening entertainment. Booking: Jungle Lodges and Resorts, 348/9 Brooklands, 13th Main, Rajmahal Vilas Extension, Bangalore. Tel: 362 820.

KERALA

Crossing the border into Kerala, it would be easy to feel that you were entering a completely different country. Kerala just does not act the same way as the rest of India.

According to legend, Kerala was a gift from the gods. Parasuma (an incarnation of Vishnu) threw his battle axe into the sea as a penance for all the bloodshed he had caused in his warlike life. Where it struck, the sea parted and the land rose to form the state. There seems to be a topographical foundation to the legend. The narrow strip of intensely fertile and intensively cultivated land that is the lifeblood of Kerala is still gradually widening as the mountains heave themselves up from the seabed.

Perhaps more than in any other area of South India, geography has had a profound influence on the culture of this long, skinny state. To the west, it is bordered by the sea, with a coastline of around 580 km and several superb, natural harbours. To the east, the boundary is formed by the formidable bulk of the Western Ghats, which effectively blocked much of the rampant empire-building and war mongering which turned most of the rest of the sub-continent into a cultural melting pot.

For over 1,000 years the area was ruled by the Chera dynasty, with occasional interruptions by the Cholas and Pandiyans. Some say that the name Kerala derives from Chera, others that it comes from the word *kera*, meaning 'crocodile'. Little is known about the Cheras in comparison with other great dynasties of the same era, partly because they did not have the same fascination with architecture as those to the north and east, partly because much of their building was in wood and has long since disappeared.

Like other Hindu peoples, Keralan society was divided into three main castes. The *Nambudiris* (Brahmans) were the priests. They achieved a far greater stranglehold on society than in almost any other area, partly, it is claimed, because any land taken in battle was promptly declared sacred and

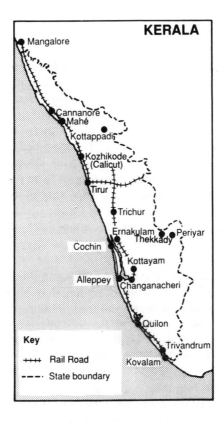

handed over to their keeping! The result today is that in Kerala, almost none of the temples are open to non-Hindus, and in the most important, even Hindus have to dress in plain white *dhotis* before entering the inner sanctuary.

The warrior class were known here as *Nairs*. Hereditary vassals of the rulers, they lived by a strict, military code of conduct similar in some ways to that of the Japanese

Samurais. Possibly because so many of the men were killed in battle, Nair inheritance law was matriarchal. The head of the family, the *Karnavar*, was male, but the family tree was traced back through the female line. All property and earnings belonging to the extended family were held in a common pot. By tradition, the ruler, or head of the family never married (at least officially), and was succeeded by his eldest sister's eldest son. This system has pretty much fallen to pieces now, but the women here do still have a level of freedom, independence and power far beyond that common in Hindu society.

The cultivators, known as *Thiyas* or *Ezhavas*, are thought by some to have come from Sri Lanka, bringing with them the coconut palm which is, even today, the mainstay of Keralan life.

From the late-tenth century, the Chola invasions began to gather pace and ferocity and under the onslaught the kingdom collapsed. In its place grew up three small kingdoms, Travancore (Venadu) in the south, Cochin in the centre, and Calicut (Kolattiri) to the north. The Zamorin ('Lord of the Sea') of Calicut slowly drew into a position of supremacy, but the three continued to battle it out between themselves until the arrival in strength of the Europeans in the seventeenth century.

Largely ignored by India, Kerala has traditionally looked to the sea. For around 3,000 years, trading ships have found their way down to this fertile coast to trade in ivory, pearls, timber and, most importantly, spices. Pepper, cardamom, cinnamon, ginger and cloves drew traders from across the world. The Egyptians, Phoenicians, Chinese, Romans and Arabs all came and made their mark on local culture.

When the Portuguese arrived in the fifteenth century, they were astonished to find a flourishing Christian church. Christianity in the region dates back to the arrival of the Apostle Thomas (Doubting Thomas) who landed in Cranganore in 52 AD. A monument still marks the spot where he is meant to have docked, while the local church, which supposedly dates back to the fourth century, contains a relic of the saint. The Romans built a temple to Augustus on the coast in the first century AD (no longer in existence), and the Chinese left behind their picturesque fishing nets and a great deal of porcelain, fragments of which can still be found on some of the beaches. Even the Jews arrived and settled in Cochin, forming themselves into an influential trading community. And while Islam entered North India with a sword, and battled its way south in a sea of blood, here it came first – and peaceably, arriving with Arab traders in the mid-seventh century. The mosque at Cranganore claims, with little justification, to date back to 664 and to be the oldest in India. Astonishingly, all these different religious groups, at daggers drawn elsewhere, lived side by side in Kerala, temples, synagogues, churches and mosques all flourishing in harmony.

The Portuguese were the first Europeans to arrive, when Vasco da Gama, at the head of three ships and 150 men, made his historic voyage to discover the sea route to India. He landed at Calicut in 1498, and the following year wrestled trading permits from the reluctant Zamorin. Portugal set up trading posts at various points along the coast, but the relationship never eased, as the Zamorin was tradition- ally dependent on the Arab traders for his wealth and the Portuguese were hell-bent on ridding the area of all Arab influence. In the early seventeenth century, the Dutch also arrived, and the Zamorin, seeing his opportunity to get rid of the Portuguese, granted them full trading rights in 1614. The following year saw the arrival of the British East India Company, who were also granted trading rights. Finally, the French pitched up, and gained themselves a toehold at Mahé. Control of the sea routes was effectively out of Indian hands as the European powers battled it out between themselves.

Over the next century, there was a free-for-all on land and at sea. The Raja of Cochin dealt with the Dutch, the Raja of Travancore looked to the British, while the Zamorin of Calicut went reluctantly back to the Portuguese. Slowly, the British gained supremacy. Meantime, Hyder Ali and Tipu Sultan began empire-building in Mysore and in 1766, Tipu Sultan crossed the Western Ghats in a bloody march south along the Malabar coast. For a while, all three kingdoms were sucked into his empire and the rulers of all three, for once united by a common enemy, looked to the British to relieve them. They drove him from the territory in 1789, and in 1792, after another defeat, Lord Cornwallis forced him to sign the Treaty of Srirangapatnam, surrendering Calicut to the British, while Travancore and Cochin were returned to their rulers, but as British puppets.

Meantime, the religious harmony which had existed for so long began to crumble. The Portuguese arrived with the Roman Catholic church, missionaries and the Inquisition, to convert, forcibly if necessary, not only the Hindus, Jews and Muslims, but the local Christians who had, until now, adhered to the Syrian tradition. They had little luck and it led to riots when they arrested the Syrian Patriarch and tried to enforce the Latin Mass. Next came Protestantism with the Dutch and British. By the late-eighteenth century, it had all settled down again into an uneasy truce under British rule, but in an infinitely more complex web of sects.

MODERN KERALA

The three kingdoms were finally joined into one state only in 1956 when borders were rearranged along linguistic lines. The local language is Malayalam, an early off-shoot of Tamil. It is one of the smallest states in the country, with an area of 38,855 square kilometre, but with a population of around 30 million, it is also one of the most densely populated.

About 20% of the population is Christian, with five separate sects – the Church of India (Anglican), Roman Catholics, the Nestorian Church, the Orthodox Syrian Church and the Mathoma Syrian Church. Another 20% is Muslim, and the remaining 60% Hindu. The Jewish colony has recently dwindled to around 30 elderly people, and there are tiny numbers of Jains and Buddhists.

Politically, it is still fascinating. In 1957, the state became the first place in the world to elect a Communist government in free elections. They have been in and out of power ever since. It is perhaps about the only place in the world where you can see the hammer and sickle flying happily from the roof of a church.

The economy has diversified now, although it is mainly agricultural. Timber and spices in particular are still important, but the coconut has taken its place as a cash crop, with copra being produced from the fruit, coir from the fibre, and furniture from the wood – along with its importance in the local diet. Coffee and rubber have both become major earners, together with the *arecanut* (*betel* nut), while the backwater area to the south of Cochin is laid out in seemingly endless rice paddies. Over the last 20 or so years, Kerala has also relied heavily on money coming in from abroad. Over half the Indians working in the Gulf were from this tiny state, and their abrupt return home in the months leading up to the Gulf War not only meant that there were a couple of hundred thousand more people to house and feed, but a massive dent was created in the local economy, which was none too strong in the first place.

In spite of its shaky finances, however, it is surprisingly successful in social welfare terms. There are few beggars in the state, which gives an impression of being prosperous, clean and tidy. The literacy rate is about 70% (around double the national average), and instead of the normal gaggles of ragged children, you will be more likely to see them neatly dressed in smart school uniforms. Keralans read about three times as many newspapers as the rest of the country, and are supplying an increasing number of its intellectuals.

To tourists who have battled their way south through massive cities and endless temples, it is a haven of peace. There are no huge cities, just an almost seamless line of towns and villages stretching along the coastal strip. As most hide under a dense green canopy of forest and palms, the misleading impression is of an almost entirely rural society. There are few major monuments of any sort and, as most of the temples won't let non-Hindus in, there is little point in trying to keep up the culture quotient. Almost all tourism is in the southern half of the state. Neither **Cranganore** (now called Kodungallore) nor **Calicut** (which, after donating its name to calico, changed it to Kozikhode) has much to draw the tourist, today. **Cochin** is now the state's largest city, but even this is relatively small in Indian terms. To the south, **Kovalam** has one of the most beautiful beaches in the world (now, tragically, under threat, courtesy of the planners). Inland, **Periyar** is a famous and popular national park with a remarkable shortage of visible animals. In spite of it all, almost everyone who visits the state falls deeply in love with it, many preferring it to any other in India.

COCHIN-ERNAKULUM

A tiny, independent state, then separate principality under British protection, Cochin only reverted to the status of an ordinary city in 1956. Built on a series of small islands, throughout its history it has relied on its harbour for its wealth, gathering in spices not only from the Indian hinterland, but acting as an entrepot for the spice trade from the East Indies.

Today the city has about 900,000 inhabitants all told, although it is officially two separate cities, the island Cochin with about 700,000 people and mainland Ernakulum, with about 200,000. In practice, however, the two have long since merged and Ernakulum is a suburb in all but name.

Cochin is still one of the busiest commercial ports in South India, and is also the Southern Command Headquarters of the Indian Navy. It also still has a remarkably polyglot local community. As a result, it has an air of cosmopolitan sophistication rarely found outside Bombay or Delhi. Even bars are relatively plentiful, although they are still not quite happy about serving women indoors. I was hustled out into the garden where I had a beer and an hour-long battle with some of the most determined, ravenous and plentiful mosquitoes it has ever been my misfortune to meet. These are one of the great drawbacks of the city. Others are its open drains (one friend fell in – not a fate to be wished on anyone), the resultant powerful odour, and the sailors, who have learned Western-style groping all too well!

Its plus points, however, far outweigh these inconveniences. It has a relaxed, friendly atmosphere, and some fascinating sights, while the old town is a maze of tiny, pretty streets, good for strolling and shopping. There are plenty of hotels and good facilities if you need to have a break from business. The harbour is a source of constant fascination, with an endless stream of traffic, from fishing boats to ferries, destroyers and merchant ships prowling the waters. It also has some of the best food in India.

GETTING THERE

Cochin is well served by **air**. Indian Airlines have two flights a day to Bombay, and daily flights to Delhi, Goa, Trivandrum, Madras, and four a week to Bangalore. Vayudoot have six flights a week each to Madras and Agatti, while Air Asiatic flies to Kodikhoze and Bombay. The airport is at the south end of Willingdon Island.

After the delights of the metre guage system in Karnataka, Cochin, at the junction of two broad guage lines, is a positive delight. The coast **railway** leads north to Mangalore, and south to Kanyakumari (and from there, right round the coast to Madras, and eventually, Calcutta (this is an extremely long way). The inland route heads first for Coimbatore, where it splits. One branch heads for for Madras, but with a branch up to Bangalore, and from there, all points north. The other crosses to Tiruchirapalli and Madurai and eventually meets up with the coastal railway again.

The result is that there are superb train connections, with daily express services to Trivandrum, Madras, Delhi, Bombay, and Mangalore, as well as less frequent express services to a host of other destinations, and regular passenger trains to most towns and cities nearby, including Quilon, Alleppey, and Kotayyam.

There are three stations all told. The **Cochin Harbour Station** on Willingdon Island is the official end of the line, but while this carries a heavy load of freight traffic, relatively few passenger trains actually come this far (Tel: 6050). The best to use is **Ernakulum Junction**, in the centre of Ernakulum. All the express trains (including those from Cochin Harbour) stop here, and it is easy to find your way across the city from the station. The station does have a few retiring rooms, but does not have a tourist counter or tourist quota, so, unless you have made your booking in advance, be prepared for some queuing (Tel: 353 100). **Ernakulum Town Station** is small, insignificant, and should be ignored unless you are looking for one of the local trains that runs from here (Tel: 353 920).

For **road** travel, Cochin is situated on the national highway which leads south to Trivandrum and north to Bombay. Via Trichur, it also connects to national highways to Bangalore and Madras.

There are plentiful **bus** services. There are four buses a day to Madurai, three to Calicut, and daily services to Bangalore, Madras, Bombay and Kanyakumari. Over 12 express buses go to Alleppey, Quilon, Kotayyam and Trivandrum each day. There are also regular services to Thekkady, Munnar, Palghat, Pondicherry, Erode, Tuticorin and Velankanni. It is also possible to pick up express services that have originated elsewhere. These all stop in Ernakulum for a break and will take you if there is a spare seat, but you cannot book in advance.

The **Ernakulum Bus Station** is beside the railway line, just north of Ernakulum Junction Railway Station. It is reasonably efficient and organised, and does have signs in English. You can make bookings up to five days in advance (Tel: 352 033).

A regular monthly **Time Table** of all buses, trains and flights is published by a local company, and is available from both the bus and train stations, as well as at most bookshops and some hotels.

GETTING AROUND

There is a pretty good **local bus** network across the city, connecting bus station, railway station, and airport with all the main centres in Mattancherry, Willingdon Island and Ernakulum. There is also a plentiful supply of **auto-rickshaws**, all miraculously with broken meters. There are also ordinary **taxis** and **tourist taxis**. Set a price for all of them before you set out. If you take any of them over to the islands, be prepared for them to charge you double, to cover the return journey as well.

Much more fun and more convenient for travel between the islands are the **ferries**. There is a regular network connecting all the islands. Each route has at least 30 crossings a day. They are also cheap, and give a great tour of the harbour en route. They stop between 9 and 10pm, so after this you will need to get a bus or hire a rickshaw or taxi.

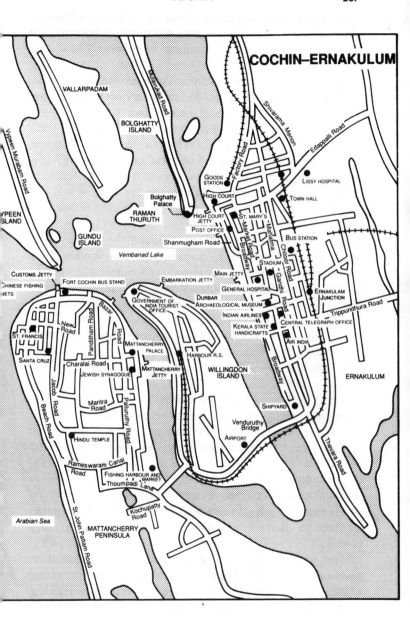

The ferry stops are clearly marked. There are two on Mattancherry – **Customs** in Fort Cochin to the north, and **Mattancherry** to the east (opposite Willingdon Island). On Willingdon Island there are three – **Terminus** to the west (opposite Mattancherry), an unnamed stop beside the **Malabar Hotel and tourist office**, and **Embarkation** in the north-east. There is one (unnamed) at the south end of **Vypeen Island**, and one (unnamed) beside the **Bolghatty Palace Hotel** at the south end of Bolghatty Island. There are three main stops in Ernakulum – **High Court Jetty** and **Sea Lord Jetty** in the north, and **Main Jetty** in the centre.

The most useful services include:

Main Jetty (Ernakulum) to Mattancherry via Customs (Fort Cochin) and Terminus (Willingdon Island);
Main Jetty (Ernakulum) to Vypeen Island via Embarkation (Willingdon Island);
Sea Lord Jetty (Ernakulum) to Vypeen Island;
Customs (Fort Cochin) to Malabar Hotel (Willingdon Island);
Customs (Fort Cochin) to Vypeen Island;
High Court Jetty (Ernakulum) to Bolghatty Island.

The KSTC runs excellent half-day **tours** of Cochin, taking in all the major sights, as well as the coir factory on Gundu Island. There are two a day, travel is by boat, and they leave from Sea Lord Jetty, Shanmughan Road, in northern Ernakulum. Booking from the Tourist Reception Centre next to the jetty (Tel: 353 234) or from the Bolghatty Palace Hotel.

GETTING YOUR BEARINGS

Mattancherry Peninsula to the south of the city curves northwards to create the original harbour. The northern end of the peninsula is known as **Fort Cochin**. This is the oldest part of the city, and has most of the tourist sights and most attractive buildings. The navy headquarters and dockyards are on the western edge of the peninsula and are forbidden to visitors.

The more modern **Ernakulum**, on the mainland, has the bus and railway stations, and most the airline offices, banks, etc, as well as most of the cheaper hotels.

Between the two is the massive **Willingdon Island,** which was created in the 1920s when the harbour channels were dredged to allow in larger ships. Apart from the tourist office and Malabar Hotel in the north, this is mainly taken up by the airport in the south, the railway and freight station, customs clearing houses and dockyards. Bridges in the south connect Mattancherry, Willingdon Island, and Ernakulum.

To the north are several other islands. The long thin **Bolghatty Island** is the closest to the mainland. Next come **Vallarpadam** and **Raman Thuruth,** which are not really part of the city and are not worth visiting. Little **Gundu Island** has a coir factory, but can only be visited on a KTDC tour. Finally, to the west, is the larger **Vypeen Island** (in practice, another peninsula, curving south to enclose the bay).

The main tourist office is on Willingdon Island, but there are also **two tourist information centres** in Ernakulum.

DON'T MISS . . .

Fort Cochin

At the northern tip of Mattancherry is the heart of the old city. The fort itself was built by the Portuguese in 1503, but was taken from them by the Dutch in 1633, and the English moved in officially from 1792. The fort itself no longer exists, but the area's charming, winding streets show all its many influences, as Dutch gables cluster next to Portuguese villas and English country cottages. The area also includes most of the interesting sights in the city. All are within walking distance for the keen, and there are plenty of buses for the less enthusiastic. There are a few good shops, but little in the way of hotels and restaurants.

Jewtown and Synagogue

Near Mattancherry Jetty, on the east side of Mattancherry. Once settled in Cochin, the white Jews huddled together in a small area, known for centuries as **Jewtown.** The narrow streets with their multi-coloured houses, Jewish street and house names, attractive shops and bustling spice warehouses, are worth lingering over.

The focus, however, must be the **Synagogue.** The earliest known synagogue was built in Kochangadi in 1344. This has long since vanished, but a stone slab with a Hebrew inscription was moved to the present site and has been incorporated into the wall of the courtyard. The first synagogue on the present site was built in 1568. This was destroyed by the Portuguese in 1662. The current building, replacing it, dates from 1664. A **Clock Tower**, built by pepper trader, Ezekiel Rahabi, in the eighteenth century dominates the lane leading towards it.

Inside, the Synagogue is a surprising riot of colour. The floor is laid out with blue and white, hand-painted, willow pattern tiles, each one different. These come from Canton in China and were also installed by Ezekiel Rahabi. There are two pulpits, one of which can be used by women, the walls are covered by brocade hangings and the ceiling is hung with huge, oil-burning chandeliers. The Old Testament Scrolls are kept in ornate silver cylinders with gold crowns. These are normally on display only during festivals, but you can get to see them if you ask, together with the copper land grants.

The synagogue's guardian speaks good English and is happy to talk and show you round. Open 10am-midday, 3–5pm. Closed Saturday and Jewish holidays. Small admission charge.

Mattancherry (Dutch) Palace

Just north of the Synagogue, next to Mattancherry Jetty. Originally built by the Portuguese in 1557, and given to Raja Veera Kerala Varma of Cochin (1537–61) in exchange for trading rights, this is a classic example of Keralan *nalukettu* architecture. The name means "four buildings", but in practice the style is a low (two-storey) rectangular building, surrounding a central courtyard. A Hindu temple dedicated to Bhagavati stands in the courtyard. The building got the name "Dutch Palace" in 1663, when the Dutch, having ousted the Portuguese, renovated it, replacing the Portuguese roof with a solid Dutch design. Neither power ever lived here.

On the first floor, the **Coronation Hall** is where the Rajas of Cochin were traditionally crowned. It now houses a collection of portraits of the Rajas, and royal memorabilia, from clothes and turbans to furniture and palanquins. The surrounding rooms, and the women's quarters downstairs,

The Cochin Jews

Two separate waves of Jews have emigrated to and settled in Kerala. The first, known locally as "black Jews", are said to have fled to Cranganore from Nebuchadnezzar in 587 BC. Whatever the truth of this, they were a settled and thriving community by the first century AD. The second group, the "white Jews", arrived in about 1,000 AD.

In the Cochin synagogue today there are a number of copper plates which tell of a land grant to the Jewish settlers by King Bhaskara Ravi Varma I, who lived from 962–1020. The grant, to one Joseph Rabban, gave him a village, Anjuvannam, near Cranganore, along with permission to use a palanquin and parasol, normally only granted to monarchy.

The "black jews" had, by this time, mainly intermarried with the local Hindu population, but the "white Jews" remained a close-knit community, in Cranganore, making their living as spice dealers. Shortly after the arrival of the Portuguese in the sixteenth century, however, a row blew up between the Jews and the Arabs about the quality of the pepper the Arabs were selling them. Whipped up by Portuguese anti-Jewish feeling, the Arabs massacred a number of Jews, and the rest fled south to seek protection from the Raja of Cochin. Here, they settled a small area on Mattancherry Island, which soon came to be known as **Jewtown**, from where they rebuilt their wealth and status as traders.

The creation of the state of Israel in 1948 spelt the end for this ancient, isolated community. Over the next few decades all the younger generation emigrated. Today, all that remains of the famous Cochin Jews is a group of fewer than 30 old people. They no longer have a rabbi, and as there are no children, it is only a matter of time before the synagogue becomes a museum and only the name Jewtown Road is left to mark their passing.

house a series of magnificent murals, dating from the late sixteenth to nineteenth centuries. Most refer to scenes from the *Ramayana* and the *Puranas*, but a few, downstairs, have less religious significance, and if not downright erotic are extremely sensual.

The **Papal Bull of Alexander Borgia**, which divided the world in two, giving the western hemisphere to Spain and the eastern hemisphere to Portugal, was read here.

Open 9am-5pm, except Fridays. Admission charge. No flash photography, and it is dark, so if you want to try, take fast film and a tripod.

Chinese Fishing Nets

North end of Mattancherry, near Customs Jetty. Introduced, according to some, by traders from the court of Kublai Khan, these cantilevered nets certainly hail from China. Chinese traders visited the area over several centuries, and in fact set up their own trading post near Calicut.

It takes several men to work one of these vast permanent structures, which are lowered into the water, then hauled up again between 15 and 30 minutes later, with a mixed haul of anything foolish enough to have swum in. The catch is separated into baskets in the area behind, which also acts as an unofficial fish market.

These are not the only Chinese fishing nets around, but almost all the others are in backwater areas and difficult to see, particularly from close to. For the visitor, these elegant nets have become a symbol of Cochin, for few can resist photographing them again and again. If possible, be there at sunset, when the silhouette against a flaming sky is truly extraordinary.

St Francis Church

North-east corner of Mattancherry (follow the coast road around from the Chinese nets). Originally a wooden church dedicated to San Antonio, this was built by Portuguese friars who arrived here with Admiral Albuquerque in 1503. It is the oldest European church in India. The current larger but somewhat faded building was erected in the mid-sixteenth century (some say in 1546, but the earliest inscription dates from 1564).

Vasco da Gama returned to Cochin as the Portuguese Viceroy in 1510, and died here in 1524. He was buried in the church, and although his body was taken to Lisbon 14 years later, his tombstone remains.

The Dutch converted the church to Protestantism in 1663, and the British changed it again, to Anglicanism, in 1795. It now belongs to the Church of South India.

The massive *punkah*, a ceiling fan worked by men hauling on its ropes, is still used during services.

Basilica of Santa Cruz
Just to the south of St Francis Church. Built in 1557, this is less important than St Francis, but is worth a look for its gaudy interior. A profusion of painting in bright colours includes the stations of the cross on the ceiling, mock marbling and garlands of flowers.

Kathakali dancers
One of the most dramatic and famous forms of Indian dance (see box), there are several places in Ernakulum which offer regular displays. Check with the Tourist Office for times and details, but make sure you get to a performance.

Kathakali

The **Kathakali dancers** of Kerala are amongst the most famous in India. Their dance is pure drama, stylised story-telling of the deeds of gods and men. Dance has always been a traditional form of Hindu worship and the line between theatre and religion is blurred. The Kathakali dance grew from the ancient Sanskrit drama, the *Kudiyattam*, which is still occasionally performed in some of the Keralan temples. Its inspiration comes both from great religious epics such as the *Ramayana* and from folk tales and village life. It also draws on the *kalarippayattu*, the martial arts tradition of the Keralan Nair population and the *theyyam* tribal dance of northern Kerala. The setting is simple, the music is provided by drums, cymbals and gongs, while the singers double as narrators.

In contrast, the costumes are magnificent. The all-male dancers wear rich, elaborate skirted costumes, together with vast headdresses and masklike make-up. The entire costume is symbolic. By tradition, for example, the "baddy" always sports a bushy red beard. The eyes are reddened by placing a seed under the lids. There are some three dozen dances in the repertoire. The movements are slight, a tradition that probably grew at least partly from the immense weight of the costumes. There are 24 main movements, *mudras*, to denote the major emotions, and literally hundreds of smaller, subtle gestures, each one, from the twitch of an eyebrow to the curl of a lip, with a specific meaning. The movements of the fingers are literally used like an alphabet. To those who can understand, the subtle inflections can be read as clearly as a page of print. However, it takes up to 20 years to learn them! Dancers generally start training at the age of five or six.

The training academy for this and other traditional dances, the **Kerala Kalamandalam**, is in Cheruthuruthi, about 3 km from Shoranur railway junction (about 34 kilometres from Trichur). It is possible to visit the centre and watch the boys being put through their paces. Sessions from 4.30am to 6.30, 8.30am-midday, and 3.30pm–5.30 pm, Monday to Friday (closed April and May). Entrance free. As there is little else to attract visitors to this rather out of the way location, however, it is probably better to go to one of the regular displays in and around Cochin and Trivandrum. The best exhibitions allow the audience to watch the dancers making up and give a short explanation both of the dance tradition and of each story before they dance it. Whatever you do, don't miss it.

Cochin Cultural Centre: 1521 Sangamom, Manniath Road, (Tel: 353 732). Plus performances in the Durbar Hall Grounds, Durbar Hall Road, (Tel: 367866).
India Foundation: 111 Kalathi Parambil Lane, off Chittor Rd (Tel: 369 471).
Art Kerala: Menon & Krishnan Annexe, Valanja.

ALSO WORTH VISITING

Bolghatty Palace
At the south end of Bolghatty Island. Built by the Dutch in 1744, this became the British residency in 1799. Crumbling and atmospheric. Now run as a hotel by the KSTC (see under **Where to Stay**).

Parishath Thamburan Museum
Durbar Hall Road, Ernakulum (Tel: 369 047). Near Ernakulum Junction station. Also known as the Cochin Museum and the Durbar Museum, this is the Old Durbar Hall, a typical example of Keralan architecture. The collection contains the usual mix of coins, sculptures, and some nineteenth-century oil paintings as well as memorabilia of the Cochin royal family.
Open 9.30am-midday 3–5.30pm, Tuesday to Sunday. Entrance free.

Museum of Kerala History and its Makers
Edapally, Cochin. The main event is a one-hour *son et lumière* which uses models to tell the story of Cochin, starting in the Neolithic period and finding its way to the present via the Romans, St Thomas, the Jews, Vasco da Gama et al. Open 10am-4pm, Tuesday to Sunday. Small admission charge.

Hill Palace Museum
Tripunithura. Small, meandering collection of paintings, carvings, arms, beds and royal left-overs. Open 9am-5pm, Tuesday to Sunday. Small admission charge.

FACT FILE

AIRLINES

Air India: MG Rd, Ernakulam. Tel: 352 465.
Indian Airlines: Durbar Hall Rd, Ernakulam. Tel: 352 065. Airport Tel: 6486/6027.
Air France: Kurusupally Rd, Ernakulam. Tel: 361 702.
British Airways: c/o TT Travels, MG Rd, Ernakulam. Tel: 361 753.
KLM, Cathay Pacific and Garuda Airlines: c/o Spencer and Co, Travel Division, MG Rd, Ernakulam. Tel: 369 165.
Pan Am: c/o Ind Am Travels, International Hotel, MG Rd, Ernakulam. Tel: 353 707.
Singapore Airlines and Swissair: c/o Aviation Travels, MG Rd, Ernakulam. Tel: 367 911/ 352 380.

BANKS

Allahaband Bank (Tel: 351 267), **Andhra Bank** (Tel: 355 427), **Bank of Baroda** (Tel: 351 205), **Central Bank of India** (Tel: 352 025), **Indian Overseas Bank** (Tel: 351 229), and **Union Bank of India** (Tel: 353 970) are all on MG Rd, Ernakulam.
Bank of India (Tel: 352 635), **State Bank of India** (Tel: 361 184), and **Syndicate Bank** (Tel: 352 883) all have branches on Shanmugham Rd, Ernakulam.
Chartered Bank (Tel: 6246), **Grindlays Bank** (Tel: 6221), and **State Bank of India** (Tel: 6134/6210) all have branches on Willingdon Island.
Dena Bank: Bazar Rd (Tel: 24952) and **Punjab National Bank** (Tel: 24464) are on Mattancherry.

COMMUNICATIONS

Central Telegraph Office: Mattancherry. Tel: 25554.
Ernakulum Telegraph Office: Jos Junction Building, 2nd Floor, MG Rd, Ernakulam. Tel: 355 601
Open 24 hours.
Head Post Office: Fort Cochin, Mattancherry (behind St Francis Church). Tel: 24247.
Poste restante facilities here.
Ernakulum Head Post Office: Hospital Rd, Ernakulam. Tel: 355 467.
There are also post and telegraph offices on Willingdon Island.

SHOPPING

Higginbotham's Books, TD Rd, and **Bhavi Books**, Convent Rd.
Kerala State Emporium (Tel: 353 063), **Kairali Handicrafts** (Tel: 354 507), **Khadi Bhavan** (Tel: 355 279), **UTC Handicrafts** (Tel: 354 420), and **Handloom Angadi** are all in MG Rd, Ernakulam.

National Textiles: Bannerji Rd, Erakulum. Tel: 354 470.

Athena Arts and **Indian Arts and Curios** are both in Jewtown, Fort Cochin, Mattancherry.

TOURIST INFORMATION

Kerala Tourist Development Corporation: Tourist Reception Centre, Shanmugham Rd, Ernakulum. Tel: 353 234.

Open 8am-6pm. Book here for KTDC tours, and they will also book tourist taxis for you.

Government of Kerala Tourist Information Centre: Old Collectorate, Park Avenue, Ernakulum.

Government of India Tourist Office: Willingdon Island, next to the Malabar Hotel. Tel: 6045.

Useful for information, and also have a **guide service**, if you prefer to go on a private tour.

WHERE TO STAY

Upmarket

Malabar Hotel: Willingdon Island. Tel: 0484–6811. Telex: 855–6661 MLBR IN.

By far the poshest hotel in town. Recently massively expanded and renovated, it now has 100 rooms. Right at the northern tip of Willingdon Island, with waterfront gardens, fabulous views across the harbour, and its own launch service across to Ernakulum.

Casino Hotel: Willingdon Island. Tel: 6821. Telex: 885–6314 SAFE IN.

Hotel Abad Plaza: MG Rd, Ernakulum. Tel: 361 636. Telex: 885–6587.

Hotel Presidency: Paramara Rd, Ernakulum. Tel: 363 100. Telex: 885–6201 TOUR IN.

Mid-range

Bolghatty Palace Hotel: Bolghatty Island. Tel: 355 003.

The old British residency, now run as a hotel by the Kerala Tourist Development Corporation. Large gardens, its own golf course, and, in a dire attempt to modernise, a number of honeymoon cottages. On the whole crumbling, but the atmosphere makes up for the inconvenience.

Bharat Hotel: Durbar Hall Rd, Ernakulum. Tel: 353 501.

Sealord Hotel: Shanmugham Rd, Ernakulum. Tel: 352 682.

International Hotel: MG Rd, Ernakulum. Tel: 353 911/560/707. Telex: 885–6698 INHO IN.

Woodlands Hotel: Woodlands Junction, MG Rd, Ernakulum. Tel: 351 372. Telex: 885–6316.

Cheap
Hotel Sea Gull: Fort Cochin, Mattancherry. Tel: 28128.
Hotel Blue Diamond: Market St, Ernakulum. Tel: 353 221.
Hotel Sangeetha: Chitoor Rd, Ernakulum. Tel: 368 487. Telex: 885–6330 PAUL IN.
Basoto Lodge: Press Club Rd, Ernakulum. Tel: 352 140.
Biju's Tourist Home: Cannon Shed Rd, Ernakulum. Tel: 369 881.

Ultra-cheap
Railway Retiring Rooms: Ernakulum Junction Station.
PWD Inspection Bungalow: Fort Cochin. Tel: 25797.
YMCA: Chitoor Rd, Enakulum. Tel: 355 620.

WHERE TO EAT

Bimbi's and **Khyber:** cnr Durbar Hall Rd/MG Rd, Ernakulum. Self-service, fast food and sweets downstairs, a proper restaurant upstairs. Both highly recommended.
Pandal Restaurant: MG Rd (opposite the Grand Hotel), Ernakulum. Good Western-style fast food (pizza and ice cream) and North Indian food.
Sealord Hotel: Shanmugham Rd, Ernakulum.
Rooftop restaurant with good fish and Chinese food.
Rice Boats: Malabar Hotel, Willingdon Island.
Excellent buffet and fish.
Ceylon Bake House: MG Rd, (opposite Woodlands Hotel), Ernakulum. Good fish and South Indian food.
Indian Coffee House: cnr Park Avenue and Cannon Shed Rd, and MG Rd (opposite **Bimbi's**), Ernakulum.
Both branches serve good, cheap South Indian snacks and meals.
The **Grand, Presidency, Woodlands, Elite,** and **Abad Plaza** hotels all have good restaurants.

THE BACKWATERS

Known as the **backwaters,** this stretch of the Kerala coastal plains in fact covers 3,200 square kilometres, from Cochin to Quilon. And far from the image of forgotten wilderness conjured up by the name, almost every square centimetre of it is cultivated, the seemingly endless rice paddies only broken occasionally by narrow banks and dykes, and, where dry land can be found, by groves of coconut and banana, mango and papaya, cashewnuts and cassava.

It is an extraordinarily beautiful area with colours that

seem at times too vivid to be real – as though someone has zapped up the contrast button a couple of notches. The pace is slow and leisurely, the towns small and the villages tiny. Heavily laden boats with sails of woven leaves navigate a silent path through narrow palm-fringed canals, or across

shallow, silvery lagoons. Children and chickens play together in the dust on the narrow dykes between houses the same width as the ledge, perched precariously above the water. The women work the fields, standing up to their waists in water. The men haul the cantilevered Chinese fishing nets in and out of the lakes, hour after hour, day after day.

Faced by such an enormous area of swampy ground, it was Tipu Sultan who, in the 1780s, began the network of canals which today takes the place of roads over much of the region. There are three main towns in the area, **Alleppey**, **Kottayam** and **Quilon**, all of which are well connected by road and rail. Elsewhere, however, the canals provide the main thoroughfares – with water buses along them to prove it.

BOAT TRIPS

The best and only really practical way to see the backwaters is by **boat**. They do stretch up as far as Cochin, and it is possible to hire a private boat or take a tour, either from here or Quilon. To do this, however, is not only to put yourself to unnecessary expense, but, around Cochin at least, you will find yourself mainly in suburban districts and will miss the best of the scenery. As you will also find yourself surrounded by other Westerners, you will also miss the delights of a day on the canals with the local people.

The **water buses** are not only incredibly cheap, but are an experience you should not miss. Everyone takes them, from besuited businessmen with briefcases, to the local schoolchildren, to the women on their way home from market with great baskets of vegetables. The passengers are all incredibly friendly and eager to talk, and we were also invited up to the wheelhouse (a climb up the wall of the toilet and across the roof) for a chat with the crew. When thrown out of there by an officious inspector; we were given the run of the flat roof for the rest of the afternoon to bask in the sun.

There are several possible routes of differing lengths.

Quilon to Alleppey: this is the longest of the journeys, taking eight hours, with only a couple of ten-minute stops for tea. Take supplies with you, particularly a plentiful supply of water, as it can get very hot. There are two departures daily in either direction, one in the morning, one at night.

Changanacherri to Alleppey: Changanacherri is on the main Cochin-Trivandrum railway line, and there are several trains a day which stop here, as well as a number of buses both from Quilon or Cochin. It is a small town with few facilities, so don't risk getting stuck overnight, but it is a good place to catch the boat for a wonderful three-hour journey to Alleppey. There are ten departures daily in each direction, and you can do it as a day-trip from either Cochin or Quilon or continue your journey on afterwards.

Kottayam to Alleppey: this is the **shortest** of the journeys, and, in part, crosses the open waters of Lake Vembanad. It takes around two and a half hours. There are about 14 boats daily in either direction.

Alleppey to Champakulam: a short trip lasting about one and a half hours, with nine departures daily.

Alleppey to Ernakulum (Cochin): there is only one, overnight departure a day for this seven-hour journey, which is also through slightly less interesting countryside (a little irrelevant at night). Choose one of the others.

Most people do choose a daytime journey, and this is without doubt the more rewarding. However, if you have time to spare, it might be worth doing a shorter night journey as well. The local *Sura's Guide* waxes lyrical on the subject: "On a cloudless night, the panorama presented to the traveller from the deck of his boat is supremely beautiful. A myriad fireflies, with their weird twinkle, light up the coastline, fringed with luxuriant vegetation, while the starry heavens reflected in the blue, limpid water below make the fairy scene complete." Can you resist?

ALLEPPEY

A pleasant market town with a population of around 220,000, Alleppey is famous for two things – as a centre of Kerala's coir industry, and for the snake boat races which take place here and in surrounding villages during the festival of *Onam* in August/September. The rest of the year, it is quiet and friendly, but with nothing in particular to recommend it apart from its water buses.

GETTING THERE

There are a great many **buses** each day – 10 from Quilon, 30 from Trivandrum and around 40 from Ernakulum. There are also regular services to Kanyakumari, Trichur and Calicut. A **rail** link with Cochin is meant to be open by now, but news of this seems somewhat sparse. The **bus station** and **jetty** are both in the centre of town, within easy walking distance of each other.

FACT FILE

WHERE TO STAY

Alleppey Prince Hotel: AS Road, National Highway 47 (2 kilometres north of the town). Tel: 3752.
Kuttanad Tourist Home: next to the bus station.
Karthika Tourist Home: just north of the canal. Tel: 2554.
Hotel Komala: just north of the canal. Tel: 3631.
PWD Inspection Bungalow: Beach Rd. Tel: 3445.

WHERE TO EAT

Arun Restaurant: Hotel Komala.
Indian Coffee House: opposite the hospital, south of the southern canal.

KOTTAYAM

A small but thriving city, chiefly because it is on the main
coast road, Kottayam stands between the backwaters and the

Festivals

Kerala is home to two of India's most famous and colourful festivals. Unfortunately, this means they have also become rather commercial in recent years, but if you can manage to be there at the right time, they should not be missed.

Western Ghats. The city itself is not particularly inspiring, but the surrounding scenery is fabulous, with rice paddies and canals to the west, and hillside plantations of rubber, tea, coffee and spices to the east. It is a useful place for tourists, with access to the backwaters and as the nearest town of any size to **Periyar National Park** (see page 286). It is a centre for Syrian Christianity and there are two interesting churches, the **Cheria Palli** (Small Church) and the **Vallia Palli** (Big Church) on a hill about 5 kilometres from the centre of town. Both are around 700 years old. The Vallia Palli has two Nestorian crosses beside the high altar.

GETTING THERE

The **express trains** between Cochin and Trivandrum all stop here and there are also regular **buses** to both Cochin and Trivandrum, as well as four a day to Thekkady and Periyar, three of which continue across to Madurai.

FACT FILE

WHERE TO STAY

Anjali Hotel: KK Rd (near the central square). Tel: 3661.
Hotel Ambassador: KK Rd. Tel: 3293.
Pallathaya Tourist Complex: beside the water.
Kumakoram Tourist Complex: Vembanad Lake.
  16 kilometres from Kottayam, on the edge of the lake, this is an old British plantation home – a lovely house in a beautiful setting.

WHERE TO EAT

Indian Coffee House: TB Rd (opposite the bus station).
Pallathaya Tourist Complex Restaurant
  Good setting, outdoors on the water's edge, and reasonable food.

Pooram

Held in Trichur (78 kilometres from Cochin), in late April or early May. This is the Malayalam month of Meddum and the start of the Malayalam new year. The festival honours two goddesses, Paramekkavu and Thiruvambady, along with eight other gods. The streets are decorated, the fireworks light up the sky and the musicians strike up, but the highlight of the festival is the parade of elephants.

Long rivalry between supporters of the two goddesses gradually led their Brahmans to the ritualised magnificence of the great **Pooram** parade. Now, each side presents 15 elephants. Supporters go into huddles for months on end to design and create ever more splendid trappings. On the morning of Pooram, the crowds gather in the massive square in front of the Vadakkunathan temple. To the accompaniment of music from the five-piece orchestra (conch, cymbals, trumpet and two drums), each side leads out its elephants, decked in gold and silver, silk and peacock feathers, lamps and palm leaves. A Brahman rides each elephant, carrying an image of the deity, shaded by a parasol. They line up in straight rows facing each other, and, as the music pounds its way to a crescendo, each side displays its decorations, until the roars of the crowd awards winner's status to one of them. After this, the elephants set off together in a massive parade which lasts much of the day, and into the evening.

There is not much point in visiting Trichur at other times of the year, as the temple is forbidden to non-Hindus and there is little else to see or do.

QUILON

It's hard to believe it today, but Quilon (pronounced "koylon") was once one of the greatest ports of the Spice Coast, with traders coming from across the world. Even Marco Polo mentions it in his account of his travels. It was considered so important that the Malayalam calendar starts with the founding of the town (which officially happened in the ninth century AD, although there was a settlement here for a good 1,000 years before that). It was even allowed to exist as a separate principality, although a vassal state of Travancore, until 1742.

Onam
Held in the Malayalam month of Chingom (August-September), this celebrates the end of the monsoon and the gathering of the harvest. It lasts for a week, leading to its climax on the night of the full moon, when, according to legend, the Asura king Mahabali returns from exile to visit his people. Celebrated throughout the state with processions of elephants, feasting, music, dance and flowers, the best place to be is in the backwater towns. It is here that the famous snake boat races are held. These massive dugouts with high, decorative prows each hold 100 oarsmen. Of them all, the most famous is the Nehru Trophy race, held in Alleppey on the second Saturday in August.

Today it is an attractive market town, with a population of about 200,000, that stands between the sea and Lake Ashtamudi. It is the centre of Kerala's cashew nut industry, as well as producing pottery, coir and aluminium. The **Thevally Palace** has long since drowned, while the Portuguese **Fort Thomas** (built in 1503 and later appropriated by the Dutch), and the British fort at nearby **Tangasseri** are both now ruined. Only the cemeteries and the lighthouse remain. This is open to the public from 3.30–5.30pm daily. Small admission charge.

Although there is little for the tourist to see, it is worth taking the time to stroll around the town, and to have a look at the maze of Chinese fishing nets which peer out over the waters of the lake.

Quilon is most famous as the southern gateway to the backwaters. As well as the water buses, it is possible to hire pedalos, rowing boats and motor boats for use on the lake from the **Quilon Boat Club** (Tel: 2519) or the **Tourist Promotion Council**, Guest House Compound (Tel: 76456).

GETTING THERE

There are excellent rail services, with several express services a day from both Trivandrum and Cochin. Services from Trivandrum to Madras and Madurai, and from Bombay to Kanya Kumari, also stop here. Choose an express train wherever possible, as the passenger trains seem even slower than usual. The **railway station** is on the north edge of the town centre.

There are also a great many **buses**, with over 20 departures a day to Trivandrum, 15 to Ernakulum, and 6 to Alleppey. There is also a daily service through to Periyar, but as this takes eight hours, do it the slow way, take a boat, and save some of the agony. The bus station is beside the boat jetty, on the southern edge of the town centre.

FACTFILE

WHERE TO STAY

There are no upmarket hotels in Quilon, but there are several perfectly comfortable cheap alternatives.

KTDC Tourist Bungalow: Tel: 76456.

2 kilometres from the centre of town, on the shores of Lake Ashtamudi. Although a little inconvenient, this is by far the best place to stay. It is a 200-year-old palace and former British residency, set in gardens beside the water.

Hotel Karthika: Tel: 76240. Telex: 886–284.

Probably the best option if you prefer to be in the centre of town.

Hotel Seabea: Tel: 2192.

Near the bus station and boat jetty.

Hotel Sudarsan: Parameswar Nagar. Tel: 3755.

Near the bus station and the boat jetty.

Iswarya Lodge: Main St. Tel: 78101.

WHERE TO EAT

Indian Coffee House: Main St.

Hotel Guru Prasad: Main St.

Iswarya Lodge Restaurant: Main St.

Village Restaurant: near the post office (evenings only).

PERIYAR NATIONAL PARK (THEKKADY)

High up in the Western Ghats, on the borders of Kerala and Tamil Nadu, **Periyar** is the most southerly of India's national parks and must be one of the most popular, with nearly 200,000 visitors a year. As most of the park is out of bounds, all tourism is centred on one development at **Thekkady**, and all game-viewing is on the lake. The result is that while the facilities are better than in most parks, it is almost always alive with people rather than animals, and if you really want to get a feel of the wilderness, you would do better to look elsewhere.

The dam across the Periyar River was constructed in 1895 by Colonel J. Peenycuick. The resultant lake covers an area of 55 square kilometres (21 square miles), and the surrounding area was turned into a sanctuary (the **Nelliampatty Sanctuary**) by the Maharajah of Travancore in 1934. This was enlarged to its present size of 777 square kilometres (299 square miles) in 1950, and in 1973 became one of 16 Project Tiger reserves.

It is an incredibly beautiful area, up in the mountains at altitudes that range from 914–1,828 metres above sea level. Almost the only flat areas are a few patches of marshland at the edge of the lake. Most of the park is covered by a mix of open grassland, semi-evergreen forest and massive primary forest, where ferns and orchids nestle under ancient hardwood trees that can reach heights of 40 metres.

There are thought to be about 40 tigers in the reserve, but don't hold your breath as even the wardens haven't seen them in years. There are also around 800 elephants, so you should get to see some of these, and *gaur* (wild oxen) are fairly common. There are also three types of deer – the sambar, barking deer and mouse deer; wild dogs; porcupines; wild boar; and four species of monkey – the lion-tailed and bonnet macaques, and the common and Nilgiri langurs. On the ground, look out for tortoises, pythons and monitor lizards, while there is a lively colony of otters on the lake. Birds include darters, cormorants, ospreys, kingfishers, kites, orioles, hill mynahs and great and grey hornbills. Other aerial creatures include flying squirrels, frogs, snakes and lizards!

The sheer volume of people has driven most of the animals away from the lake, and while the experts continue to insist that the park is well stocked, game-viewing these days is poor. The best time to go is between March and May, at the end of the dry season, when the forest pools have dried up, the grass is short and the animals are forced back to the water's edge.

GETTING THERE

The only way to get to Thekkady is by **road**. The nearest airports are Madurai (145 kilometres away) and Cochin (208 kilometres away), while the nearest railway station is at Kottayam (114 kilometres to the west). Whichever way you approach the park, from east or west, you are in for a long drive. Thekkady is at the top of the Western Ghats and the roads twist their way upwards in an excruciatingly slow, if dramatic fashion, through forests and plantations. The views are fabulous.

Kottayam is the nearest town of any size. Six **buses** run from here each day, taking four hours to do the journey. There are also four a day from Madurai (four hours), three a day from Ernakulam (six hours) and Trivandrum (eight hours), and daily services from Kovalam (nine hours) and Kodaikanal (six hours).

All buses officially run to and from Kumily, but the bus station here is little more than a patch of scrub land and in practice they all continue to Thekkady, stopping outside the Aranya Nivas Hotel.

GETTING YOUR BEARINGS

Periyar National Park is centred on **Periyar Lake**. The nearest village is **Kumily**, 3 kilometres to the north-west of the park boundary, but the main tourist centre is **Thekkady**, a KTDC development with several hotels, on the northern shore of the lake. All sightseeing trips, boats and walks are based here. Everything here is within easy walking distance, but take a torch at night.

GETTING AROUND

Even if you have your own car, you are not permitted to use it within the boundaries of the national park. If you don't want to walk, or wait for the bus to take you down to the lake, there are **jeeps**, both private and shared, for hire in Kumily. It is also possible to hire **bicycles** here and in Thekkady itself.

Almost all sightseeing is by **boat**. Huge motor launches, carrying up to 60 people leave every two hours between 7am–3pm, on two-hour tours. These are the cheapest way to go out, but should be avoided as they are almost always full and incredibly noisy, and almost guaranteed to frighten away any of the animals you might otherwise expect to see. Pay a bit more and you can hire a smaller boat, either privately or with a few others, from the **Aranya Nivas Hotel,** or the **Wildlife Preservation Officer,** both in Thekkady. There is a small charge per person on top of the boat hire, you have to pay for camera permits, and you will probably also have to give the guide a tip at the end of the trip.

It is also possible to hire a guide for **walking trips** within the park, and there are a number of **viewing platforms.** Watch out for leeches on jungle walks.

FACT FILE

WHERE TO STAY

Periyar is one of the most popular of India's national parks and accommodation can be difficult to find, particularly over weekends and local holidays. It is worth booking in advance.

Mid-range
Aranya Nivas Hotel: Thekkady, Tel: Kumily 23.
   Run by the ITDC, this is the centre of most activity and also has useful postal facilities, bank and exchange.
Lake Palace Hotel: Edapalayam. Tel: Kumily 24.
   Also run by the KTDC, this is the most attractive of the hotels, a former hunting lodge with only 6 rooms, on a small island in the lake. Fun, but a little inconvenient. The last boat across leaves at 4 pm, so if you are planning to stay here, make sure you arrive in time. The room rate includes full board and there is a bar, shop, bank and postal facilities.

Cheap
Periyar House: Thekkady. Tel: 26.
   The third, and cheapest, of the KTDC hotels, with simple rooms, some dormitory accommodation and a fairly basic restaurant.
Hotel Ambadi: halfway between Kumily and Thekkady, beside the Forest Checkpoint. Tel: Kumily 11.
   Reasonable cheap hotel and restaurant, plus a few cottages.
Hotel Lake Queen: Kumily. Tel: Kumily 84.
Muckumkal Lodge: Kumily. Tel: Kumily 70.

WHERE TO EAT

Coffee Inn: halfway between Kumily and Thekkady.

Otherwise, all the hotels have restaurants, and will also serve those who are not staying there, if you want to ring the changes.

TRIVANDRUM

Trivandrum became the capital of Travancore in 1750, when Raja Marthanda Varma moved his centre of government here from Padmanabhapuram (now in Tamil Nadu). It remained the state capital with the founding of Kerala in 1956.

The city derives its name from Thiru-Anantha-Puram, which means "the home of the sacred serpent, Anantha", who is the coiled serpent on which Vishnu reclines. Vishnu is known here as Sri Padmanabha, and not only the temple but the entire state was dedicated to him by the Raja, in atonement for his misdeeds during a whole series of wars.

Today Trivandrum, built like Rome on seven hills, has a population of around 700,000. There the resemblance ends, however, for it still feels like a small, rather sleepy town, with narrow lanes, red roofs, and plenty of woods and greenery. The only regular shock to its laid-back atmosphere is an almost constant stream of demonstrations which invade the streets, occasionally erupting into violence. The main outcome of the high education levels in Kerala is a political awareness that outstrips almost every other area's. It is an attractive town, but holds little to entice the tourist. It is most useful as a gateway to Kovalam, and other nearby areas of South India.

GETTING THERE

For air traveller, Indian Airlines have daily services to Madras, Delhi, Bombay, and Bangalore, three a week to Cochin, and services to Goa and Tiruchirapalli. Indian Airlines International also have three flights a week from here to Male (Maldives) and weekly flights to Colombo (Sri Lanka). Vayudoot have three flights a week to Bangalore; and Air Lanka have five flights a week to Colombo. Air India fly from here to Delhi, Bombay, and Madras, as well as offering direct flights to various Gulf destinations.

The **airport**, which is on the coast, 6 kilometres from the city centre, is particularly chaotic, although efforts are being made to bring a little order into the situation. Local buses (No. 14) run out here frequently; otherwise take a taxi or auto-rickshaw.

Trivandrum is on the main broad guage coastal line, and has superb **rail** connections. There are daily express trains to Delhi (52 hours) and Bombay (45 hours), as well as the closer destinations of Madras, Mangalore, Coimbatore and Bangalore. Several trains a day between Cochin and Kanyakumari also stop here, and at Quilon and Kottayam.

The **station** is on Station Road at the southern end of MG Rd. The **Advance Reservations Office** is upstairs in the ticket office building, just to the side of the main station building. There is no tourist counter, so ignore the queues and head straight for the Chief Reservations Supervisor's Office at the top of the stairs. He is very helpful and there is a generous tourist quota here. The office is open from 7am–1pm, 1.30–7.30pm from Monday to Saturday, and 9am–5pm on Sundays (no advance reservations). There are good retiring rooms here (Tel: 62966/63066).

Trivandrum is on the main, coastal national highway. There are daily long-distance **bus** services to Madras and Bangalore, and three departures a day for Periyar. There are also services to Coimbatore, Cuddalore, Erode and Madurai. Ten buses a day go to Kanyakumari, and even more go as far as Nagercoil. There are about 12 departures a day for Ernakulum, all of which stop at Quilon, and most of which go through either Alleppey or Kottayam. Long-distance buses leave from the chaotic **Central Bus Station**, opposite the railway station. Buses for Kovalam (25 a day) leave from Fort Bus Depot, on MG Rd, south of the railway station, (Bus enquiries: 67756).

GETTING AROUND

There are plenty of **local buses**, which are cheap, but usually extremely crowded. It is also often difficult to find out any information on routes and timetables. There are a great many **auto-rickshaws** about, all with broken meters. Set a price before you leave. There are also **yellow-top** and **tourist taxis** if you prefer.

The KTDC runs day-long city **tours**, which also take in Kovalam Beach, as well as daily tours to Kanyakumari, and excruciating two-day tours to Periyar. These are bookable at any KTDC information counter (see Fact File).

GETTING YOUR BEARINGS

Trivandrum sprawls over a fairly large area, but almost everything you need is clustered around MG Road, which runs north-south through the centre of the city. The **railway station** and main **bus station** are together at the southern end of MG Road. Just to the south of these are the Sri **Padmanabhaswamy temple** and **Fort Bus Station**, which is the depot for all local buses. The museums are clustered together in the **Zoological Park** on Museum Road, just off the northern end of MG Road.

ALSO WORTH SEEING

There is nothing in Trivandrum that is essential viewing, although you can find enough to keep you happy if you have a day to spare. Most tourists simply pass through on their way to **Kovalam** (see page 296).

Sri Padmanabhaswamy Temple

Built in 1733 on the site of a much older temple by Raja Marthanda Varmi to house an image of Padmanabha (Vishnu) reclining on the sacred serpent, Anantha. It has 368 sculpted granite pillars, together with a number of murals and other statues, in the main hall. This, however, is out of bounds to non-Hindus who are forbidden to enter even the court-yard. Even Hindu men have to change into plain white *dhotis* before doing so. It is worth going to have a look at the outside, as the highly ornate, seven-storey *gopuram* is reflected in a large tank and makes an attractive picture.

Napier Museum

This small museum is worth a visit. The building itself is a remarkably jolly confection that has stirred together traditional and colonial styles and come out with a very eccentric roofline. The collection includes some 400 bronzes, mostly dating from the Chola, Vijayanagar and Nayak periods, many of them superb examples of Keralan craft. There are also a number of Keralan wood and ivory carvings, some traditional dress, and the ubiquitous mementoes of the royal family. Open 9am–5pm, Tuesday, Thursday to Sunday, and 1–4.45pm, Wednesday. Closed Monday. Small entry fee.

Sri Chitra Art Gallery

In the grounds of the Napier Museum. Collection of Mughul, Rajput and Tanjore miniatures, other types of Indian art, including some work by Raja Ravi Varma, and paintings from various Far Eastern countries, including China, Japan and Indonesia. Open 10am–5pm, except Monday, and 1–5pm Wednesday. Small admission charge.

Other museums in Trivandrum include the **Museum of Science and Technology**, near the Mascot Hotel, the **Children's Museum**, near Thycaud, and the Oriental Manuscript Library at the University, Kariavattom, which has a huge collection of palm leaf manuscripts. All open 10am–5pm, closed Monday. Small entry fee.

Botanical garden and zoo

Just behind the Napier Museum, with some of the best laid out and tended gardens in India. Zoo less idyllic. Open 9am–4.15pm, Tuesday to Sunday.

FACT FILE

AIRLINES

Indian Airlines: Air Centre, Mascot Junction. Tel: 66370/60181/62288/61776. Airport tel: 72228.
Vayudoot: c/o Airtravel Enterprises, LMS Junction. Tel: 60690. Airport tel: 71351,

Air India: Museum Rd, Vellayambalam Circle. Tel: 64837. Airport tel: 71426.
Air Lanka: Geethanjali Building, Geethanjali Hospital Rd, Vazhuthacaud. Tel: 66475/63267.
Gulf Air: c/o Jet Air Travels, Panavila Junction. Tel: 67514/68003.
Maldives Airways: c/o S&J Sales Corporation, Glass House Building, Panavila Junction. Tel: 66105.

BANKS

Bank of Baroda: MG Rd. Tel: 65923.
Canara Bank: Spencer Junction. Tel: 68501.
Central Bank of India: MG Rd. Tel: 68547.
Federal Bank: Palayam. Tel: 62645.
Indian Overseas Bank: Ayurveda College Junction. Tel: 68489.
Punjab National Bank: Statute Junction. Tel: 61697.
Reserve Bank of India: Kowkidar. Tel: 60676.
State Bank of India: Nr Secretariat. Tel: 66683.
State Bank of Travancore: Marikar Building. Tel: 68344.

COMMUNICATIONS

Central Telegraph Office: Statute Rd (just off MG Rd). Tel: 61494. Open 24 hours.
GPO: Palayalam (on a narrow street, just west of MG Rd). Tel: 61494.
Poste restante counter open from 8am–6pm.

SHOPPING

Higginbotham's Book Store: MG Rd. Tel: 79122.
Kairali Government Emporium: opp. Secretariat, MG Rd. Tel: 60127.
SMSM Handicrafts Emporium: behind Secretariat. Tel: 63358.

TOURIST INFORMATION

Government of Kerala Tourism Information Centre: Park View. Tel: 61132.
Guide service available from here. There are also Kerala tourism information counters at the **airport** (Tel: 71085), and the **Chaithram Hotel,** near the railway and bus stations (Tel: 67224).
Kerala Tourism Development Corporation: Tourist Reception Centre, Thampanoor. Tel: 75031.
There is also a **Government of India Tourist Information Counter** at the airport (tel: 71085).

VISA EXTENSIONS

City Police Commissioner: Residency Rd, Thycaud. Tel: 60555. Open 10am–5pm Monday to Saturday.
Superintendent of Police (Rural): Kowkidar. Tel: 61296.

WHERE TO STAY

Upmarket
Hotel Luciya Continental: East Fort. Tel: 73445, Telex: 435–330 LUCY IN.

Between the airport and the city centre.
Mascot Hotel: Museum Rd. Tel: 68990. Telex: 0433–229 KTDC IN.
Run by the KTDC. Boring but competent.

Mid-range
Hotel Horizon: Aristo Rd. Tel: 66888. Telex: 0435–346 HRZN IN.
Hotel Pankaj: MG Rd. opp. Secretariat. Tel: 76257. Telex: 0884–323 PKNJ IN.

Cheap
Chaithram Hotel: Station Rd.
Near the station. Run by the KTDC.
Hotel Highland: Manjalikulam Rd (near the station). Tel: 78440.
Manacaud Tourist Paradise: just off Station Rd. Tel: 75360.

Ultra-cheap
Railway Retiring Rooms: Trivandrum Station. Tel: 63869.
YMCA Guest House: Palatam (behind the Secretariat). Tel: 68059.
Youth Hostel: Veli. Tel: 71364.
Incredibly cheap, but a little way from the centre of town, on Veli Lake, so you pay in fares what you save on a bed.

WHERE TO EAT
More upmarket
Galaxy: Hotel Horizon, Aristo Rd.
Rooftop restaurant serving Indian, continental and Chinese. There is also an air-conditioned restaurant, **Mira**, in the hotel.
Hotel Luciya Continental: East Fort.
Good South Indian food.

Cheaper
Indian Coffee House: MG Rd.
2 branches, one near the Secretariat, one just south of the railway station.
Kalandriya: MG Rd.
Aryul Jyoti: MG Rd.

KOVALAM

Kovalam Beach is certainly the most beautiful in India, and, at the moment knocks spots off the more famous Goa. The white-gold sand stretches in all for several kilometres, but is broken up into smaller bays by rocky promontories. There is only one resort hotel so far and the smaller hotels and cottages huddle amongst the palms. The sand is relatively narrow, but continues in places into the palm groves to provide plenty of shade within easy reach of the water. The village proper sprawls along the road above the beach, within easy walking distance, but out of sight. Sari-clad women prowl the sands selling fruit to visitors, flat baskets piled high with pineapples, mangoes and coconuts on their heads. Tucked under the palms, a row of tiny, ramshackle beachfront cafés glory in such names as Woodstock, the Black Cat, Velvet Dawn, and even the Giggling Sausage.

At dawn, the villagers swarm like bees down to the beach to wrestle ashore huge nets filled with writhing fish and translucent purple jellyfish. The mussel fishermen, small, wiry figures clad only in *dhotis*, and armed with great baskets, drag their log canoes towards the water. And as the sky finally fades to a brilliant blue, the cafés open in a clatter of pots and pans.

During the day, if basking isn't enough for you, the fruit ladies are always game for a chat, and the fishermen will often take you out, if you are brave enough to venture offshore in a canoe that is little more than a few logs tied together with a bit of string. It's worth doing, although it is a little alarming setting out to sea sitting up to your waist in water. Take a T-shirt, as the sun is ferocious. The experience of surfing back in should not be missed. The sea is great for swimming, with a gently shelving sand bar, but be wary of the currents if you plan to go out of your depth, and keep an eye out for the jellyfish. The purple ones are safe, the little orange ones are not. Boats and other watersports are available at the Ashok Resort.

Sadly, since my first visit – and probably because of people like me waxing lyrical in print – Kovalam has been growing steadily more commercialised. The number of people and the noise level have both grown. The worst excesses of the developers have been avoided so far, but the number of hotels increases year by year, parasols have appeared and and the beach now has resident lifeguards. Not too bad? The latest idiocy is a plan to widen the beach – knocking down all the cafés in the process and probably destroying most of the atmosphere that has made the place special. Go now, and hopefully you won't be too late.

GETTING THERE

The best way to get here is from Trivandrum, about 16 kilometres to the north. There are around 25 **buses** a day (No. 111 from Fort Bus Depot). Alternatively, take a **taxi** or **auto-rickshaw**. Some are shared and will wait to fill up (or overfill), the rest will screw you for as much as they can possibly get. Haggle hard and set the price before you set out.

There are also direct buses from Ernakulum, Kanyakumari, Quilon and even one a day from Periyar.

The **bus stand** is on the main road above the Ashok Resort. If you are planning to go to one of the more southerly hotels, this will still leave you with a fairly healthy walk. There are a few auto-rickshaws and taxis, which hang around the Ashok Resort and Rockholm Hotel. Otherwise, you will have to walk.

GETTING YOUR BEARINGS

There are three main bays, stretching along about 4 kilometres. The most northerly is the least developed, with only some cottages so far, although quite a few new buildings are going up around here. The **Ashok Resort** stands on the headland between this and the middle bay. The southern bay is the one with most of the small cafés and cheap hotels. The

lighthouse on the promontory at the southern end of the bay is open to visitors every afternoon for a small charge. It offers a superb view.

Kovalam village stretches out along the main road behind the beach. The bookstall, post office and general stores are all near the bus stand behind the Ashok Resort. There are also a number of tailors' stalls who will whip up clothes cheaply and quickly for you, and several shops selling souvenirs from as far afield as Tibet and Kashmir.

OUT OF TOWN

The two most common places to visit from here are the **Padmanabhapuram Palace** and **Kanyakumari**. Both are in Tamil Nadu (see page 392 for details).

FACT FILE

WHERE TO STAY

Luxury
Kovalam Ashok Beach Resort: Tel: 68010/65323. Telex: 0435–216.

Run by the ITDC. The only major hotel in Kovalam, this is a five-storey hotel built to an award winning design by Charles Correa. It has recently doubled in size and now has 125 rooms, about half of them cottages. All mod-cons, including rudimentary watersports equipment, and a yoga and massage centre. The State Bank of India has a branch here that can be used by all visitors to the area.

Mid-range
Rockholm Hotel: Lighthouse Rd. Tel: Vizhinjam 306/406/407.

Small, but extremely comfortable hotel beside the lighthouse, with wonderful views over the beaches and the cliffs to the south.

Cheap
There are a wide range of good, cheap hotels. Amongst the best are the **Sea Weed Hotel**, the **Paradise Rock Lodge** and the **Hotel Samudra Tara** (run by the ITDC), which are all near the lighthouse, at the southern end of the beach. Further north, the **Sea Rock Hotel** is near the middle headland, while the **Hotel Blue Sea**, the **Hotel Palm Garden**, and the **Hotel Raja** are about the best in the village, away from the beach.

There are also large numbers of cottages, particularly along the southern bay. These are all cheap, although the price varies, both with the season and how naive the customer seems. The quality, ownership and general pecking order tends to change rapidly, so the best bet is to get there with daylight to spare and inspect a few.

WHERE TO EAT

The grandest menus are to be found at the Ashok, but the quality doesn't always match up. The **Rockholm Hotel** has a good restaurant with an outdoor terrace. The best food here however is the simplest – to be found in any of the little beachfront cafés. They are all much of a muchness and people tend to choose according to the name, the ambience, or pure instinct. Most do a mix of Western and Indian dishes and will happily serve you toast and porridge for breakfast. Obviously, they tend to concentrate on fish, so fresh it is practically swimming, and they can normally provide, or at least order, some of the more luxurious species, such as lobster. Fruit salad is another speciality, chopped to order, and the pineapple pancakes and mango *lassis* are experiences to be remembered.

Treat the meal as a leisurely pastime. You will probably have to wait quite a while. But then, can you think of anything better to do on a tropical evening than to sit on the shore under a star-strewn sky, sipping a beer and waiting for the shark and chips to arrive?

TAMIL NADU

The south-eastern corner of India is taken up by the huge state of Tamil Nadu, which, at 130,000 square kilometres, is almost the size of England. The population, at around 54 million, is similar too. Tamil Nadu simply means the "land of the Tamils". The Tamils themselves call their country Dravida (from which the word Dravidian is taken). They are the oldest of the many peoples inhabiting India, probably arriving in the area in around 4,000 BC. They are also hard-working, extremely proud of their vast cultural heritage, and very politically aware. Wary of the mainly northern-led central government which they see as trying to strip them of their traditional culture, their built-in mistrust has flared frequently into real violence. The last tragic incident, early in 1991, was the dramatic assassination in Madras of Rajiv Gandhi.

There are some 18 minor tribal groups in the state. The best known of them, the Todas, live in small grass and bamboo villages in the Nilgiri Hills around Ooty. Still following an animist tradition, they worship the goddess Tiekirzi, who invented the buffalo, and her brother, On. Other groups include the Badagas, Kotas, Kurumbas and Irulas. The vast majority of the population however is Tamil and most (89%) of them are Hindu. Six % are Christian, and only 5% Muslim. There are bare handfuls of Buddhists and Jains.

Little is known about the earliest history of the state, although Madurai is known to have existed as a major city for more than 2,500 years. For most of the last 2,000 years it has been dominated by two dynasties, the Cholas and the Pandyas. Until the fourth century AD, the position remained fairly stable, with the Cholas in control of the north of the state, the Pandyas ruling the south, and the Keralan Cheras ruling

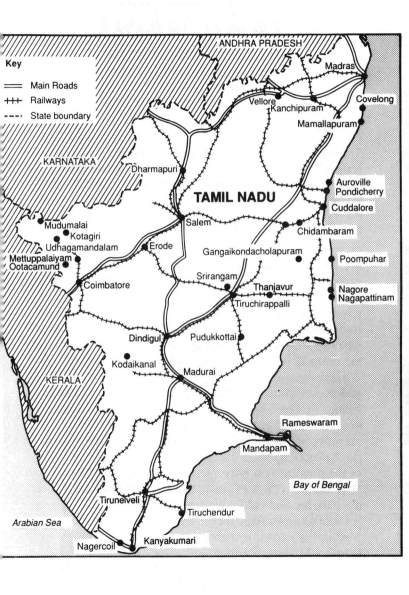

Tamil

The Tamil language was in use long before the Aryan invasion in c. 1500 BC brought Hinduism to the sub-continent. The alphabet dates back to around 1,000 BC and borrows heavily from Semitic scripts of the eastern Mediterranean. It has 31 letters, with 12 vowels, 18 consonants and one anaswara. There are no equivalents for w, x and z. The flowery script is written, like Hebrew, from right to left. The language has become a focus of Tamil nationalist identity and much of the discontent in the area has been caused by northern efforts to turn Hindi into India's one official language of government. In Tamil Nadu, they are quick to point out, 85% of the population speaks Tamil, another 10% speaks Telegu — and that only leaves 5 percent for India's other 62 languages, and Hindi is only one of them. This is not the place to try out our few proudly learnt Hindi phrases!

---

a small area to the west. With the emergence of the Pallava dynasty, however, things became unsettled. No one is too sure where the Pallavas came from, some suggesting that they were a tribe from Vengi, others that they were really Parthians (Pahlavas) from West India. Legend has it that a young prince fell in love with a Naga woman, but had to leave her. He told her to tie a twig to the body of her child and set it adrift. When he found it he would recognise the child as hers and give it part of his kingdom. And, in the best of traditions, so it came to pass, and the Pallavas (meaning "young twig") got their kingdom, with its capital at Kanchipuram.

During the second half of the seventh century, a series of empire-building wars between the Pallavas and the Chalukyans broke out. The honours were fairly evenly matched until 731, when the Chalukyas and Gangas joined forces, defeating the Pallavas and killing the king. The dynasty struggled on, but had lost its real power.

With their collapse, the Chola family began to rise again. In the mid-ninth century, they conquered the area around Thanjavur and set up an independent kingdom. In 907, Parantaka I came to the throne and captured Madurai. For the next 300 years they fought almost everyone they could find to fight – the Rashtrakutas, a revived Chalukyan kingdom, the Yavadas (from the Aurangabad area), Kakatiyas (from Andra), the Hoysalas and the Pandyas. Their fortunes fluctuated, but from the late-tenth century they made great strides, with Rajendra I even campaigning as far north as the banks of the river Ganges, as far south as Ceylon, and even managing for a time to conquer the Straits of Molucca. But the constant fighting sapped their energies and finances and when, at the end of the twelfth century, they found themselves fighting on two fronts, against the Hoysalas to the west, and the Pandyas to the south, it was too much for them, and they too sank back into relative obscurity.

The Pandyas now took over as the major power in the region, but their moment of glory was relatively shortlived, owing to the arrival of the Delhi Sultanate in the thirteenth century. Tamil Nadu was never part of the Muslim empire, but with the foundation of the Vijayanagar dynasty in 1336, the Pandyas, along with the other great families, became feudal vassals, with the Nayaks as their local governors.

The golden age of Tamil power might have ended, but it had left a lasting legacy. Like other southern dynasties of the same era, the Tamil kings were great builders. Like Karnataka, Tamil Nadu is littered with temples, many of them architecturally magnificent, a great many of them vast. Only the most important are listed here, as there are literally thousands, and they could take a lifetime to see.

As on the east coast, the next major development came with the arrival of the Europeans. The Portuguese were again the first to arrive in 1520. Shortly afterwards, the Dutch founded a settlement at Pulicut, just north of Madras. The Danes set up shop at Tranquebar, and in 1639 the British founded Fort George and the city of Madras, while in 1673 the French installed themselves at Pondicherry. The settlers proceeded, in their usual inimitable fashion, to fight each other over trade routes and territories, and slowly but surely, as elsewhere, the British won out and Tamil Nadu got sucked into the Raj. At Independence, the state of Madras included not only modern Tamil Nadu, but parts of Kerala and Andra Pradesh. It was only during the redrawing of India's map along linguistic lines in 1956 that it took on its

present shape, and it was 1969 before it changed its name
to Tamil Nadu.

MADRAS

In 1639, the Raja of Chandragiri gave Francis Day, a trader
with the East India Company, a grant of land on which to
build a warehouse and factory. It was only one of many such
grants that had been handed out over the last century to all
the various European powers who were trying to leap onto
the Indian trading bandwagon. Nor was its site, in the village
of Madraspattnam, on the north bank of the Cooum River
estuary, anything to write home about. It was just a piece of
flat land, about three miles long and one mile wide, which
wasn't doing anything much at the time. In order to keep an
eye on all the squabbling foreigners, the Raja then built himself
a settlement just to the north, calling it Channapatnam.

The British built a wall around their fledgling settlement
and on St George's Day (April 23) 1640 officially christened
it Fort St George. They then began to trade in earnest, and the
fort soon became one of the major centres for the East India
Company's activities in India, although it was ruled officially
from Java. A secondary town, known as George Town, soon
grew up outside the walls of the fort, and gradually merged
with Chennapatnam. In 1683, **Madras**, as it was coming to
be known, was given independence from Java and in 1688
James II granted it a municipal charter, the first to be given
to a town in India.

By 1693, the surrounding area had fallen under the
domination of the Mughuls. Governor Elihu Yale (who
went on to found Yale University) did a deal with Emperor
Aurangzeb and took possession of Egmore, Purasawalkam
and Tondiarpet. In 1746, Madras was briefly occupied by
the French, but was returned in 1748 as part of the terms
of the Treaty of Aix-la-Chapelle. In 1749 other local villages,
including Mylapore, San Thome, Perambur and Ennore, fell
into British hands and were all swallowed up by the rapidly
growing city.

Until this time Calcutta, Madras and Bombay had all been

administered separately, and in a spirit of ferocious rivalry. In 1793 Calcutta won, and the administration for all of British India was moved here. Nevertheless Madras continued to grow and flourish, one of the youngest and most successful cities on the sub-continent.

Today it has a population of about 5.5 million, and is the fourth largest city in India, sprawing out in all directions over the flat land along the coast and up the river valley. Courtesy of the Victorians, it has some splendidly monumental municipal buildings, and a number of broad avenues and gardens. There is relatively little for the tourist, however, especially when it is compared to the fabulous temple cities only a few kilometres away. The city does work pretty efficiently, in comparison to some in the north, but it somehow feels uncentred and chaotic. While it is an extremely useful centre as a business stop and transport junction, it does not warrant a stay of more than a couple of days.

GETTING THERE

Getting to Madras is incredibly easy. It not only has superb **air**, **bus** and **rail** connections with the rest of India, but is the main international airport in the south, with direct flights from London and New York, as well as a number of Far Eastern destinations.

By air
International
Air India has weekly flights to London, New York and Jeddah, and daily flights to Singapore and Kuala Lumpur. British Airways has two flights a week to London. Singapore Airlines has three flights a week to Singapore. Air Lanka flies five times a week to Colombo. Malaysian Airlines has five flights a week to Kuala Lumpur, three of them via Penang, and Indian Airlines has nine flights a week to Colombo and daily flights to Singapore.
Domestic
Air India has eleven flights a week to Bombay, and four a week to Delhi. Indian Airlines has five flights a day to Bangalore, three a day to Bombay, two a day to Hyderabad and Calcutta, and daily flights to Delhi, Coimbatore, Trivandrum,

Vishakapatnam and Cochin. They also run eleven a week to Tiruchirapalli and Madurai, four a week to Port Blair, and three a week to Ahmadebad. Vayudoot have daily flights to Coimbatore; six a week to Neyveli, Pondicherry, Tirupati, Bangalore, Thanjavur, Calicut and Tiruchipalli; three a week to Vijayawada, Rajahmundry, Hubli, Trivandrum, Cochin and Agatti.

Meenambakkam Airport is 17 kilometres south-west of the city centre. There are separate **international** and **domestic** terminals, next-door to each other, and both relatively new and well-organised, although my hotel refused to let me leave for the airport until they had checked that the plane was actually going to leave. They were very surprised when it was on time. (For up-to-date flight information, Tel: 433 954.) Also double-check which terminal to use, as some departures, to Delhi and Bombay, in particular are the first leg of an international flight. Baggage has to be security X-rayed and sealed before you can check in, but they were prepared to search film by hand.

A **fixed fare taxi** system operates from both terminals. Another option is the **airport bus** which runs, via the Indian Airlines office and all the major hotels, to a stop at the Hotel Imperial, beside Egmore Station, 30 times a day.

Suburban trains from Egmore Station also run regularly through the day. The stop you need is Tirusulam, which is opposite the airport. There are also a number of **local buses** from Parry's Corner which pass here, but they are generally crowded, slow and not worth the hassle.

By rail

Headquarters of the **Southern Railways**, considered by many to be the best of India's regional networks, Madras has excellent rail connections. Broad guage lines go north to Delhi and Calcutta, and west to Bangalore and Bombay. Metre guage services head south to Tiruchirapalli, Madurai, Kanyakumari, and all points en route. There are also broad and metre guage and electric local and suburban trains.

There are two express services a day to Delhi (40 hours), and one a day to Calcutta (27 hours), Bombay (24 hours), Varanasi, Hyderabad, Bangalore, Tirupathi, Rameswaram,

Tiruchirapalli, Mettuppalayam (for Ooty), and Cochin. Calcutta, Bombay and Trivandrum also have daily mail trains, and there are more frequent, if slower, services to most major centres in Tamil Nadu.

There are three main **stations** in Madras, with a minibus link between Central and Egmore that should theoretically connect all important trains.

Madras Central is a large pink and white building on VOC Road, between the Buckingham Canal and Fort St George. This is strictly broad guage. All the main trains to the north and west leave from here. It is also the main headquarters and houses the **Foreign Tourist Bureau**. This is on the second floor of the new Advanced Reservations Building just to the side of the main station. It is possible to buy Indrail passes here and there is a tourist information officer who will help you find your way around the vagaries of the timetable, as well as an efficient computerised booking system. This office will handle all broad guage bookings and any metre guage bookings that fall within the tourist quota. Other 1st class metre guage bookings are handled in the main station, while the 2nd class metre guage ticket office is in a small, scruffy annexe round the side. The FTB is open from 7am–1pm and 1.30–7.30pm, Monday to Saturday, and 7am–1pm on Sundays (Tel: 563 535).

Other facilities at Central include Tamil Nadu and TDTC tourist information counters, retiring rooms, a variety of restaurants, snack bars and shops, a pharmacy, post and telegraph office with public phones, and left luggage.

Egmore Station is the oldest of the stations here, a massive redbrick Victorian pile on Gandhi-Irwin Road. This is the metre guage station, handling most trains within Tamil Nadu itself, as well as some of the surburban trains (including the airport connection). You can make bookings here for all the metre guage services, with the booking office open from 7.30am–1pm and 1.30–7.30pm, Monday to Saturday, and 7.30am–1pm on Sundays (Tel: 566 565). If you wish to make your life easier, however, and to be sure of getting a place on the tourist quota, it is better to make all bookings at Central.

Madras Beach Station is on North Beach Road, Georgetown. This is the main surburban station, with a mix of broad and metre guage and electrified EMU lines. As a tourist, you are fairly unlikely to need to travel from here.

There is also a **rail booking counter** at the international airport, and a **railway information desk** at the domestic terminal.

By road

Madras is at the junction of four national highways – to Bangalore and Bombay, Calcutta, Trivandrum via Rameswaram, and Trichur. It is also well connected by road to other nearby towns and tourist places. The roads in Tamil Nadu are meant to be some of the best in the country – but it is the only state where I have also nearly concussed myself by hitting the ceiling while crossing a particularly splendid pothole.

The state-run **bus** service is known as the Thiruvalluvar Transport Corporation (TTC) and this, along with a number of private operators, run huge numbers of long-distance buses, both in and out of the state. There are 17 departures a day for Bangalore, 16 for Madurai, 20 for Pondicherry, 12 a day to Thanjavur, and 22 a day to Tiruchirapalli. In addition, there are six a day to Chidambaram, three a day to Tirupathi, four a day to Trivandrum, and one a day to Cochin, Hyderabad, Mysore, Ooty, Rameswaram and Kanyakumari. There are also regular services to Kanchipuram, Mamallapuran, and other nearby towns.

All inter-state and some long-distance buses leave from the well-organised **Esplanade Bus Station** (also known as the Express bus station), behind the High Court Building in Georgetown. This has a computerised advance booking office upstairs in the main reservations building, open from 7am–9pm daily. It also publishes a useful route map and guide (Tel: 561 835).

The **Tamil State bus stand** behind Popham's Broadway, also in Georgetown, is a very different kettle of fish, a heaving, smelly, disorganised heap of a place with little visible logic, nothing in English, and even the numbers of the buses in Tamil. Most of the services within Tamil Nadu leave from here, however, so chances are that you can't avoid it. You can at least get details of when the buses go from Esplanade, but about the only way to get yourself on to a bus is to allow one of the army of small boys to take you in hand.

By boat

There are regular twice-weekly sailings from Madras to the Andaman and Nicobar islands. The journey takes just under three days. Tourists are only allowed on to South Andaman Island, and even for that have to have a permit (available from the Foreigners' Registration Office in Madras). You will need the permit before you can buy a ticket. Tickets are available from the Shipping Corporation of India, Rajaji Salai, North Beach Road (Tel: 514 401).

There are persistent rumours of a regular passenger service to Singapore, but they have been around for several years now, with no sign of any action. Rumours of a coastal service up the east coast seem equally mythical.

GETTING YOUR BEARINGS

Madras is divided fairly conveniently into several areas, bordered to the east by the coast, and split in half by the Cooum River. The oldest part of the city is **Fort George** and **Georgetown**, on the coast, just to the north of the river.

Both bus stations are here, together with a number of smaller hotels and restaurants. The centre of this area is at **Parry's Corner** (beside the High Court Building), at the intersection of Popham's Broadway and NSC Bose Road.

The working heart of the city is **Egmore** which crosses the river a little further inland. Egmore and Central Stations are in the north of this area, along with the museum. The main shopping and business street, **Anna Salai**, runs across the district from the south-west up to Fort St George in the north-east. Most of the hotels, of all price categories, are also in this area, with the greatest concentration of cheaper places around Egmore station. Several more hotels are scattered on or around **Nungambakkam High Road**, to the south-west of Egmore, while **San Thome**, the **aquarium** and **Guindy Park** are in the far south.

Like Bombay, Madras has a little trouble with its names. All the maps might call a place by a new name but the inhabitants, who continue to call it by another, will stare at you in blank astonishment if that is what you ask for. Amongst the worst offenders are the Anna Salai, which is also known as Mount Road; Prakasam Road, Georgetown, which is usually known as Popham's Broadway; Periyar EVR Salai, which everyone calls Poonamallee High Road; Kamaraj Salai, which used to be South Beach Road, and Rajaji Salai, which was formerly North Beach Road. As these are probably some of the major roads in the city, you could be in trouble without both versions.

GETTING AROUND

Madras extends over a total area of around 180 square kilometres, and even the centre covers a pretty large area. It is fairly impractical to try and get around on foot.

Local buses are operated by the **Pallavan Transport Corporation** (PTC). Buses are frequent, regular, and rarely overcrowded, although it is probably worth trying to avoid rush hour. The PTC headquarters are on Anna Salai (Tel: 566 063), but other major centres for local buses include **Egmore** and **Central Stations** and **Parry's Corner**. Buses with yellow boards, or marked LSS, are limited stopping services, so are useful for longer journeys. There are also shuttle buses between the two main stations, and regular departures for the airport from Egmore Station which take in some of the main hotels.

Local trains run between Mount Beach Station and Tambaram. Services are fast and frequent, and can be useful for getting to Guindy and San Thome, but are probably not worth the effort for journeys within the centre of town. A metro system is in the early planning stages, but for the foreseeable future is going to cause more problems than it solves, as they dig up half the city to put it in place.

There are some **yellow-top taxis**, usually hanging around the better hotels, but they are not as common as in other major cities. You can always book one via hotel reception, but they can be difficult to find on the street. They will usually use the meter but will probably try very hard to persuade you that there is a good reason for a hefty surcharge. **Tourist taxis** are available via the hotels, some travel agents, and the tourist offices.

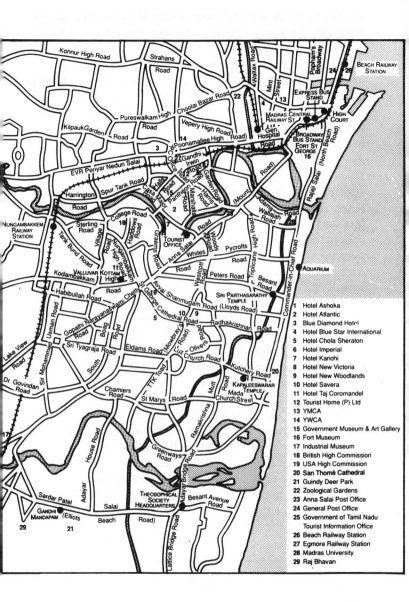

1 Hotel Ashoka
2 Hotel Atlantic
3 Blue Diamond Hotel
4 Hotel Blue Star International
5 Hotel Chola Sheraton
6 Hotel Imperial
7 Hotel Kanchi
8 Hotel New Victoria
9 Hotel New Woodlands
10 Hotel Savera
11 Hotel Taj Coromandel
12 Tourist Home (P) Ltd
13 YMCA
14 YWCA
15 Government Museum & Art Gallery
16 Fort Museum
17 Industrial Museum
18 British High Commission
19 USA High Commission
20 San Thomé Cathedral
21 Guindy Deer Park
22 Zoological Gardens
23 Anna Salai Post Office
24 General Post Office
25 Government of Tamil Nadu
   Tourist Information Office
26 Beach Railway Station
27 Egmore Railway Station
28 Madras University
29 Raj Bhavan

There are plenty of **auto-rickshaws** and, for shorter journeys, **cycle-rickshaws**. Haggle before travelling and haggle hard. You might persuade an auto-rickshaw driver to use a meter, but it is a rare event, and they all have the city knack of assuming you are three times as rich as you really are.

Both the TTDC (state) and ITDC (all-India) run **tours** in and from Madras. The TTDC has two half-day and one full-day city tours daily, while the ITDC runs a half-day city tour each afternoon. There are also daily full-day tours to Kanchipuram, Thirukkalikindram, Mamallapuran and Tirupati, as well weekend tours of the main temple cities, and week long tours of Tamil Nadu and South India. (For addresses, see under **Fact File** on page 320).

DON'T MISS ...

Fort St George

Beside the sea, on the north bank of the Kovam River, this is the site of the original British settlement at Madraspattnam. First built in 1640, the old fort was demolished in 1711, when the current hefty walls and many of the buildings, such as the hospital and mint, were erected. It became the headquarters of the East India Company's Eastern Central Government in 1652, was blockaded by the Dutch in 1673, and captured briefly by the French in 1756–8. It reached its current form by 1781. The southern half of the fort is still a working army post and, as such, is closed to the public. The rather elegant **Factory House** to the north currently houses the State Secretariat and Legislative Assembly. This was originally built in 1666, but has been considerably altered since then. The flagstaff in front of the building is the tallest in the country, a 46 metre-high mast from a ship wrecked off the coast in the seventeenth century. There were originally 32 of the polished black granite pillars forming a colonnade up to the building. They were all looted by the French, but the British managed to retrieve and reinstall 24 of them.

The **Fort Museum** is housed in the former Officers' Mess. It has a small but interesting collection of Raj memorabilia, and in the Banqueting Hall upstairs there are a number of portraits of former governors of Madras and other city dignitaries. Open 9am–5pm, except Fridays. Entry free.

St Mary's Church

Built with money raised by public subscription and consecrated in 1680, this is the oldest Anglican church east of Suez, and the oldest surviving British building in India. The spire was completed in 1710, and the sanctuary at the east end is a nineteenth-century addition. The attractive vaulted ceiling with its white stucco rosettes hides a bomb-proofed roof constuction, while the louvred panels in the side walls were designed to open up and turn it into a breezy pavilion in hot weather. The painting of the Last Supper, over the altar, is attributed to the school of Raphael. It is thought to have been looted from a French church in Pondicherry. There are a number of fascinating monuments around the walls, which make good reading. Both Robert Clive and Elihu Yale were married here. For those interested in Raj history, it is possible to consult the church records. The **British cemetery**, which is both the St Mary's Cemetery and the War Graves' Cemetery, is on Pallavam Road, near Central Station. It is one of the largest in India. Open every day.

Clive's House, next to the church, is now the home of the Archaeological Survey of India. One room, known as **Clive's Corner**, is open to the public, and has a number of fascinating photos and letters.

Government Museum and Art Gallery

Pantheon Road, near Egmore Station. Originally built in the grounds of the eighteenth-century Pantheon, which has now vanished. The main museum is housed in a round, red and white Victorian building, rather like a mini-Albert Hall. It was founded in 1851 and has since grown to be one of the finest in the country, with three separate collections of archaeology, art and bronzes.

The most important of the three is the collection of Indian bronzes, one of the finest in the sub-continent and for once well displayed. Most date from the late Pallava and Chola periods (ninth to twelfth centuries) and, if you are prepared to spend the time, offer a good explanation of Hindu religious iconography. The archaeology section has exhibits collected from all over South India, with some prehistoric displays and works from the Chola, Vijayanagar, Chalukya and Hoysala periods. The art gallery has ivory carvings, Rajput and Mughul miniatures, and a number of later paintings. On the second floor is a gallery of modern art, opened in 1984. There are also smaller sections on geology, botany, zoology, and anthropology. Open 9am–5pm, except Fridays and public holidays. Entrance free.

Basilica of San Thome and St Thomas Mount

According to legend, St Thomas (who arrived in Kerala in 52 AD) worked his way across the continent and eventually fetched up in Mylapore. He certainly managed to achieve some conversions, although not on the same scale as his success in the west, but in doing so, fell foul of the authorities.

Clive of India

Robert Clive was born in 1725 into a middle-class English family who found it hard to cope with his rebellious streak and breathed a sigh of relief when, in 1743, he joined the East India Company as a clerk and set out for Madras. Here he found a British colony involved in constant skirmishing with the French and various local Indian rulers, and soon discovered an aptitude for irregular warfare and double-dealing. In 1748 a power struggle for the Hyderabadi throne blew up. The French supported one candidate, the British automatically looked to the other. Deadlock seemed inevitable as both sides geared up for a fight. Clive's big opportunity arrived when the head of the British forces refused the command. Ever willing to grab a chance, Clive took over, and with only 210 men seized the town of Arcot and managed to hold it against French counter-attacks for 53 days. As a result the French and their candidate eventually lost out, and Britain gained effective control of a large area of southern and central India. Clive returned to Madras where, in 1753, he married Margaret Meskylene.

In 1756 Calcutta was captured by Siraj-ud-Daula, the Nawab of Bengal. Clive promptly headed north and, in January 1757, took it back. He then began to hear rumours both of the Nawab's fabulous wealth, and of plots to replace him. He promptly chose the most amenable of the contenders for the throne, backed him, and at the Battle of Plassey utterly routed the Nawab's armies. Britain gained control of Bengal, Clive received titles both in Britain (Baron of Plassey) and from the Mughuls in India (*Sabat Jung* – literally "one tried in battle"), and a hefty personal fortune of £234,000 and land grants worth £30,000 a year. Until 1760 he remained the power behind the throne, just about keeping the other colonists in check while they all did their best to bleed Bengal dry. He was recalled to Britain in 1760.

Four years later the situation was so bad he was sent back as Governor and Commander-in-Chief of Bengal to sort things out. For a time he managed to control the activities of the Calcutta merchants, but his own fingers continued to dabble in many different pies and he was named in an enquiry into the appalling state of affairs in India. Recalled again in 1767, he was brought before Parliament to defend himself in 1773. He managed to clear his name, but committed suicide the following year.

He took refuge on a hill (St Thomas Mount, on the airport road, just beyond Guindy Park), but was shot by an arrow and bled to death. Some say it was just a hunting accident, but he has always been claimed by the church as one of the early martyrs. He was buried on the coast.

His grave was discovered by Armenian Christians in the sixth century, and they built a church on the spot. This was rebuilt by the Portuguese in 1523, and was in turn replaced by the current neo-gothic creation in 1898. This was turned into a basilica in 1956, and in 1957 shared its dedication with Our Lady of Mylapore, who was created joint patron saint of the city. Light and elegant on the outside, the church is gaudily cheerful inside and even has a digital clock bearing the neon legend "Jesus Saves"! The side chapel, now dedicated to Our Lady of Mylapore, is said once to have been the home of St Francis Xavier, and the spot where he was tormented by demons. The Basilica of San Thome is at the south end of Marina Beach.

Valluvar Kottam

Just off Nungambakkam High Road, Egmore. Opened in 1976 in the grounds of what used to be the Governor's Residence, this is part memorial, part auditorium. The auditorium is said to be one of the biggest in Asia. The memorial is to the great Tamil philosopher, poet and saint, Thiruvalluvar. Beside the auditorium is a massive, granite temple car drawn by two stone elephants, each 7 foot tall. All 1,330 verses of Thiruvalluvar's greatest work, the *Thirrukural*, are carved on granite slabs on 67 pillars. The octagonal shrine on the roof of the auditorium contains an image of Thiruvalluvar seated in a chariot. His three raised fingers represent the different aspects of his work – poetry, philosophy and religion. Open 9am–7pm daily. Small admission charge.

Marina Beach

Madras is inordinately proud of its 18-kilometre beach, which they are proud to tell you is the second longest in the world. It is wide, open, completely shadeless, unsuitable for swimming and, sadly, the only badly littered beach I have ever seen in India. It is worth a drive along the city centre section, however, as the Beach Road offers good views of several of Madras's most attractive buildings.

Start in the north at the 1844 **lighthouse**. No longer in use, except as the official benchmark for Madras, it is shaped like a Doric column. Next comes the **High Court Building**, built in 1892 in the Indo-Saracenic style. This is on the site of Chennapatnam village (once known to the British as "Black Town", because this is where the Indians lived). It is said to be the second largest law court in the world (the largest is in London) and is a bright red maze of domes, spires, minarets, and any other sort of decoration the architects could cram in. The central red tower was constructed for use as a lighthouse, and remained in use until 1977. It is nearly 50 metres tall, and can be seen for 30 kilometres. It is possible to have a look around inside, where there is some equally over the top stained glass, woodwork and furniture. Court No. 13 is reckoned to be the best. Open 10.45am–1.45pm and 2.30–4.30pm, Monday to Saturday.

Continuing south, you reach the **fort** (see page 313) and the Cooum River. On the south bank of the river is Anna Square, where Dr C.N. Annadurai, former and extremely popular Chief Minister of Tamil Nadu, is buried. A memorial pillar stands nearby, along with the **Anna Samadhi**, a monument shaped like the curved tusks of an elephant, which marks the gateway to the park.

Just below this is the **aquarium**. It's open from 2–8pm, Monday to Saturday, and 8am–8pm on Sundays and holidays, but is a horrible place and is not recommended.

Next comes the altogether more magnificent **University Building**, designed by Robert Chisholm in 1864, combining Italianate and Saracenic themes. The University of Madras, which was established in 1874, is one of the oldest in India. Next along is the **Senate House**, which was completed in 1879, followed by a modern building, **Ezhilagam**. The **Chepauk Palace**, built by Philip Stowey in 1768 in the Mughul style this is sadly now hidden behind the modern buildings, but the keen can wander round the back for a look.

Continuing southwards are the **Presidency Hall**, also designed by Robert Chisholm; the **University Examination Hall**; **Vivekananda House**, which was formerly an ice house, used to store blocks of ice sent over from Canada and the USA until they invented the fridge; the **Lady Willingdon Training College for Women**; **Queen Mary's College for Women**, the **Office of the Director-General of Police**, and **All India Radio**. At the tail end of all these is the ugly modern lighthouse.

If you wish to continue down further, you will reach San Thome Basilica.

ALSO WORTH VISITING

Kapaleeswarar Temple

Off Kutchery Road, in the south of the city. Although this temple does contain fragments of inscriptions dating back to 1250, it was in fact only built in 1566 by the Vijayanagar kings. The architectural style is typical of the period, and while the brightly coloured, 37 metre-high *gopuram* might seem a little startling, this is in fact correct. All the *gopurams* would have been painted when first built.

The earlier temple which it replaced was badly damaged by the Portuguese. It is thought to have been on the shore, in the spot now occupied by the Basilica of San Thome.

The temple is dedicated to Shiva in the form of a peacock (a couple of scraggy peacocks are kept in the grounds), and to the goddess Kappagambal. It is best known however as the site of a famous miracle which took place in the seventh century, when Saint Ghanasambandar prayed to Kapaleeswarar and brought a girl, Poomparai, back to life. Non-Hindus are only allowed into the outer courtyard.

Sri Parthasarathy Temple

On Triplicane High Road, originally built in the eighth century by the Pallavas, this is the oldest building in Madras. It has however been considerably altered over the centuries, by the Pandyas and Cholas, and, in the early-sixteenth century, by the Vijayanagars. Dedicated to Vishnu in the form of Parthasarathy, the charioteer of the epic hero Arjuna (his story forms part of the *Mahabharata*), it houses images of five incarnations of Vishnu, the most famous of which is of a wounded Krishna as the charioteer, with his wife and brothers. Non-Hindus are not even allowed into the main courtyard.

Guindy Park and Snake Park

On Sander Vallabhai Patel Road (Elliot Beach Road), in the south of the city, **Guindy Park**, formed from the Raj Bhavan estate (the Governor's Residence), is the largest in Madras and has several different sections. **Government House is an attractive single storey building**, built in 1817. Near this and the road stand a number of **memorials**: to Mahatma Gandhi, to General Rajagopalachari (better known as "Rajaji"), the first Governor of Tamil Nadu, and to K. Kamaraj, one of the greatest movers in the Independence struggle.

The **deer park** contains a number of species including black buck, spotted deer, civet cats, jackals, mongooses and a variety of monkeys. The **snake park** has a variety of snakes as well as other reptiles such as turtles and monitor lizards. Snakes on display include kraits, cobras, puff adders, vipers and pythons. A demonstration is given on the hour every hour, from 10am onwards. There is also a **children's park**. The park is open from 8.30am–5.30pm daily.

Theosophical Society

On the south bank of the Adyar River estuary. The Society was founded in New York in 1875 by Madame Blavatsky and Colonel Olcott. The headquarters were moved to Madras in 1882, and here they have remained since, housed in an elegant mansion surrounded by 120 hectares of beautiful gardens. These house a number of shrines belonging to different faiths and a Serene Garden of Remembrance dedicated to the founders. The 400-year-old Banyan tree in the grounds spreads over an area of 40,000 square feet and is thought to be the largest in the world. The library has some 17,000 books, including a valuable collection of oriental palm leaf and parchment manuscripts. Open 8–11am and 2–5pm, Monday to Friday, and 8–11am, Saturday.

Other buildings worth looking out for include the **Wesleyan Church** (Popham's Broadway), the **Armenian Church of the Holy Virgin Mary** (Armenian Street), **Pachaiyappa's Hall** (just west of the High Court Building), **Rajaji Hall** (Adams Road), **Wallajah Mosque** (Triplicane Road), and the **Thousand Lights Mosque** (corner of Anna Salai and Peters Road).

FACT FILE

AIRLINES

There are some variations, but most airline offices are open from 9.30am–5.30pm, Monday to Friday, and 9.30am–1pm Saturday.

Air Canada, Garuda, JAL, Kenya Airways: c/o Global Travels, 733 Anna Salai. Tel: 867 957.

Air France: 769 Anna Salai. Tel: 868 377.

Air India: 19 Marshalls Rd, Egmore. Tel: 474 477.

Air Lanka: Hotel Connemara Annex, Binny's Rd. Tel: 865 301.

Alitalia, Zambia Airways: c/o Ajanta Tours & Travel, Khivraj Mansions, 738 Anna Salai. Tel: 861 406.

Bangladeshi Biman, Philippine Airlines: c/o Jetair, 55 Monteith Rd. Tel: 861 810.

British Airways: Fagun Mansion, 26 Commander-in-Chief Rd, Egmore. Tel: 477 388.

Cathay Pacific, KLM: c/o Spencer & Co, Hotel Connemara, Binny's Rd. Tel: 811 051.

Eastern Airlines, Ethiopian Airlines, Iberia, LOT Polish Airlines, Royal Nepal Airlines: c/o STIC Travels, Hotel Chola Sheraton, 10 Cathedral Rd. Tel: 473 347.

Egypt Air, Yemen Air: c/o BAP Travels, 135 Anna Salai. Tel: 849 913.

Gulf Air: Red Cross Building. Tel: 867 872.

Indian Airlines: 19 Marshalls Rd, Egmore. Tel: 477 977/478 745.

Lufthansa: 171 Anna Salai. Tel: 869 095.

Malaysian Airline System: 189 Anna Salai. Tel: 868 970.

Maldives Airways: c/o Crossworld Tours, Rosy Tower, 7 Nungambakkam High Rd. Tel: 471 497.

North-West Airlines: 1 White's Rd. Tel: 87703.

Pan Am: c/o Indam Travels, 163–4 Anna Salai. Tel: 868 493.

Pakistan International Airways: c/o Swaman, 63 Pantheon Rd. Tel: 810 619.

Qantas: G-3 Eldorado Building, 112 Nungambakkam High Rd. Tel: 478 680.

Sabena: Regency House, 250 Anna Salai. Tel: 451 598.

Scandinavian Airlines, Thai International (SAS): c/o Swan Travel, Aarti Buildings, 189 Anna Salai. Tel: 450 400.

Singapore Airlines: 167 Anna Salai. Tel: 862 871.

Swissair: 191 Anna Salai. Tel: 862 692.

TWA: c/o Air Transportation, 68 Pantheon Rd. Tel: 812 775.

Vayudoot: 1st Floor, Wellington Estate, Commander-in-Chief Rd. Tel: 869 901. Airport no. 435 521.

BANKS

There are a few minor variations, but most banks are open from 10am–2pm, Monday to Friday, and 10am–Midday Saturday.

Allahabad Bank: Anna Theatre Building, 41 Anna Salai. Tel: 477 262.

Bank of America: 748 Anna Salai. Tel: 810 856.

Bank of Baroda: 738a Anna Salai. Tel: 812 504.

Bank of India: 827 Anna Salai. Tel: 88664.

Also branch at 46 Cathedral Rd. Tel: 478 091.

Canara Bank: 781 Anna Salai. Tel: 812 071.

Also branch at 23 Mowbrays Rd. Tel: 452 769.

First National City Bank: 768 Anna Salai. Tel: 810 756.

Grindlays Bank: 104 Anna Salai. Tel: 811 168.

Also branch at 3a Padmanabha Nagar. Tel: 411 092.

Indian Bank: 612 Anna Salai. Tel: 475 081.

Also branches at Purasawalkam High Rd. Tel: 661 413; and Commander-in-Chief Rd. Tel: 470 661.

Indian Overseas Bank: 762 Anna Salai. Tel: 82041.

Also branch at 109 Nungambakkam High Rd. Tel: 473 989; 58 Pantheon Rd. Tel: 867 234; and 473 Poonamallee High Rd. Tel: 666 141.

State Bank of India: 103 Anna Salai. Tel: 840 393.

Also at the international airport.

Thomas Cook: 20 North Beach Rd. Tel: 524 976.

United Bank of India: 675 Anna Salai. Tel: 812 112.

CONSULATES

France (Hon. Consul): 3rd Floor, VD Swami House, 26 Cathedral Rd. Tel: 476 854.

Open 9.30am–5pm

Germany: 22 Commander-in-Chief Rd. Tel: 471 747.

Open 9am–midday.

Italy (Hon. Consul): 5th Floor, Sudarsan Building, 86 Chamiers Rd. Tel: 452 329/451 691.

Open 10am–5pm.

Japan: 60 Spur Tank Rd, Chetpet. Tel: 865 594.

Open 9am–5pm.

Malaysia: 287 TTK Rd. Tel: 453 580.

Open 8am–4pm

Norway, (Hon. Consul): 44–5 Rajaji Salai. Tel: 517 950.

Open 10am–5pm.

Singapore: 2nd Floor, Apex Plaza, 3 Nungambakkam High Rd. Tel: 473 795/476 393.

Open 9am–midday.

Spain (Hon. Consul): Lawdale, 8 Nimmo Rd, Santhome. Tel: 72008.

Open 9.30am–12.30pm.

Sri Lanka: 9D Nawab Habibullah Avenue, Anderson Rd. Tel: 472 270/470 831.

Open 9am–5pm
Sweden (Hon. Consul):   6 Cathedral Rd. Tel: 472 040, etxn 60.
Open 9.30–1pm
UK: 24 Anderson Rd, Nungambakkam. Tel: 473 136.
Open 8.30am–4pm
USA: 220 Anna Salai. Tel: 473 040.
Open 8.30am–5.15pm.

Austria, Belgium, Brazil, Czechoslovakia, Denmark, Finland, Hungary, the Philippines, Romania, Turkey and the USSR also have diplomatic representation here.

COMMUNICATIONS

GPO: Rajaji Salai (North Beach Rd), and **Anna Rd Post Office:** Anna Salai.

Both offices have *poste restante* facilities and 24-hour telegraph offices.

DHL International Courier Service: 44/5 Pantheon Rd. Tel: 825 4102/04/06.

Open 9.30am–6pm.

Globe Grabbers: Shop 17, Parsn Manere, Gemini Circle, 602 Anna Salai. Tel: 825 1414/825 1717.

Commercial pay phone centre.

ENTERTAINMENT

Hello Madras is a useful monthly publication, giving listings of all sorts of addresses and activities. Available from tourist offices, hotels and some bookshops. The local daily, *The Hindu*, also has good entertainment listings.

Madras Music Academy: 115–E Mowbray Rd (Tel: 475 619) has regular traditional dance, music and drama performances.

SHOPPING

Books

Higginbotham's: 2 branches at 814 Anna Salai (Tel: 831 841), and F39 Anna Nagar E.

Landmark: 3 Nungambakkam High Rd. Tel: 479 637.

Kennedy Book House: 1/55 Anna Salai. Tel: 831 797.

Fabrics

India Silk House: 846 Anna Salai. Tel: 568 930.

Handloom House: 7 Rattan Bazaar. Tel: 357 756.

Co-optrex: Kuvalagan, NSC Bose Rd.

Also has branches in most other areas of Madras.

Radha Silks Emporium: 1 Sannathi St, Mylapore. Tel: 71187.

Kumaran Silks: Panagal Salai Park. Tel: 443 544.

Souvenirs
Indian Arts Museum: Agarchand Mansion, 151 Anna Salai. Tel: 868 683/861 560.

Open 9.30am–8.30pm.

Victoria Technical Institute: 765 Anna Salai. Tel: 863 131.

Open 9.30am–6.30pm, Monday to Friday; 9.30am–1.30pm, Sunday.

Pompuhar (Tamil Nadu Government Emporium): 818 Anna Salai. Tel: 832 724.

Open 10am–10pm.

SMCS: 14A College Rd. Tel: 476 997.

Open 9am–8pm.

There are a number of other state emporia along Anna Salai, including **Haryana, Kashmir, Kerala, Karnataka, Andra Pradesh,** and **W. Bengal.**

TOURIST INFORMATION

Government of India Tourist Office: 154 Anna Salai. Tel: 869 685.

Open 9am–6pm, Monday to Friday; 9am–1pm Saturday.

Also tourist information counters at the **domestic air terminal** (Tel: 431 686, open 24 hours), and the **international air terminal** (open to meet incoming flights).

India Tourism Development Corporation (ITDC): 29 Victoria Crescent, Commander-in-Chief Rd.

Open 6am–8pm, Monday to Saturday, 6am–2pm, Sunday. Book here for ITDC tours.

Tamil Nadu Government Tourist Office: 143 Anna Salai. Tel: 840 752.

Open 10am–5pm daily.

Tamil Nadu Tourist Development Corporation (TTDC): 143 Anna Salai. Tel: 849 803.

Open 10am–5pm daily. Book TTDC tours here.

Also a tourist information counter at **Central Railway Station** (Tel: 563 351). Sales counter open Sundays only.

The following regions all have tourist offices at 28 C-in-C Rd: **Himachal Pradesh** (Tel: 472 966); **Kerala** (Tel: 479 862); **Rajasthan** (Tel: 472 093); **Uttar Pradesh** (Tel: 479 726).

Other state tourist offices include **Gujurat,** 2nd Floor, Mount Chambers, 758 Anna Salai (Tel: 825 172); **Haryana,** 700 Anna Salai (Tel: 860 475); **Jammu and Kashmir,** 1st Floor, 837 Anna Salai; and **W. Bengal,** 787 Anna Salai (Tel: 87612).

VISA EXTENSIONS

Chief Immigration Office: Foreigners Regional Registration Office, 9 Village Rd. Tel: 475 424/478 210/477 036.

Open 9.30am–6.30pm, Monday to Friday. Visa extensions and permits for the Andaman Islands from here.

WHERE TO STAY

Luxury

Trident: 1/24 GST Rd. Tel: 434 747. Telex: 041-26055.

First of a new, slightly cheaper chain being developed by the Oberoi Group to cater mainly for business trade. Extremely comfortable and elegant and, most importantly, right near the airport, so it is more convenient than the inner city hotels if your flight is at an awkward time. They also do 12-hour lets if you have a day to kill while waiting for a flight, and offer free airport transfers.

Hotel Connemara: Binny's Rd, off Anna Salai. Tel: 860 123. Telex: 041–8197 CH IN

Built as the town house of the Nawabs of Wallajah and converted into a hotel in the 1930s. Recently renovated and now run by the Taj Group, but still wonderfully atmospheric, and the most interesting place to stay in Madras, if you can afford it.

Taj Coromandel: 17 Nungambakkam High Rd. Tel: 474 849. Telex: 417 194 TAJM IN.

Run by the Taj Group. Probably the best hotel in town, but modern and a little soulless. There are regular traditional dance displays here in the evenings.

Chola Sheraton: 10 Cathedral Rd. Tel: 473 347. Telex: 041–7200 WELC IN.

Part of the Welcomgroup. Also extremely comfortable, modern and unatmospheric.

Park Sheraton: 132 TTK Rd. Tel: 452 525. Telex: 041–6868/8881.

Also run by the Welcomgroup, and similar in standard and style to the Chola.

Upmarket

Hotel Savera: 69 Dr Radhakrishnan Rd (Edward Elliots Rd), Mylapore. Tel: 474 700. Telex: 041–6869.

Hotel Ambassador Pallava: 53 Monteith Rd, Egmore. Tel: 868 584/862 061.

President Hotel: 16 Dr Radhakkrishnan Rd (Edward Elliot Rd), Mylapore. Tel: 842 211/832 211. Telex: 041–6699 ARIF IN.

Madras International Hotel: 693 Anna Salai. Tel: 861 811. Telex: 041–7373 ARU IN.

Mid-range

New Victoria Hotel: 3 Kennet Lane, Egmore. Tel: 567 738. Telex: 041–7897 VICKY IN.

Imperial Hotel: 14 Whannels Rd, Egmore. Tel: 566 176.

Cheap
New Woodlands Hotel: 72 Dr Radhakrishnan Rd (Edward Elliot Rd), Mylapore. Tel: 473 111. Telex: 041–6914 MS IN.
Hotel Kanchi: 28 Commander-in-Chief Rd, Egmore. Tel: 471 100.
Broadlands Hotel: 16 Vallabha Agraharam St, off Triplicane Rd. Tel: 845 573/848 131.
Hotel Peacock: 1089 Poonamallee High Rd. Tel: 39081. Telex: 041–8169.
Hotel Maris: 9 Cathedral Rd. Tel: 470 541. Telex: 041–6380 MARS IN.
Hotel Ram Prasad: 22 Gandhi Irwin Rd, Egmore. Tel: 567 875.

Ultra-cheap
TTDC Youth Hostel: 2nd Avenue, Indira Nagar. Tel: 412 882.
Tourist Hostel: Andhra Mahila Sabha, 38 Adayar Bridge Rd. Tel: 416 001.
YWCA Guest House: 1086 Poonamallee High Rd. Tel: 39920.
YMCA: 14 Westcott Rd, Royapettah (Tel: 811 158), and 17 Ritherdon Rd, Vepery (Tel: 32831).
Salvation Army's Red Guest House: 15 Ritherdon Rd, Vepery. Tel: 38148.

WHERE TO EAT

More Upmarket
Most of the best restaurants in Madras are at the posh hotels (see above for addresses). They include:
Park Sheraton – The Gatsby (multi-cuisine, with live folk music at lunchtime, disco at night); **The Khyber** (poolside, specialising in Indian-style grills and barbecues); and **The Residency** (Indian, Chinese and continental).
Connemara – The Kolam, restaurant and grill. This has the best buffet in town, and also has a good pastry/cake shop.
Taj Coromandal – The Mysore (Indian), **The Golden Dragon** (Chinese), and **The Pavilion** (a 24-hour coffee shop).
Chola Sheraton – Peshawri (Indian), **The Sagari** (Chinese), and **The Mercara** (24-hour coffee shop).
Cascade: Kakani Towers, 15 Khader Nawaz Khan Rd. Tel: 471 412.
   Thai, Malay and Japanese food.
Fiesta: Spencer's Building, 769 Anna Salai. Tel: 810 051, extn 853/893.
   Indian, continental and Chinese food.

Cheaper
Chungking Chinese Restaurant: 67 Anna Salai. 86134
China Town: 74 Cathedral Rd. Tel: 476 221.
Woodlands Drive-In Restaurant: 30 Cathedral Rd. Tel: 471 981.

Mathura Restaurant: Tarapore Towers (2nd Floor), 827 Anna Salai.
Tel: 831 777.
Dasaprakash: 100 Poonamallee High Rd. Tel: 825 5111.
   Also has an ice-cream parlour.

Fast Food
Cakes "n" Bakes: 22 Nungambakkan High Rd. Tel: 477 075.
   Fast food.
Chit Chat: 557 Anna Salai. Tel: 451 880.
Snappy: 74 Cathedral Rd. Tel: 475 770.

NORTHERN TAMIL NADU

KANCHIPURAM

Kanchipuram is the seat of the Hindu *math* (the equivalent of the Pope), HH Sankaracharaya, who has his home in the nearby village of Kaladi. As such it is one of the seven sacred cities of India (the others are Haridwar, Ujjain, Varanasi, Mathura, Ayodhya and Dwaraka). Since the third century BC, it has also been a seat of learning for both Hindus and Buddhists. The great Buddhist saint, Bodhidharma, who was responsible for taking Buddhism to the Far East, lived and worked here in the sixth century AD, and for a while it became one of the great centres of Indian Buddhism, with some 100 temples and 10,000 monks.

In the sixth century AD, the Pallavas established the city as their capital. With the ascendancy of the Cholas, it remained as their northern capital, and even the Vijayanagars upheld its importance.

The net result for the visitor is that this small city, of around 200,000 people, has about 1,000 temples all told. Only about 80 of them in reasonable order, however, and even fewer are still in use today. No one expects you to visit them all, but do allow a full day for a visit, as it would be a shame only to see the most important ones listed below. If you have the time, you can wander the streets and pop into any more that grab your fancy as you pass. You will also able to do justice to the silk if you have enough time to drool as well as shop.

GETTING THERE

By far the easiest way to get here is from Madras, 71 kilometres away.

Kanchipuram is on a metre guage line with reasonably frequent **trains** into Madras Beach Station via Chengalpattu. Going west, services connect with Arakkonam, on the Madras-Bangalore line. The **railway station** is on the eastern edge of the town.

Kanchipuram is on the main national highway between Madras and Bangalore. There are pretty good **bus** connections, with regular services from Madras (the dreaded State bus stand behind Popham's Broadway), as well as four direct services a day to Mamallapuram (64 kilometres), plus many more buses to Chingleput that connect with services to Mamallapuram. There are also less frequent direct services to Tiruchirapalli, Pondicherry, Kanyakumari, Bangalore, Vellore, Tirupati, Tiruttani and Tiruvannamalai.

The **bus stand** is in the centre of town, on the corner of Nellukkara St and Kossa St.

Tourist taxis from Madras are an easy, if slightly more expensive, way of getting to and around Kanchipuram, while the city is also included on some TTDC and ITDC **tours**, although, as these take in Mamallapuram and a couple of other stops as well in the day, they are not only hurried but you will be exceedingly over-templed.

GETTING AROUND
It is not really possible to get around on foot, as things are just a bit too spread out. There are some **taxis** and **auto-rickshaws**. The other alternative is to engage a **cycle-rickshaw** for the day. Make sure you set a price before you start. If you find a driver who speaks decent English, you could even find you have a tour guide thrown in (although do double check before you take the facts as gospel). The drawback is that you will have to agree to go to his brother's/mother's/cousin's silk workshop. You can hire a **bicycle** from beside the bus stand.

GETTING YOUR BEARINGS
Kanchipuram is built on the north bank of the Vegavathi River. The **Railway station** is on the eastern edge of the town, about 2.5 kilometres from the river. The **bus station** is in the centre of town, about 1 kilometre from the railway station. The hotels and the temples are all scattered within a 3-kilometre radius of the bus station. There is no one district that has all the amenities, and although I've seen four maps, none of them bears more than the slightest resemblance to another. It's time to give up and let the rickshaw driver take you round.

DON'T MISS . . .
Kailasanatha Temple
On Putteri Street, on the western edge of the city. Begun by the Pallava king, Rajasimha, and finished by his son, Najendra, in the late-seventh, early-eighth centuries, this is one of the earliest surviving temples in Kanchipuram, and the only one not to have been altered by later additions. Built of sandstone, and dedicated to Shiva, it is a slightly more sophisticated version of the temples at Mamallapuram, with seven *rathas* (monolithic temple chariots), each showing different aspects of Shiva. The main rectangular temple has several intricately carved panels, including one showing a dance contest between

Shiva and Parvati, while faint traces of eighth-century frescoes are still visible on some of the inner walls. There is a *lingam* in the inner sanctuary. The outer wall of the enclosure holds 58 small shrines, showing different aspects of Shiva, each with a *nandi* at its feet. The eight opposite the entrance are said to have been built by the queens of Rajasimha.

Sri Vaikuntha Perumal Temple
Near the corner of East Raja Street and Kamakshi Amman Sannathi Street, in the centre of town, near the railway station. This was built by Pallava kings, Parameshwara and Nandivarma Malla, between 674 and 800 AD, and is dedicated to Vishnu. The cloisters are formed of a series of lion columns that foreshadow the great 1,000 pillar halls that became a hallmark of Chola temple building. Bas relief panels and inscriptions on the inner side of the parapet tell the history of the Pallava dynasty, with battle scenes of their wars with the Chalukyas and Gangas. The unusual sanctum is in the form of a free-standing, three-storey tower, each storey holding an image of Vishnu in the reclining, sitting and standing positions.

Ekambareswara Temple
In the north-west corner of the city, between North and West Made Streets, this is the largest of the Kanchipuram temples. Originally built by the Pallava kings, and dedicated to Shiva, it has been in continuous use for the last 1,300 years. Additions and alterations by both the Cholas and Vijayanagars have, however, changed it beyond all recognition, and there is little left to show its early origins.

The temple is huge, covering an area of 9 hectares, with five enclosures, and a 1,000-pillar hall. The massive, granite outer walls and 59 metre-high *gopuram* were built by Vijayanagar king Krishna Devaraya between 1509–25. Its sculptures include several portraits of both him and his wife.

Non-Hindus are only allowed into one enclosure, which contains a mango tree that is claimed to be 3,500 years old. It still bears fruit, and it is said that the fruit from each of the four branches (which represent the four *vegas* or Hindu scriptures) tastes different. Eka Amra Natha (the Lord of the Mango Tree) is the temple's presiding deity.

The inner sanctum contains a *lingam* said to have been created by Parvati herself as a penance for playing a trick on her husband. The temple was also used as a fortress during Clive's Arcot campaign.

There is a small entrance and camera charge.

Sri Kamakshi Amman Temple

In the centre of town, just off Odai Street. Again built originally by the Pallavas, and heavily altered, this is now, to all intents and purposes, a fourteenth-century Chola temple. Dedicated unusually to the goddess Kamakshi (Durga-Parvati), who is also the patron goddess of Kanchipuram, this is one of only three holy centres in India for followers of Shakti, the Hindu mother-goddess cult which sees the female (Durga) as the active and accessible and the male (Shiva) as the passive, remote energy. Other Shakti centres are in Madurai and Varanasi.

The temple has some fine carvings, and a golden *gopuram*, but is best known for a magnificent wooden temple car which is paraded during the temple car festival in February/March each year. The rest of the time it is kept partly covered in Gandhi Street.

Sri Varadaraja Perumal Temple

Just off Thirukatchinambi Koil Road, near the river, to the south-east of the city. Also known as the **Devarajaswamy temple**, this is built on an elephant-shaped hillock called Hastagiri, on which Brahma himself is said to have made a sacrifice.

Another massive temple, dedicated to Vishnu, this was built by the Vijayanagar kings in the sixteenth century. It has a 1,000-pillar hall, two *gopurams* and a famous ornamental chain said to be carved from a single piece of stone.

There is a small entrance and camera charge.

ALSO WORTH VISITING

Weavers

Kanchipuram is one of the main centres in southern India for both silk and cotton weaving, with some 5,000 families in the town involved (see box). For a more authoritative tour, or if you want to buy, contact the Weavers' Service Centre, 20 Railway Station Rd. Tel: 2530.

FACT FILE

WHERE TO STAY

Hotel Tamil Nadu: 78 Kamakshiamman Sannadhi St. Tel: 2561.
  Virtually opposite the railway station, this is run by the TTDC, is also known as the Ashok Traveller's Lodge, and is the most upmarket place in town.
Sri Rama Lodge: 19–20 Nellukkara St. Tel: 3195/2395.
  Very basic, near the bus station.
Sri Krishna Lodge: 68a Nellukkara St. Tel: 2831.
  Very basic, near the bus station.
  Most people visit Kanchipuram on a day trip, either from Madras or Mamallapuram.

WHERE TO EAT

The Hotel Tamil Nadu has the best food in town. Otherwise, there are a number of small, fairly grubby cafés in the vicinity of the bus station. Take your pick.

MAMALLAPURAM (MAHABILAPURAM)

It's not often that you find the ideal spot for a longish stay in India, but **Mamallapuram** comes close. It has a good beach and swimming, a small village with beach houses, cheap hotels and a range of better resorts for those who like their comfort – and some of the oldest and most beautiful of all Tamil Nadu's many temples. Add to this the fact that Madras is within easy reach, so you can go in for the day if you need to take care of any business, and it becomes close to perfect.

The name of the village has caused some confusion. For the

Southern silk and cotton

Most of us think of Indian cotton as that flimsy, flyaway loose weave which is used to make cheap shirts and dresses. This is to do it an injustice. India grows 23 different varieties of cotton of all qualities and has over 3 million handlooms, as well as a large number of factories involved in processing and weaving it. Madras was the centre of the British cotton trade in India and long ago gave its name to Madras cotton, one of the heaviest and finest cotton cloths in the world. The penalty for tourists is that the city is probably the most expensive place in India to go fabric shopping.

Hundreds of thousands of people in Tamil Nadu still make their living from weaving, whether it be the simple cotton *lunghi*, or fabulous, heavy brocaded cloths, developed originally under the Pallavas in the fourth century AD for use in the temples. Kanchipuram in particular has long since had a reputation for these splendid, elaborately patterned brocades, known as *zari*. Some use a cotton warp and silk weft, others are all silk, but most include a generous proportion of gold or silver thread. It can take two weavers working together nearly a month to produce a sari, so prices are not cheap and these are more often than not bought as wedding gowns or as India's equivalent of an Yves St Laurent original. A good weaver can turn out two cheap cotton *lunghis* a day, and a simple, everyday silk sari will probably take about a day's work.

There are some 5,000 households devoted to weaving in Kanchipuram, usually with the entire family involved. Any one of them will be happy to show you around and explain how they work. If you want to buy, it is probably better to wait and go to the Weavers' Service Centres, the co-op headquarters and shops in Kanchipuram and Madras, where you will have a better range and more realistic prices.

last 100 years or so, it has been known as Mahabilapuram, but the ancient name, which has now been officially revived, is Mamallapuram. Either will do however as both are recognised. The origins of the name are equally disputed. One theory says that it is named after the Pallava king Narasimha who was also known by the praise name "Mahamalla" (great wrestler). Others say that it was the site of Vishnu's victory over the giant, Mahabali.

There was a thriving seaport here as early as the first century AD, and it remained a significant town up until the sixteenth century, with such diverse travellers as Ptolemy and Marco Polo mentioning it in their memoirs. It was during the Pallava period, from the sixth to eighth centuries, that it really came into its own, however, as the royal family's southern capital. It might now have shrunk into a small village, with no ships but a few tiny fishing vessels, but a hive of building activity over this period left it with one of the greatest concentrations of temple art in India, with fourteen cave temples, eight monolithic rathas, a host of other fragmentary sculptures, and, of course, the famous **Shore Temples**. Temple building appears to have begun during the reign of Narasimha II (630–68), and to have continued until the death of Rajasimha in 728.

GETTING THERE

The nearest **airport** is Madras, 58 kilometres to the north. The nearest **railway station** is at Chengalpattu, from where there are regular buses. Train services are slow and relatively infrequent, however, and your journey will be faster and easier if you get a **bus** direct from Madras. PTC services leave the ghastly State Bus Stand in Madras about every 30 minutes, and there are also private buses from Parry's Corner (see page 308). The journey takes about 2 1/2 hours. There are also five buses a day from Pondicherry, if you are coming up from the south (also 2 1/2 hours), and four direct services a day to Kanchipuram, if you want to avoid Madras. Alternatively, splash out and hire a taxi, and do the journey in about an hour.

GETTING AROUND

The more glamorous resorts are somewhat spread out, the furthest around 10 kilometres away at Covelong. The resorts will organise **taxis** for those who want them, and if you walk up to the main road, most of the **buses** pass the gates. Once in Mamallapuram itself, everything is within walking distance, except, perhaps, the 5 *rathas*. There are plenty of **auto-rickshaws** and **cycle-rickshaws** in the centre of the village, and even more small boys who are prepared to go and get you one, if you are somewhere else.

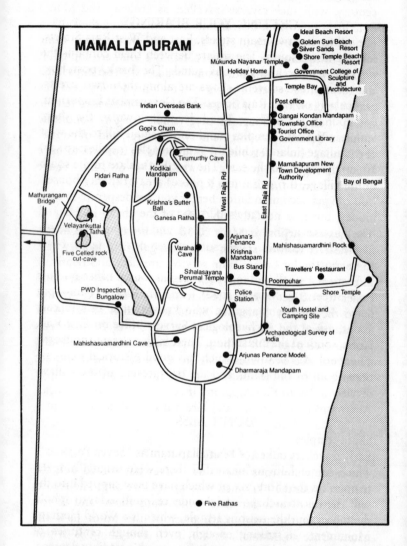

MAMALLAPURAM

Ideal Beach Resort
Golden Sun Beach
Silver Sands Resort
Shore Temple Beach Resort
Mukunda Nayanar Temple
Holiday Home
Government College of Sculpture and Architecture
Temple Bay
Post office
Gangai Kondan Mandapam
Township Office
Tourist Office
Government Library
Mamallapuram New Town Development Authority
Indian Overseas Bank
Gopi's Churn
Tirumurthy Cave
Kodikai Mandapam
Pidari Ratha
West Raja Rd
East Raja Rd
Bay of Bengal
Mathurangam Bridge
Krishna's Butter Ball
Ganesa Ratha
Velayankuttai Tatha
Five Celled rock cut-cave
Varaha Cave
Arjuna's Penance
Krishna Mandapam
Bus Stand
Mahishasuamardhini Rock
Sihalasayana Perumal Temple
Travellers' Restaurant
Poompuhar
PWD Inspection Bungalow
Police Station
Shore Temple
Youth Hostel and Camping Site
Mahishasuamardhini Cave
Archaeological Survey of India
Arjunas Penance Model
Dharmaraja Mandapam

● Five Rathas

There is also a **bicycle hire** shop on the main road, near the bus station. Rates are cheap, the land is generally flat, and there is less likelihood than in many other places of your being flattened by the local traffic.

Take a torch with you in the evenings, as the street lighting is negligible at best and seems to be confined to two streets.

GETTING YOUR BEARINGS

The village has two main streets, East and West Raja Streets, running north-south. The square between them contains the working temple and the **bus stand**. The **bank, post box**, and most of the souvenir shops are along these two streets, particularly on East Raja Street. The **Government Emporium**, Poompuhar, is on Shore Road, leading down to the **shore temples**. The **cave temples** stand on the small hill to the west of the village (inland) while the shore temples (needless to say) are on the beach to the east. The **Five Rathas** are to the south of the village, through a much poorer area of shanty houses. You can get accommodation here if you are desperate to save money, but it is not advised. Most of the cheap hotels and beach houses are between the village and the sea, to the north of the shore temples. The resorts stretch out along the coast to the north.

There is a small and fairly ineffectual **tourist office** on East Raja Street (the Madras road). (Tel: 32. Open 10am–5pm daily). If you want a guide who knows what he's talking about, ask at the **Archaeological Survey Office** on East Raja Street, south of the bus station. There is also a state-sponsored guidebook to the town, which has good historical explanations, both of the sights and the background of the Pallava dynasty.

DON'T MISS . . .

Shore temples

Early travellers talked of Mamallapuram as "Seven Pagodas", which some claim to mean that there were originally seven temples on the shore, six of which have now slipped into the sea. There is no archaeological evidence found so far to uphold the theory, but the existing temple, which is a World Heritage Monument, is striking enough, even though centuries of battering by wind and waves have caused incredible damage, destroying much of the detail of the wealth of sculpture. A massive breakwater has now been constructed behind the temples to try and limit damage.

The whole is set in one large temple courtyard, surrounded by statues of bulls and lions. There are three shrines, with, unusually, Shiva and Vishnu sharing their quarters. The oldest of the shrines is the rectangular central one, which has lost its spire. This is dedicated to Vishnu and contains an image of him in repose, as well as various incidents from his life on the outer walls. The two pyramidal shrines are dedicated to Shiva. There are also the remains of a number of *mandapams* and other buildings within the courtyard.

Arjuna's Penance

This is a massive bas relief, 27 metres long and 9 metres high, carved along the curve of the hill just behind the bus stand. It is thought to be one of the largest in the world.

It is commonly known as *Arjuna's Penance*, but there is some doubt as to whether this is really the case. One of five Pandya brothers who had lost their kingdom, Arjuna, one of the heroes of the *Mahabharatha*, made a penance to ask Shiva for a miraculous weapon with which he could defeat his enemies. When Shiva appeared to grant him his request, all the animals in the world came to watch. The other interpretation claims that the praying figure is in fact Bhagiratha, an ancestor of Rama whose own ancestors had been turned into ash by an angry sage. In order to redeem their souls, they had to be washed by the waters of the Ganges, but as the flood would be devestating, Bhagiratha prayed to Shiva for assistance. Shiva received the full weight of water in his hair and trickled it through slowly, watched by all the gods.

Whichever interpretation is correct, it is an artistic master-piece. Dominated by the massive elephants, it is a mass of detail, with extraordinarily lively animals, people, and gods, all gathered together. Even the natural cleft in the rock has been drawn into the sculpture. The remains of a water tank at the top of the cliff above the break lead many to think that this was turned into a waterfall to represent the falling waters of the Ganges.

Krishna Mandapam
Just along the road to the south of Arjuna's Penance. A rock cut temple of the mid-seventh century, this has a fine panel telling a story from the life of Krishna. He persuaded the villagers to ignore Indra, the god of rain. Indra, in his fury, called down terrific storms and threatened to destroy the countryside. The horrified villagers turned to Krishna for help, and he solemnly uprooted a nearby mountain and held it over them like an umbrella for the next week. They remained safe, but the rest of India was devastated. The *mandapa* at the front is a later addition.

There is a second, unfinished relief of Arjuna's Penance at the southern end of the hill, behind the old lighthouse.

The cave temples
The rock cut temples are clustered together, along with a number of other fragmentary sculptures, on the massive granite outcrop to the west of the village. A path which starts near Arjuna's Penance leads up to the top and round the most important of them. Only the most important are described below. There are small explanatory plaques beside several others.

As you walk up, you will see a vast granite boulder lodged, somewhat precariously, on the edge of a smooth rocky slope. This is known as **Krishna's Butterball** (reason unknown). Far from being dangerous, it has been there forever and even the Pallavas, 1,200 years ago, failed to shift it, in spite of using men, horses and even elephants.

Next to this is the **Ganesha Ratha**, a small, free-standing monolithic shrine, carved between 665–80. It is the only complete *ratha* in Mamallapuram. It has an inscription which shows that it was originally dedicated to Shiva. The *lingam* was removed, and the statue of Ganesha added more recently.

Turn left along the path at the top, and the first temple you meet (on your left) is the **Varaha temple**. This has a small rock cut shrine with a *mandapam* and bathing tank in front. It was dedicated to Vishnu, and was probably carved between 640–74. There are four fine bas relief panels: on the north wall, Vishnu is emerging from the sea, after rescuing the goddess Earth; on the south wall he is shown as Vamana the dwarf who grew to an incredible size to fight the giant Mahabali. The other panels are of Lakshmi (east) and Durga (west).

Follow the path, and there are two turnings off to the left. The first leads to the **Rayala Gopuram**, the second down to the road, beside the **Krishna Mandapam**. Continuing along the path at the top, the next major temple is the **Mahishamardini Cave**, built between 640–74 and dedicated to Shiva. It is a triple-celled temple with a *mandapam* in front. The central panel shows a family group of Shiva, Parvathi and Skanda, with Nandi at their feet and Brahma and Vishnu in the background. The southern panel shows Vishnu in repose, the northern depicts the fight between Durga and the buffalo-headed demon, Mahishasura.

The five rathas

Also known as the **Pancha rathas**, after the five Pandya brothers of the *Mahabharatha*, these stand clustered together, about 1 kilometre south of the main village. Monolithic temple cars, they are some of the earliest examples of what later became one of the main architectural features of southern temples. Four, the **Draupathi ratha**, the **Arjuna ratha**, the **Bhima ratha** and the **Dharmaraja ratha**, stand in a row, aligned north-south, while the fifth, the **Nakula-Shadeva ratha and stone elephant** stands on its own to the west. Together they give a quick run-down of all the different types of temple architecture, from the *gopurams* of Hindu temples, to the *stupas* of the Buddhists, that were beginning to appear in the south.

ALSO WORTH SEEING

School of sculpture
East Raja Street. This is the official state school of sculpture. It is hard to miss, as the entire town rings to the sound of chisels on stone, and every second shop seems to be a workshop, where current and former pupils turn out vast quantities of work to feed the souvenir market. Almost everything they produce is simple copying of ancient religious art, although you do occasionally find someone experimenting with something more innovative. Price carefully before you buy. I was offered a temple horse by one sculptor at a "very good price, because I made it myself" – it was only three times the price of an identical model in the souvenir shop next-door. The school is open from 9am–1pm, and 2–6 pm, except Tuesdays.

Nethaji museum
West Raja Street, near Arjuna's Penance. A tiny archaeological museum with fragments of sculptures found in the area.

OUT OF TOWN

Tiger cave
On the coast, 5 kilometres north of Mamallapuram. To get there, take the Madras bus, hire a bicycle, or walk up the beach. A Pallava cave temple and group of *rathas*, built at much the same time as the temples in the village. It gets its name from the magnificent frieze of snarling tigers that surrounds the entrance to the cave temple.

Crocodile bank

At Vadannammeli village, 20 kilometres north of Mamallapuram, just off the main Madras road. Backed by the World Wildlife Fund, Crocodile Bank was set up in 1976 to provide a captive breeding program for the three, rapidly vanishing species of native Indian crocodiles.

There are three species of crocodile native to India. The most common is the large **saltwater** crocodile. The **mugger** or marsh crocodile is more adaptable, living anywhere from small, freshwater streams, through brackish swamps, to the river estuaries. The **gharial**, which is a fish-eater that naturally lives only in the major river estuaries, is now almost extinct, except for captive populations.

The program has been a resounding success and crocodiles are now regularly released back into the wild. Other species have also arrived (some even coming in from Thailand and Africa) and Crocodile Bank now has around 2,000 crocodiles, of six different species here as well as a number of other reptiles, including tortoises, turtles and snakes.

Open 8.30am–5.30pm daily. Admission charge.

Cholamandal artists' village

Forty kilometres north of Mamallapuram on the main Madras Road. Officially much closer to Madras, this nevertheless makes a good excursion from Mamallapuram. Created as a co-operative by a former head of the Madras School of Arts, painters, sculptors, and even photographers from all over South India have gathered in this tiny village and have turned it into a hive of artistic activity. Most will welcome you into their workshops and studios and there is a gallery where you can buy paintings, drawings, sculpture, batiks and graphics. Open 6am–8pm. There is also an open air theatre where regular dance, music and drama performances are staged.

Tirukkalukkunram

Sixteen kilometres from Mamallapuram, on the road to Chengalpattu. Once there, you are faced by a climb up about 400 steep stone steps, but at the top is a small but important Pallava temple that has been a major pilgrimage site for centuries. Each day at noon two kites arrive to be fed by a priest on a mixture of sweet rice and ghee. No one knows why they come, but they (or their ancestors) have arrived every day for centuries. A Dutch writer, Havert, talks of witnessing their lunch in 1681. Legend says that they are two ascetics who upset Shiva and were turned into birds. Each day, they start in Varanasi and make their way south to Rameswaram, making pit stops at several particularly favoured temples en route. They will have to continue in this way until the end of the present Kali age – which is several thousand years off.

Vedanthangal bird sanctuary

Fifty kilometres south-west of Mamallapuram, off the main Tiruchipalli Road. The nearest railway station is at Maduranthakam, 15 kilometres away. The ITDC run tours to the sanctuary in season.

Originally established in 1798, the official sanctuary covers only 30 hectares of marshy land on the edge of Lake Vedantangal. Unofficially, the birds' breeding ground covers an area of about 10 square kilometres, with several habitats, including woodland, marsh, and open grass, as well as several other lakes. It is an extraordinarily crowded place, with up to 100,000 birds of 100 different species being recorded at peak season. Amongst the more common species are sandpipers, wagtails, teals, ibis, shags, cormorants, spoonbills, darters, coots, ducks, egrets, herons and mallards. As many of them are migratory, the best time to visit is from November to February, at the height of the breeding season.

There are viewing platforms near the lake and basic accommodation is available at the **Sanctuary Rest House**. Book through the Wildlife Warden, 50 4th Main Rd, Candhi-Nagar, Adyar, Madras. Tel: 413 947.

FACT FILE

WHERE TO STAY

Luxury
Fisherman's Cove: Covelong Beach, Chingleput District. Tel: 04114–
6268. Telex: c/o 041–7194 TAJM IN.
Actually about 20 kilometres north of Mamallapuram itself. This is
run by the Taj Group with their customary flair, and is the only really
upmarket beach resort in the area.

Mid-range
Silversands: about 2 kilometres north of the village, on the Covelong
Rd. Tel: 04113–228/283. Telex: 041–8082 SAND IN.
The largest of the resorts, with a range of accommodation from
simple singles to cottages.
Temple Bay Ashok: about 1 kilometre north of the village, on the
Covelong Rd. Tel: 251/257.
Run by the ITDC, with rooms and cottages.
Shore Temple Beach Resort: near the shore temples, in the centre of
the village. Tel: 235/268.
Run by the ITDC. Also with rooms and cottages.
Ideal Beach Resort: about 4 kilometres north of the village, on the
Covelong Rd. Tel: 240/243.
Small, friendly but a little out of the way.

Cheap
Silver Inn: behind the Silversands Resort, about 2 kilometres north of
the village. Tel: 228/283.
The cheap annexe to the posher resort.
Shore Temple Youth Hostel: beside the shore temples. Tel: 287.
Run by the ITDC, this is a cheap version of the posher resort, with
cottages, dormitory beds, and a campsite.
There are several small hotels and lodges in the centre of the village.
Apart from being away from the sea, they are fine. Amongst the best
are the **Mamalla Bhavan**, the **Uma Lodge**, the **Hotel Surya**, and the
Mamalla Lodge.
Many of the small restaurants have a few rooms to let, and there
are also a number of beach houses and rooms in private houses
available. Mostly, their owners will find you at the bus stop. The
quality varies enormously, as do the prices (particularly according
to season), so have a look and haggle hard before committing
yourself.

WHERE TO EAT

If you really want to splash out, make the trek up to Fisherman's Cove. Nearer to the village, the Silversands outdoor restaurant seems to rate most highly.

A multitude of tiny restaurants have sprung up between the village and the sea. The food in most of them is excellent, if simple, and the service slow but always friendly. My particular favourites are Tina's Blue View Restaurant (upstairs with a good view and a lending library/book exchange), and the Rose Garden (where I was given a magic show with my breakfast). Others that come recommended are the Sunrise, Papillon, Village and Surya.

PONDICHERRY

The French arrived on the east coast of India in 1664, setting up their trading station at Pondicherry. From here, they started trying to empire build, but spent considerably more time and energy squabbling with the British. Once the dust settled, they were left with four small outposts – Pondicherry and Karaikal in Tamil Nadu, Mahé (on the Kerala coast), and Yanam in Andra Pradesh. They kept hold of them until 1954, when they saw the writing on the wall and handed them over to the Indian government just before they could be thrown out. Today, the four are officially ruled together as the Union State of Pondicherry.

There is thought to have been a town here as far back as 1500 BC when it was a centre of Vedic scholarship, and the Vedic sage Agastyamuni had an *ashram* here. The Romans had a trading post here in the first century AD, and there was a Sanskrit University on the site in the ninth century. By the time the French arrived, however, it was no more than a small fishing village. The modern town shows no signs of its lengthy history, however, and is laid out in a neat grid, with a startlingly European feel. India is trying to take over, and slowly but surely the street vendors and tiny shops are occupying the pavements, but there is still a very alien sense of regimentation, while the police wear kepis and you are still likely to hear plenty of French spoken in the streets – albeit with a decidedly eccentric accent.

The major influence in the town these days is the Sri

Aurobindo ashram, which is the major landowner and employer (see below and box). There is little of any real importance to see here other than the *ashram*, but it is an attractive city where you can spend an enjoyable and lazy day or two.

GETTING THERE

Pondicherry does have a railway station, on the southern edge of town. Its only link however is on a short but excruciatingly slow spur from Villupuram, with only two trains a day, and it is much better to take the **bus**. The nearest town with a more frequent train service is Cuddalore, from where you can get a train down to Thanjavur and Trichy. The actual station to use, if you are coming up from the south, is Thirupathiripulitur. This is the stop after Cuddalore Junction. The bus stand for services to Pondicherry is right next to the station, and buses seem to run almost continuously.

Pondicherry is not on a national highway, so journeys can be even more bumpy than usual. It is well served by buses, with hourly services to Madras, seven a day to Chidambaram, four a day to Mamallapuram, two a day to Tiruvannamalai and Bangalore, and daily services to Madurai, and Ooty.

There are two **bus stations**, more or less next-door to each other on the Villapuram Road to the west of the city. One belongs exclusively to the Thiruvalluvar Bus Company (TTC), Tel: 26513. The other, the Moffusil Bus Stand, handles all the other bus companies, state-run and private (Tel: 26919). The TTC stand is well labelled and has computerised booking, the Moffusil is a jungle. Nothing is in English, the booking staff don't seem to speak it, and there aren't even any recognisable bays. Fall back on the small boys who are eager to help, or you will never get away.

GETTING AROUND

The area around the sea front is small enough for you to get everywhere on foot. Alternatively, there are a number of places hiring out **bicycles**, which are also the best way to get to Auroville.

There are some **auto-rickshaws** around, but while you find plenty at the back of the town, they are remarkably few and far between near the sea, and when you do find one, they tend to try and hold you to ransom. Public transport consists of a collection of illogical three-wheelers that cram in too many people and set off on some sort of route known only to the driver.

GETTING YOUR BEARINGS

The planned (grid) city of Pondicherry is roughly oval in shape, surrounded like all good French towns by a peripheral boulevard. This is split roughly in three, running north-south. A third of the way back from the sea is a **canal** (called the "ditch" on local maps!), and two-thirds of the way back is a main thoroughfare, **Mahatma Gandhi Road**. Almost everything of interest to tourists is in the third nearest the sea, where the atmosphere of colonial France seems to remain intact, with calm, empty streets and well-maintained mansions. Behind the canal, India abruptly catches up. The main **ashram** complex is two blocks back from the sea in the north of the city. The monuments and the park are halfway down. The tourist information bureau is on the front towards the south.

The road along the front is officially known as Goubert Salai, but is equally likely to be known as Beach Road.

DON'T MISS . . .

Sri Aurobindo ashram

The heart of this huge operation (see box). The main building contains a marble *samadhi* where Sri Aurobindo and The Mother are buried.

Reception service in Francois Martin Street. Open 8am–midday, 2–6pm; Central Bureau in Marine Street, open 6am–4.30pm daily. Tel: 24836. If enough people are interested, the *ashram* will lay on a guided tour, leaving from the main gate at 8.45am.

Sea front

A stepped, concreted and neatly brushed promenade that looks as if it stepped right out of Europe, complete with a snack bar and ice cream sellers. Great for a stroll, but don't try swimming as the water is less than healthy. Halfway along Goubert Salai are the old pier and lighthouse, the war memorial and Gandhi Memorial, with an avenue stretching back into the attractive, shady Government Park. Behind this is the eighteenth-century Raj Niwas, formerly the Governor's Residence.

Pondicherry museum

1 Rue Romain Rolland, on the south side of Government Park. The best of the galleries houses a collection of Pallava, Chola and Vijayanagar sculptures; the next best is the French gallery, which tells the story of Pondicherry's colonial past. Others include art, archaeology, geology and crafts. Open 10am–5pm, except Monday. Entrance free.

OUT OF TOWN

Auroville

Eight kilometres north of Pondicherry. This is the centre of The Mother's dream of all nations and cultures living together in creative harmony. It hasn't quite worked out like that (see box), but it is still interesting. They welcome people who are genuinely interested, but are not too fond of casual sightseers and cynics. There are also three guided tours a week. Ask at the Auroville Information Centre in La Boutique d'Auroville on Nehru Street in Pondicherry (Tel: 27264).

FACT FILE

BANKS
State Bank of India: 5 Suffern St. Tel: 24102.
United Commercial Bank: Mal Labourdounais. Tel: 23252.
Indian Overseas Bank: 168 Nehru St. Tel: 24027.
Indian Bank: 65 Mission St. Tel: 26403.
Canara Bank: 16 Nehru St. Tel: 24354.

COMMUNICATIONS
Head Post Office: Rangapallai St. Tel: 25532.
Central Telegraph Office: Rangapallai St. Tel: 25850.
Post and Telegraph Office: (Bazaar Branch), Nehru St.
Sri Aurobindo Ashram Post and Telegraph Office: Kalatheeswaram Koil St.

CONSULATE

France: 2 Marine St. Tel: 24058.

SHOPPING

Higginbotham's Books: 12 Ambur Salai.
Public Handloom Article Centre: 32 Rue Suffern.
Orient Bazaar: 4 Curzon St.
The best place in town if you are looking for antiques.
Co-optex (Handloom): 28 Nehru St.
Poompuhar: 1st Floor, 51 Nehru St.
The Tamil Nadu state emporium.
Hand Made Paper Factory: Sardar Vallabai Patel Salai.
The *ashram* also runs a number of other shops around the city, selling books, fabrics and handicrafts.

TOURIST INFORMATION

Tourist Office and Pondicherry Tourist Development Corporation: Goubert Salai (south end). Tel: 24575/23590.

WHERE TO STAY

There are no luxury or upmarket hotels in Pondicherry, but there are several very good cheaper places.

Mid-range

Pondicherry Ashok Beach Resort: Kalapet. Tel: 85–460.
12 kilometres along the coast. Custom-built as a beach resort and run by the PTDC.

Cheap

Grand Hotel d'Europe: 12 Suffern Rd.
Wonderful old courtyard building. A hotel since 1891, and still run by a Frenchman.
Ajantha Guest House: Goubert Salai.
Pleasant small hotel at the south end of the seafront.
Hotel Surguru: SV Patel Rd. Tel: 29022.
Aristo Guest House: 50A Mission St. Tel: 26728.
Ellora Lodge: 27 Rangapallai St. Tel: 24474.
Hotel Bristol: 23–4 Brindavan. Tel: 23954.
The following are all good, but are run by the *ashram*, so there are strict rules against smoking and alcohol.
Sea Side Guest House: 10 Goubert Salai. Tel: 24496.
North end of the city. Rambling old mansion with huge rooms.
Park Guest House: Goubert Salai. Tel: 24412.
Modern hotel on the sea front to the south of the city.
International Guest House: Gingy Salai. Tel: 25200.

Ultra-cheap

Government Tourist Home: Uppalam Rd. Tel: 26376/7/8.
Yatri Nivas: Kennedy Nagar. Tel: 29474.

Sri Aurobindo

Aurobindo Ghosh was born in Calcutta in 1872, sent to England to be educated at the age of seven, and remained there until he graduated from King's College, Cambridge. In 1893, he returned to India as an administrative official of the Maharajah of Baroda. Shortly afterwards, he became actively involved in the Independence movement, and from 1906 onwards became one of its leaders — an activity for which he was imprisoned by the British.

He had plenty of time to think during his year in captivity and soon began to shift his values in favour of the spiritual. In 1910, he gave up politics altogether and retired to Pondicherry to devote himself to philosophy and the study of yoga. His basic belief was simple. Man might consider himself superior to animals, but is still ruled by the animal's instincts and material behaviour. Therefore the so-called superiority of man is simply an intermediate stage. Man must continue to work towards "the evolution of another kind and form of life which would in the final end be moved by a higher spiritual consciousness and embody a greater life of the spirit". This was to be achieved by yoga, meditation, spiritual and temporal study, and physical work.

Aurobindo's fame spread and the *ashram* grew around him. However the real guiding force behind its expansion was a Frenchwoman, Mirra Alfassa, simply known to most as The Mother. Born in Paris in 1878, she first arrived in Pondicherry in 1914, as a disciple of Aurobindo, but soon began to take over much of the organisation of his life and collaborated with him on several of his books. In 1926, Aurobindo retired from any active participation in the *ashram* and she took over total responsibility not only for the administration, but for the spiritual guidance of its disciples. He died in 1950, but the *ashram* continued successfully under her leadership. She died in 1973.

Today, the *ashram* owns some 400 buildings in Pondicherry (a goodly portion of the town), and has 2,000 permanent members, as well as huge numbers of visitors. It is also the major employer in the area, with its own farms, construction companies, oil and flour mills, foundry, sheet-metal works, garages, electrical repair shops, shoe makers, laundry, schools, hospital, publishing house, papermakers, printing presses, etc. There are also craft workshops for, amongst other things, weaving, embroidery, batik, pottery, and incense-making. The economic power it wields is staggering, leaving it none too popular with many of the locals, who are left with little or no say in how their community is run.

The *ashram* is perhaps even more famous, however, for the notoriety surrounding its second centre, Auroville, 8 kilometres north of the town. This was The Mother's great dream, designed to be a community of some 50,000 souls from every corner of the globe, come together to live in peace and harmony. Laid out by French architect Roger Anger, it is divided into four zones – residential, cultural, industrial and international – and delights in such names as Hope, Fraternité, Promesse, Discipline, Fertile, Aspiration and Sérenité.

It opened in a massive flourish in 1968, with a ceremony attended by representatives of 121 countries, all of whom brought a handful of their native earth. This was all poured into one great urn, which now forms the centrepiece of the Matri Mandir monument, as a symbol of universal oneness.

Money and volunteers poured in and construction began in earnest, but it all came to a grinding halt when The Mother died only five years later. Immediately, a power struggle blew up between the Sri Aurobindo Society (who run the *ashram*) and the community at Auroville, who wished to run their own affairs. Over the next 15 years, it literally became a battle ground, the violence becoming so bad that the police had to be called in twice. Everyone lobbied furiously, claims of corruption, free sex and drug taking were bandied back and forth and local and national governments became involved. When, in 1976, the Society tried to starve out the Aurovillians by witholding funds, France, Germany and the United States were drawn into the dispute, providing food parcels to stop their citizens from starving. In 1980, central government took charge and even nationalised the project. In 1988, they set up a new panel of nine people to run Auroville. Things have now calmed down, and construction has begun again, but no one has yet managed to reach a final settlement and it is all a far cry from The Mother's original concept.

There is now a resident community of about 700, who are working on computer, sports and agricultural research, as well as handicrafts, village industry, education and health.

Youth Hostel: Solai Nagar. Tel: 23495.

WHERE TO EAT

More upmarket

Alliance Française: Goubert Salai (south end).
Evenings only, with good French food.

Grand Hotel d'Europe: 12 Suffern St.
French food.

Cheaper

Ajantha Guest House: Goubert Salai (south end).
Pleasant rooftop restaurant with Indian and continental food.

Hotel Aristo: 36e Nehru St.
Rooftop restaurant with the best Indian food around, plus continental and Chinese.

Sea Gull Restaurant: (opp. Port Office), Rue Dumas.
Formerly the Fiesta. Run by the PTDC.

Snow Lion Restaurant: 224 St Louis St.
Mainly Chinese and Tibetan food.

Indian Coffee House: Nehru St.

Blue Dragon Chinese Restaurant: Rue Dumas.

CENTRAL TAMIL NADU

OOTACAMUND (UDHAGAMANDALAM)

Officially renamed Udhagamandalam, this town is usually known as Ootacamund, and, more often than not, is referred to by the diminutive, Ooty. It stands at a height of 2268 metres in the Nilgiri Hills (Blue Mountains), between the Eastern and Western Ghats, on the corner where Tamil Nadu, Karnataka and Kerala all meet. Because of this, and because it is isolated from other tourist areas in Tamil Nadu, people usually include a visit to Ooty when travelling between Mysore and Cochin, rather than trying to get here from the east coast.

Ooty was founded by the British in the early-nineteenth century so that the wives and children could escape to the hills during the stifling monsoon weather. It wasn't the first of the hill stations in the area, but it rapidly became the largest and most important and has long since awarded itself the title of "queen of hill stations". The Indian rulers followed, several of them, including the Maharajahs of Mysore, Hyderabad, Baroda and Jodphur, building palaces here. A couple of these are now hotels, but none has the same splendour as palaces elsewhere, and they are really little more than rather tatty country houses. The population today is around 110,000.

The mountainous area around the town is the traditional homeland of a number of India's ethnic minorities, amongst them the buffalo-worshipping Todas, the Kotas, the Kurumbas, the Panias and the Irulas, who are chiefly famous for farming snakes for their venom. Numbers are down to a few thousand now, and many are moving away and abandoning their traditional lifestyles, but it is still possible to find their shrines.

There is little specific to see in the town itself, but it is worth a visit for its general atmosphere – a crumbling remnant of the old Raj that seems somehow to have been fossilised in the 1930s. As you wind your way up from the plains, the landscape and crops change, through tea and coffee plantations to closely cultivated terraces filled with those British staples, carrots, cabbage and potatoes. The weather gets cooler and damper, and will quite probably shroud you in some typically British mist and drizzle. (This is not as bad as it seems, and is actually quite a welcome relief after weeks of temperatures in the 30s and 40s). The houses look English, from thatched cottages with roses round the door to good old neo-Tudor. The statue of Queen Victoria still stands proud in the central square – which is called Charing Cross. The hotels serve you hot buttered toast and Horlicks in front of roaring log fires and you sleep under heavy quilts that smell of mothballs. And just to help that autumnal feel, one of the town's main products is eucalyptus oil, which fills the streets with the scent of cold cures.

Even the people are different. The Indian lady we stopped to ask for directions turned out to be called Hannah, and have a husband called Alfred. Later that evening, we fell in with an Anglo-Indian party. The men wore tweed jackets with leather patches, the women wore cardigans over their saris and had blue-rinsed hair. And, as the town is thought to have a particularly healthy climate, it is an educational centre. One of India's top public schools is based here, filling the streets with polite school boys with smart blazers and perfect Oxford accents. The shops, catering to this youthful trade, are filled with such traditional delicacies as rock-like rock cakes and fudge.

The many Indian tourists who come to Ooty are usually there to walk, ride, play golf or go boating and generally have one of those traditional, lazy holidays with no culture and plenty of fresh air. It seems ideal!

GETTING THERE

The nearest airports are at Mysore to the north and Coimbatore to the south.

A rack and pinion "toy train" winds down the southern slopes of the hills from Ooty, to connect up with the main broad guage line at Mettupalayam. The "up" train leaves Mettupalayam at 7.45am; the "down" train leaves Ooty at 2.55pm. It connects with mainline services through to Madras and, via Coimbatore, to Cochin. This famous railway is one of the main reasons why many people come. (See under **Don't Miss** for more details).

The **railway station** is at the west end of the lake, near the race course and the centre of town.

Ooty is connected by **road** to Mysore and Coimbatore as well as to the smaller towns in the immediate area. From the north, the only way to get there is by road, and although there is a railway to the south, this is limited to infrequent passenger services, so all freight and almost everyone has to travel by road. As a result, the road is fairly well maintained, but those who get car-sick beware – there are 36 hairpin bends between Mudumulai and Ooty alone.

There are plenty of **buses** into and out of Ooty, many of them run by the regional transport authority, Cheran. There are services every 10 minutes to Coonoor, every 20 minutes to Coimbatore, hourly services to Kotagiri, eight a day to Calicut, five a day to Mysore (this goes through Mudumulai) and Bangalore, and daily services to Madras, Kanyakumari, Pondicherry, Cannanore and Palani. Many of the buses going north are extremely full, and the journey to Mysore takes five hours. Unless you fight hard for a seat, you are likely to have to stand the whole way.

The **bus station** is almost directly opposite the train station, between the lake and the race course, in the centre of town.

GETTING AROUND

For such a small place, Ooty is surprisingly spread out and while one of the points of coming here is to walk, and almost everything is within a fairly hearty walking distance, you might find you need a ride, in at least one direction, or if you have your luggage. There are plenty of **auto-rickshaws** and **cycle-rickshaws** for journeys within the town. For trips further out, however, these are not powerful enough to cope with the gradient, and you will probably have to use a **taxi**. It is also possible to hire **bicycles**.

The TTDC and the Cheran Transport Corporation both run **tours** of Ooty and the surrounding area. TTDC tours leave from the Hotel Tamil Nadu, CTC tours leave from the Central Bus Stand. Avoid the ones that include Mudumulai, as you won't see any game anyway, and you'll have to do those awful hairpin bends twice in one day.

GETTING YOUR BEARINGS

Ooty sprawls round a large bowl in the hills. The central valley runs from the west, and goes due east for a while before turning north-east. **Ooty Lake** takes up the eastern end. Next come the railway and bus stations, and then the racecourse. As it twists to the north, the main shopping area of Commercial Road leads up to Charing Cross. The **Botanical Gardens** are in the far north-east. The better hotels are mainly at the western end of town (near the lake), the cheaper ones are, with some exceptions, in the area just north of Commercial Road.

The **Tourist Information Office** is in the **Super Market** Buildings, Charing Cross. Tel: 2416.

DON'T MISS . . .

Blue mountain railway
This has to be one of the great little railways of the world. The line up from Mettupalayam was first suggested as early as 1854. It took some time to get going, however, and reached Coonoor (halfway to Ooty) in 1899. It was extended up to Ooty in 1908. One of the engines still working was put into service in 1925, the others were built in 1952. The distinctive yellow and blue carriages date back to the 1920s.

The journey is 46 kilometres long, and very slow. It takes 4^1/2 hours on the way up, and 3^1/2 on the way down. The line crosses 250 bridges (many of them with rather alarming fresh air between the sleepers), and goes through 16 tunnels. The views the whole way are stupendous. It's best to sit on the left on the way up, on the right on the way down. You will almost certainly see monkeys, and there are elephants in the area.

Stops include Kallar, where the rack and pinion is brought into action (or released), Hillgrove, Coonoor, which (for steam fanatics) has the shunting yards and maintenance sheds, and the tiny settlement of Lovedale.

Botanical gardens

4 kilometres north-east of the railway station, off Woodehouse Road. These 22-hectare gardens were originally founded by the Marquis of Tweeddale, who brought over a gardener from Kew to transform the town's small kitchen gardens. He succeeded dramatically, and today these are a superb example of British-style municipal gardens, with lush green lawns, neat, colourful beds and a fabulous collection of mature trees, gathered from across the world. The mini-lake at the bottom has a 20-million-year-old fossilised tree trunk.

Just behind the main gardens is the old Governor's Residence, now known as the **Raj Bhavan**. This was designed by Chandos for the Duke of Buckinghamshire in 1877, and is modelled on his family home, Stowe.

Perhaps best of all, however, the botanical gardens are one of the film industry's favourite locations, and you will often find them shooting those wonderful song and dance routines that are the backbone of Hindi movies. Great entertainment.

ALSO WORTH VISITING

Ooty lake

Just west of the railway station. This is an artificial irrigation tank built between 1823 and 1825 by the then Collector, John Sullivan. It has shrunk slightly since then, but is still about 2^1/2 kilometres long. You can rent boats from the Tourist Café on the north shore. The problem with the lake is that first, it is terribly polluted and rather whiffy, and second, it is the focus of most day and weekend tripping and tends to be noisy and overcrowded.

OUT OF TOWN

Dodabetta peak

About 10 kilometres east of town, this is 2623 metres high and is the highest peak in Tamil Nadu, and the second highest in the Western Ghats. The road up leads through the tea plantations. At the top, there is an **observatory** with a micro-telescope. The views are amazing. On clear days, it is said you can see as far as Mysore. It is, however, just as likely to be shrouded in dense cloud, when you will be lucky to see your own feet.

FACT FILE

WHERE TO STAY
Prices in some hotels literally double in high season.

Upmarket
Savoy Hotel: Club Rd. Tel: 4142. Telex: 0853–240 SAHO IN. About 1.5 kilometres north of the railway station. Low, colonial-style building with surrounding verandahs and some separate cottages. Run by Taj, so efficient, but fairly expensive.

Mid-range
Fernhill Palace: just south of Ooty Lake. Tel: 3097/2055. Telex: 0853–246 FERN IN.
The former summer palace of the Maharajah of Mysore, set away from the town in the forests. Plenty of decaying grandeur.

Cheap
YWCA: Ettines Rd, Anandagiri. Tel: 2218.
Just south of the racecourse.
Reflections: North Lake Rd. Tel: 3834.
Hotel Tamil Nadu: Commercial Rd. Tel: 2543/4.
The TTDU hotel for the area.
Hotel Sanjay: Charing Cross. Tel: 3160.

WHERE TO EAT
Savoy Hotel: Club Rd. Tel: 4142.
Probably the best food in town. The buffet cuts down the cost.
Shinkow's Chinese Restaurant: 42 Commissioner's Rd. Tel: 2811.

Good food – Indian and continental as well as Chinese – at very reasonable prices.

The **Kaveri**, the **Ritz**, and the **Blue Hills** are all near Charing Cross, and all do reasonable, cheap, non-veg Indian food.

MUDUMULAI NATIONAL PARK

Nestled in the foothills of the Western Ghats, at an altitude of around 1,000m, Mudumulai is part of a massive reserve which also includes **Bandipur** and **Nagarahole** in Karnataka (see page 253) and **Wynad** in Kerala. It was established in 1938 and later extended to cover 322 square kilometres (124 square miles). The main Mysore-Ooty road runs right through the middle, past the park office and main lodge.

Everyone says that it has good game-viewing, but when I was there, they had a notice up saying: "Wild animals are shy, do not be sorry if you do not see one". My haul was three elephants (two tame), a peacock, some hens and a herd of cows. We did hear some more elephants in the distance, and got there just too late to see a bear (you know, the one that got away). The time was well spent, even so. The scenery is fantastic, and the sense of peace after all those Indian cities was worth more than an ox, wild or not.

If you are luckier than me, there are meant to be extensive herds of elephants, chital and gaur, as well as wild boar, wild dog, sambar, pangolin, civet, and even tiger and panther, and most other relatively common Indian animals. There is also a wide variety of birds, including peacocks, hornbills, woodpeckers, parakeets, warblers, babblers and mynas. Reptiles include crocodiles, monitor lizards, pythons and cobras, so be careful where you put your feet.

GETTING THERE

The only way to get there is by **road**. The Mysore-Ooty **bus** passes through five times a day. The journey is roughly 2½ hours either way.

Nilgiri tea

Tea is big business in India, with more than 13,000 estates employing over a million people. The famous plantations are in the north — in Darjeeling and Assam — but the southern Nilgiri hills have been catching up fast, and, with a milder climate and double monsoon, are the only place on the sub-continent where they can harvest year round. Nearly half the crop, however, is picked between September and December, and the very finest teas are picked in December and January.

There is only one species of tea bush, the **camellia sinensis**. Everything from the climate, the soil, the altitude, and when the tea is picked can affect the flavour, however, and the Nilgiri, with its wide range of landscapes and soil types, produces a broad range of flavours. The blends are created by different curing methods, using various proportions of leaf, bud and flower, and even, for more perfumed varieties, adding essential oils. Nilgiri tea is mild, delicate and refreshing. It would be hard to create a strong enough brew to stand a spoon in.

GETTING AROUND

It is possible to hire a **jeep** or **minibus** from the reception centre, and you can walk within a reasonable area of your lodge, although you must take extreme care. Wild animals are dangerous, however sweet they look, and however much of a cliché it is to say so. Even if you escaped with a simple bite you could get rabies, while you are a long way from help if you get bitten by a snake. If you prefer to get out of range, try an elephant. Advance bookings can be made through any Tamil Nadu Tourist Office, and via the Wildlife Warden, Mahalingam Building, Coonoor Rd, Ooty. Tel: 3114. There is a small admission and camera charge.

DON'T MISS . . .

Elephant school

There is an elephant training school at **Theppakkadu**, just across the river from the Lodge, with both captive bred and captured animals. Go down during the day, and you can watch them being taught the skills necessary to work in a logging camp, take tourists for a ride, or even to become a temple elephant, giving blessings in exchange for cash. In the early evening (about 5.30pm), they are all taken down to the river for a bath. It is possible to book game viewing rides on elephant back – one of the very best ways to see the animals. These go out between 6–8am, and 4.30–6pm. You must book your ride in advance.

FACT FILE

FOOD AND LODGING

Theppakkadu
This is the main park administration centre, beside the road, the bus stop and the elephant school.

The **Reception Centre**, the **TTDC Youth Hostel** (Tel: Masinagudi 49), and the **Range Office** all have some dormitory beds. If you prefer a room to yourself, other lodges here include the **Sylvan Lodge**, the Forest Service's **Log House**, and the **Abhayaranyam Rest House**. There is food available at the Youth Hostel and the Sylvan Lodge only.

Masinagudi
This is a separate village, about 8 kilometres east of Theppakkadu. The accommodation here is more upmarket, with several small, privately operated lodges, still in the cheap to mid-range price category.
Bamboo Banks: Tel: 22.
You must have your own transport, unless you can arrange for them to collect you from somewhere. Bookings to Bamboo Banks, Masinagudi, PO Nilgiris, Tamil Nadu.
Mountania Lodge: Tel: 37.
Jungle Trails Lodge: Tel: 56.
Right out in the bush, about 8 kilometres further east from Masinagudi. Difficult to get at, but friendly, welcoming and with fantastic views.

CHIDAMBARAM

Chidambaram takes its name from two words – *chid*, which, according to Saiva philosophy, means human thinking consciousness, and *ambaram*, the expanse of the skies or heaven. Thus the city believes itself to be the centre from which all human knowledge expands. This role, it claims, comes from an episode in the life of Shiva.

Kali (Parvati) was once the patron goddess of the city, but Shiva came to visit two devotees. Kali, upset by his intrusion, challenged him to a dance contest, winner take all. Vishnu acted as referee and judge. For some time they were neck and neck, but then Shiva began to dance the *Ananda Tandava*, the dance of bliss that tells the story of the entire life cycle of the universe, and is so pure it can only be danced at the centre of the world. Kali could not hope to compete, and she left to set up her temple outside the gates of the city, where it remains to this day (the *Thillai Kali Amman*). Since then, Chidambaram has been dedicated to Shiva, in the form of Nataraja, Lord of the Dance.

Chidambaram is now a town of about 75,000 people on the northern edge of the Coleroon River, which is itself part of the Thanjavur Delta. It has its own university, and is also considered a centre for the study of dance, poetry and music.

GETTING THERE

Chidambaram is about 70 kilometres south of Pondicherry. It is on the coastal metre guage line that has through **rail** connections to Madras, Thanjavur, Tiruchirapalli and Rameswaram. If you are heading south from Pondicherry, pick up the train in Cuddalore. There are several services a day, both express and passenger.

The **railway station** is about 1.5 kilometres to the south-east of the town, on the other side of the canal.

Chidambaram is on the **road** which links Pondicherry with Thanjavur and Tiruchirapalli. It is not a national highway, but is reasonable driving. The state-run TTC runs plenty of **buses**, with hourly services to Madras and Pondicherry, and regular services to Thanjavur, Trichy, Nagapattinam and Madurai.

The **bus station** is in the centre of town, about three blocks east of the temple.

GETTING AROUND

There are **cycle-rickshaws** available at the railway station to take you into town. Once in the centre, everything is within easy walking distance.

There is a **tourist information office** on Railway Feeder
Road. (Tel: 2739).

DON'T MISS ...

Nataraja Temple

Right in the centre of town, surrounded on all sides by a
broad avenue designed to show off the festival processions, the
temple covers a total area of around 13 hectares (40 acres). Its
history extends as far back as 500 AD when Emperor Hiranya
Varna Chakravarti was miraculously cured of leprosy here
and built the temple in gratitude. It is known to have existed
as far back as the tenth century, but the current layout dates
from the reign of Vikrama Chola and his son, Kulottunga
Chola II in the twelfth century.

The courtyard is enclosed by two rings of high walls, with
massive *gopurams* over each of the four entrance gateways.
The East Gate, which is the oldest and the main entrance,
dates from about 1250. The North and South are the largest,
reaching a height of around 45 metres. The North was built
by Vijayanagar King Krishna Devaraya between 1509 and
1530. There are portraits of him and the four architects
involved on the tower. A series of panel reliefs of women
on the inner walls of the *gopurams* catalogue all 108 poses
of the *Bharata-natyam* dance tradition (see page 363).

The outer enclosure contains the **Sivaganga Tank** and the
Raja Sabha, a 1,000-pillar *mandapam* built between 1595 and
1685, as well as shrines to Parvati and Ganesha. The more
sacred inner enclosure has four halls. The temple management
use the **Deva Sabha** as a meeting hall. The hall of wisdom, the
Chit Sabha is the main hall for worshipping Shiva. It has a
roof of gold tiles, and houses the **Asaka Lingam**, an invisible
lingam said to stand at the exact heart of the universe, in a
small inner sanctum behind the image. The golden hall, the
Kanakha Sabha, also with a golden roof, houses the famous
image of Nataraja, Lord of Dance. It represents the five acts of
Shiva: the drum in the right hand stands for creation; the right
hand itself, in a gesture of protection, stands for sustenance;
the fire in the left leg symbolises destruction; the right leg is
firmly on the back of a dwarf to represent concealment; and

the raised left leg and left arm pointing towards it represent the Grace of God. The halo of fire stands for cosmic space and the light of knowledge. The hall of dance, the **Nritta Sabha**, has 56 pillars carved with dancing figures.

The temple is run by the local Brahman community, who are known as *Dikshitars*. As they rely on contributions, they are perhaps more insistent than most about offering their services as a guide. Use one, however, as non-Hindus are officially not allowed into the inner sanctuaries, and the only way to get past the ban is to have a guide.

The best time to visit is for the evening *puja* (6pm), which is particularly colourful. The main temple festival is held in January each year, but the time to come is in February/March for the **Natyanjali Festival**. This lasts five days, when dancers from all over India arrive to pay homage to and dance for the Lord of Dance.

The temple is open from 4am-midday and 4.30–9pm daily. Entry is free, although you will have to leave something for the shoeminder, and you will almost certainly have to make a donation, even if you don't take on a guide.

FACT FILE

FOOD AND LODGING
Hotel Tamil Nadu: Railway Feeder Rd. Tel: 2323.
The best in town, although still simple. Run by the TTDC.
The Star Lodge: South Car St. Tel: 2743.
Hotel Raja Rajan: West Car St. Tel: 2690

THANJAVUR

Once upon a time there was a city called Alakai which was troubled by demons named Thanja Tharaka and Dhandaka. The great sage, Parasaka, came here to do penance and asked Lord Vishnu to protect the town. Vishnu and Durga arrived and killed the demons, but as Thanja died, he asked that the place be named after him. This was done, and so Thanjavur was born. It is also commonly referred to as Tanjore.

Today, Thanjavur is a city of about 200,000 people, situated halfway between Tiruchirapalli and the coast, in an area of rice plantations on the Cauvery Delta. It became politically important in the eighth century when the first of the revived Chola dynasty captured it, proclaimed independence from their Pallava overlords, and made it their capital. From here, they came to rule an empire that stretched from Bombay to

Puri in the north, and as far south as Sri Lanka. And as befits a monarchy that claims direct descent from the sun, they lived in lavish fashion, as patrons of the arts and builders on a massive scale. Along with the famous Sri Brihadeeswarar Temple, the town has some 70 other smaller ones, and many of the towns in the surrounding area also have fine examples of Chola temples.

Thanjavur remained the Chola capital until the thirteenth century, and on the dynasty's decline, continued as a regional capital throughout the Pandya, Vijayanagar, Nayak and Maratha periods. The city only began to fade in importance when the British shifted the emphasis to the coast.

Bharata-Natayam

The Tamil classical dance, **Bharata-natayam**, is one of India's greatest dance traditions. It took on a recognisable form only around 300 years ago, and reached its current state at the court of Thanjavur in the eighteenth and nineteenth centuries. For its inspiration however, it harks back to the sculptures of the tenth century. It is usually a solo dance performed by a woman. Dances are divided into two main strands, the **sringara** or erotic, and **bhakti** or devotional. Each has a poetic or emotional theme, which is then interpreted in a series of variations. The basic postures are formal and severely disciplined by the demands of line and balance, as though one of those miraculous sculptures had come to life and was flowing with infinite grace from one pose to the next, while drama is added by the dancer leaping, turning and striking the floor with her heels. It is closely related to the (male) **Bhagvata Mela** dance-dramas, and the (female) **Kuruvanji** folk operettas, both of which are still performed in Tamil Nadu.

The music is in the classical Carnatic tradition and the dancer is accompanied by a singer and an orchestra made up of a single drum, cymbals, flute, *veena* (a stringed, fretted instrument common to the area) and the violin (which entered the repertoire courtesy of the Europeans).

The dances are performed in many of the temples, particularly over festivals, but if you wish to see a performance at other times, there are several venues in Madras.

GETTING THERE

Thanjavur does have a small **airport**, with Vayudoot services to Madras and Madurai. Alternatively, fly to Trichy, 60 kilometres west and get a bus or train from there.

Thanjavur is on the metre guage coastal **rail** line from Madras to Tiruchirapally. There are daily "express" services, and more frequent passenger services every day to Chidambaram, Cuddalore (for Pondicherry), and Madras (9 hours). There is also a daily express for Rameswaram. The easiest way to get here is from Trichy, which is only 1^1/2 hours away by express. There are also frequent passenger services on this stretch.

The **railway station** is about 2^1/2 kilometres from the centre of town, south of the Anicut Canal.

There are good **bus** connections, with 12 daily departures for Madras, 2 a day to Pondicherry, and daily services to Madurai and Tirupathi. There are departures to Trichy and Kumbakonam every 15 minutes.

There are two **bus stations** next to each other on Hospital Road, between the Anicut Canal and the old city walls. The Thiruvalluvar Bus Stand handles all long distance traffic. This is moderately well organised, although there are no signs in English. There is a computerised booking office which is open from 7am–9pm. The Municipal Bus Stand next door is a zoo. Unfortunately, this is where the Trichy buses leave from.

GETTING AROUND

There are a few **taxis**, **tourist taxis**, and **auto-rickshaws**, but **cycle-rickshaws** are much more common. The drivers seem more pleasant than in many other towns, although you should still be careful to set a price before starting. Mine came sightseeing with me and proved a very informative guide. It is possible to get around on foot, but you will be in for quite a hike.

GETTING YOUR BEARINGS

The old city is between the Vadavar River to the north, and the Grand Anicut Canal to the south. The streets of the old city are within a circular road, which actually follows the line of the old city walls, although these have long since gone. The **palace** is in the centre of the old city, the **temple** is to the south-west, just beside the Anicut Canal. The bus station is on the southern edge of the old city, by the north bank of the canal. The railway station is south of the canal, linked to the old city by **Gandhiji Road**, also knows as Railway Station Road. Most of the hotels are on Gandhiji Road, as is the **tourist office**, which is beside the Hotel Tamil Nadu. There are **banks** on South Main Street, next to the palace, and Hospital Road, next to the bus station. The souvenir shops, which include a branch of **Poompuhar**, the state emporium, are all on Gandhiji Road.

DON'T MISS . . .

Sri Brahadeeswarar Temple

The main reason for coming to Thanjavur is to see this fabulous temple, which most consider to be the finest of all the great Chola temples of Tamil Nadu. It is extraordinarily beautiful, built of granite, but with warm, red-gold tones and a unity of design that makes it truly breathtaking. It has been designated a World Heritage Site.

The temple was built by the great Chola emperor, Rajaraja I (985–1014), between 1003 and 1009, as a temple-fortress. It covers an area of 400 acres, and is surrounded by massive rectangular walls and a wide moat. The main entrance is in the east, guarded by two relatively small *gopuram*.

The focus of the entire temple, however, is the **Peruvudayar temple**, the inner shrine dedicated to Shiva. This is topped by a 14-storey, 62 metres (216 foot) high tower, the tallest in India. Every inch of the surface is carved, until you reach the winged granite dome which is its crowning glory. This is said to weigh 81 tons. An earth ramp 6 kilometres long was needed to put it in place (in much the same way as the Pharaohs put the finishing touches to the pyramids). Inside, the *lingam* is also claimed to be one of the largest in India, standing a total of 15 foot high, with a base stone 54 foot in circumference, and an upper stone 23½ foot round. It is said to have needed assistance from the gods to complete. The inner walls are surrounded by a series of frescoes showing different aspects of Shiva and scenes from the lives of saints. Above these, a series of statues of dancing women catalogue the 108 poses of the *Bharata-natyam*.

Guarding the entrance to the shrine is a monolithic statue of Nandi the bull. This is itself 6 metres long, nearly 4 metres high and weighs around 20 tons. It is the second largest in the country. Thanjavur has no rocky outcrops that could produce a stone of this size, and it is thought to have been brought here from near Tiruchirapalli. Legend has it that once the bull was set in place, it began to grow, getting bigger and bigger until it was threatening the temple, and the alarmed people drove an iron nail into its back to stop it.

There are several other smaller temples and pavillions within the courtyard, together with more mundane monastic buildings around the edge of the cloisters. Keep an eye open for the various inscriptions on the walls, which not only imortalise many of those involved in building the temple (including the architect, Rajaraja Perum Taccan), but also many of those who have donated treasure to it. There is also a small **Archaelogical Museum**, which gives a fascinating account of the temple's restoration and a history of the Chola empire. There is a huge tank, the **Seppunaikan Tank**, behind the walls to the west, and a smaller, sacred tank, the **Sivaganga Tank**, in the temple courtyard, within a 100-pillared *mandapa*.

The temple is open from 6am–midday and 4–8.30pm daily. The museum is open from 9am–midday and 4–8pm daily. There is a small admission charge for the museum, but the temple itself is free, although you may be expected to make a donation.

City Palace

Built by Servappa Nayak in about 1540 AD, with later Maratha additions, this is a vast rabbit warren of a palace which houses, amongst other things, the Archaeological Survey office and Thanjavur University. You enter through an attractive garden courtyard, the cloisters of which now house the **Rajaraja Museum**, with a particularly fine collection of Chola bronzes and stone sculptures. There are several magnificent bronzes of Nataraja, the dancing Shiva, amongst them. Behind this is the **Sadr Madi**, a five-storey building erected by Serfoji II in 1800, and behind this still is the massive arsenal tower, which was built in the shape of a *gopuram* for camouflage. This belongs to the Nayak period, but remained in use as a watchtower and bell tower until 1855. It is possible to climb up inside, and there are good views from the top.

The **Durbar Hall** was originally built during the Maratha period, but was remodelled in Sahaji in 1684. It consists of two *mandapam*, a rear raised one with a vaulted roof and granite pillars, and a front one with a sloping wooden-tiled roof. The ceiling is decorated with stucco figures representing the ten atavars of Vishnu, royal portraits and hunting scenes. There is also glass decoration.

Behind this is the **Saraswathi Mahal library**, which has a collection of some 40,000 manuscripts, rare books and first editions, including 8,000 palm leaf manuscripts, many of them sadly in poor condition.

The museum is open 9am–midday and 3–6pm, except Friday. The library is open 10am–1pm and 2–5pm, except Wednesday. There's a small admission charge.

FACT FILE

WHERE TO STAY

Hotel Parisutham: 55 Grand Anicut Canal Rd. Tel: 21466.
Telex: 0468–220 PTS IN.
The best hotel in town.
Hotel Tamil Nadu: Gandhiji Rd. Tel: 21024/21325.
Run by the TTDC. Simple, but attractive, with a central courtyard garden. They also have a cheaper **annex** building on Tiruchirapalli Rd. Tel: 20365.
Ashoka Lodge: 93 Abrahem Pandither Rd. Tel: 20021.
Traveller's Lodge: Vallam Rd.
Run by the ITDC.

WHERE TO EAT

The Hotel Parisutham serves the best food in town, with two restaurants, **Les Repas** (Chinese) and the **Geetha** (non-veg Indian).
Golden Restaurant: Hospital Rd.
Air-conditioned dining room and a roof-top terrace, serving good, cheap vegetarian meals.
Sathars: Hospital Rd.
Near the bus stand. Tandoori food.

TIRUCHIRAPALLI (TRICHY)

Tiruchirapalli claims to have got its name in memory of a battle between Shiva and the three-headed demon, Trisiras, at a place called Tiruchi. The name literally means "City of the Three-Headed Demon". Most people these days have given up and just call it Trichy.

On the confluence of two major rivers, the Cauvery and Cooleron, there has been a major trading post here for at least 2,000 years. The city was first fortified in the second century BC and it is mentioned by Ptolemy at this same period.

It became more important however with the ascendancy of the Nayaks, in the sixteenth century, who were responsible for building the current fort, and much of the existing town. It has been well and truly fought over along the way, by Cholas, Cheras, Pandyas, Vijayanagars, Nayaks, Marathas and even the French and British.

Today, it is a city of around 500,000 people. As a major rail centre (the railway arrived in 1864), it is a thriving industrial city, making amongst other things, cigars, artificial diamonds, and *bidis*, the traditional Indian cigarettes, which most swear have about one flake of tobacco amidst all the other sweepings.

GETTING THERE

There are six flights a week to Colombo, Sri Lanka (four on Indian Airlines, two on Air Lanka). Indian Airlines fly six times a week to Madras, Madurai and Trivandrum.

The **airport** is 7 kilometres south-east of the city centre. Plenty of local buses run from here into the Central Bus Station. Look for numbers 7, 63, 63A, 122 or 128. The journey takes about 30 minutes. Otherwise, hire yourself an auto-rickshaw or taxi.

Trichy is a major **rail** junction, on both the main broad guage line from Madras to Madurai, and the metre guage services which head up to Madras, via Thanjavur, down to Rameswaram along the coast, and west to Erode. As a result, there is a plentiful choice of services, and you have to take a little care to select the right one. If, for instance, you are planning to head straight for Madras, the last thing you want is the metre guage line, even if it says it's an express.

There are six express services to Madras each day, and plenty going south, most of them stopping at Madurai, some going as far as Rameswaram. There are also regular express services on the coastal route to Thanjavur and Chidambaram and through services to Bangalore, Quilon, Coimbatore, Cochin and Mangalore. Slower passenger trains also run to all these destinations.

Trichy has a total of six **railway stations**, although almost every train you are likely to use will come into **Tiruchirapalli**

Junction, which is in the south-east corner of the city centre. This handles broad and metre guage lines. There is a separate

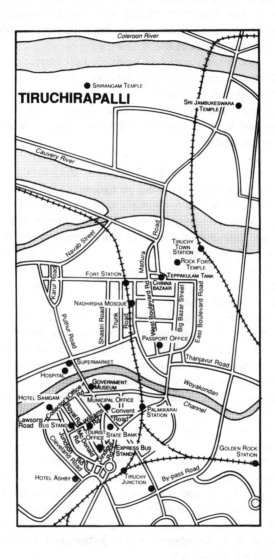

advance booking office in a new building to the left of the station forecourt. This is open from 7am–1pm, and 1.30–8 pm daily. Counter No 3 deals with foreign tourists. There is a tourist information counter in the forecourt.

Other stations which might be useful are **Srirangam Station**, which is the closest to Srirangam Temple; **Tiruchirapalli Town**, which is the closest to the Rock Temple; and **Golden Rock Station**, which is the closest to the airport.

Trichy is on the national highway between Madras and Madurai, and has reasonable **road** connections to all the other major centres in the south.

The state **bus** company, Thiruvalluvar, runs buses to Thanjavur every 15 minutes, frequent services to Madurai, 30 buses a day to Madras, two a day to Kanyakumari and Tirupathi, and regular services to Bangalore, Pondicherry, Kanchipuram, Vellore, Rameswaram, Kodaikanal, Coimbatore, Nagercoil and Nagapattinam. Some are express services, so look out for these if you are faced with a long journey. Other buses that have not originated in Trichy also stop here and will take you up if they have space, but you cannot book these in advance.

There are two **bus stations**. All TTC buses leave from the **Express Bus Stand** on the corner of Junction Road and Dindigul Road in the city centre. This is relatively organised and has computerised advance booking facilities. The **Central Bus Stand**, a few minutes' walk away on the corner of Williams Road and Royal Road, handles all other services, and local buses. This has no visible sense of order, no signs in English and no advance booking. Rely on the goodwill of the crowds to get you to the right place. They normally succeed.

GETTING AROUND

The **local bus** service is, for once, relatively organised and uncluttered. Services leave from the **Central Bus Station** on the corner of Williams Road and Royal Road – the least pleasant aspect of the journey. Bus No. B1 goes to or near the Rock Temple, Sri Jambukeswara Temple and the Srirangam Temple.

There are plenty of **auto-rickshaws** around, who are all used to doing the sightseeing tour if you hire them for a day or half-day. Fix a price before you set out, then hold firm. Mine first tried to up the price halfway round, then tried to leave out one of the temples.

The final alternative is to hire a **bicycle**. The ground is flat, but, on the downside, the traffic is lethal in parts of the city.

GETTING YOUR BEARINGS

Trichy is set just south of the Cauvery and Coleroon Rivers. The **Srirangam Temple** is actually on an island between the two rivers, about 10 kilometres north of the centre of town. The centre of the old city is around the **Rock Fort** and **Chinna Bazaar**, which are just south of the river. The heart of the modern city has shifted still further south, however, to the southern edge of the **Woyakondan Canal**, in what used to be the British cantonment. The railway station, both bus stations, and many of the hotels are within a short distance of each other at the southern end of this area. These can be managed on foot, but you will need transport for any sightseeing.

DON'T MISS . . .

Rock Temple and Fort

This is the major, and very dramatic, landmark, that you will see on approaching Trichy, a vast lump of sheer granite rising out of an otherwise flat plain. It was originally fortified by the Chola kings of the Sangam period (second century BC to second century AD), but the current fort was constructed by the Nayak kings in about 1660. Over the centuries, it has seen plenty of action, right up until the eighteenth century when it became the site of a battle between the French and British during the Carnatic Wars.

The entrance is through a small tunnel in the rock face, where you find yourself nose to nose in the gloom with a temple elephant who will bless you, if you tip him. You have to leave your shoes at the bottom. There is a climb of 437 rock-cut steps through the mountain. You pass a number of temples en route, including several finely carved cave temples built during the reign of the Pallava king, Mahendra Varman I, between 600 and 630 AD. You can also see the line of the eleventh-century defences. The largest of the temples on the way up is the Shaiva **Thayumanavarswamy temple**, which has a 100-pillar hall, a gilded *vimana* (tower), and a *lingam* carved from the solid rock. Right at the summit, 84 metres above the city, is the free-standing **Vinayaka temple**, dedicated to Ganesha.

Although you can peer round the doorways, non-Hindus are not allowed into any of the temples proper, so the main reason for trekking up here is to have a look at the view. It is worth it, with both rivers, the other main temples and the entire city laid out at your feet.

At the foot of the fort is the large **Teppakaulam Tank**, surrounded by the colourful bustle of the Chinna Bazaar and Big Bazaar.

Srirangam Temple

Officially called the **Sri Rangansthaswamy temple**, this is one of the largest temples in India, covering a total of 250 hectares on an island between the Cauvery and Coleroon Rivers.

Although it dates back to the Chola period, the temple has been the focus of much attention, and from the fourteenth to seventeenth centuries it became a hive of building activity, until it has grown to its present massive size, with seven concentric rings of walls and 21 *gopuram*. The huge, brightly coloured *gopuram* that looms over the main entrance was only completed in 1980.

The temple behaves more like a town, with the three outer

circles housing a teeming bazaar and the homes of a large colony of local Brahmans. The temple proper starts at the entrance to the fourth circle.

Here, more than anywhere, it is worth hiring a guide. Temple priests and a number of freelances hang around the ticket office. I was taken round by an archaeology student who was supplementing his income over the vacs. He spoke wonderful English, knew incredible amounts about the temple and was great fun. Set a price before you start out.

It is impossible to describe the whole temple, but there are one or two things to watch out for. The 1,000-pillar hall of the fifteenth-century **Narayana temple** has, in fact, 960 pillars. Amongst them are some of the most spectacular carvings in South India, with a series portraying the ten atavars of Vishnu, and the famous **Horse Court**, with a series of intricately detailed studies of riders on rearing stallions. Look out also for the thirteenth-century **Krishna temple**, and buy an extra ticket to climb the walls for a panoramic view over the whole temple, including the golden *vimanas* of the inner courtyards.

The small original temple (now the inner sanctum and closed to non-Hindus) dates back to the Chola period. It contains an image of Vishnu as Ranganatha, reclining in the coils of the snake, Anantha. Water is brought to him each day in silver vessels, accompanied by music and a procession of temple elephants.

There is a small **museum and art gallery** beside the ticket office.

The temple is open from 6.15am–1pm and 3.15–8.45pm daily. The ticket office and shoeminder are beside the entrance to the fourth circle. There is a small admission and a camera charge, and you will need to buy an extra ticket from the art gallery in order to go up on the walls (wear socks, the stone is horribly hot up there).

ALSO WORTH VISITING
Sri Jambukeswara Temple
Two kilometres east of Srirangam Temple, also on Cauvery Island. A much smaller temple (although it does have five

concentric walls and seven *gopuram*), dedicated to Shiva. The *lingam* is almost completely submerged by water which flows from an underground spring nearby. The temple is also known as the Thiruvannaikaval Temple, in honour of an elephant which once came here to worship. Begun in the Chola period (sixth to ninth centuries) this has also been considerably altered, and now dates mainly from the fourteenth to seventeenth centuries. There are a number of interesting sculptures and ceiling paintings. Open 6am–1pm and 4–7.30pm, daily. There is a small admission and camera charge, and non-Hindus are not allowed into the inner sanctum.

Government Museum

Bharatiyar Rd, 19/2 Promenade Rd, Cantonment. Varied collection of sculpture, art, anthropology, archaeology, crafts, coins, geology and natural history. Open 9am–12.30pm and 2–5pm, except Fridays. Entrance free.

FACT FILE

AIRLINES

Air Lanka: c/o Hotel Lakshmi, 34 Alexandria Rd. Tel: 27952/28844.
Indian Airlines, Railway Cooperative Building, Dindigul Rd: Tel: 23116/26288. Airport no. 27563.

BANKS

Bank of India: West Boulevard Rd. Tel: 24331.
Central Bank of India: West Boulevard Rd. Tel: 24136.
Indian Bank: Big Bazaar St. Tel: 24106.
Indian Overseas Bank: Birds Rd. Tel: 25795.
State Bank of India: Cantonment. Tel: 25172.

COMMUNICATIONS

Head Post and Telegraph Office: Madurai Rd. Tel: 25717.
RMS Post Office: Railway Junction.
Open 5.30am–10pm.

SHOPPING

Poompuhar (Tamil Nadu state emporium): nr Main Guard Gate.
Tel: 24895.
Open 10am–1pm and 3–8pm.
Khadi Kraft: opp. railway station, Junction Rd. Tel: 40814.
Open 9.30am–1.30pm and 4–8pm
Also Big Bazaar St.

TOURIST INFORMATION

Government of Tamil Nadu Tourist Office: Hotel Tamil Nadu Complex, Cantonment. Tel: 25336.
Open 10.30am–5.30pm, Monday to Saturday.
There are also **tourist information counters** at Tiruchirapalli Railway Junction (open 7am to 9pm) and at the airport.

VISA EXTENSIONS

Foreigners' Registration Office: Government Multi-Storeyed Building, Kajamalai.
Passport Office: Water Tank Complex, West Boulevard Rd. Tel: 29515.

WHERE TO STAY

Mid-range
Sangam Hotel: Collector's Office Rd. Tel: 25202. Telex: 0455–221.
Hotel Rajali: 2/14 Macdonald Rd, Cantonment. Tel: 41301.
Telex: 0445–279.

Cheap
Hotel Aristo: 2 Dindigul Rd, Cantonment. Tel: 26565.
Hotel Ashby: 17A Junction Rd. Tel: 23652.
Old and crumbling Raj hotel.
Hotel Tamil Nadu: Macdonald Rd, Cantonment. Tel: 40383.
Run by the TTDC.

Ultra-cheap
Ashok Traveller's Lodge: Race Course Rd. Tel: 23498.
A second, cheaper unit of the Hotel Tamil Nadu, with dormitory beds.
Some way from the city centre, nearer to the airport.
Railway Retiring Rooms: Railway Junction.
Municipal Tourist Bungalow: Central Bus Stand. Tel: 41680.

WHERE TO EAT

Chorogo Restaurant: Hotel Rajali, Macdonald Rd.
Chinese, Indian and continental. The Chinese food is particularly good.
Selvam Lodge: Junction Rd.
Rooftop restaurant serving South Indian food.
Vasantha Bhavan Restaurant: Junction Rd.
Good, basic vegetarian *thalis*, plus a few omlettes.

SOUTHERM TAMIL NADU

MADURAI

Madurai is thought to be one of the oldest cities in India, having been inhabited continuously for at least 2,500 years. As capital of the Pandya kingdom, it is mentioned in dispatches by the Greek ambassador Megasthenes in 320 BC, by Pliny in 77 AD, by Ptolemy in 140 AD, Marco Polo in 1293 and Ibn Batuta in 1333.

According to legend, Indra the King of Gods built a *lingam* and gave homage to Shiva in a forest clearing near a lotus pond. Some time later, the Pandyan king Kulasekhara built a great temple on this holy place, and clearing the forest around it, built a city whose streets fanned out like the petals of a lotus flower. On the day the city was to receive its name, Shiva himself appeared, and nectar showered down from his hair onto the blessed city below. From that time on, the city has been known as Madhurapuri, the "city of nectar".

The city has had a chequered historical past, but until very recently always remained the capital of the region. It was the Pandya capital until 920 AD when it was captured by the Cholas. The Pandyas got it back in 1223, only to lose it again in 1323 to the Delhi Sultanate. In 1371 they were in turn ousted by the Vijayanagars who put in a Nayak Governor. In 1530, it became independent again when the Nayaks broke away from their overlords and set up their own kingdom. It only lost its status in 1801 when the British took control and the regional capital shifted to Madras.

Today the city has a population of about 900,000. It is heavily industrialised, although life still tends to revolve around the temple. It also has a great tradition as a centre of learning and the arts. The Tamil Sangam, the association of Tamil poets, was founded here. It is a teeming, bustling, noisy, colourful city that feels as if it is permanently *en fête*.

There are two major festivals each year. The **Float Festival** at Vandiyur Mariamman Teppakulam in January/February marks the birthday of Thirumalai Nayak. The **Chitrai Festival** in April/May is a ten-day celebration to mark the wedding of Shiva and Meenakshi.

GETTING THERE

By **air** Indian Airlines run daily flights to Madras, and three flights a week to Bangalore. Vayudoot fly to Madras, Cochin, Coimbatore and Thanjavur.

The **airport** is six kilometres south of the city centre. The Pandyan Roadways Corporation run an airport bus from the city centre, picking up at the top hotels en route. Otherwise, you need to get a taxi or auto-rickshaw.

Madurai is at the junction of two metre guage **rail** lines, north to Trichy (where it connects with the broad guage) and Madras, east to Rameswaram, and south to Quilon. There are fairly definite plans afoot however to extend the broad guage line south. As it is, there are around 18 express services a day, to Madras, Rameswaram, Tirunelveli (for Kanyakumari), Quilon, Tiruchirapalli, Bangalore and Tirupathi. There are also more frequent passenger trains to nearby towns such as Trichy and Thanjavur.

Madurai Junction Railway Station is on West Veli Street, the western edge of the old city, only a few minutes' walk from the temple. There is no separate Foreign Tourists' Bureau, but the **Rail Tourist Information Counter** in the main lobby should be able to help. This is open from 6am–6pm. The Upper Class booking office is to the right. Open 9.30am – 1pm and 2–5pm. Tel: 37597.

Madurai is at the junction of two national highways, the north-south **road** from Madras to Kanyakumari, which also comes through Trichy, and the eastern spur to Rameswaram. It also has reasonable road connections to other towns in the nearby area.

There are plenty of **buses** serving Madurai; the only problem can be finding them, as there are five different bus companies and three bus stations. Amongst others, services go to Madras (16 daily), Thanjavur and Trivandrum (eight daily), Kodaikanal (seven daily), Kanyakumari (three daily), Ernakulam (two daily), and Pondicherry, Vellore, Bangalore, Courtallam, Palani, Periyar, Trichy, and Tiruchendur. A number of other buses that have originated elsewhere also stop here, and will take you up if they have space, although you can't book them in advance.

The **Thiruvalluvar Bus Stand** and the **State Bus Stand** (also known as the Periyar Bus Stand), are next-door to each other at the southern end of West Veli Street, near both the railway station and the temple. Most long-distance buses go from the Thiruvalluvar stand. This has an advance booking office open daily from 7am–9pm. Local and city buses, and buses for Kodaikanal, leave from the State Bus Stand. The **Anna Bus Stand** is 3 kilometres away, on the north bank of the river. Buses for Thanjavur, Tiruchirapalli and Rameswaram leave from here.

Tel. enquiries: Thiruvalluvar – 25354; Mofussil – 36818; Periyar – 35293; Pandyan – 43622; Rani Mungammal – 33740.

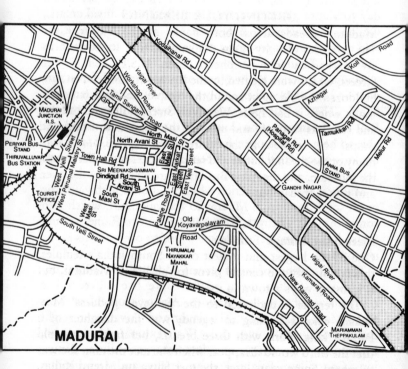

GETTING AROUND

The temple, the bus stand and railway station are all within walking distance, but everything else is too spread out to do on foot.

There are reasonable **local bus** services from the State bus stand. Useful numbers include Nos 1 and 2 to the Hotel Tamil Nadu and Gandhi Museum, and No. 3 to the Anna Bus Stand.

Alternatively, there are plenty of **taxis, auto-rickshaws** and **cycle-rickshaws,** none of which ever seem to have heard of a meter. Bargain hard and set a price before you go and be warned – if you give a posh hotel as your destination, you can expect the sticking point to be roughly double the correct fare.

GETTING YOUR BEARINGS

Madurai spreads across both banks of the Vaigai River. The compact old city is on the south bank. Its boundaries are marked by four peripheral roads, N,S,E, and W Veli Streets, which were created by the British in 1840, when they bulldozed the old moat round the temple, and laid out these roads where it had been. West Veli Street holds the **railway** and two **bus stations,** and most of the important offices and shops. The **temple** is at the centre of this square, along with many of the cheaper hotels and restaurants. The posher hotels, the museum, and the **Anna Bus Stand** are all north of the river, and rather spread out.

DON'T MISS . . .

Meenakshi Amman Temple

One of the largest and jolliest of all South India's temples, this is not only the central pivot for all life in Madurai, but is in many ways a town in itself.

The temple is dedicated to the 'fish-eyed goddess' Meenakshi who, according to legend; was the daughter of a Pandya king. Born with three breasts, her father was told that the third would disappear when she met the man she was to marry. Some years later, she met Shiva on Mount Kailas, and this duly happened. Eight days afterwards, he arrived in Madurai in the form of Lord Sundareshwara and amidst great feasting, they were married. The event is still celebrated in the town's main festival each year.

It is an ancient temple, with a history that goes back some 2,000 years, although much of the current building was the work of the Nayaks of the sixteenth and seventeenth centuries. It covers an area of 6 hectares, enclosed by massive rectangular walls, with a huge painted *gopuram* at each of the compass points. The East Tower dates back to 1256, and was built by the Pandya King, Jatavarman Sundara Pandyam. The west Tower is also Pandya, dating from the fourteenth century. The North Tower is thought to be sixteenth-century. The

South Tower, built in 1559 by Siramala Sevvanthichetty, is the tallest, at 50 metres. It is possible to climb this if you buy an extra ticket, and it is well worth the effort, as you get a wonderful view over the whole temple and the city. Inside this main ring life goes on, with priests, pilgrims and tourists threading their way between colourful market stalls set out beneath the sculpted columns.

The main entrance today is in the east wall, just south of the east *gopuram*. A number of authorised guides hang around here (along with a great many unauthorized ones), and if you really want to find anything out, it is worth hiring one. The temple is magnificent if you just want to wander round, but it is also large and confusing.

The first hall as you enter is the **Ashta Shakthi Mandapam**, with statues of the eight different manifestations of the goddess Shakti (Durga-Parvati as centre of the mother-goddess cult). In the north-east corner (turn right on entering) is the **Veeravasantharayar Mandapam**, built by the elder brother of Thirumalai Nayak. Behind this is the magnificent **Hall of 1,000 Pillars**, built in the mid-sixteenth century. Each of its 985 pillars is different in design. The **temple art museum** is housed in the hall. It has a wonderful collection of bronzes, stone sculptures and relief panels along with a lengthy and confusing description of the Hindu pantheon.

Just beyond this, on the north side, is a cluster of five groups of musical pillars. Each is monolithic, but is carved into the form of 22 flutes. If struck, each produces a different note, and it is possible to play them like a musical instrument.

The inner temple, past a second ring of five, slightly smaller *gopuram*, is divided into three main enclosures. The first (centre-south, opposite the south *gopuram*) is the **Chitra Mandapam**, at the centre of which is the **Golden Lotus Tank** – the sacred spot upon which Madurai was founded.

Legend has it that during the great days of the Tamil Sangam, all works of literature were thrown into this tank. Those that pleased the gods floated and were deemed to be great, those that sank were considered worthless. The north gallery of the *mandapam* is decorated with seventeenth-century murals describing the 64 miracles of Shiva. The south gallery has marble panels inscribed with readings from the Tamil Book of Ethics.

To the west of this, the **Yali Mandapam** has pillars carved in the form of the mythical beast, the Yali, along with a statue of the seventeenth-century Nayak queen, Rani Mangammal. This leads through to the inner sanctum of the Meenakshi Shrine, which stands on its own, surrounded by several other, smaller shrines.

Going north from here, a small *gopuram* leads through to the Sundareshwarar Shrine, passing a giant statue of Ganesh found 3 kilometres away, and erected here by Thirumalai Nayak. To the east of the inner sanctum, the **Kambathadi Mandapam** houses a fine sculpture of the marriage of Meenakshi and Sundareshwarar being blessed by Vishnu, Brahma and all 24 attributions of Shiva.

The temple is officially open from 5 am–midday and 4–10 pm. If you wish to take photos, however, you have to pay more and go in during the closed period from 12.30–4 pm. As it is much quieter then, it's worth paying the extra.

There are musical concerts beside the Meenakshi Shrine every evening from 6–7.30 and 9–10 pm. At 9.15 every evening, a procession takes the image of Sundareshwarar over to Meenakshi's shrine to spend the night with her, and another at 6 am takes him back to his own quarters for the day. There is usually plenty to see anyway, as generous donations are all marked by a procession, the largest bringing out the golden thrones and elephants.

Thirumalai Nayakkar Mahal

About 1 kilometre south-east of the Meenakshi Temple. This was the palace of Thirumalai Nayak (1623–59), who is considered by most to be the greatest of the Nayak Kings, responsible also for much of the building in the temple. It was built in 1636 in the Mughul style. Only about a quarter of it still remains today, as Tirumalai's grandson dismantled much of it to reuse when he moved to Tiruchirapalli, and more was destroyed by the British. Only the entrance gate and two pavillions remain intact. These are still very impressive, however, and have recently been heavily restored by the Archaeological Survey of India. The **Swarga Vilasam** (celestial

Abode) is an octagonal pavilion, built of bricks and mortar, with stuccoed arcades, columns up to 20 metres tall, and a vast dome that has no visible means of support. The **Nataka Salai** to the north-west, is a dance hall, while to the west, were the women's quarters.

The palace is open from 8am–midday and 1–4pm daily, with a small admission charge. Drama and dance performances are held during the day in the central courtyard, and there are two *son-et-lumière* performances each evening. The English language performance is from 6.45 to 7.45pm daily. Small admission charge.

Gandhi Museum and Government Museum

On the north bank, about 5 kilometres north of the city centre. Both these museums are housed together in the seventeenth-century palace of the Rani Mangammal. The Gandhi Museum is by far the better of the two, with photographs, paintings and sculptures associated with the Mahatma, as well as a good explanation of his life, a pair of his spectacles and, belatedly, in a bullet proof glass case, the blood-stained *dhoti* in which he was shot. (Also see page 151.)

The museum also has displays of Indian history, South Indian Handicrafts, and a small art gallery. Open 9am–midday, 1.30–6pm, except Fridays.

FACT FILE

AIRLINES

Air India: opp. railway station, West Veli St. Tel: 24947.
Indian Airlines: TVS Building, 7A West Veli St. Tel: 22795. Airport no. 37433.
Vayudoot: c/o Travel Lok, Kamaraj Rd, Vilakunthun. Tel: 34343.

BANKS

Allahabad Bank: 1–2 Amman Sannathi. Tel: 33664.
Bank of India: 5 East Avanimoola St. Tel: 25938.
Andhra Bank: 25 West Chiba St. Tel: 33640.
Central Bank of India: 15 Meenakshi Koil St. Tel: 37457/8.
State Bank of India: 6 West Veli St. Tel: 22850/33899.
Indian Bank: 100–101 East Avana Imoola St. Tel: 22133.
Punjab National Bank: 47 North Chitra St. Tel: 24529.

Vijaya Bank: 76 West Avana Imoola St. Tel: 32089/36978.

COMMUNICATIONS

Head Post Office: Town, north end of West Veli St. Tel: 27080.
Head Post Office: Tallakulum. Tel: 42263.
Central Telegraph Office: Tallakulum. Tel: 42275.

SHOPPING

Souvenirs
All India Handicrafts Emporium: 39–41 Town Hall Rd. Tel: 30742.
Poompuhar (Tamil Nadu State Emporium): West Veli St. Tel: 25517.
Khadi Gramodyog Bhandar: West Veli St.
Pandyan Co-operative Super-Market: Palace Rd. Tel: 31582.
Surabhi (Kerala Handicrafts Emporium): West Veli Rd.

Textiles
Co-optex (Tamil Nadu Handlooms): Opposite South Tower and West Tower St.
Hajee Moosa: 18–19E Chitrai St (near East Gate). Tel: 32118.
Femina: 10–11W Chitrai St. Tel: 32485.

TOURIST INFORMATION

Government of Tamil Nadu Tourist Office: 180 West Veli St (near Central Bus Stand). Tel: 22957.
Open 10am–5.30pm, Monday to Saturday, and 10am–1pm, Sunday.
There are also **tourist information counters** at Madurai Railway Junction (Tel: 24535), and Madurai Airport.

WHERE TO STAY

Upmarket
Pandyan Hotel: Race Course Rd. Tel: 42470, Telex: 0445–214 COSY IN.
About 5 kilometres north of the old city. All mod cons.
Hotel Madurai Ashok: Alagar Koil Rd. Tel: 42531. Telex: 0445–297.
About 5 kilometres north of the old city. Run by the ITDC, with all facilities.

Cheap
Hotel Supreme: 110 West Perumal Maistry St. Tel: 36331. Telex: 0445–232 LOOM IN.
Hotel Prem Nivas: 102 West Perumal Maistry St. Tel: 37531.
Hotel Tamil Nadu Star: Alagar Koil Rd. Tel: 42461.
Run by the TTDC. This is in the north of the city, away from the city, away from the centre. NB: This is not the Hotel Tamil Nadu in the centre of town, which is also run by the TTDC, but is not recommended.
Hotel Aarathy: 9 Perumalkoil West Mada St. Tel: 31571.

New College House: 2 Town Hall Rd. Tel: 24311.
Hotel Devi: 20 West Avani St. Tel: 36388.

WHERE TO EAT

For something more upmarket, you will have to try either the **Ashok** or the **Pandyan** Hotels. The Ashok has a good buffet.

Otherwise, there are a number of reasonable, cheap restaurants on Town Hall Rd. Amongst the best are the **Taj**, the **Mahal**, the **Indo-Ceylon**, the **Amutham**, and the dining room at **New College House**.

KODAIKANAL

Kodaikanal is perched at 2343 metres on top of the Panali Hills, part of the Western Ghats. It was first settled in 1845 by American missionaries who had progressively been chased off the plains and the foothills by malaria. A proposal in 1861 to turn it into a sanitorium fell through because access was so difficult, and by 1883 it still had a population of only 600. Things then began to improve, however, as its situation was recognised as being healthy. People began to retire up here, and schools followed. Today, like its larger sister, Ooty, it is an educational centre of some repute.

It is a small town, with only around 25,000 inhabitants, and there is little to do in the way of sightseeing. Nevertheless it is extremely pretty, with a good complement of English cottages and cottage gardens, and is surrounded by breathtaking scenery and a rich collection of fauna (particularly birds, of which 114 species have been catalogued) and flora. It even has a unique plant, the kurinji plant (*Strobilanthes kunthianus*), which only produces its purple flowers once every 12 years – 1992 and 2004 are your best bets!

Kodaikanal is increasingly popular as a tourist destination for those who want a lazy holiday in a pleasant, cool climate with nothing much to do but mooch around on the lake or go for walks. As a resuscitation stop for battle-weary travellers, it can't be beaten.

GETTING THERE

There is a railway station called Kodaikanal Road, but don't let it fool you, it's still 80 kilometres away from the town.

Unless you have hired a car, the only practicable way to get here is by **bus**. If you do decide to take the train as far as Kodai Road, there are regular buses all day from here, as well as from nearby Dindigul and Palani. The easiest option, however, is to take a direct bus from Madurai, 120 kilometres away. There are eight departures a day. There are also through services to Cuddalore, Madras, Trichy, Coimbatore, Thekkady (for the Periyar National Park), and Bangalore.

The **bus station** is right in the centre of town.

GETTING AROUND

The town itself is easy to get around on foot. If you want to go some distance, there are a few **taxis**. Set a price before you go. Alternatively, if you feel you can brave the hills, hire a **bicycle** from the shop near the intersection at the top end of the bazaar.

GETTING YOUR BEARINGS

Kodaikanal is set in a bowl in the hills, surrounding the lake. The centre of town is very compact, huddled at the east end. The **bus stand**, two **banks**, and the **post office** are all in Bazaar Road (officially known as Anna Salai), along with six souvenir shops and the market. The very cheap hotels and restaurants are all here too; the better ones spread out around the edges, most of them within 15 minutes' walk.

DON'T MISS . . .

Kodaikanal Lake

It would be hard to miss this, as it is the focus of the entire town. An artificial reservoir, it was dammed by Sir Vere Henry Levinge in 1863, and now covers an area of 25 hectares in the valley bottom. It is possible to hire boats and pedalos from the boat house on the east shore, but as the lake is thoroughly polluted, swimming and fishing (or at least eating your catch) are not recommended. You can also hire horses here.

WALKS

These are the main reason for coming to Kodaikanal and there are a number of places which provide you with a goal that is not miles away. Amongst the best are:

Coaker's Walk: along a steep slope on the southern side of the lake to an observatory with a telescope. There is a fantastic view over the plains (mist permitting) and you can see Madurai on a clear day.

Bear Shola Falls: about 2 kilometres from the bus stand, are pretty waterfalls that make a good picnic place.

The Kurinji Andavar Temple: north-east of town, past the **Chettiar Park**, attractive, well-maintained botanical gardens. There is an observatory with a telescope beside the temple, with excellent views over the plains, and the Palani and Vagai Dams (again, mist permitting).

Pillar Rocks: three massive granite formations, over 120 metres high, that stand dramatically next to each other. They are about 7 kilometres from town.

There are also a number of dolmens and other prehistoric sites scattered around the area.

Solar Laboratory

Founded in 1898, on the highest point in Kodaikanal (2347 metres), this is the only astro-physical research laboratory in India. It has a small museum. In April, May, and June, it is open to visitors from 10am–12.30pm and 7–9pm, Monday to Friday. Out of season, it is only open on Friday mornings from 10am–midday. It is about 7 kilometres from the bus stand, past the west end of the lake.

Shrenbaganur Museum

This is a small flora and fauna museum founded in 1895 and maintained by the Sacred Heart Theological Seminary. The museum is interesting, but far more so is the **orchid house**, which contains some 300 different species. It is about 6 kilometres from the bus stand, east along Law Ghat's Road. Open 10–11.30am and 3.30–5pm, except Sundays.

FACT FILE

WHERE TO STAY

Upmarket
Carlton Hotel: Boathouse Rd. Tel: 252.

Mid-range
Sornam Apartments: Fernhill Rd. Tel: 431.

Cheap
Garden Manor: Lake Rd. Tel: 525
Hotel Sunrise: by the post office. Tel: 358.
Hotel Tamil Nadu: Fernhill Rd. Tel: 481.
Run by the TTDC. Also has 5-bed family rooms and an attached **Youth Hostel**.
Taj Lodge: Coaker's Walk.
Greenlands Youth Hostel: Coaker's Walk.

WHERE TO EAT

The only "posh" meals in town are at the **Carlton Hotel**, which also does buffets. The **Tamil Nadu** and the **Garden Manor** both do good food – Indian, Chinese and continental.

Otherwise, there is a collection of small restaurants in the centre of town. Amongst the best are the **Kodai Milk Bar**, the **Tibetan Brothers**, **Kwality Icecream** and the **Silver Inn**, all on Hospital Rd. The **Pakia Deepam** at the bus stand does good Indian food.

RAMESWARAM

Rameswaram is one of the major holy places of India because this is the action-packed centre of the epic *Ramayana*, the story of Rama's struggle to release his wife Sita from the clutches of Ravana, the demon king of Sri Lanka, assisted by his faithful ally, the monkey god Hanuman. As such, it is a place of pilgrimage to followers of both Shiva and Vishnu.

The town actually stands on the eastern side of Dhanushkodi Island, just off the mainland, and is the nearest point in India to Sri Lanka. When it runs, the Sri Lanka ferry crosses from here, but this has been suspended for some years now, and there are no plans to reinstate it until such time as the trouble in Sri Lanka has settled down. Rameswaram has a population of around 15,000.

GETTING THERE

The nearest airport is at Madurai, 173 kilometres away.

There is a metre guage **rail** link from Madurai to Rameswaram, across the Pambam Bridge. Through rail services run each day to Madurai, Madras, Coimbatore, and Tirupathi.

The **railway station** is on the southern edge of town. The **reservation counters** open from 7am–1pm and 1.30–6pm daily.

Rameswaram is connected to Madurai by a national **highway**. The way on to the island is via the splendid new Indira Gandhi Bridge, which took 14 years to build and was finally completed in 1988.

The **Central Bus Stand** is neither central, being 2 kilometres west of the town, nor a proper bus station, really only aspiring to being a patch of empty ground with some buses on it. Nevertheless, it gets a lot of use with 16 buses a day to Madurai, six daily to Trichy, two daily to Pondicherry, and daily services to Kanyakumari, Madras, Tiruchendur, Ramanathapuram and Thanjavur.

Thiruvalluvar (the state bus company) run a **booking office** in West Car Street, in the centre of town. Open 7am–9pm daily. There is no booking service at the bus stand, but for enquiries Tel: 251.

GETTING AROUND

Local buses run almost constantly between the bus stand and the temple. There are plenty of **auto-rickshaws, cyclerickshaws** and **tongas**. Set a price before you go. Alternatively, you can hire a **bicycle** in West Car Street.

There are some **taxis** and **jeeps** available from the railway station and the hotels.

GETTING YOUR BEARINGS

The **temple** is on the shore, right in the centre of town, surrounded by North, South, East and West Car Streets. These are the main shopping and business areas, with two

banks, three souvenir shops and the bus booking office. There
is a **Government of Tamil Nadu Tourist Office** on West Car
Street, open 10am–5pm (Tel: 371). There is also a **tourist
information counter** at the railway station, which opens to
meet incoming trains. The **Hotel Tamil Nadu** is a little bit
north of the town. The **post and telegraph office** is on Mela
Street, a short way west, on the way to the bus stand. Open
9.30am–5.30pm (Tel: 225).

DON'T MISS . . .

Ramanathaswamy Temple

Although there has been a temple on this site for much longer,
the earliest temple buildings still in existence date back to the
late Chola period (twelfth century AD), and most of them were
built by the Nayaks in the sixteenth and seventeenth centuries.
It is built on the spot where Rama came to do penance to Shiva
for the sin he committed in killing Ravana.

The temple covers a total of 15 acres, surrounded on three
sides by high rectangular walls. The eastern side, facing the
sea, is made up of a colonnade, while the east *gopuram* is on
the inner wall beyond. The north and south *gopuram* were
built in 1420 by Vijayanagar ruler, Keerana Raya.　The east
was begun in 1640, but only completed this century. This is
the tallest of the four, reaching a total height of 53 metres.
The west *gopuram* is relatively modern.

The most dramatic element of the temple however is the
colonnades which surround the inner sanctum. Lined by
4 metre-high pillars, decorated with scrollwork and lotus
leaves, they stretch for a total of 1220 metres. The longest
single colonnade is over 200 metres long. The north and
south corridors are most dramatic, as the march of the
pillars seems to bend perspective into infinity. They lead
towards the inner shrines which house the Ranathaswamy
and Parvati *lingams*. Non-Hindus are not allowed to enter
the inner sanctum. Near the east *gopuram*, there are statues
of Nandi and Hanuman, and two Nayak kings, Visvanatha
and Krishnama.

The sea at **Agnitheertham**, about 100 yards from the temple,
is particularly calm and is used for sacred bathing.

ALSO WORTH VISITING

Kothandaramaswamy Temple

Near the southern tip of the island, about 8 kilometres from Rameswaram Village. This is said to be the place where Vibhishana, the brother of the demon king, Ravana, came to apologise to Rama for his brother's behaviour in abducting Sita. The story is told in a series of paintings inside the temple.

A further legend grew up around it in 1964, when a cyclone washed away most of the area surrounding it, leaving the temple as the only building left standing.

Right at the tip of the peninsula, beyond the temple, there is a good bathing pool, and there are coral reefs which you can reach if you persuade one of the local fishermen to take you out. If you plan to snorkel here, be careful as the coral is extremely fragile and dies if touched.

Gandhamadana Parvatam

At all of 30 metres, this is the highest point on the island, about 2 kilometres north of Rameswaram village. It is said to be the place from which Hanuman, his tail ablaze, made a great leap across the sea to destroy Sri Lanka. The rather uninspiring **Ramjharoka Temple** is built around some of Rama's footprints. There is a good view from the terrace.

FACT FILE

WHERE TO STAY

Hotel Tamil Nadu: on the beach. Tel: 277.
Run by the ITDC. Also has a **Youth Hostel** attached. Book in advance, as this is nearly always full.
Hotel Maharajah: 7 Middle St. Tel: 271.
Santhya Lodge: 1 West Car St. Tel: 329
Alankar Tourist Home: West Car St.
Devasthanam Lodges and Cottages: Bookings to Executive Officer, Devasthanam. Tel: 241.
115 cottages at varying price ranges.

WHERE TO EAT

The **Hotel Tamil Nadu** and the **Devasthanam Trust** restaurant opposite the east gate of the temple are the best bet. Otherwise, there are several rather dingy restaurants on West and South Car Streets. The best amongst them are reckoned to be the **Ashok Bhavan**, the **Vasantha Vihar**, and the **Vasantha Bhawan**.

KANYAKUMARI

Kanyakumari stands on Cape Cormorin, the southernmost tip of India, an important place for those who like tidy endings, but also one of the major Hindu holy places of South India.

The town got its name from the goddess, Devi Kanya, manifestation of Parvati. She came here to marry Shiva, but the town was plagued by the king of demons, Banasura, who could only be killed by a virgin. The gods put their heads together, and on the day of the wedding, made the cocks crow early to trick Shiva into believing that the auspicious moment for his wedding had passed. He went away dejected, and the goddess took a vow of perpetual celibacy. She, of course, went on to slay Banasura. The rice which was to be thrown at the wedding became the many-coloured sands of Kanyakumari.

Three seas, the Arabian Sea, the Indian Ocean and the Bay of Bengal, all meet at Cape Cormorin, and each of the three has brought its own sands with it, to create a kaleidoscope of red and black and gold. The sunrises and sunsets across the triple sea are thought to be so fine that times are posted in the station, which also has a special observation point on its roof, and a siren is sounded to warn people so that they can gather to watch the spectacle. At the full moon, the sunset and the moonrise happen at the same time, and on the full moon in April, the sun and the moon are visible on the same horizon.

It is a small town, with a permanent population of only around 17,000, although this is always swelled by the many pilgrims who come to bathe at the **Kumari Ghats**, right at the tip of the cape. It also, sadly, has a great deal of the atmosphere that seems to go with a shifting population, and is loud, littered and slightly tired.

Rama's penance

Once Rama had finally vanquished Ravana, and retrieved his wife, he was told to do penance for killing the demon king. He sent his faithful aid, Hanuman, up to Mount Kailasa to find him a *lingam*, but when the auspicious moment arrived, Hanuman had still not returned. Instead, Sita made him a *lingam* from the sand on the beach. When Hanuman returned bearing the *lingam* with him, he was desolate to find he was too late and threatened to kill himself. To comfort him, Rama told him to remove Sita's *lingam*, and put his own in its place. He tried to pick it up and when he failed, wrapped his tail around it and leaped towards the heavens. The mountains shook, the skies cracked, but the *lingam* would not budge and Hanuman eventually fell unconscious back to earth. Rama wept to see his friend in such a state and when the monkey god finally came round told him to put the *lingam* where he had fallen, saying that he, Rama, would make all who came to make *puja* pay homage first to Hanuman's *lingam*. Today, the two still stand side by side in the Ramanathaswamy Temple and pilgrims still worship first at Hanuman's *lingam*, then at Sita's.

GETTING THERE

The nearest airport is 80 kilometres away at Trivandrum.

Railway Kanyakumari is the southern end of the broad guage line which runs most of the way down the west coast of India. Not many trains come here, but those there are do some impressive distances, with a daily express service to Bombay (2149 kilometres) and, once a week, the Jammu Tawi Express to Kashmir, via Madras and Delhi. This train takes 86 hours (just under four days) to do 3,726 kilometres, and is the longest single train route in India. There are also daily passenger services to Trivandrum, Nagercoil and Tirunelveli. If you want to go up the east coast, Tirunelveli, 81 kilometres north, connects up with the metre guage line to Madurai and Madras.

The extremely grand **railway station** is about 1 kilometre north of the centre of town. The booking office is open from 8am–midday and 2–4pm, but it doesn't have a large quota, so if you are wanting to do a long journey, it's worth reserving at a larger station before you get here.

Kanyakumari is on the national highways that run north to Trivandrum in the west and Madurai and Madras in the east. Thiruvalluvar, the state **bus** company, runs services to most of the major cities in the south, with daily services to Madras, Pondicherry, Tiruchirapalli, Madurai, Turchendur, Tuticorin, and Mandapam (for Rameswaram). There are also more frequent local services to Nagercoil, Kovalam and Trivandrum.

The **bus station** is about 500 metres west of the town. It is a grand affair with a reservations office (open 7am–9pm), restaurant, waiting rooms and even retiring rooms. Even better, it has proper timetables, written in English.

GETTING AROUND

You can walk everywhere, but things are a bit spread out unless you are feeling keen. There are plenty of **cycle-rickshaws** and some **taxis** as an alternative. Set a price before you get in. A **ferry** service to Vivekananda Rock leaves every half-hour from 7–11am and 2–5pm from the jetty near the centre of town.

GETTING YOUR BEARINGS

There are two main through roads in the town, one leading north to the **railway station**, one leading west, past the **lighthouse** to the **bus station**. Most of the hotels and the main shopping centre are near the junction of the two. The **banks** and **post office** are both north of the town centre, on the way to the railway station. The **temple** is on the shore at the southern end of town. There is a **tourist office** at the Hotel Tamil Nadu, Beach Road, near the Gandhi Mandapam. The **Co-optex** and **Khadi Krafts** shops are both near here also, while **Poompuhar**, the state emporium, is on Sannathi Street.

DON'T MISS . . .

Kanyakumari Temple

Dedicated to the goddess Devi Kanya, this stands right on the shore, next to the bathing ghats. The image of the goddess has two diamond nose rings, replacements given to the temple sixty years ago by the Maharajah of Trivandrum for the ones stolen earlier by the English. It is said that the ring shone so brightly that a British ship mistook it for the lighthouse and was wrecked on Vivekananda Rock. The temple is open from 4.30–11.45am and 5.30–8.45pm. Non-Hindus are not allowed into the inner sanctum.

GANDHI MANDAPAM

Mahatma Gandhi was particularly fond of Kanyakumari, of which he wrote: "I am writing this at the Cape in front of the sea, where three waters meet and furnish a sight unequalled in the world. For this is no port of call for vessels. Like the Goddess, the waters around here are virgin."

On his death, part of his ashes were brought here to be scattered out to sea, and the memorial has now been built over the place where his urn was displayed. It is carefully designed so that at noon on the 2 October, the Mahatma's birthday, the sun streams through a tiny opening to bathe the exact spot in light.

VIVEKANANDA MEMORIAL

Swami Vivekananda was a great Hindu saint and philosopher from Bengal who, in 1892, swam out to the rock and sat on it for a long while to meditate. He returned, inspired, to preach in New York, and then to found the Ramakrishna Mission in Madras. The memorial was built in 1970, using elements of all the different architectural styles in India. The sacred *om* is written in flourescent green on the walls of the meditation hall.

Also on the rock is the **Sri Padaparai**, the sacred footprints of the goddess Kanya. It is also possible to climb the **lighthouse**, which has the best views in town. Unfortunately, for unspecified security reasons, you are not allowed to take photos.

The rock is open from 7–11am and 2–5pm, except Tuesdays. There are separate small entry charges for the memorial and the lighthouse. You are not allowed to smoke or eat.

OUT OF TOWN

Padmanabhapuram Palace

45 kilometres from Kanyakumari, on the main road to Kovalam and Trivandrum. Although it is officially now in Tamil Nadu, this was, until 1750, the capital of the south Keralan kingdom of Travancore. The name means "the town of the lotus at Vishnu's navel". The **palace**, which is set within fort walls in six acres of gardens, was built in 1550.

A low, elegant wooden courtyard building, with steep-pitched roof, this is probably the finest remaining example of typically Keralan architecture. The whole building is full of magnificent, delicate carvings of teak and rosewood. In particular, have a look at those in the **Council Chamber**, which also has highly polished black floors. There are some wonderful seventeenth- and eighteenth-century murals on the top floor, similar to those in the Mattancherry Palace, Cochin. Open 9am–5pm, except Monday. Small admission charge.

The **Ramaswamy Temple** next door has 45 carved panels telling the entire epic story of the *Ramayana*.

Suchindrum Temple

13 kilometres west of Kanyakumari, on the main road to
Kovalam and Trivandrum. The **Thanumalayam Temple** is
sacred to Shiva, Vishnu and Brahma. It is from here that Shiva
is said to have travelled to marry Kanya. It dates back originally to the Pandyan period (nineteenth to twelfth centuries
AD), but has been considerably altered by Tirumala Nayak in
the seventeenth century. The temple is enclosed by a rectangular courtyard, with a 41metre (seven-storey) high *gopuram*
over the main entrance. Inside, there are 30 shrines.

In the **Konnayadi Shrine** there is a 2,300 year old laurel
tree, at the foot of which stand three *lingams* which are
said to have sprouted naturally. The **Alangara Mandapam**
has musical pillars, one of which resembles a drum beat. A
5^{1}/2 metre-tall image of the monkey god, Hanuman, stands
opposite statues of Rama and Sita, while images of the
devadasis (temple maidens) holding lamps flank the pillared
corridors. These are the second longest in the country.

The temple was used as a sanctuary by various different
dynasties, all of whom endowed it with treasure. Today,
therefore, it is massively wealthy, but its golden thrones and
jewelled statues are only brought out during festivals.

FACT FILE

WHERE TO STAY

Hotel Sangam: Main Rd. Tel: 351.
Hotel Tamil Nadu: Beach Rd. Tel: 222.
Run by the TTDC, who also have a slightly cheaper **guest house**, a bit
further from the beach (Tel: 257), and a **Youth Hostel** nearby.
Kerala House: Beach Rd. Tel: 229.
Run by the KTDC.
Manickhan Tourist Home and the **DKV Lodge**: both near the
Vinayaka Kovil Temple.
Retiring rooms at the railway and bus stations.

WHERE TO EAT

The **Hotel Tamil Nadu**, the **Manickhan**, the **Palace Hotel**, and the
Chicken Corner have the best food, all much on a par. Otherwise try
grazing from the pavement stalls at the main intersection.

GLOSSARY OF COMMON INDIAN TERMINOLOGY

Acha – (also spelled *atcha*) OK

Ashoka – great Indian emperor from Orissa in 3rd century BC

ashram – literally "refuge". A spiritual community. The four main stages of life are also known as *ashrama*

Aryans – people from Iran who invaded India in c.1500 BC, introducing Hinduism and the caste system

atavar – incarnation of a god

attar – perfume

ayah – children's nanny

ayatollah – Shi'ite Muslim religious leader

baba – term of respect, most commonly used for one's father or for religious leaders

bagh – garden

baksheesh – that irritating "little something" asked for as a tip, a bribe, a gesture of goodwill, or for no reason at all

bandh – strike (as in industrial action)

bazaar – market

bearer – servant, ranging from a porter to a butler

begum – high-ranking Muslim woman

beedis – (also spelled *bidis*) tiny, hand-rolled cigarettes

betel nut – mildly intoxicating and addictive nut chewed by many in India

Bhagvan – the one-god, soul of the universe

bhakti – personal devotion and acts of worship

bhang – dried marijuana leaves and flowering shoots. Also sometimes used to describe a party

bharata natyam – classical dance from Tamil Nadu

bodhisattva – disciple of the Buddha

Brahma – the Hindu god of creation

Brahmans – priestly caste, the highest caste in the Indian system

cantonment – originally the military and administrative district of a town, today used more generally to describe the area of town lived in by the British during the Raj

caste – the Indian class system

chai – tea

chaitya – sacred enclosure, Buddhist hall of worship

Chalukyas – dynasty of South Indian rulers

chappals – leather sandals

chappati – simple, griddle-baked unleavened bread

charas – marijuana resin

charpoi – Indian rope bed

Cholas – dynasty of South Indian rulers from Tamil Nadu area

chowk – courtyard, marketplace

crore – 10 million (100 *lakhs*). Indian form of counting

dacoit – member of a huge gang of armed bandits in North India

dabbah – layered metal container used for transporting food; a tiffin carrier

dabbahwallah – men who ferry the packed lunches round Bombay

dargah – shrine of a Muslim saint

Deccan Plateau – vast high agricultural plain in central India

Delhi Sultanate – first Muslim empire in India, from 1192–1526 AD

devi – a goddess

devata – the minor gods of the Hindu pantheon

dhal – common food dish made from lentils, ranging in consistency from a thin soup to a thick purée

dhobi – laundry

dhobiwallah – the man who does the laundry

dhoti – white loin cloth commonly worn by men

dosa – large thin pancake of fermented rice flour and *dal*. Popular snack food from South India

Dravidian Culture – South Indian megalithic society from c.500BC–100 AD

durbar – government meeting or court audience

Durga – terrible aspect of the goddess Parvati

fakir – ascetic holy man. Term used by both Muslims and Hindus

feni – Goanese liqueur, made from cashew or coconut

Ganesh – elephant-headed god of wisdom and prosperity. Son of Shiva and Parvati

ganja – local name for marijuana

Garuda – eagle, the vehicle of the god Vishnu

ghat – literally "step". Used both for the steps leading down to a river, lake or tank, and for mountains

ghee – (also spelled *ghi*). Clarified butter, commonly used in Indian cooking

godown – warehouse

gopuram – highly carved, pyramidal gateway tower, mainly found in southern Hindu temples

guru – Hindu spiritual teacher

Haji – Muslim who has made the pigrimage (*haj*) to Mecca.

Harappa Culture – alternative name for the Indus Valley Civilisation (see below)

Hanuman – the monkey god, mainly known as the assistant of Rama

Harijan – literally "Children of God". Name given to the untouchable castes by Mahatma Gandhi

Hindi – the main spoken language of India, and (along with English), the language of government

hookah – water-cooled bubble pipe

howdah – elaborate, often canopied, seat for riding an elephant

Hoysalas – dynasty of South Indian rulers from southern Deccan

idlis – dumplings made from fermented rice flour

Indus Valley Civilisation – North Indian culture from c.2,300–1,700 BC

imam – Muslim religious teacher/leader

imambara – tomb of a Shi'ite Muslim holy man

jaggery – dark brown molasses made from palm syrup

jatra – (also spelled *zatra*). Goanese temple festivals

ji – suffix added to a name as a term of respect, e.g. Gandhiji

juggernauts – huge, highly decorated Hindu temple chariots

Kali – the most terrible aspect of the goddess Parvati, the goddess of death and destruction

kama – desire, love, worldly pleasure. One of the four goals in life according to Hindu philosophy

karma – Fate, those aspects of life which determine your future incarnations

kathakali – Keralan dance-drama

Krishna – the 7th incarnation of Vishnu, a merry god who loved women

kshatriyas – the caste of warriors and rulers

kulfi – Indian ice cream flavoured with pistachio and cardamom

lakh – 100,000. India form of counting

Laksmhi – (also spelled *Laxmi*). Hindu goddess of wealth and good fortune

lama – Tibetan Buddhist holy man

lassi – thin yoghurt drink

lingam – phallic symbol used mainly in worship of Shiva

lok sabha – the lower, directly elected house of the Indian national parliament

lunghi – the piece of material worn sarong-style all over South India

Mahabharata – epic poem describing the civil war between the Pandavas and Kurus, written down in the fourth to second centuries BC. One of the great classics of Hindu literature

mahal – house or palace

maharaja – great king or ruler

maharani – queen, consort of the maharajah

Mahatma – literally 'great soul'. Title of respect

mahout – elephant keeper

maidan – open grassy area or park in town

Marathas – ruling family from the Deccan, founders of a great empire in the sixteenth and seventeenth centuries AD

marathi – main language in Maharashtra

marg – road

masala – mixed spice

masjid – the principal mosque in any town

Mauryan Empire – first great Indian empire, from 321–185 BC

mela – fair (as in festival or market)

memsahib – respectful term of address for married women. Commonly used towards Western women

mihrab – prayer niche in a mosque

minaret – turret on a mosque used for calling the faithful to prayer

monsoon – rainy season, stretching from about June to September

mosque – Muslim place of worship

muezzin – the Muslim man who calls the faithful to prayer, five times a day

Mughuls – great Muslim dynasty which ruled North India from 1526–1761 AD

murg – chicken

Namaste – common Hindu greeting

nan – baked leavened bread

Nandi – the bull ridden by the god Shiva

nawab – a local ruler or minor prince

nimbu paani – drink of fresh lime and soda water

nirvana – the highest goal of Buddhist achievement, the state of perfection and release from the cycle of rebirth.

paani – water

paise – smallest unit of Indian currency. 100 *paise* to Rs1 (approx. 4,700 to £1)

Pallavas – South Indian dynasty

pan/paan – leaf wrapped around betel nut and spices, sold by street sellers and chewed as a mild intoxicant

Pandyas – South Indian dynasty

paratha – bread layered with butter, sometimes stuffed with meat or vegetables

Parsees – Zoroastrian worshippers, originally from Persia, now settled mainly in Bombay

Parvati – goddess at the centre of the mother goddess cult. Wife of Shiva and sister of Vishnu

pucka – correct, genuine, proper

puja – act of worship

pundit – (also spelled *pandit*). Term of respect for an expert, a teacher or professor

punkah – huge fan of cloth or palm weave worked by a rope

purdah – curtain screen to shield the women's quarters. Now also the state of isolation in which some women women live. Muslim term and practice also adopted by some Hindus

pyjama – baggy trousers

Raj – rule. Usually used to describe the colonial period of British India

raja – a ruler or prince

rajya sabha – upper house of the Indian national parliament, representing the federal states

Rama – the 8th incarnation of Vishnu

Ramayana – epic poem, now one of the classics of Hindu literature, that tells of the exploits of the super-hero, Rama, as he struggles to rescue his wife, Sita, from the Demon King of Lanka

raja – king

rani – queen

rath – (also known as *rathi*). Chariot or temple now used to describe the wooden temple chariots in which the temple idols are paraded during festivals. Also the war chariots of the Maharathi, and the stone chariots of Pallava shrines

rickshaw – method of passenger transport, for two to three people, with a small engine, or pulled by men on foot or bicycle

rupee – main unit of currency. About 47 *rupees* to £1 sterling

saddhu – Hindu ascetic holy man

sahib – 'Sir'. Term of respect usually accorded to Western men

Sanskrit – ancient Indian language, brought to the sub-continent by the Aryan peoples *sari* – traditional form of dress of Indian women, one long length of cloth draped around the body

shalwar kamiz – also known as a Punjabi suit. The loose pyjama-style baggy trousers and long shirt commonly worn in India.

scheduled castes – modern official name for the lowest castes

sepoy – private in the infantry of the Indian army

Shaiva – followers of Shiva

Shiva – Hindu god, the Destroyer

shudras – Aryan name for the lowest or "out" castes

sikhara – spire or tower on a Hindu temple

Sita – wife of Rama, held as the ideal of Hindu womanhood

sitar – stringed musical instrument

Slave Dynasty – another name for the Delhi Sultanate (see above)

stupa – rounded Buddhist reliquary mound

suttee – (also spelled *sati*). Literally "honourable woman", but also used to describe the now illegal Hindu practice whereby a widow flings herself onto her husband's funeral pyre

swami – literally "lord of the self". Title given to an initiated monk

sweeper – lowest level of servant, responsible for heavy cleaning, including latrines

Tamil – the people and language of south-east India

thali – a full set meal, consisting of rice or bread, three or four small dishes of curry and some pickle. Also the name of the metal tray on which it is served

tiffin – a snack meal. Also used to describe lunch. Incorrectly adopted by the British to describe tea

toddy – South Indian alcoholic drink made from coconut

tonga – horse-drawn passenger vehicle

Vaishnava – followers of Vishnu

vaishyas – the caste of cultivators and landowners

Vishnu – Hindu god, the Preserver

wallah – literally "man" or "fellow"

Yavadas – imperial dynasty from the northern Deccan

FURTHER READING

HISTORY AND SOCIETY

A History of India:
Vol 1 – The Discovery of India to 1526, by Romila Thapar
Vol 2 – Sixteenth century to Twentieth century, by Percival
Spear (Penguin)

The Wonder That Was India, by A.L. Basham
(Sidgwick and Jackson)

From Raj to Rajiv – 40 Years of Indian Independence
(BBC Books)

India File by Trevor Fishlock.
(John Murray.)

Tribes of India – The Struggle for Survival, by Christoph von
Furer-Haimendorf
(OUP)

The Nehrus and the Gandhis, by Tariq Ali.
(Picador)

Freedom at Midnight by Larry Collins and Dominique Pierre
(Grafton)

Highness – The Maharajahs of India, by Ann Morrow
(Grafton)

Plain Tales from the Raj, ed. by Charles Allen
(Future)

RELIGION

A Handbook of Living Religions, ed. by John R. Hinnells
(Penguin)

GUIDES

Indian Wildlife (Insight Guide), ed. by Samuel Israel and Toby Sinclair
(Apa Production)

India – A Travel Survival
(Lonely Planet)

South Asian Handbook, ed. by Robert Bradnock
(Trade and Travel)

Southern India
(Nelles Guides/Robertson McCarta)

India in Luxury by Louise Nicholson
(Century Hutchinson)

TRAVEL BOOKS AND FICTION

Numerous novels and travel books have been written about India over the centuries, but almost every single one of them has concentrated on the north. They will give something of the flavour of the country, however, so a few of the best are listed below. If some of the more obvious titles are not here, it is because I felt that they were too firmly fixed in another area.

An Indian Summer by James Cameron

Chasing the Monsoon by Alexander Frater

An Area of Darkness by V.S. Naipaul.

A Passage to India by E.M. Forster

Midnight's Children by Salman Rushdie

Into India by John Keay.

The Great Railway Bazaar by Paul Theroux

The Raj Quartet and *Staying On* by Paul Scott

INDEX